D0628818

THE ANCIENT NEAR EAST

 **is**

**Harcourt
College Publishers**

A Harcourt Higher Learning Company

Now you will find Harcourt Brace's
distinguished innovation, leadership, and
support under a different name . . . a new
brand that continues our unsurpassed
quality, service, and commitment to
education.

We are combining the strengths of our
college imprints into one worldwide
brand: 🌀Harcourt

Our mission is to make learning
accessible to anyone, anywhere,
anytime—reinforcing our commitment
to lifelong learning.

We are now Harcourt College Publishers.
Ask for us by name.

**One Company
"Where Learning
Comes to Life."**

**www.harcourtcollege.com
www.harcourt.com**

THE ANCIENT NEAR EAST

939.4
Dun

WILLIAM E. DUNSTAN
NORTH CAROLINA STATE UNIVERSITY

NORTH BAY
PUBLIC LIBRARY
NORTH BAY
PUBLIC LIBRARY
DISCARDED
NOV 9 2007

HARCOURT BRACE COLLEGE PUBLISHERS

FORT WORTH   PHILADELPHIA   SAN DIEGO   NEW YORK   ORLANDO   AUSTIN   SAN ANTONIO

TORONTO   MONTREAL   LONDON   SYDNEY   TOKYO

Publisher	Christopher P. Klein
Senior Acquisitions Editor	David C. Tatom
Product Manager	Steve Drummond
Developmental Editor	Christopher Nelson
Project Editor	Betsy Cummings
Senior Production Manager	Kathleen Ferguson
Art Director	Vicki Whistler

Cover image: Josephine Powell, photographer. Rome, Italy.

Copyright © 1998 by Harcourt Brace & Company

All rights reserved. No part of this publication may be reproduced or transmitted in any form or by any means, electronic or mechanical, including photocopy, recording, or any information storage and retrieval system, without permission in writing from the publisher.

Requests for permission to make copies of any part of the work should be mailed to: Permissions Department, Harcourt Brace & Company, 6277 Sea Harbor Drive, Orlando, Florida 32887-6777.

(Copyrights and acknowledgments begin on page 307, which constitutes a continuation of this copyright page.)

Harcourt Brace College Publishers may provide complimentary instructional aids and supplements or supplement packages to those adopters qualified under our adoption policy. Please contact your sales representative for more information. If as an adopter or potential user you receive supplements you do not need, please return to your sales representative or send them to: Attn: Returns Department, Troy Warehouse, 465 South Lincoln Drive, Troy, MO 63379.

Address for Editorial Correspondence:
Harcourt Brace College Publishers, 301 Commerce Street, Suite 3700, Fort Worth, TX 76102.

Address for Orders:
Harcourt Brace & Company, 6277 Sea Harbor Drive, Orlando, FL 32887-6777.
1-800-782-4479.

Library of Congress Catalog Card Number: 97-71994

ISBN: 0-03-035299-1

Printed in the United States of America

0 1 2 3 4 5 6 016 0 9 8 7 6 5 4 3

To my mother, Ida Powell Fuller Dunstan,
to whom this volume is dedicated, I owe more than words can convey.

CONTENTS

PREFACE

Advanced societies flourished in the Near East long before the emergence of Greece and Rome. Although gaps and uncertainties remain, archaeological discoveries continue to illuminate the fascinating Near East of preclassical antiquity. The transition from hunting and gathering to farming took place in the region. The inhabitants of the Near East developed the earliest known cities, monumental architecture, metalworking, writing systems, wheeled vehicles, kingdoms, and empires. Civilization arose almost simultaneously in Mesopotamia and Egypt, with important later achievements taking place in Anatolia, Syria, Palestine, and Persia. The peoples of the Near East developed skills and techniques that nourished the classical Greek culture and strongly color modern ways of life. They produced literature and ideas now embedded in great religions, thus contributing to contemporary beliefs. Our debt to the brilliant civilizations of the Near East is undeniable.

This study serves as the first volume of a three-part comprehensive overview of the Near Eastern and Greco-Roman worlds. Written for the student of history and the general reader, *The Ancient Near East* brings together the findings of historians, anthropologists, archaelogists, linguists, geographers, art historians, scientists, and other specialists. The book begins with an examination of prehistory, the long span before the invention of writing, with evidence based on the material remains left by early inhabitants. Warranting more than cursory analysis, the prehistoric world witnessed many crucial developments in the shaping of humanity. Later chapters focus on social and cultural themes while broadly outlining Near Eastern political and military developments, as documented by textual sources, artifacts, and architecture. *The Ancient Near East* is intended to be thought-provoking and does not shy away from controversial issues and topics. The aim throughout is to kindle the reader's interest in examining more specialized works, a number of which are listed in the bibliography.

ACKNOWLEDGMENTS

My warmest thanks are due to colleagues, friends, and students for their valuable suggestions, especially Professor Clark Spencer Larsen of the University of North Carolina, who read the first draft of Chapters 1 and 2, and Professor Reginald H. Sack of North Carolina State University, who read Chapters 3 through 7. I would like to thank the reviewers of the manuscript, who contributed to the quality of the publication by their advice and corrections: Jack Balcer, Ohio State University; John W. Dahmus, Stephen F. Austin State University; John K. Evans, University of Minnesota; P. Corby Finney, University of Missouri—St. Louis; Pericles B. Georges, Lake Forest College; Eleanor G. Huzar, Michigan State University; Donald Kyle, University of Texas at Arlington; George E. Pesely, University of Northern Iowa; Kenneth S. Sacks, Brown University; Thomas Turley, Santa Clara University; Glee E. Wilson, Kent State University; and L. J. Worley. Any faults or omissions are my own. Access to the superb holdings of the Walter Royal Davis Library at the University of North Carolina at Chapel Hill greatly aided in preparing the text. A number of librarians and staff members provided generous assistance, especially Bernice Bergup, Humanities Reference Librarian, and Jean S. Greene, Circulation Day Desk Supervisor. Finally, I must express particular appreciation for the efforts of the outstanding editorial team at Harcourt Brace: David C. Tatom, Fritz Schanz, Christopher B. Nelson, Carla Clardy, Betsy Cummings, Vicki Whistler, Kathy Ferguson, and Shirley Webster.

THE ANCIENT NEAR EAST

CHAPTER I

Tracing Early Humanity

Astrophysicists estimate that the age of the universe is between ten and twenty billion years. Other scientists tell us organic life emerged on earth billions of years in the past. The earliest humanlike creatures had appeared by five million years ago, and our own species, *Homo sapiens,* goes back at least two hundred thousand years. Although countless questions remain about our early ancestors, paleoanthropologists and archaeologists continue to make astounding discoveries about remote ages. Thus future investigators will write with far more certainty than we can about the veiled mysteries of the origins of human life.

Our understanding of the broad sweep of the human past is a multidisciplinary enterprise involving the interpretation of a wide variety of remnants of life left scattered over and under the landscape, including tools, weapons, jewelry, pottery, architecture, sculpture, paintings, graves, fossils, and written records. As we move backward to the mists of time, however, these sources become increasingly scarce. Historians usually refer to the immense period of human existence prior to the development of writing some 5000 years ago as *prehistory*, the span of which almost totally eclipses the epoch of recorded history. Whether investigating prehistory or recorded history, historians attempt to reconstruct and explain the story of earlier events. Evidence in prehistory is material, drawn from artifacts and sites. Inferences flowing from these discoveries are more credible when they concern shelter or diet, less so in terms of reconstructing religious beliefs or political and family structures. Because of the inherent difficulties in analyzing the various remnants of life, historians acknowledge that history is an inexact science offering only approximate knowledge of the human chronicle.

We should recognize, however, that the exacting and difficult task of reconstructing the human narrative is of profound importance for providing even a limited understanding of the past or the present. Contemporary civilization in the West has been shaped largely by cultural inheritances from the various peoples of the ancient Mediterranean world and beyond. Among them were the humans of prehistory, who successfully coped with existence through a variety of lifestyles and exhibited remarkable characteristics and skills enabling them to survive and to reproduce over countless millennia. To know them is to know ourselves.

THE ADVENT OF MODERN
EVOLUTIONARY THEORY

The nineteenth century witnessed bitter controversy over one of the most signifi-cant questions ever asked: Did God create humanity "in his own image" during the course of a day, as proclaimed in the first chapter of the biblical book of Genesis, or were human beings the product of a gradual evolution from lower forms of life? At the beginning of the century most people believed the world was only a few thou-sand years old. James Ussher, a seventeenth-century Irish scholar and Anglican archbishop, had devised a famous system of biblical chronology, estimating that God created the world 4004 years before the birth of Jesus. Subsequently, this date was inserted in margins of the Authorized Version of the Bible and came to acquire the infallibility that many people ascribe to Scripture itself. As fossils of extinct plants and animals were found in ever-deeper geologic strata, however, some inves-tigators became aware that the earth was far older than Ussher had imagined. In his *Principles of Geology*, which appeared in three volumes from 1830 to 1833, Sir Charles Lyell presented evidence hinting at the immense age of the earth. The next logical step was to question the age of human beings as well.

CHARLES DARWIN (1809–1882)

Among the readers of Lyell's celebrated work on geology was English-born Charles Darwin, who served as the naturalist during a five-year scientific exploration aboard H.M.S. *Beagle* in the 1830s. To gather data on the wildlife of many lands, the expe-dition sailed to the coasts of South America and then continued to the Galápagos Islands, Tahiti, Australia, and South Africa. Thus Darwin became acquainted at firsthand with the great variation of living organisms, and he began to wonder how different species of the same animal might have developed distinct physical features. In time, his observations convinced him that each species had slowly evolved from other forms.

Darwin realized the idea of an evolution of species was a fundamental contra-diction to the biblical account of a creator-god bringing forth all things in a matter of several days. For more than twenty years he hesitated to make his conclusions public, fearing the power of the biblical view of creation might compel committed believers to attack him. Finally, in 1859, he gathered his resolve and outlined his theories concerning the evolution of plants and animals in his renowned treatise, *On the Origin of Species by Means of Natural Selection*, telling of the rise, the devel-opment, and even the disappearance of thousands of species.

To explain how evolution took place, Darwin proposed the mechanism of nat-ural selection. This is the view, in simplified terms, that organisms best adapted by favorable variation to a particular environment tend to live longer, to reproduce more frequently, and to pass their traits on to the next generation, while others tend to disappear. Darwin suggested that over long periods of time these successful varia-tions may produce great differences, resulting in new species. Despite his obvious courage in presenting these findings to the public, he was extremely cautious. The evidence he offered to support his hypotheses was limited to plants and some animals but did not include humans. Darwin referred to the origin of human beings only once in his entire book, a single hesitant sentence in his conclusion: "Light will be thrown on the origin of man and his history." The implication was clear, however, and nobody missed it.

Later, in 1871, Darwin published *The Descent of Man* to complete his theory of evolution with a detailed explanation of the emergence of human beings. In this work he argued that humans, far from being the result of a special creation, had been subject to the same evolutionary processes as any other animal. Nowhere did he claim humans are descended from apes, arguing instead that both species have a common ancestor. Darwin suggested humans had developed their physical characteristics as well as their ethical nature and religious beliefs in response to the requirements of survival. Thus neither the origins nor the character of human beings requires the existence of a deity for explanation. Although evolutionary evidence was sufficiently convincing to persuade many people to interpret the Bible metaphorically, the religious fundamentalists held to their unshakable belief in the literal truth of the biblical account. Their anguish and outrage led to years of bitter controversy, marked by repeated charges that Darwin's findings were the work of Satan.

Even before Darwin had published his conclusions, however, supporting evidence had already come to light. In 1856 the fossilized bones of an early form of human were discovered near Düsseldorf in the Neander Valley of western Germany. The German word for valley is *Tal*—spelled *Thal* in nineteenth-century German—and the creatures represented by these bones became known as the Neanderthals. Living during one of the most critical periods in the history of human development, the Neanderthals as we know them had evolved in Europe by around 130,000 years ago. They were anatomically more robust than modern human beings but were clearly humans and not apes. Their existence offered evidence that both they and modern humans had evolved from a common ancestor.

Although investigators have not yet unearthed a total series of steps in the fossil record, the preponderance of evidence for evolution is overwhelming. The evolutionary principle has become central to all the modern biological sciences. In the meantime twentieth-century discoveries about how hereditary material is transmitted from one generation to the next has given us a much more complete picture about how evolution operates, while new scientific methods have led to far greater accuracy in dating sites and remains.

TECHNIQUES FOR DATING THE PAST

RELATIVE DATING

Stratigraphy, Bone Dating, Morphology, Paleomagnetic Dating.   Relative dating establishes a chronological order from oldest to most recent for specimens or deposits. The investigator employing this method places a fossil, artifact, or sedimentary layer in a time sequence in relationship to other fossils, artifacts, or layers. Although this does not provide the actual age of a particular prehistoric specimen, scientists are often successful in cross-relating one object to another whose age is more precisely known. One technique of relative dating is *stratigraphy*, the study of the sequence of layers at a site in an attempt to arrange the buried fossils and artifacts in relative chronological order. In an undisturbed site, the oldest layer should be at the bottom and the most recent at the top. Another technique, *bone dating*, is important at disturbed sites for determining the contemporaneity of bones with other bones found there. This method depends on groundwater seepage through the bones, the result of which is a gradual build-up of fluorine or uranium deposits. The investigator determines the relative age of a bone by comparing its fluorine content or radioactivity with bones of known age at the site. Sometimes a bone not found with organic material or embedded in a stratum can be dated by its *morphology*—its form and structure—especially if the fossil has a well-documented evolutionary history. Another technique, *paleomagnetic dating*, is based upon the periodic past reversals of the earth's magnetic poles. Magnetic particles in sediments—particularly lavas—retain the polarity they had when laid down. This helps researchers determine the relative ages of bones or artifacts that were buried in the sediments at the time they formed.

ABSOLUTE DATING

Radiocarbon and Potassium-Argon Dating.   Absolute (or chronometric) dating provides the age of a specimen in calendar years. The best-known and one of the most useful of all dating techniques is *radiocarbon dating*, a method linked to the radioactive carbon (carbon 14) present in bones, shells, wood, leather, cloth, ash, or other organic matter. All living organisms absorb radioactive carbon, which they surrender after death at a constant and known rate. Investigators measure the amount of residual carbon 14 to estimate the date at which the organism died. The method is fairly accurate for dating organic materials ranging from about 500 to 75,000 years ago. Another technique, *potassium-argon dating*, is of crucial importance for determining the age of volcanic rocks and, indirectly, the earliest human remains. This method involves measuring the steady disintegration in volcanic materials of radioactive potassium (potassium 40) into the gas argon (argon 40) and is reasonably accurate for deposits ranging from around 500,000 to several billion years ago. One obvious drawback of the technique is its dependence on volcanic materials. Yet potassium-argon dating is ideal for investigating extremely early human fossils and artifacts found in areas once volcanically active, as in East Africa, for the objects can be dated relatively after first determining the age of the volcanic material.

Fission-Track and Thermoluminescence Dating.   Scientists are working to find reliable methods to bridge the gap of almost 500,000 years between radiocarbon and potassium-argon dating. One of these is another radioactive decay technique, *fission-track dating*, which is used for determining the age of certain minerals and natural glasses found in volcanic ash by measuring the radiation damage that has been done to a sample by the spontaneous fission of uranium 238. A single fission burns a minute tunnel called a track in the crystal, and the distinctive mark is actually visible under a microscope. Because the number of tracks increases with age and the concentration of uranium, the dual measurements of track density and uranium content permit calculating the age of the sample. The technique may have application for dating volcanic substances ranging from about 100,000 to ten million years ago. Another method, *thermoluminescence dating,* is employed for dating pottery, clay figurines, campfire stones, and other crystalline materials subjected in the past to intense heat, resulting in a loss of energy that had been gradually trapped inside by exposure to radiation. The buildup of energy begins again after the firing and gradually increases with time. This method involves the controlled heating of a sample to release the new buildup of energy, the intensity of light emitted indicating when the initial heating took place. In principle, the technique can be applied for dating crystalline materials ranging from a few thousand to one million years ago. These and numerous other methods of dating have radically lengthened the known time span of human evolution and have dramatically expanded knowledge about our early ancestors.

THE BIOLOGICAL AND CULTURAL EVOLUTION OF EARLY HUMANS

ANCESTORS IN THE TREES: THE FIRST PRIMATES

Paleoanthropologists continue to uncover extraordinary evidence of human evolution. Renowned investigators—exemplified by the Leakey family and Donald Johanson—have discovered important fossil remains in East Africa and have compiled an extensive literature on the subject; thus only a bare outline of the evolutionary story need be traced here. Scientists tell us the earth lacked life entirely for billions of years, until living cells arose from their chemical constituents around four billion years ago. Paleontologists working in western Australia have discovered traces of primitive algae and bacteria in rocks that are at least three and one-half billion years old. For additional billions of years the earth was home to lower forms of life such as vegetation, insects, and fish. A number of air-breathing fish developed into amphibians with limbs, and from these came reptiles, some evolving into birds, others into mammals.

Perhaps some fifty to sixty million years ago the first true primates appeared on our planet. What makes primates different from other mammals? They have hands capable of grasping and manipulating objects, nails rather than claws at the tips of their fingers, short snouts, and forward-facing eyes with stereoscopic vision. The first primates lived aloft in the protective shelter of trees, as do most surviving primate species. They were the ancestors of all living primates, including monkeys, apes, and humans. Tree dwelling enhanced their prehensile abilities. Somewhat in the manner of squirrels, these early tree-dwelling primates adopted hand feeding, which led to a reduction of the snout and consequently to more forward-facing eyes and stereoscopic vision. Because of these features, they relied more heavily on sight than smell for exploring their environment. This in turn encouraged the development of new areas in the brain.

THE EVOLVING HOMINIDS

Over vast tracts of time, our early tree-dwelling ancestors gave rise to subfamilies of primates such as monkeys and apes. Eventually the ancestral line of humans and apes diverged. The fossil record indicates that creatures approaching the biological features of modern humans evolved in Africa. With considerable confidence, investigators now trace the lineage of hominids—modern human beings and their humanlike ancestors—back at least five million years. About this time a drying trend in Africa diminished the rain forests and gave rise to grasslands. Our ancestors no longer had the protection of trees but lived in the dangerous open countryside, and they made several notable terrestrial adaptations as a means of survival. We saw they had already developed stereoscopic vision in the trees. Next their legs and feet changed. Instead of walking on all fours, they began to adopt an erect posture permitting bipedal walking. Bipedalism freed the hands of our progenitors for carrying things and later for toolmaking. Additionally, their hands became increasingly dexterous. Each hand included an opposable thumb, one that can touch the tips of all the other fingers. This ability meant our distant ancestors could employ a *precision grip*—the holding of objects by the tips of the fingers and the thumb—permitting the development of artistic creations and writing. They could also use a *power grip*—the wrapping of the thumb and fingers around an object—permitting the manipulation of tools and weapons.

We do not know when meat first assumed importance in the human diet. Judging from the wear of their teeth and other evidence, some of the earlier hominids were vegetarians, though eventually meat eating was adopted. In the meantime, the hominid brain became increasingly complex and large, necessitating some widening of the female pelvis and the birth canal, but there was a limit because extreme widening would have hindered bipedalism. Thus hominid infants were born while still physically underdeveloped and remained dependent for a very long time on their mothers. Paleoanthropologists used to think this extended period of infant and child dependency fostered a sexual division of labor among the earlier hominids. They argued that females carrying children were more restricted than males in roaming about seeking food, though able to gather fruit, nuts, berries, and grain. According to one version of this hypothesis, males went off hunting while females collected plant foods, all bringing their contributions back to a common place for processing and sharing. Many investigators now seriously question the hunting theme, doubting that the hominids of two million years ago were capable of killing and butchering their prey. Instead, they find evidence that the earlier hominids were scavengers stealing into the territory of carnivores to obtain the defleshed bones of recent kills for marrow. Adherents of this view place increasing emphasis on the gathering of food by both males and females, suggesting the latter may have transported their infants in a carrying device to free their hands.

HOMO ERECTUS

Paleoanthropologists working in East Africa have unearthed the remains of hominid fossils at least five million years old. During this far distant period a number of hominid species apparently developed, flourished for a while, and then disappeared. Investigators have identified several successive species—they are termed *Ardipithecus ramidus, Australopithecus afarensis, Australopithecus africanus, Australopithecus robustus, Australopithecus boisei, Homo habilis, Homo erectus,* and *Homo sapiens*—but their interrelationships remain elusive and puzzling. The last three of these are classified in our genus *Homo* (man), characterized by a notable expansion of the brain. Fossil remains indicate that the species known as *Homo erectus* (upright man) appeared between one and one-half and two million years ago. The achievements of these people far surpassed those of earlier hominids. Although strongly built *Homo erectus* was quite similar to modern human beings from the neck downward, the skull was thick and low, with prominent brow ridges and a protruding jaw. The average cranial capacity of the species was under 1000 cubic centimeters—considerably less than the modern human average of 1450—but the *Homo erectus* skull and brain continued to expand with time.

Culture.   The physical variations of early human beings are vastly less significant to the historian than the manner of their lives. This brings us to a consideration of culture, a distinguishing mark of humanity. Anthropologists have defined the term in numerous ways, but most regard culture as the pattern of learned values, behavior, and beliefs built up by a group of people and transmitted from one generation to another. Each culture fosters its own characteristic mode of thinking and living, while discouraging others. The vast scope of culture includes the means people employ for securing food and shelter, devising tools and weapons, responding to the supernatural, and interacting socially. The diverse cultures of our early ancestors arose, expanded, and declined, though leaving a heritage of traits in other cultures through absorption.

Improved Tool Technology.   The use of tools is one of the most important components of a culture. We know *Homo habilis* fashioned all-purpose implements from stone. Members of the successive *Homo erectus* cultures, on the other hand, tailored their tools for specific purposes. Investigators have found a wide range of stone tools used for cutting, scraping, chopping, piercing, and pounding, activities associated with the preparation of plant and animal foods. Several sites have yielded bone and wooden implements as well. The evidence of extensive butchery suggests a major increase in the consumption of meat, and future excavations may show that *Homo erectus* employed wooden spears for hunting.

Use of Fire.   Although the members of the species were still predominantly forgers and scavengers, perhaps they engaged in a degree of big-game hunting. Evidence suggests that at least some of them learned to control fire for warming and illuminating their living spaces as well as cooking food and warding off predators. They may have used fire to frighten animals such as mammoths into muddy bogs or other traps, then butchering the helpless creatures. Hunting in this fashion required cooperation and planning among the hunters. Yet we must not confuse cooperation with a lack of more exotic practices, at least from the modern perspective. Although fierce debate rages over the issue, a number of investigators argue that *Homo erectus*

Reconstruction of
Homo habilis.

practiced cannibalism. Excavators have found many split and charred human bones, perhaps suggesting these people liked human marrow, though preferring to eat the fatty tissue cooked.

Vocal Development.   Apparently *Homo erectus* lived in small groups or bands, each band probably interbreeding with others. Any group activities depended upon following instructions, perhaps by watching and imitating or by responding to vocal commands. We do not know whether *Homo erectus* was capable of fully articulate speech. A number of paleoanthropologists have concluded that spoken language in some rudimentary form emerged some two million years ago, but others support a relatively recent date of around 40,000 or 50,000 years in the past. Language, whenever it developed, was a monumental human achievement, enabling people to share their knowledge, their experiences, and their feelings. The use of speech was decisive in the development of culture and its transmission from one generation to another. Through language, parents not only taught their children to make tools but also inculcated proper rules of conduct and correct religious beliefs.

Migration from Africa.   Paleoanthropologists now believe *Homo erectus* originated in Africa and became the first hominid to leave the continent, migrating to Asia and Europe. Evidence of the species has been found in Africa and across much of the rest of the Old World, especially Southeast Asia. Perhaps a growing population had exhausted the resources in Africa, causing some groups of *Homo erectus* to move into unexplored regions very early, at least one million years ago, possibly much earlier. With their increased brain size, systematic toolmaking, and use of fire, they were able to adapt to new environments and occupy habitats unknown to previous hominids.

THE PALEOLITHIC AGE
(c. 3,000,000–10,000 bp)

The remote dimensions of time cited in prehistory are mere approximations. Dates in the narrative that are earlier than around 10,000 years ago are expressed in years Before Present, conventionally abbreviated bp. Following increasingly frequent scholarly practice, later dates are indicated by the abbreviations bce, Before the Common Era, and ce, Common Era, in place of bc and ad. Historians usually divide the entire span of human technology into two great but roughly delineated periods—an age of stone and an age of metals—terms referring to the prevalent medium used in the manufacture of tools and weapons. While the age of stone generally falls within the prehistoric era before the invention of writing, the age of metals corresponds to the historic era based upon written records. Nineteenth-century investigators separated the age of stone into three stages: the Paleolithic (Old Stone) Age, the Mesolithic (Middle Stone) Age, and the Neolithic (New Stone) Age. Such designations emphasize only one cultural element of a span of time—not necessarily the one of greatest historical significance—and the dates for the three ages vary widely from one part of the world to another. Nevertheless the terms Paleolithic, Mesolithic, and Neolithic have become conventional and are usually retained, though the second of the three is now generally restricted to developments in northwestern Europe.

The Effects of Glaciation

The Paleolithic Age lasted from the time of the earliest toolmaking hominids—they lived at least three million years ago—to about 10,000 years ago in some parts of the world. An epoch of chipped stone tools, the Old Stone Age witnessed the

Reconstruction of *Homo erectus*.

spread of the evolving human species to almost every corner of the earth. In response perhaps to subtle changes in the radiation of the sun or to other cosmic phenomena, the period was characterized by wide fluctuations in climate and environment. On at least four different occasions during an enormous span of prehistoric time known as the Pleistocene geological epoch, lasting from almost two million years ago to 10,000 years ago, the Northern Hemisphere witnessed major advances of great ice sheets—the Ice Ages—followed by warmer periods of glacial retreat. A drop of just a few degrees in the northern latitudes was sufficient to prevent winter snows from melting the following summer. Then the snows of the next winter would pile on top. About 500,000 years ago much of northern Europe was buried under mile-high glacial ice, which had also pushed deep into North America. At their maximum thrust, ice sheets and glaciers covered nearly one-third of the land surface of the Northern Hemisphere. The oceans shrank and sea levels plummeted far below their present depths as water became locked up in continental ice sheets. What is now Britain and continental Europe were joined by a land bridge, as was North America and Asia, Australia and New Guinea.

The last major period of glaciation, albeit ebbing and advancing several times, held the northern latitudes in its firm grip from roughly 70,000 to 10,000 years ago. During the interglacial eras the fauna and flora of warmer zones inched northward. The retreat and melting of ice resulted in vast quantities of water being deposited in Europe and elsewhere in the Northern Hemisphere, changing what had been a relatively arid area into one of great river systems, dense forests, and moist grasslands. Such an environment supported reindeer, bison, horses, mammoths, woolly rhinoceroses, and cave bears, as well as lions, wolves, deer, hyenas, Arctic foxes, panthers, and other mammals eaten by the hominids. All animals were wild at this time and some were extremely dangerous, but over thousands of years such creatures, along with changing vegetational zones, had lured *Homo erectus* up from warm Africa into temperate Asia and Europe.

ABSENCE OF PERMANENT SETTLEMENTS AND AGRICULTURE

Unaware of the methods of an agricultural existence, early Paleolithic people did not establish permanent settlements. *Homo erectus* bands made camps, where they probably remained for at least several days butchering animals and sharing meat and edible plants. The ground must have sufficed for resting and sleeping during the summer and in warmer climates. In cool northern regions, however, *Homo erectus* sometimes inhabited rock shelters or caves and apparently raised tentlike huts of interlocking leafy branches anchored by rocks. A basic feature of each hut was a central hearth sheltered from wind by a circle of stones.

THE EVOLUTION OF ARCHAIC AND MODERN *HOMO SAPIENS*

Rival Theories.   The elusive *Homo erectus*, seemingly the only surviving hominid species on earth by one million years ago, vanishes from the fossil record around 150,000 years ago. *Homo erectus* had already started evolving toward more anatomically modern humans by 400,000 years ago. About 300,000 years ago a new human species known as *Homo sapiens* (wise man) begins to appear in increasing numbers and variation. Apparently this species first evolved as a form of archaic *Homo sapiens*, later as the subspecies *Homo sapiens sapiens* (doubly wise man), fully modern humans. A fundamental question for paleoanthropologists concerns the evolutionary descent of *Homo sapiens sapiens*. The issue has spawned two main competing scientific theories to explain the transition to anatomically modern humans. According to one hypothesis, *Homo erectus* migrated from Africa at least one million years ago, populating the entire Old World and also providing the basis for further evolution

Reconstruction of a 4,000,000-year-old oval hut of interlocking branches at Terra Amata on the Mediterranean shore of France.

both within and outside Africa. The proponents of this view suggest that *Homo erectus* populations in various geographical regions gradually evolved into the archaic *Homo sapiens*, from which came the subspecies *Homo sapiens sapiens*. Thus modern Europeans would have originated in Europe, modern Africans in Africa, and modern Chinese in eastern Asia. This helps to explain why regional forms of *Homo erectus* had common physiological features that became even more pronounced with the successive emergence of archaic *Homo sapiens* and *Homo sapiens sapiens*.

The other camp contends that anatomically modern humans evolved from the archaic *Homo sapiens*—but *only in Africa*—and then embarked upon a major wave of migration (the second from the continent) around 100,000 years ago to replace all existing mortals and to populate the entire earth. This theory is based on research carried out by molecular biologists. Their study of the genetic codes in tiny structures outside the nucleus of the human cell (the mitochondrial DNA) supports an African origin for *Homo sapiens sapiens*. The origin of our mitochondrial DNA, itself inherited largely or entirely from the mother, stretches into the remote past without interruption from a long succession of mothers. The biologists argue that a primeval woman in Africa, whom they call Eve, was the mother of every one of us. The proponents of both theories agree that all human beings alive today are interconnected by a flow of genes and that their common ancestor arose in Africa. Their dispute

This artistic reconstruction of a Neanderthal face contrasts with the former customary image of the hominid as a brutish, primitive creature.

concerns whether the common *African* ancestor was *Homo erectus* or *Homo sapiens*. As research methods improve and more fossils are found, undoubtedly a more clear-cut picture will emerge about the evolutionary descent of fully modern humans.

WHO WERE THE NEANDERTHALS?

Before the appearance of *Homo sapiens sapiens* in Europe, the continent was occupied by the enigmatic Neanderthals, who are established in the fossil record between about 130,000 and 30,000 years ago. Although the origin of the Neanderthals cannot yet be traced with any certainty, most paleoanthropologists think they evolved gradually across Europe and western Asia from a late form of *Homo erectus* or an archaic *Homo sapiens*. The scientific community is deeply divided concerning *Homo neanderthalensis*. Did they evolve into people like us, as suggested by investigators holding that archaic *Homo sapiens* descended from *Homo erectus* in various regions of the world, or were they an evolutionary dead end, as argued by those concluding that anatomically modern humans emerged only in Africa and migrated to replace other mortals?

Rugged individuals who survived in the shadow of ice sheets during the last period of major glaciation, the Neanderthals ranged from what is now southern France to Israel and Iraq. They were short and powerful in build, with massive skeletons, broad chests, and large hands and feet. We know nothing of their skin pigmentation, but their muscular bodies supported heads of considerable size that featured thick skulls, great brow ridges, low and sloping foreheads, small cheekbones, large front teeth, and enormous noses. The middle of the Neanderthal face was characterized by its extreme protrusion and spacious nasal cavities, perhaps an adaptation for warming bitterly cold inhaled air. The brain was equal to or slightly larger than the average today, but some investigators make the disputed suggestion that the Neanderthals lacked certain crucial mental abilities enjoyed by anatomically modern humans.

Neanderthal Technology: Mousterian Flake Tools.   The Neanderthals are generally associated with the manufacture of a variety of tools termed Mousterian. This tool industry was relatively advanced but remained unchanged during the long existence of the Neanderthal people. Named for the village of Le Moustier in southwestern France, where representative examples of the tools were first found, the Mousterian tradition produced a variety of carefully shaped stone implements. The characteristic technique involved striking flakes from a prepared core of flint, then retouching them to make specialized tools. Archaeologists have found remains of Mousterian tools over a vast area, extending from western Europe to North Africa and southwest Asia. Neanderthal populations were able to influence their environment with such implements. They could compete with larger and stronger animals, for example, or easily trap smaller ones. The Neanderthals were skilled hunters, using stone-tipped wooden spears to prey upon large creatures such as reindeer, mammoths, bison, cave bears, horses, and wooly rhinoceroses. They employed various implements for hunting swans and ducks and others for fishing. Using their serviceable tools, the Neanderthals could skin animals, work with wood, and carry out other chores essential for their way of life.

Bands of Neanderthal hunter-food gatherers seem to have moved seasonally, apparently in pursuit of prey. They were the first people to move into truly cold climates, enduring miserable winters and short summers as they pushed northward behind the retreating glaciers. They must have worn the skins of animals they hunted, for the rigors of winter would have compelled wearing clothing for survival. Most Neanderthals found refuge from the bitter cold in rock shelters and in caves, but excavators have discovered sites in eastern Europe where people raised large huts having a framework of branches. Apparently the numerous heavy mammoth bones found nearby were employed as weights to hold down animal skins covering the dwellings.

Neanderthal Burials.   Some anthropologists think the Neanderthals lacked family units. They argue the men roamed about hunting and were reluctant to share their meat with women, who generally took care of themselves and ate plant foods. According to this view, men and women employed different tools and engaged in different tasks, and their impoverished interaction hindered planning for the future or making effective use of the natural resources around them. This theory of limited social behavior is strongly challenged by other investigators who suggest Neanderthal burials indicate a degree of caring for their kind. The Neanderthals were the first people who systematically buried their dead. Anthropologists and archaeologists have discovered a number of their burial sites in Europe and southwest Asia, almost always in caves. A find at Shanidar cave in northern Iraq has aroused considerable speculation about the possibility of funeral rites. Did a group of Neanderthal mourners bring wild-flowers to this burial site? Pollen analysis suggests the body at Shanidar was laid on a bed of branches and surrounded with flowers, including certain varieties still known locally for their medicinal properties. Many researchers have taken this evidence to mean that the Neanderthals assigned importance to a person's life and death, perhaps even believing in a hereafter. The occasional recovery of stone tools and other objects apparently associated with these burials has been interpreted as offerings to supernatural beings in the next world or as personal possessions needed for survival in an existence after death. Corpses were painted with an earthly mineral oxide known as red ocher and positioned carefully with the knees drawn up and the arms folded over the heart. The Neanderthals may have believed the use of red ocher, as the color of blood, provided a magical means for reestablishing life.

PALEOLITHIC RELIGION AND MAGIC

Animism. Although the details of beliefs and rites in the distant past cannot be recovered from the archaeological evidence, investigators offer tempting interpretations on the overall picture of Paleolithic religious patterns. The people of the period seem to have been convinced that natural phenomena, natural objects, and heavenly bodies are endowed with spirits, a belief now called animism. Perhaps they believed natural forces such as rain, wind, thunder, and lightning were alive and capable of acting with a purpose. Were floods, earthquakes, volcanic eruptions, eclipses, and comets not manifestations of supernatural powers intervening in human affairs? Did animate objects such as trees and such inanimate objects as rocks, mountains, rivers, and stars not possess consciousness? Paleolithic people must have believed the spirits could be flattered from time to time by human actions or be easily offended. To appease the supernatural, humans seem to have made offerings or sacrifices. Apparently certain ministrants gradually emerged as specialists in communicating with the natural forces on behalf of the people through rituals, trances, and chants. These intermediaries, known today by names such as shamans and priests, also probably offered explanations for the three great mysteries of life, namely, birth, existence, and death.

Fertility, Death, and Life Cults. In time, various cults emerged to help mortals cope with the triad of great mysteries and other concerns. Some investigators identify three major classes of cults: fertility, death, and life cults. Fertility cults emphasize birth and are absorbed with the regeneration of plants, animals, and people. Death cults are primarily concerned with a future beyond mortal existence and are characterized by prominent tombs and elaborate burials. Life cults emphasize life on earth and are not preoccupied by questions about the origin of life or the hereafter. Although life cults have been relatively rare in the human chronicle, the religion of the classical Greeks—while not ignoring the power of fertility—was essentially such a cult and took a rather casual attitude about the possibility of a future beyond mortal existence.

Clearly, Paleolithic peoples believed in powers they did not understand. They probably appealed to the supernatural through both magic and religion. Some investigators, though acknowledging that the two elements were closely intertwined, make a broad distinction between Paleolithic religion and magic, viewing the former as an attempt to appease gods or spirits to obtain favor, the latter as an endeavor to control the world through special techniques believed to channel supernatural power. Thus the prehistoric magician may have sought to manipulate events or nature by means of an incantation (the ritual recitation of a formula of words supposed to produce a desired effect), an amulet (something worn for protection or power), or an imitation (the mimicking of a desired result in an attempt to bring it about). Perhaps the practitioner of magic also resorted to divination, the attempt to foresee future events. Some scholars suggest prehistoric magicians may have attempted to control the world not only to benefit themselves and their people but also to harm anyone identified as an enemy.

UPPER PALEOLITHIC CULTURES: A SPECTACULAR FLOWERING OF ARTISTIC AND RELIGIOUS EXPRESSION (c. 35,000–10,000 BP)

ANATOMICALLY MODERN *HOMO SAPIENS* IN WESTERN EUROPE

The latter phase of the Paleolithic Age, referred to as Upper Paleolithic, lasted from about 35,000 to 10,000 years ago, a time when people virtually indistinguishable from modern humans lived in Europe, Africa, and Asia. Thus they were representatives of the subspecies *Homo sapiens sapiens*. Those who succeeded the Neanderthals in western Europe are sometimes called the Cro-Magnons, named for a site in southern France where their bones were first unearthed. Although anatomically modern, these people exhibited relatively robust cranial capacities averaging about 1600 centimeters in volume, somewhat larger than the typical human skull today.

The Disappearance of the Neanderthals from the Fossil Record (c. 30,000 BP). We saw that paleoanthropologists are divided concerning the Neanderthals. One group of investigators suggests a pattern of continuous evolution of late Neanderthals into early modern humans. Advocates of an opposing view point out that the Neanderthals and early modern humans coexisted in Europe and other places for a period of time. They find no compelling fossil evidence of a gradual blending between the two populations, but a steady disappearance of the Neanderthal people, as though modern humans filtered into western Europe some 40,000 years ago to replace them with some slight competitive edge. Within 10,000 years the Neanderthals were gone.

CAVE ART

The short period of the early modern humans in western Europe witnessed an amazing sequence of cultures and a striking efflorescence of art in the form of extraordinary

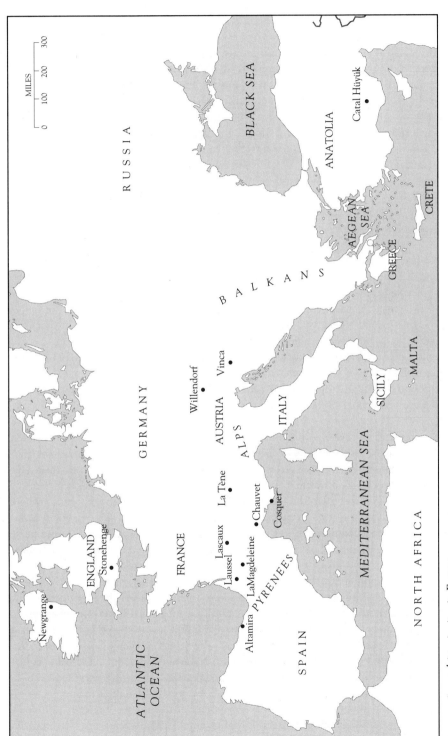

Some major prehistoric sites in Europe.

murals and decorations on the walls and roofs of their caves. Artisans created a profusion of images—chiefly animal figures—some engraved with sharp stone tools, others painted. Since the initial discovery in the 1870s, investigators have found about two hundred painted and engraved caves from the Upper Paleolithic period in western Europe, the vast majority being in France and Spain. Two of the most celebrated are the caves of Altamira in northern Spain and of Lascaux in southwestern-central France. Late twentieth-century discoveries yielded a couple of additional major caves in southern France. In 1985 a diver found a great cave named Cosquer on the coast of southeastern France near Marseilles, its entrance now submerged 120 feet below the Mediterranean. Subsequent explorations revealed Cosquer was decorated with hand stencils and paintings of a wide range of fauna believed to be 27,000 years old. The other vast cave network, Chauvet, was discovered in 1994 near the town of Vallon-Pont-d'Arc in southern France. Chauvet contains hundreds of Upper Paleolithic paintings and engravings so superbly made and preserved that investigators describe them as one of the most important archaeological finds of the twentieth century. Created some 20,000 years ago, the images are unique because the majority of the depicted animals—wooly-haired rhinoceroses, bears, and lions—were not regularly hunted or eaten by Upper Paleolithic peoples.

Magnificent Lascaux, dated 17,000 years ago, is the most famous of the Upper Paleolithic decorated caves. Artists ventured deep inside Lascaux to create accurate renderings of the game animals most important to them, including bison, aurochs (wild cattle), mammoths, horses, ibex (wild goats), and deer. The spectacular, lifelike animal figures were made with considerable care, though the images in such dark and remote settings could be seen only by torchlight or by the sputtering light of primitive animal-fat lamps.

Hunting Magic.   Scholars offer many theories for the purpose of cave art, the oldest of which explains the images as part of the rituals of hunting magic, presumably performed to increase the chances of a successful hunt. Paleolithic peoples must have regarded images as powerful, even dangerous. Artists in the caves often painted game animals with spears and arrows entering their bodies at critical points, perhaps evidence of an imitation. They may have believed drawing images of wounded animals would make the hunters successful, or painting a herd of animals would make game more plentiful. The artists also depicted animals feared as predators, including lions, hyenas, and bears, commonly showing them wounded by spears or arrows, possibly to bring about their magical destruction. Other animals appear trapped in drawings of rectangular enclosures. Some investigators suggest the placement of the pictures may have been significant. In many caves one painting was superimposed upon another, exemplified by four layers of images at a spot in Lascaux, though much empty wall space lies nearby. Perhaps the artists favored placement of paintings on spots seemingly bringing good luck in former hunts, for all ritual involves duplicating as closely as possible a prescribed practice yielding success in the past.

Magic dances may have been performed before the potent paintings as imitations to bring about successful hunts. A number of the images have been chipped, possibly by blows dancing hunters or shamans made with spears. Investigators ex-

Cave paintings in the Hall of Bulls, Lascaux (Dordogne), France. c. 15,000 BCE.

ploring a cave in the Pyrenees found the remains of numerous modeled clay animals, some punctured with holes, presumably caused by the throwing of spears in a hunting ritual. The most famous of these animal statues represents a bear. Its body may have been draped with a bear skin to increase the lifelike appearance, and the skull of a real bear seems to have been attached with a wooden peg. At Chauvet explorers found the skull of a bear on a large rock, possibly some sort of altar.

Initiation Ceremonies.   Most prehistorians now reject a single interpretation for the cave art and seek diverse explanations. Some argue that one likely use of the caves was for initiation ceremonies. Quite a few of the painted chambers were accessible only by crawling through long, tortuous passages or by crossing underground streams, possibly to keep out the uninitiated. Contemporary societies throughout the world employ ceremonies called rites of passage to mark key points along the way of life such as birth, puberty, marriage, and death. As a parallel, perhaps the caves served as imposing settings where young people who had reached puberty underwent initiation ceremonies marking their passage from childhood to the sexual life of an adult. Investigators exploring a cave in western Europe found traces of ancient footprints whose size suggest children or young adolescents.

Other Images.   Although much of the art of prehistoric peoples is intrinsically related to belief, its cultural and religious significance remains puzzling. Occasional man-beast figures on cave walls combine animal or bird heads with partially human bodies, variously interpreted as costumed dancers, godlike beings, or powerful shamans. In terms of human representation, the Upper Paleolithic painters rarely created naturalistic images, usually distorting bodies or rendering them as stick figures. The artists frequently created vivid images of human hands by blowing paint from a hollow tube over an outstretched hand employed as a stencil. Were the human hands signs of membership in a cult or community? The fingers are sometimes mysteriously missing, possibly a macabre note. A few investigators suggest that at least some of the animals and various cryptic geometrical signs found in the caves are sexual in nature, being magic representations intended to induce fertility. Pairs of animals often appear together, sometimes mating. Perhaps the animals shown with seemingly swollen bellies have reached a state of advanced pregnancy. Overall, an almost limitless range of hypotheses can be offered, though not systematically tested, to explain the puzzling animal images and the abstract signs and symbols scattered throughout the paintings.

Painting Techniques.   Whatever the meaning of the murals, the skill of the painters and the beauty of their polychromatic images is astounding. The artists often incorporated natural features of the cave walls in their compositions to suggest the bulging flank of an animal or some other physical attribute. They began by drawing an outline with charcoal, then painting the interior spaces with colors of the earth (yellow, brown, reddish-brown, and black) as well as white and violet. Paleolithic artists seem to have prepared their paint pigments by grinding natural deposits to a fine powder and then mixing them together to achieve the desired colors, finally adding a base of water, saliva, or animal fat. Apparently paints were applied with fingers, pointed tools, blowpipes, pads made of moss and fur, and possibly by rapidly spitting chewed pigments on the walls. Once applied, the colors were slowly absorbed by the rock face to give the paintings their phenomenal durability. Many of the images of animals are exceptionally naturalistic and vivid, though involving only a minimum amount of painting. So bold and clear, the creatures seem almost painted from life, the very essence of animal presence.

Adornments, Decorated Objects, and Musical Instruments

Upper Paleolithic artistic expression was not confined to cave paintings. Specialists made pendants, rings, bracelets, and anklets from bone, shell, mammoth tusk, tooth, and stone. They improved the quality of life by fashioning such materials into fishhooks and eyed needles, as well as fine harpoons with barbed heads for stabbing salmon. Upper Paleolithic peoples frequently decorated weapons and other implements with geometric figures and images of animals, fish, and plants. Their artifacts included the spear thrower, a device greatly increasing the velocity and killing range of spears. According to one highly controversial theory, the seemingly random notches and markings engraved on certain portable objects found over a wide area in Europe actually represent a notational system, possibly a form of lunar calendar used to predict the changing seasons. Other important finds include bone flutes, rattles, drums, and other musical instruments, perhaps played during various rites as well as for pleasure.

IMPACT OF WOMEN ON UPPER PALEOLITHIC RELIGION

Identification with the Moon.   Archaeologists have found numerous renderings of vulvae and erect penises at Upper Paleolithic sites. The probable purpose of these genitalic representations, not strictly erotic, was to portray female and male attributes. Perhaps a vulva symbolized fruitfulness, a penis strength. No doubt Paleolithic peoples lacked a complete understanding of the connection between sexual relations and conception. Apparently they believed women had some strange connection with the moon giving them mysterious regenerative powers, an identification probably related to the process of menstruation. The usual menstrual cycle of twenty-eight days approximates the cycle of the moon known as the lunar (or synodic) month. Lasting about twenty-nine and one-half days, the lunar month marks the interval between one phase of the moon and its recurrence. An even more uncanny correspondence between the cycles of the moon and the menstrual cycle is represented by the sidereal month of almost twenty-eight days, the period elapsing before the moon returns to the same position in the sky. Reminding us that ancient observations of lunar cycles led to the first widespread measure of time, the word *moon* is rooted in the base *me*, meaning "to measure," and the word *menstruation* comes from the same base.

The Venuses.   Excavators have found numerous sculptured female images—the so-called Venuses— in Upper Paleolithic sites from the Pyrenees to the Urals. These take the form of figurines (statuettes) and reliefs (carved figures raised from a background plane). The figurines were made of varied materials such as stone, ivory, antler, and fired clay. The famous relief known as the *Venus of Laussel*, which was recovered at a site of the same name in southwestern France, depicts a frontal view of a naked, faceless female holding a crescent bison horn marked with thirteen lines (the number of sidereal months in a year). Archaeologists have unearthed many similar female images, all with featureless faces. The majority have exaggerated genitalia and appear pregnant with enormously swollen bellies and breasts. The most widely known of these is a tiny limestone figurine called the *Venus of Willendorf*, found near the village of the same name in Austria. Dated 25,000 to 30,000 years age, the *Venus of Willendorf* has a faceless head crowned by tight curls of hair and displays the prominent genitalia characteristic of all the female images. Her rudimentary arms rest upon her huge breasts, while her belly bulges enormously and her thighs appear quite swollen. At one time her short legs must have ended in miniscule feet, now broken off, and only traces survive of the pigments originally covering her body.

Researchers offer various theories to explain the female figurines and reliefs. A recurrent interpretation regards the Venuses as representations of a great mother-goddess. Perhaps they signify an association of lunar and menstrual cycles. Were they were magical symbols employed in fertility rites to promote successful pregnancy

Venus of Willendorf. Rendered in limestone, this small sculpture in the round typifies the female forms often called "Venus figures," with exaggerated breasts, buttocks, abdomen, and genitalia, other features being minimized. This piece, dating c. 25,000 BCE, is now in the Naturhistorisches Museum, Vienna.

and safe birth for both animals and humans? Did they reflect Upper Paleolithic mythology and lore relating to female processes such as maturation, menstruation, copulation, pregnancy, birth, and lactation? Regardless of the precise meaning of the Venuses, their physical characteristics seem to indicate fertility was a constant theme.

Many prehistorians suggest the Venuses evolved into the vast series of carved female figures of Neolithic date—often interpreted as goddesses of fertility—whose bare-breasted form frequently appears with symbols representing the moon, hunting, and fertility. The Venuses may have been ancestral to several goddesses in classical Greece, one of whom was Artemis, a virgin associated with the moon, hunting, and agriculture. In Rome a possible descendant of the carved female figure was Diana, the ancient Italian moon goddess, who came to be identified with Artemis and was associated with chastity, hunting, and women in childbirth. Some scholars find a reflection of the Venuses in Mary of the Christian religion, a mother figure associated with virginity and sometimes depicted with her feet on the moon.

TOTEMISM

The importance of animals for survival during the Upper Paleolithic period may have resulted in some totemism, commonly defined as the identification of a group with an animal. Apparently early humans perceived a certain kinship with other creatures. Perhaps some groups designated a specific animal with qualities they admired as their ancestor or patron god. According to this view, one population might have chosen the cave bear as its totem, another the reindeer. The theory suggests the animal was sacred to the group and could be killed only under special circumstances such as a ceremonial holy meal—an essential element of almost every known religion—when people may have eaten its flesh to acquire its qualities and performed rites to thank the sacrificed creature for being a channel of divinity. Many scholars hypothesize that the animal depictions in the Upper Paleolithic caves are totemic emblems.

CHAPTER II

The Transition from Hunting and Gathering to Farming

About 15,000 years ago the last Ice Age began to retreat, finally ending around 10,000 years ago after several periods of oscillation. Temperatures rose worldwide and the glaciers made their final retreat, producing fundamental changes in Europe, the northern part of Africa, and southwest Asia. The climate in Europe became rainier, leading to the gradual replacement of grasslands with dense forests, while great grazing herds of mammoths and other animals that were adapted to cold and ice became extinct or moved north. The rainfall pattern also changed in northern Africa, creating an environment of semiarid grasslands and shallow lakes in what is now the Sahara Desert. This region dried up rapidly after 8000 years ago (6000 BCE), and the Sahara Desert gradually emerged, rendering life considerably more difficult for both people and animals. In the meantime, warmer and wetter conditions in southwest Asia brought flourishing woodlands as well as wild cereal grasses and other food resources capable of being domesticated. The climatic changes paralleled a momentous period of transition in southwest Asia, dated from around 10,500 to 6000 years ago (8500–4000 BCE), when humans in the region gradually learned to plant grain for a harvest the following year and discovered the secrets of breeding animals. Thus they switched from subsistence wholly by hunting and gathering to subsistence by food production based on plant and animal domestication. These changes, by no means smooth or rapid, stretched over many centuries and began at different times from place to place in southwest Asia and elsewhere.

THE NEOLITHIC AGE AND THE EARLY FARMERS IN THE ASIAN NEAR EAST (c. 10,500–6000 BP, OR 8500–4000 BCE)

Generally, archaeologists refer to southwest Asia and Egypt as the Near East. Our immediate concern is with the Asian part of the Near East during the Neolithic period. The term Neolithic implies new and advanced stone-working methods but is now more commonly used to designate the transition in a region from dependence upon wild sources of food for survival to dependence on domesticated plants and animals, first attested in the Asian Near East.

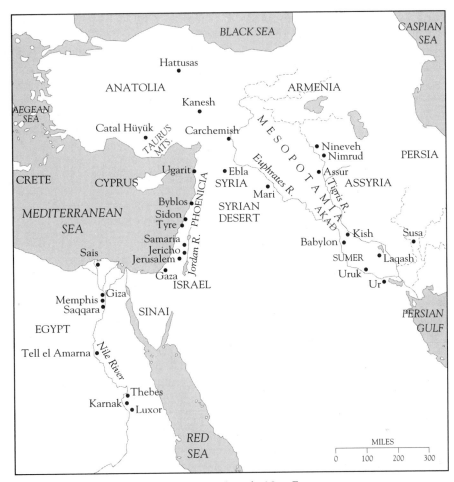

Some major prehistoric and early historic sites in the Near East.

THE NATUFIANS AND THE SETTLEMENT OF PREAGRICULTURAL VILLAGES (C. 12,000–10,500 BP, OR 10,000–8500 BCE)

Perhaps the most important element in the transition to food production in the Asian Near East was the establishment of preagricultural settled communities, generally near springs, lakes, or coasts providing fish and game. Although the inhabitants subsisted in part on hunting and gathering, they also harvested a wide variety of wild cereal grasses, the most widespread being wild barley. The clearest early evidence for this development is found in the lands bordering the eastern shores of the Mediterranean. The people of the area—prehistorians call them the Natufians—occupied much of the coastal strip from southern Turkey through Israel from roughly 12,000 to 10,500 years ago (10,000–8500 BCE), the period just before the development of agriculture. Their culture was characterized by fairly permanent villages of circular dwellings on stone foundations, though some of the Natufians continued to live in caves or rock shelters. Their society seems to have been matrilineal, that is, descent was traced through the female line. These people hunted the small antelopes known as gazelles, but they acquired much of their food by reaping the wild cereals of the area with straight bone sickles set with many-toothed flint blades, processing the harvested kernels with pounding and grinding stones. They constructed roughly-plastered pits under their houses, apparently for the storage of surplus grain. Remains from several Natufian sites offer conclusive evidence for the domestication of the dog from the wolf about 12,000 years ago (10,000 BCE), much earlier than any other animal. Apparently the Natufians were on the verge of discovering the secrets of raising livestock and cultivating land for the production of crops.

NEOLITHIC JERICHO (C. 10,500–7000 BP, OR 8500–5000 BCE)

Evidence of a Budding Farming Economy. One of the important sites associated with the Natufian culture is the ancient village of Jericho, situated just north of the famous salt lake between Israel and Jordan known as the Dead Sea. Many hundreds of feet below sea level, Jericho served around 11,000 years ago (9000 BCE) as a customary campsite of Natufian hunter-gatherers, who were drawn to its bubbling freshwater spring supporting a nearby oasis of luxuriant vegetation. A long period of settlement took place under their descendants, who presided over important technological advances and the transition to agriculture. Jericho witnessed a spectacular building program around 10,000 years ago (8000 BCE), the inhabitants constructing numerous round or oval sun-dried brick houses with conical roofs and stone foundations. Indicating strong leadership, they encircled their settlement with a finely built massive stone wall, strengthened by an imposing circular tower whose excavated remains stand about thirty feet high. The massive tower is almost solid but includes an internal flight of stairs, an engineering marvel for the day. The walls may have served to protect the settlement from slides of mud during rainfall rather than enemy attack. Investigators offer a range of speculations about the tower, some suggesting a design for military defense, others a place of religious activities. If the former theory is correct, the tower represents the earliest known stone fortification. Jericho covered an area of at least eight acres, suggesting a population of between two and three thousand. The size also implies the domestication and cultivation of cereal grasses in the rich soil of the oasis, as indicated by the discovery of grains of domesticated wheat and barley. The inhabitants probably irrigated the soil by means of their copious spring, which provides water even today.

Evidence of Religious Beliefs and Holy Places. Mysteriously, Jericho seems to have been abandoned around 7500 BCE. New settlers arrived shortly thereafter, but their occupation was of a different character. Apparently they introduced domesticated animals such as sheep and goats, which provided them with meat, clothing, milk, and fat for fuel. They constructed rectangular sun-dried brick houses resting on stone foundations and having plastered walls and floors. Their architecture included a large columned building whose walls contained sockets for huge poles—perhaps totem poles—suggesting a shrine or sanctuary. The inhabitants of early agricultural settlements frequently built shrines, taken as evidence for the existence both of organized religion and a priestly class. Excavators at the Jericho shrine found a female figurine—seemingly depicting a deity—and several others of animals, all probably associated with a fertility cult.

Decorated Skulls.   The prominence of decorated skulls at Jericho and other sites in the eastern Mediterranean may reflect some form of ancestor worship. The people at Jericho and elsewhere buried the dead within their settlements, frequently under the floors of their houses, after first severing the head. Some heads were deposited separately, while others remained unburied. Artisans developed an extraordinary form of portraiture by re-creating the features of the deceased on the skulls of the unburied heads. The technique involved covering the skull with molded plaster, applying sprightly colors, and setting cowrie shells in the eye sockets. Perhaps the people believed a spirit located in the head could survive the death of the body, the restored heads serving as dwelling places for deceased ancestors. Whatever their purpose, the riveting plastered and painted skulls were on display in the houses of Jericho.

Pottery.   The second phase of the history of Jericho ended about 6000 BCE, and the archaeological remains offer scant evidence of human occupation for the next millennium. Around 5000 BCE another Neolithic group inhabited the site. These people used pottery, introduced from elsewhere in the Near East. We do not know when or where ceramic vessels were first crafted. Although investigators have found a number of baked clay Venus figures at Upper Paleolithic sites in eastern Europe dated around 20,000 to 30,000 years ago, the hunter-gatherers of the period used convenient light containers such as baskets, bags, and gourds on their frequent wanderings rather than heavy, fragile pottery. The widespread use of clay vessels is a hallmark of the Neolithic and its settled lifestyle. Farmers living in the communities of the New East were making ceramic ware by at least 6000 BCE. The invention of pottery greatly enriched human life, providing durable vessels for the cooking and serving of food and for the storing and carrying of dry materials and liquids.

At first the ware was crudely formed. Perhaps early people had experimented by lining baskets with clay and noticed that the coating hardened after standing near a fire or under the sun. Artisans were soon coating baskets or gourds with clay and baking them to produce a variety of vessels for cooking food. Before long, specialists were making durable pots of innumerable sizes and shapes by an exacting process of carefully preparing, slowly molding, and cautiously firing clay. Another decisive step in the development of sound pottery was taken when artisans began glazing the porous surface of the ware to facilitate the retention of liquid, an innovation permitting the boiling of food. Over the centuries finer shapes and textures were obtained as potters refined their clays and learned to make better vessels by firing their wares in ovens rather than on open fires.

Ceramic articles were shaped by hand during the Neolithic period, for the invention of the potter's wheel would await the beginning of the succeeding Bronze

Age. Prehistoric pottery is distinctive and often aesthetically pleasing. Early Neolithic clay vessels were either burnished or incised, but artisans working later in the period applied painted designs. The ware of each local area was characterized by its own unique decorations, which changed over time. Although pottery is easily broken, pottery fragments—potsherds—are virtually indestructible, even when all else perishes. Archaeologists and prehistorians carefully study potsherds in order to trace the changes in pottery styles, information that is useful in approximating the dates of sites relative to each other. They also investigate the spread of pottery motifs and shapes to discern the transmission of techniques from place to place.

ÇATAL HÜYÜK (c. 6500–5500 BCE)

Jericho is far from unique as an early farming settlement in southwest Asia. Many sites are known from the Levant—the eastern shores of the Mediterranean—to the Zagros Mountains and their foothills along and across what is now the Iraq-Iran border. One region providing a highly favorable environment for human habitation during the Neolithic period was Anatolia, or Asia Minor, the Asian and greater part of modern Turkey. The largest and most complex Neolithic site discovered in Anatolia was once a small bustling town on the southern plateau. Prehistorians call the town Çatal Hüyük, *hüyük* being the Turkish word for a mound formed by a succession of settlements built on top of one another. We should keep in mind that farming sites in the Asian Near East were often occupied for thousands of years. The building and rebuilding activities at the same settlement resulted in the accumulation of considerable debris that gradually formed enormous mounds known in English as tells, which still dot the landscape of southwest Asia. The fifty-foot sequence of deposits at Çatal Hüyük reveals a high level of Neolithic culture, though the town was rebuilt at least twelve times, perhaps when the population increased or the sun-dried brick dwellings began to crumble. At the height of its prosperity around 6000 BCE, Çatal Hüyük covered about thirty-two acres and included an estimated thousand houses and perhaps a population of around five or six thousand.

Agriculture and Technology.   Farming was advanced in the town. The people enjoyed a surplus of food by growing vast quantities of peas, lentils, wheat, and barley, and by gathering apples, almonds, acorns, hackberries, and pistachio nuts. They are the first agriculturalists in the Near East known unquestionably to have kept herds of domesticated cattle. Moreover, their level of technology was remarkably high. By weaving animal or plant fibers into textiles, they created strikingly beautiful rugs with vivid decorative patterns. Apparently the process of weaving cloth had been invented early in the Neolithic period, perhaps by transferring the methods of basketry to the long fleece of sheep or plant fibers. The inhabitants of Çatal Hüyük produced attractive carved wooden bowls and boxes, making other receptacles of stone, bone, and wicker. Limited quantities of undecorated pottery vessels were on hand, probably considered useful for cooking. They fashioned knives, spoons, ladles, and similar utensils from bone, while they manufactured a great number of tools and

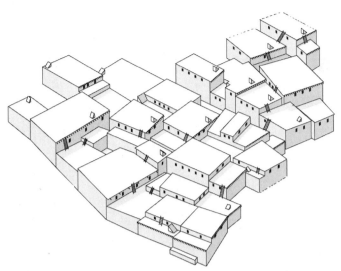

This schematic reconstruction shows houses at Çatal Hüyük
c. 6000 BCE. Access was across the rooftops.

weapons from flint and additional materials. Artisans in the town employed shell, bone, animal teeth, stone, and occasionally copper or lead to create jewelry for both men and women, including necklaces, bracelets, armlets, and anklets. After adorning their bodies, people could admire themselves in polished mirrors made from a dark but translucent volcanic glass known as obsidian, also used in the manufacture of chipped tools and other objects. Much of the prosperity of Çatal Hüyük resulted from its proximity to obsidian-rich mountains, permitting the town to become a center of trade in this natural glass. We know from archaeological remains that after 8000 BCE trade accelerated greatly in the Near East, with farmers exchanging numerous items—exemplified by turquoise, serpentine, jadeite, and marine shells—from settlement to settlement by barter transactions.

Architecture.   The inhabitants of Çatal Hüyük lived in rectangular, sun-dried brick and timber houses built directly against one another, separated at intervals by small courtyards. The absence of doorways—perhaps as a security measure—suggests people entered their houses through an opening in the flat roof, wooden ladders providing access. Streets did not exist in the town, and all communication was at the rooftop level, where in good weather activities such as food processing must have taken place. The outermost dwellings created a useful perimeter wall, intended either for defense or to protect the inhabitants against unexpected flooding. In addition to hearths and ovens, rooms were furnished with built-in benches and low platforms for sleeping, sitting, or working, all made of sun-dried bricks and then plastered. Corpses were buried beneath the sleeping platforms, though the bodies seem to have been exposed in the open air prior to burial to permit vultures to strip away the flesh.

Reconstruction of a shrine at Çatal Hüyük, dating c. 6150 BCE. The wall painting depicts vultures pecking at human bodies.

Artistic and Religious Expression.   Remains at Çatal Hüyük indicate strong belief in the magical potency of images. Scores of rooms contain wall paintings, plaster reliefs, and statuary. These must have been used as shrines for the performance of specific rituals. Their carefully plastered walls preserve the earliest known paintings on a fabricated surface. Several of the shrines include wall paintings that apparently reflect the uncertainties and fears revolving around life and death, some showing huge diving vultures attacking and devouring headless human figures.

Life-Producing Female Figures.   Much of the art shows a strong and an overt preoccupation with fertility and the regeneration of life, matters of profound importance to the Neolithic farmers at Çatal Hüyük and linking them to the Paleolithic past. Plaster reliefs of pregnant women with upturned arms and legs may represent supernatural beings with power over regeneration. Many figurines carved in stone or modeled in clay show women with enormous breasts and abundant bellies. One female figure appears with a hand between her legs, plainly a representation of childbirth. Such sculptures may have been used by mortal women as channels of supernatural force to assist them with the act of bearing offspring. Another figurine portrays a woman sitting as she begins to give birth, her hands resting upon a pair of formidable wild animals. Perhaps she signifies a deity protecting hunters and providing them with wild game. Clearly, these life-producing mothers were central figures in the religious life of Çatal Hüyük, and they may be expressions of a powerful mother-goddess, often regarded as a descendant of the Paleolithic Venuses.

Evidence of a Bull Cult.   The female fertility figure was associated with a remarkable bull cult. The bull is a natural symbol of power and later appears as a deity in places such as Egypt, Mesopotamia, and Crete. A series of plaster reliefs at Çatal Hüyük portrays women giving birth to the heads of bulls. Some shrines are adorned with rows of paired bull horns mounted on the floor, facing sculptured heads of bulls attached to the wall, all possibly representing supernatural power and fertility. Equally striking is the combination of the horn of a bull with the breast of a woman, perhaps intended as the joining of male and female symbols of regeneration.

Landscape of a Volcanic Eruption.   One of the most extraordinary of all the wall paintings from Çatal Hüyük is the earliest known landscape. This maplike image shows the town in the deadly path of molten lava from a volcano high overhead, possibly based on a legend about a catastrophic eruption before the time of the artist. Although the viewer sees the town—represented by a series of closely spaced rectangles—from above, the volcano and its blobs of lava appear in profile, perhaps the unsystematic perspective being employed to ensure the recognizability of all elements of the scene. Whenever the volcano erupted, the terrified inhabitants must have regarded the natural event as a manifestation of divine power. Çatal Hüyük was abandoned around 5500 BCE, though the reason for the decline and fall of the town remains a mystery.

THE PRELUDE TO THE NEOLITHIC PERIOD IN EUROPE: MESOLITHIC HUNTER-GATHERERS (c. 8000–4000 BCE)

The term *Mesolithic* applies to postglacial times in Europe from around 8000 BCE until farming was introduced to the northwest part of the continent about 4000 BCE, a period of numerous flourishing hunter-gather groups. The available game had changed drastically in Europe by the beginning of the epoch. Upper Paleolithic peoples had followed migratory herds of large animals, especially reindeer, but such creatures became scarce in the Mesolithic, having migrated northward with the climatic changes.

CULTURAL DEVELOPMENTS

Mesolithic Technology.   Humans of the Mesolithic developed new weapons and different hunting techniques designed more for slaying individual animals than preying upon herds. Yet stalking and killing animals sheltered in the dark woods of postglacial Europe—deer, elk, aurochs, and wild pigs—was vastly more difficult than herd hunting, and the diet of Mesolithic people increasingly depended upon capturing small game and collecting plant foods such as nuts and wild cereal grasses. Numerous hunter-gatherers found convenient homes along coasts, estuaries, and lakes, where they could live off fish and mollusks. Such groups seem to have eaten oysters and other edible shellfish with relish, for they left behind thick mounds of discarded

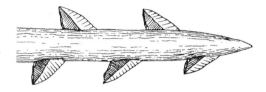

Microliths were used as components of many Mesolithic tools, exemplified by the mounted barbs of this arrow.

shells and other refuse known as shell middens. They developed useful implements, exemplified by nets, barbless fishhooks, harpoons, chisels, and gouges. They also devised the simple dugout canoe, which was hewn or burned from a single log. Mesolithic people living inland produced the sledge, the simplest kind of land vehicle, and made bows and arrows for hunting. In the far north, skis provided a rapid means of transportation.

Microliths. The Mesolithic period witnessed a trend toward lighter and smaller tools made with microliths, which came into use almost everywhere in the world after the last Ice Age. Employed to some extent in Upper Paleolithic times, microliths were small razorlike flakes, commonly of flint, designed to be mounted along grooves in wood or bone to give a jagged cutting edge to arrows, harpoons, and sickles.

Artistic Stress on Human Themes. The decreasing reliance of people on wild animals is reflected in a striking artistic development, a new concern for human themes. Artists working at numerous rock shelters in the hills on the Mediterranean coast of Spain began to emphasize both single and group human action. Their works, painted in silhouette, are generally diminutive and usually confined to a single tone of red or other earth color. Although these Mesolithic images lack the expressive presence of the secluded Upper Paleolithic cave paintings, they exhibit a marked anecdotal and dynamic quality. Typifying the Mesolithic painting style, a nine-inch-wide rock painting on the Gasulla Gorge shows five marching or dancing warriors taking rhythmic leaping strides, their dramatic profiles starkly enhanced not only by their bows and arrows but also by the feathered headdress of the leader. Other artistic remains indicate Mesolithic people ornamented some of their tools with finely engraved designs, and they wore amber and stone pendants.

THE NEOLITHIC AGE AND THE EARLY FARMERS IN EUROPE (c. 7000–4000 bce)

The Southeastern Region

After having developed in the Asian Near East, farming slowly spread across Europe, from southeast to northwest, during a three-thousand-year period beginning around 7000 bce. The oldest European farming communities emerged in the southeast—Crete, the Aegean Islands, and the Greek mainland—with many similarities to those of the Asian Near East, from which current evidence suggests most of the early domesticated animals and crops of the region were introduced. The transformation to farming in southeast Europe may have resulted from colonists entering the region from Anatolia or, less likely, from native societies adopting staples and skills after contact with peoples to the east.

The Central and Northwestern Regions

The period from around 6500 to 4000 BCE witnessed the spread of farming to central and northwestern Europe, regions marked by strong contrasts between summer and winter temperatures. The colder climates of the north dictated a summer growing season, unlike the warm Mediterranean shores permitting plant maturation during the winter. Wheat and barley were the main crops in central and northwestern Europe—others did not adapt as well to the more frigid conditions—while pigs and cattle were the most important domesticated animals. The land was tilled with simple digging sticks and wooden hoes. Although sun-dried brick houses were fairly durable under the limited precipitation of southwest Asia and southeast Europe, timber or stone was essential in rainy Europe.

The Bandkeramik. The early Neolithic farmers in central Europe are known as the Bandkeramik, a term derived from the distinctive incised, linear bands they used for decorating their pottery. The Bandkeramik constructed long, rectangular houses of timber, with sloping roofs jutting out to shield the walls from rain. The walls were often made of wattle and daub—upright poles interwoven with sticks or tree branches and then plastered with mud or a mixture of mud and cow dung—and the floors were supported by posts sunk into the earth. Apparently the dwellings sheltered families as well as their animals and grain. Built some distance apart in farming hamlets, the Bandkeramik houses were equipped with tables, beds, and other furniture.

The Megalith Builders of Western Europe (c. 4800–1800 BCE)

Communal Tombs. The merging of farming and native hunter-gatherer populations resulted in considerable regional differentiation in Europe. Even before agriculture was well established on the western shores of Europe, people in the area had begun erecting immense, puzzling stone structures called megaliths. Built in several forms, the megaliths include monumental communal tombs, which were roofed and walled with huge stone slabs and boulders. Apparently the earliest of the stone tombs was the dolmen, a burial chamber made of several large standing stones and a flat roofing slab. The entire dolmen was often buried under a mound of earth, though most of these coverings have washed away over time. Two kinds of giant tombs developed from the dolmen in northern and western Europe, the passage grave and the gallery grave. The passage grave—thousands still diversify the landscape in France and the British Isles—was entered through a long corridor leading to a circular chamber covered by a constructed mound of earth. The chamber might

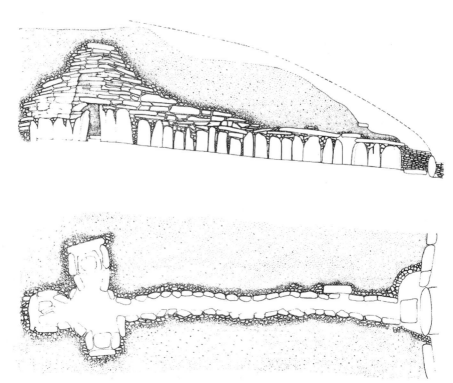

The magnificent passage tomb of Newgrange in County Meath in Ireland, shown in elevation at the top and plan at the bottom, was erected about 2500 BCE. The narrow passage to the burial chamber at the center of the great mound is some sixty feet long, and the corbeled vault of the chamber reaches a height of about twenty feet.

include an impressive corbeled vault, that is, an arched roof composed of many rings of stones, each projecting slightly inward beyond the one directly below until they close at the top. Such a vault was held together by the weight from the earthen mound above. The gallery grave, the other type developing from the dolmen, lacked an entrance corridor, the burial chamber or chambers forming the entire internal structure.

Stonehenge.   Another megalithic innovation was the erection of massive standing stones known as menhirs, examples of which may or may not be associated with graves. Menhirs were set up in a wide variety of dimensions, either alone or in rows or circles. Although these great prehistoric monuments probably served as religious meeting places, we can only guess what beliefs inspired their construction. One of the most impressive of these is the great circular setting of huge upright stones at Stonehenge on the Salisbury Plain in southern England, built in several phases from around 3300 to 1800 BCE. The northeast axis of the complex is aligned with the sunrise at the summer solstice, prompting much speculation that Stonehenge was a place of sun worship.

Maltese Temples.   The small Mediterranean islands of Malta are famous for their temples, dated about 3500 to 2500 BCE, which are among the earliest free-standing stone buildings in the world. Megalithic structures, the Maltese temples were made of enormous stone blocks resting on one another without mortar. Their portals were constructed on the simple post-and-lintel system, created by placing a large horizontal stone, or lintel, upon two upright stones. Generally, the interior stone walls were corbeled (projecting one beyond the other) to create sloping sides that probably supported wooden roofs.

NEOLITHIC RELIGIOUS, SOCIAL, AND ECONOMIC DEVELOPMENTS

RELIGION

We can make only a few general suppositions about the religious beliefs and practices of the early farmers. Apparently they thought spirits exercised power over nature, agriculture, and the village. They must have deemed a priesthood essential for interceding with these supernatural beings on behalf of humans. Although investigators are unable to recover the details of myths that flourished before literature recorded them, stories concerning the supernatural must have been told and retold in Neolithic times. One apparent function of these myths was to explain the great mysteries of creation, life, and death. Another was to provide religious and moral instruction for each rising generation.

Likelihood of a Pantheon.   Many scholars suggest the farming communities developed a pantheon linked to possible cults of natural elements, ancestors, and fertility. Perhaps some deities in Neolithic mythologies personified the sun, the moon, the stars, and the seasons. We saw that the plastered skulls of Jericho may have been associated with a cult of ancestors. Female figurines proliferated in Europe and the Near East during the Neolithic. These images have attracted considerable attention and prompted a wide range of interpretations. Judging from later Near Eastern mythologies—probably elaborations of Neolithic myths—early farmers may have looked upon the earth as a great mother-goddess presiding over plant, animal, and human fertility. The farmers were dependent on the earth as the provider of agricultural necessities and were concerned with the reproductive aspect of nature. Barebreasted female figurines often appear with symbols representing the moon, hunting, and farming. Perhaps figurines depicting two seated male figures found in some Neolithic sites were connected with plant regeneration. One is youthful and robust and has an erect penis. Did he preside over the flourishing of vegetation? The other, represented as an old man, may have been the god of dying vegetation. In the succeeding Bronze Age, the mother-goddess is associated with a god of vegetation, her youthful lover who eventually dies but comes to life again in a cycle of death and resurrection paralleling the withering of vegetation in the fall and its flourishing in the spring.

THE ACCELERATION OF COMPLEX SOCIAL AND ECONOMIC TRENDS

Although originating with the hunter-gatherers of the past, a number of complex social and economic trends accelerated under the impact of farming during the Neolithic period, several of which we have already noticed. Perhaps the most significant of these are (1) sedentism, (2) social inequality, (3) warfare, (4) population expansion, (5) food surplus, (6) long-distance trade, (7) occupational specialization, and (8) technological innovation.

Sedentism, Social Inequality, and Warfare.   With the adoption of agriculture in the Near East, Europe, and other regions of the world, people became sedentary, living in permanent villages rather than hunting and gathering in small bands. Some farmers were more successful than others. This encouraged the expansion of social and economic classes, which became increasingly differentiated in privilege, function, and responsibility. Perhaps even among the earliest hominids, some males and females achieved greater social status and influence than others, thereby forming incipient ruling classes. The powers and prerogatives of the ruling classes must have increased with the advent of concentrated populations in permanent villages. Apparently the elite gained a pivotal position in both trade and decision making, permitting them to erect barriers limiting the access of other groups to resources. Although direct evidence is lacking, a number of anthropologists suggest the Neolithic farming societies were under the leadership of village chiefs, who not only served as judges to settle disputes but also functioned as kings to lead fighters during periods of warfare. In the view of one well-known hypothesis, settled life resulted in ongoing warfare. As settlements grew and required increasing resources, so this argument goes, the inhabitants began raiding the fields and looting the villages of their neighbors to acquire additional acreage and other forms of wealth.

Population Expansion.   Although the human population increased after the adoption of sedentism and agriculture, the greater numbers seem to reflect an increase in child production rather than a higher rate of adult life expectancy. The transition from hunting and gathering to farming did not come without its costs. Despite popular beliefs about progress, a growing body of evidence based on skeletal and dental patterns suggests a reduction in the quality of life among early agricultural populations, with greater incidence of infectious disease, vitamin and mineral deficiency, protein-calorie malnutrition, stature reduction, and poor dental health. Apparently the hunter-gatherers had enjoyed a more nutritious and well-balanced diet than early farmers, the latter sacrificing variety for quantity. Moreover, even when technological improvements increased food production, the privileged classes did not widely share the benefits with other groups.

Food Surplus and Long-Distance Trade.   By adopting a settled life, people learned to grow more grain than they could eat. They developed the key ability of storing surplus food for consumption over extended periods of time, thereby preventing starvation through the long winters of northern climates. Fragments of pottery found at numerous Neolithic sites offer evidence that people stored grain, wine, oil, and other staples. Meanwhile some farmers built rudimentary silos or grain bins. Although Neolithic villagers grew or made many items themselves, the privileged classes controlling trade had to barter with outsiders for essential goods such as salt. The existence of trade with people in faraway places is indicated by the presence at many sites of exotic objects and materials. Trade brought Neolithic communities into touch with one another and made possible the spread of new ideas and techniques.

Occupational Specialization and Technological Innovation.   An agricultural surplus freed some people from the necessity of producing food, permitting them to turn their attention to trade or the production of goods that made life more pleasant and comfortable. Thus the Neolithic period witnessed an increasing degree of occupational specialization, with some individuals spending most of their working hours acquiring or processing food through farming, hunting, fishing, or food preparation, but with others manufacturing items such as tools, weapons, or pottery. Agricultural needs stimulated the invention of new or improved techniques and implements. Specialists who created tools and weapons continued the traditional practice of chipping and flaking, but they introduced the technique of grinding and polishing stone. Other artisans crafted pottery—an excellent channel of artistic expression— for the cooking and storage of food. Potters learned to make better ware by firing their vessels in an oven. The development of pottery and the oven allowed people to cook food in a greater variety of ways. They could prepare grain, for example, as bread, porridge, or beer. Neolithic villagers also developed the spindle and loom for the spinning and weaving of flax, cotton, and wool, permitting people to wear apparel made of woven textiles. By around 7000 BCE, artisans in southern Anatolia were hammering cold lumps of copper into necklaces, pins, and borers. Metalsmiths working in the latter part of the Neolithic discovered the secrets of smelting copper, but the story of metallurgy is more appropriately told with the rise of civilization in the next two chapters.

NEOLITHIC WOMEN

The lack of clear archaeological evidence has led to much speculation about the effect of early farming on women. Some researchers theorize that women had provided the bulk of the diet during the Paleolithic period by gathering plant foods, thereby enjoying much respect and equal status with men. Men were preoccupied with hunting, according to one popular argument, and women became the first Neolithic farmers by experimenting with the planting of grain, soon learning to cultivate land with a weighted digging stick functioning as a crude hoe. This scheme suggests women also oversaw the rationing and storing of surplus food, the means whereby villagers survived through the rigorous winters of northern regions. The lack of evidence notwithstanding, some investigators theorize women's domestic activities prompted them to invent baskets and pottery as containers for food and drink. Another unproven claim argues that women discovered the process of spinning thread and weaving textiles.

Major Developments in Human Prehistory

Years Before Present	Africa	Near East	Europe
5,000,000	Early Hominids		
1,800,000	Homo erectus		
1,000,000		Homo erectus	Homo erectus
300,000	Archaic Homo sapiens		
130,000			Neanderthals
100,000	Modern Homo sapiens	Archaic Homo sapiens and Neanderthals	
50,000		Modern Homo sapiens	
40,000			Modern Homo sapiens (Cro-Magnons)
30,000			Terminal Neanderthals
12,000		Natufians	
10,500		Farming	
10,000			Mesolithic Hunter-Gatherers
9000			Farming in southeast Europe
7000	Farming in the Nile Valley		

We know simple hoeing was being superseded by plow agriculture in the Near East and Europe during the period from roughly 3500 to 2500 BCE. A number of prehistorians suggest this development profoundly altered the status of women because they lacked the strength to operate the heavy Neolithic plow. They point out that early depictions of plowing scenes show men leading and guiding the bulky implement. According to this theory, women must have helped in the fields, but their responsibilities now centered on food preparation and textile and clothing production.

Apparently men were involved not only in large-scale planting and harvesting but also in most herding of animals. Animal domestication must have resulted in a clearer understanding of the role of the male in producing offspring, for people had many opportunities to observe that female animals gave birth only after contact with male members of their species. Did this knowledge erode the probable age-old view that women were endowed with power over life itself? Certain writers suggest the various ongoing developments in agriculture lowered the status of women, while that of men was enhanced by their involvement in various male activities away from the home, such as the herding of animals and warfare, responsibilities offering them extensive knowledge of the outside world. As populations multiplied and land became more valuable, warfare seems to have become increasingly important for adding landed wealth to the community.

Although the archaeological record offers no proof, a number of contemporary investigators echo the well-known nineteenth-century theory that women had exercised dominant authority in the early Neolithic farming societies. If such matriarchies ever existed in the distant past, patriarchies were well established by the time written records first appear in the Near East and Egypt in the late fourth millennium BCE. As the patriarch of the family, the father exercised considerable sway over wives, children, and property. The nurturing mother, however, must have exercised paramount authority over the child during the period of early training, teaching the first vocabulary, admonishing loyalty to the community, inculcating beliefs about the supernatural, and ingraining the values and aspirations of society. The influence of the mother was indelible.

By around 3000 BCE, farming settlements were numerous in various regions of the world, including southwest Asia, Europe, Egypt, India, Thailand, China, Mexico, and Peru. Although the social landscape was complex, life in such agricultural villages represented the basic pattern of farm existence through the ages. Farmyards abounded with dogs, pigs, and other domesticated animals. Farmers spent long hours in far pastures herding sheep and following cattle. Besides the arduous cycle of sowing and reaping, their responsibilities included tending cleared fields by driving away roaming animals and pulling up weeds. An endless round of lambing and calving, milking and shearing, spinning and weaving, churning and cooking awaited farming people—young or old—from dawn until dusk. These close-knit communities were tied to the land physically and spiritually in a timeless pastoral existence, their people worshipping the same gods, respecting the same customs and taboos, and cherishing the same values. By this time a more elaborate way of life known as civilization had begun to appear in the great river valleys of Mesopotamia and along the Nile, ushering in a new phase in the human narrative. We now turn to Mesopotamia to trace the gradual transition from the agricultural village to an urban civilized society.

CHAPTER III

THE RISE OF THE FIRST URBAN CIVILIZATION: SUMER IN SOUTHERN MESOPOTAMIA

The Near East embraces the meeting point of Africa, Asia, and Europe at the eastern end of the Mediterranean Sea. A number of modern states lie here, including Turkey, Iraq, Iran, Syria, Lebanon, Israel, Jordan, and Saudi Arabia. Students of antiquity often employ other names for some of these lands that are more relevant to ancient cultural patterns: Palestine for the area now occupied by Israel and Jordan, Arabia for Saudi Arabia and the other states of the Arabian Peninsula, Phoenicia for Lebanon, Anatolia or Asia Minor for the part of Turkey lying in Asia, the Levant for the eastern shores of the Mediterranean, and Mesopotamia for the great river valleys in Iraq. Additionally, based on ancient Greek terminology, many scholars continue to use the name Persia for Iran.

The classical Greeks delighted in coining terms and phrases. Many of the words we encounter in the study of ancient history are derived from their language. One of these—Mesopotamia—is from a Greek term meaning "between the rivers," referring to the land between the Tigris and the great bend of the middle Euphrates. Later the region was more broadly defined as a large geographical unit framed by the valleys of the two famous rivers and extending from the mountains of Anatolia in the northwest to the Persian Gulf in the southeast. Although Mesopotamia is almost devoid of stone or timber for building and is generally hot and dry, the southern part of this riverine land witnessed the emergence of the world's earliest civilization around 3500 BCE. Shortly thereafter civilizations arose in major river valleys elsewhere, first along the great Nile, then beside the course of the Indus on the Indian subcontinent and on the banks of the Yellow (Hwang Ho) and Yangtze rivers in China.

ATTRIBUTES OF THE EARLY MESOPOTAMIAN AND EGYPTIAN CIVILIZATIONS

Our encounter with the term *civilization* points to another salient chapter in the human narrative. A derivative of the Latin *civilis*—of which one meaning is "pertaining to a city"—this word civilization can be confusing. In many places a decidedly urban life did arise with the emergence of civilization, yet ancient Egypt and some other lands witnessed *civilized* people generally living not in cities but in mere villages. We should keep in mind, moreover, that the advent of civilization was a complex, wide-ranging process requiring many centuries of development.

40

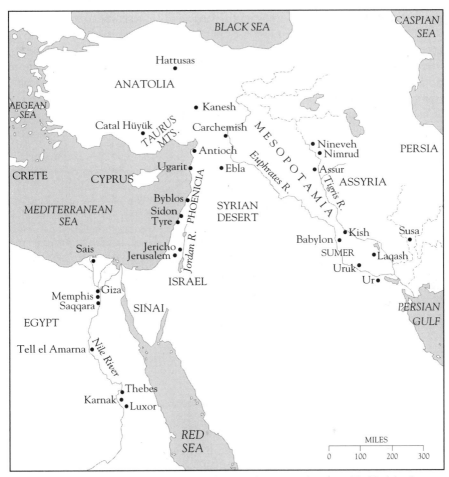

Some major sites in the ancient Near East, from prehistory to the second half of the first millennium BCE.

Although formulating a precise definition for the word civilization is virtually impossible, investigators have identified several fundamental attributes distinguishing the Mesopotamian and Egyptian civilizations from prehistoric cultures. Perhaps nine of the suggested attributes are most significant. First, these civilizations enjoyed increased agricultural efficiency based on sophisticated techniques such as artificial irrigation of crops, thereby sustaining large food surpluses and high population densities. Second, they were centralized states controlling specific regional territories. Third, they took the form of theocracies, with the ruler considered either a god or a representative of one or more deities. Fourth, they sustained their economies by the centralized accumulation of taxation and tribute, permitting the support of non-farming specialists such as priests and artisans on a full-time basis. Fifth, they were stratified into distinct social classes marked by great differences in wealth, ranging from vast throngs of commoners and slaves to a tiny ruling elite. Sixth, they achieved major technological innovations, particularly in response to transportation needs, inventing devices such as sailing craft and the wheel, and later they developed a tradition of metallurgy for producing tools and forging weapons. Seventh, they engaged in a much greater volume of long-distance trade, now beginning to rival agriculture in importance. Eighth, they used some form of writing, probably stimulated by increased trade, itself necessitating a system of rudimentary record keeping. Ninth, they built distinctive monumental architecture in the form of religious centers, royal palaces, or great tombs.

THE GEOGRAPHICAL SETTING OF MESOPOTAMIA

Geography and climate combined to produce a more pessimistic and gloomy attitude among the Mesopotamians than the Egyptians, whose remarkable civilization is traced in chapters 6 and 7. The great Tigris and Euphrates rivers forming the boundaries of Mesopotamia, the heart of modern Iraq, fail to serve as effective obstacles to invasion, and countless intruders have crossed this land. Flowing roughly southeastward, each river rolls a thousand miles and more to the Persian Gulf through hilly country and vast plains flanked by a wide desert region on the southwest and by the Zagros Mountains on the northeast. The rivers are separated by about two hundred miles of open steppe at the points they enter Iraq, the Tigris to the east and the Euphrates to the west. Near modern Baghdad the rivers almost meet but diverge again until uniting at a spot more than a hundred miles above the Gulf, into which they empty with one mouth.

In contrast to the highlands of northern Mesopotamia, southern Mesopotamia, extending from around fifty miles above Baghdad down to the Gulf, is a flat alluvial plain where the Tigris and Euphrates run slowly. The rivers flow with such a low gradient south of Baghdad that they meander dramatically, resulting in the formation of extensive marshes, swamps, and shallow lakes. Sometime between the months of April and June the two rivers overflow and spread rich silt over the land, accounting for the typical fertility of the area in ancient times. Yet the spring flooding depends on the variable amount of rain and snow that has fallen on distant mountains. This means the time, intensity, and volume of the overflow is unpredictable, and the rise of water can be sudden and catastrophic for both humans and animals.

The inhabitants of southern Mesopotamia faced additional anguish if a few years of low flooding led to drought and famine. Another problem involved the overflow of the rivers, for the inundation occurred too late to water winter crops, too early for summer produce. Occasional but devastating winter storms came in the form of sudden, unpredictable rains, and the permanent lakes and marshes of the area served as a ready breeding ground for armies of mosquitoes. The climate was harsh and cold in the winter and miserably hot in the summer, when a searing sun and parching wind rendered much of the soil hard and dry, unsuitable for cultivation for months at a time. In short, southern Mesopotamia was a rather inhospitable land of extreme contrasts, ranging from swamp to desert. Under such circumstances, the people of the area were faced with the necessity of irrigating their fields by means of a network of well-maintained dikes and canals. Because faulty irrigation techniques could quickly leave the area saline and sterile, a strong form of government was essential for overseeing the development and maintenance of a serviceable system for supplying the land with water. Such governments exercised only local sway for many centuries, however, partly because the stagnant pools, reed swamps, and dried mud flats of southern Mesopotamia created a geographical maze hindering political unification.

Despite the geographical and climatic disadvantages of Mesopotamia, its floodplain witnessed crucial developments leading to the earliest undisputed urban civilized society. Yet the early Mesopotamians were eventually forgotten, for much of the evidence supporting their existence became deeply buried in the earth. Seventeenth-century European travelers to Mesopotamia brought back accounts of mysterious tells and puzzling inscribed clay tablets. They did not realize the tells—low mounds formed by the gradual crumbling of sun-dried bricks used in ancient construction—stood over the sites of former Mesopotamian cities. The very existence of the early inhabitants of southern Mesopotamia remained unknown until nineteenth-century archaeological exploration uncovered astonishing remnants of their cradle of civilization.

THE BIRTH AND EARLY DEVELOPMENT OF CIVILIZATION IN SUMER (c. 5500–2350 BCE)

Only the northern part of Mesopotamia is blessed with adequate seasonal rainfall for nonirrigation farming. The first agricultural communities appeared here around 7000 BCE. Three loosely successive but generally overlapping cultures named for sites and distinguished by pottery styles—the Hassuna, Samarra, and vigorous Halaf—flourished in the area during the sixth and the second half of the fifth millennia BCE. In terms of southern Mesopotamia, known as Sumer in the most ancient usage, present evidence suggests agricultural communities emerged before 5500 BCE. Perhaps settlers had been attracted to the south by its fertile silt and availability of water for crops. All along the lower reaches of the meandering Euphrates were natural levees of rich sediment built up over time as the river flooded its banks. Farmers in Sumer adopted a simple method of irrigation by diverting floodwaters from the Euphrates and the Tigris across their fields, then draining them to prevent salt from accumulating in the soil.

THE UBAID PERIOD (c. 5500–4000 BCE): A PATTERN OF PREDOMINATING TEMPLES

Although we do not know what the earliest farmers of southern Mesopotamia called themselves, prehistorians sometimes refer to them as the Ubaid people (named after Tell al-`Ubaid, a low mound marking the site of an ancient village on the Euphrates near the ruined city of Ur). During the Ubaid period, people engaged in irrigation-based farming and produced surpluses supporting specialists in pottery, weaving, and metalwork. Because stone is extremely rare in southern Mesopotamia and must be imported, its use was limited to heavy tools and personal adornment. The Ubaid people made axes and many additional implements of a hard, fired clay known as terra cotta. In the meantime they carried on an extensive trade with other places for cherished luxuries such as gold and lapis lazuli, a highly prized deep-blue mineral used as a gem or for ornamentation and the making of pigments.

THE UBAID TEMPLES

The Priestly Class.   The Ubaid people took several important steps toward urbanization. They built their villages and towns with the available materials of sun-dried bricks and reeds. Many of their houses took the form of modest reed structures supported by wooden poles, but these extraordinary people developed distinctive, strongly built temples for the deities believed to protect their communities. Temples dominated every Ubaid settlement of any size, where a powerful priestly class apparently directed both society and economy.

Eridu.   Archaeologists excavating a Ubaid settlement at the southern tip of Sumer known as Eridu discovered what seems to be the earliest temple of the site under several layers of subsequent religious structures. This shrine took the form of a rectangular sun-dried brick building, about fifteen feet long, and exhibited features similar to those of later temples in Sumer, especially a niche for the deity's cult statue, an altar located before the divine figure, and an offering stand in the center of the room. Soon the Ubaid people were erecting larger temples at Eridu and elsewhere in Sumer, each containing a central room—usually referred to as a cella or naos—surrounded by a number of subsidiary chambers. By the middle of the fourth millennium BCE, designers at Eridu had built a temple on a lofty sun-dried brick platform, devotees reaching the shrine itself by ascending a staircase to the entrance. This towered temple style seems to have served as the model for the later ziggurat, a roughly pyramidal structure of monumental size supporting a shrine at the top.

THE URUK PERIOD (c. 4000–2900 BCE): DEVELOPMENT OF THE WORLD'S FIRST CITIES

The Ubaid culture spread throughout Mesopotamia and even beyond, though each local area assumed a somewhat distinctive character. Ubaid settlements were the forerunners of those of the succeeding Uruk period, named for the large and impressive site of Uruk (biblical Erech, modern Warka). The Uruk phase, dating from around 4000 to 2900 BCE, reflects cultural developments in Sumer during the gradual emergence of civilization. Of the relatively few sites associated with the Ubaid tradition, we already find evidence of some clustering in the pattern of settlement. Both the number of settlements and the degree of clustering increased strikingly during the Uruk phase, which was marked by the rise of the earliest large cities and the advent of writing. Uruk itself was settled almost a hundred miles north of Eridu

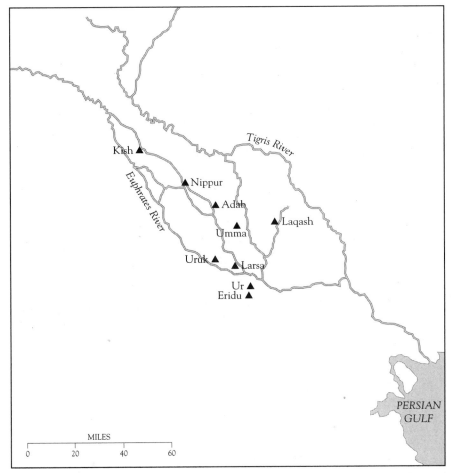

The principal urban centers of Sumer.

on the banks of the Euphrates during the Ubaid period, and the small town in-creased in size to become one of the world's first cities. Satellite villages, each served by a separate irrigation system, extended at least six miles beyond Uruk and helped to increase agricultural production. Uruk was packed with houses built along nar-row, winding streets, all overshadowed by great temple complexes.

THE URUK TEMPLES

The White Temple. Several temples from Uruk are reasonably well preserved. About 3300 BCE, builders at Uruk erected a small brick temple on the summit of a monumental sloping platform towering about forty feet above the plain, a tradi-tion from the Ubaid period. The walls of the platform were sheathed in brick and its

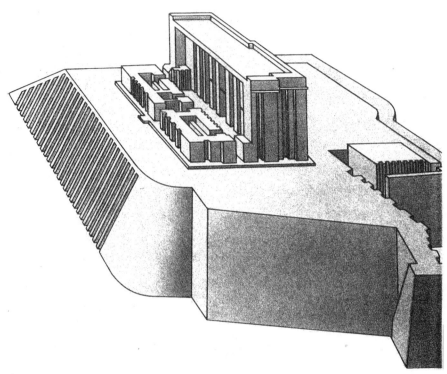

Cutaway reconstruction of the so-called White Temple at Uruk (modern Warka), dating c. 3000 BCE. This summit shrine took the form of a rectangular chamber covered with white plaster.

corners directed toward the four cardinal points. The temple at the top, thought to have been dedicated to the sky-god An, was painted a gleaming white. Not surprisingly, archaeologists nicknamed the shrine the White Temple. Stairs and ramps led from the ground to the shrine, within which priests offered sacrifices to An on an altar located before his statue. A number of scholars have suggested that the loftiness of the temple stemmed from a fundamental Mesopotamian belief that mountaintops served as the dwelling places of gods, or at least were closer to the sacred dwelling places than the land below. Accordingly, the image of a transcendent divine being could be properly housed only on a monumental platform, in effect an artificial mountain.

The Evolution of Writing (c. 3300–1500 bce)

The gradual transition from prehistory to history occurs with the invention of writing and the consequent ability of people to record contemporary events for posterity. For the historian, writing is the paramount mark of civilization. The earliest writing system in the world is thought to have developed at Uruk and other cities of

Sumer in connection with the economic framework. The temple administration of the Uruk period—like that of the preceding Ubaid phase—seems to have largely controlled the economy, supervising both agriculture and long-distance trade. From a practical need to compile inventories and record economic transactions, temple administrators in Sumer developed writing in its simplest form near the end of the fourth millennium BCE. Writing was used chiefly for recording economic transactions for many centuries but by the middle of the third millennium BCE had evolved into a flexible instrument allowing scribes to reproduce complicated texts.

Precursors of Writing.   For thousands of years, villagers in the Near East had been using small geometric clay objects known to historians as tokens as a means of recording transactions involving various items of trade, such as sheep or barley. Apparently the sizes and shapes of the tokens came to signify both the commodity itself and the quantity of the transaction. Later, the practice developed of keeping the tokens of a single transaction together in a clay ball. Another important step involved inscribing the surface of certain balls with the shapes of the enclosed clay pieces, a very early example of pressing symbols onto clay.

Pictograms and Ideograms.   By around 3300 BCE, temple administrators in Sumer had found they could eliminate the tokens and balls by inscribing marks on small clay tablets to represent both the commodity and the quantity of a transaction. These uncomplicated drawings are known as pictograms, each of which was a simple picture of a familiar object, exemplified by a fish or a cow. The pictograms were accompanied by strokes or circles expressing numbers. The range of communication was soon expanded by employing the signs to signify not only the objects depicted but also the ideas associated with them. In the latter sense, the signs are known as ideograms. The picture of the human foot, for example, might represent just a foot (a pictogram) or mean *to walk* (an ideogram), while that of the sun might denote the heavenly body itself or signify allied concepts such as *day* or *brightness*.

Phonograms and Determinatives.   The next step in the evolution of Sumerian writing occurred at the end of the Uruk period, when scribes began using a sign to stand for the sound value of the object portrayed, usually equivalent to a syllable. The introduction of such sound signs, known as phonograms, permitted writers to reproduce actual speech. The sign for an arrow was pronounced *ti*, for example, and so the depiction of an arrow suggested that sound. Now the scribes were able to write any word in their language. Using a rough equivalent in English, the word *football* would be formed by two phonograms representing the sounds made when saying *foot* and *ball*. Besides the phonograms, scribes also ushered in unpronounced signs we call determinatives, which greatly helped the reader by clarifying the range of meaning of certain words.

Clay Tablets.   Clay was readily available in the region to serve as a writing material. When clay tablets were dried in the sun, they became sufficiently durable to last indefinitely. Eventually people learned to fire their more important documents, making them rock hard and virtually indestructible. The process of writing was relatively simple. Using a reed stylus whittled to a sharp point, the early scribes engraved curving lines on the surface of the soft clay. At first they entered their writing in incised squares or between inscribed vertical lines. In the latter case, their writing took the form of vertical columns, which were begun at the upper right-hand corner of the tablet and were read downward and from right to left. Probably to minimize the possibility of smudging the wet clay, scribes began turning their tablets sideways, writing in horizontal rows from left to right. As a result of this development, occurring after 3000 BCE, the signs themselves appeared sideways and were read from left to right and from top to bottom.

Cuneiform.   In the meantime the pointed stylus was discarded in favor of one cut to a triangular, or wedge-shaped, tip. Abandoning the old curved lines for straight ones, the scribes pressed the sharp edge of the stylus inward with greater pressure at the beginning of each short stroke, causing its "head" to be wedge shaped and thus wider than the remainder of the line. Gradually the signs became more geometric and abstract until they developed into conventional groups of wedges bearing no resemblance to objects. This system of writing came to be called cuneiform, a term derived from the Latin word *cuneus*, meaning wedge or wedge-shaped. Because of the diverse and complex symbols used in cuneiform writing—ideograms, phonograms, determinatives, and others—the number of signs far exceeded those in an alphabetic form of writing. With its hundreds of characters, the complicated script would remain the exclusive possession of a class of learned scribes.

Cuneiform was passed on to a number of ancient peoples. The script was used almost exclusively for recording a wide range of languages throughout the Near East until about 1500 BCE and in a diminishing degree for another fifteen hundred years. Thus cuneiform provides us with the principal record of human existence for a substantial part of the historical era.

SUMERIANS PREDOMINANT IN SOUTHERN MESOPOTAMIA

Once scribes adopted the system of spelling out words syllabically at the end of the Uruk period, their language can be recognized as Sumerian. The term Sumerian is fundamentally a linguistic concept denoting the prevailing language of southern Mesopotamia at the time, and any reference to Sumerians should be construed as the Sumerian-speaking people, not members of a particular ethnic group. We should keep in mind also that our words Sumerian and Sumer are derived from a name of the ancient Akkadians for the southern part of Mesopotamia.

The Sumerians are a linguistic puzzle because their largely monosyllabic language has never been convincingly related to any other known tongue. Moreover, many unresolved questions surround the identity of the early Sumerian speakers and their place of origin. Scholars dispute whether they came from some other region or

EARLIEST PICTOGRAPHS (3000 BCE)	DENOTATION OF PICTOGRAPHS	PICTOGRAPHS IN ROTATED POSITION	CUNEIFORM SIGNS C. 1900 BCE	BASIC LOGOGRAPHIC VALUES	
				READING	MEANING
	Head and body of man			lú	Man
	Head with mouth indicated			ka	Mouth
	Bowl of food			ninda	Food, bread
	Mouth + food			kú	To eat
	Stream of water			a	Water
	Mouth + water			nag	To drink
	Fish			kua	Fish
	Bird			mušen	Bird
	Head of an ass			anše	Ass
	Ear of barley			še	Barley

The evolution from a pictographic script to an early cuneiform script, and then to Late Assyrian cuneiform.

NORTH BAY PUBLIC LIBRARY

NORTH BAY DISCARDED PUBLIC LIBRARY

were direct descendants of the Ubaid people. Supporters of the former theory mention the possibility an earlier predominant language in southern Mesopotamia, suggested by the non-Sumerian names of early settlements such as Ur, Uruk, Lagash, Nippur, and Kish. Favoring the competing view is the apparent social and religious continuity from the Ubaid to the Uruk periods, as well as the absence of any hint in Sumerian texts of an earlier homeland or an invasion into Sumer.

SEMITES PREDOMINANT IN CENTRAL MESOPOTAMIA

Sumerian was not the only language spoken in Mesopotamia. By the beginning of historic times Sumerians held sway in the extreme south, but Semites were there also, and the latter were predominant in central Mesopotamia (later known as Akkad). The term Semites denotes any people whose native language is one of the closely related Semitic tongues. In the manner of references to Sumerians, any mention of Semites should be construed as Semitic speakers, not members of a specific ethnic group. Although we are not certain where the Semites in Mesopotamia originated, scholars suggest they came from territories to the west, north, and possibly east, bringing about an important cross-fertilization of cultures.

THE URBAN CENTERS OF SUMER

Agricultural Abundance.   During the centuries following the invention of writing, Sumer attained unprecedented heights of material wealth and political power. Perhaps based on a blend of diverse cultures, the region also witnessed significant achievements in architecture, technology, education, and literature. In the meantime the prosperous settlements of Sumer were growing into increasingly powerful urban centers surrounded by vast expanses of land devoted to farming. We saw that the lower half of Mesopotamia, which ordinarily witnessed eight rainless months following winter, required an extensive artificial irrigation system during the dry, merciless months of summer. The Sumerians fed their intricate network of canals from reservoirs, keeping the latter filled by using sweeps, or long poles that were counterweighted for raising buckets of water from the river. Sheer agricultural effort usually meant that food was plentiful in Sumer, and the typical abundance led to an increase in population and an expansion of farmland. Such growth necessitated community cooperation and effort in the mandatory tasks of enlarging, extending, cleaning, and repairing the irrigation canals and reservoirs.

A Powerful Priesthood.   The Sumerians believed the fertility of the soil and the timely flooding of the rivers depended on the benevolence of the gods. The inhabitants of every settlement envisioned one special deity—a sort of patron god—as the protector and owner of their city. The prestige of the chief god rose and fell with the political fortunes of the city. During the Uruk period, the priests of the temple—the deity's manor house on high—dominated both the spiritual and economic landscape on behalf of the supernatural ruler.

THE EARLY DYNASTIC PERIOD (c. 2900–2350 bce)

The Sumerian City-States

A clearer picture of the Sumerian settlements emerges in the third millennium bce. By then, Sumer included a dozen or more prosperous cities, with a shifting of political power from priests to successive dynasties of kings or priest-kings. Thus the era from around 2900 to 2350 bce is called the Early Dynastic period. During this time each city served as the heart of a politico-religious unit functioning as a petty state, usually referred to as a city-state, ranging in population from about 10,000 to 50,000. Like the old settlements, every city-state was theoretically owned by its patron god. Such a state included the city as well as its suburbs, dependent towns and villages, and rural territory, a total expanse of a few hundred square miles at the most. The land surrounding the city was absolutely essential for maintaining the power and economic strength of the city-state, which was based in part on intensive agriculture. Each city-state was independent and frequently engaged in offensive warfare with other city-states to protect its irrigation rights and to enlarge its territory. Imagine the difficulties when two cities were in sight of one another, as were Ur and Uruk, for invasion might come at any moment, perhaps leading to the total destruction of crops in the field.

The Rise of Kingship

The En, Ensi, *and* Lugal.   A number of different titles for rulers are known in Sumerian, though meanings remain somewhat obscure. The most common are *en, ensi,* and *lugal.* The first, generally translated lord, seems to indicate both secular and religious authority. In other states the ruler bore the title *ensi,* roughly equivalent to our term governor. A number of rulers called themselves *lugal,* literally meaning great man, apparently the closest approximation of the three to the idea of actual kingship. We find evidence that in some cases the *lugal* acted as a sovereign over several city-states, while the *ensi* served as his vassal.

The *lugal* administered justice, directed external affairs, and probably acted in many cities as chief priest. His role was critical, for the struggles of the various city-states were growing increasingly violent, and nomads to the east and west were pressing against Sumer. The ruler's wife—known as *nin* (lady)—took an active role in the public and religious life of the city. Gradually kingship, with all of its prerogatives, evolved into a hereditary institution that was believed to have been instituted by the deities on high.

The Theory Concerning Assemblies of Citizens.   A number of scholars suggest a parallel between the political system and certain Sumerian myths telling of a supreme god seeking advice from a council of seven exalted gods and presiding over an assembly of all the deities during times of crisis. Perhaps the early kings in some cities consulted local assemblies of citizens on occasion. If such political bodies did function in an earlier day, they were left with only vestigial responsibilities by the end of the Early Dynastic period.

The Power and Duties of the King.   The palace eventually rose decisively above the temple both in wealth and influence, and the kings gained control over temple estates. In the meantime the kings established impressive standing armies. Every military force included heavily armed infantry troops, who attacked opponents in formation, while the chariot served as the main offensive weapon. A solid-wheeled and rather clumsy vehicle drawn by a team of four asses, the chariot carried both a driver and a soldier, the latter armed with a battle-ax and a quiver of spears. Besides creating powerful armies, the kings also built huge palace complexes, some containing a hundred or more rooms for the royal family, court officials, guards, servants, and guests. The ruler served sumptuous banquets to distinguished visitors, who enjoyed court entertainment featuring music, dancing, and poetic recitals by bards singing to the lyre.

The Sumerian King List

Sumerian religion taught that kingship was a gift of the gods to humankind. This is the view of the famous Sumerian King List, an all-important document listing Sumerian kings—some legendary and some historical—ruling in the third millennium BCE, though the present form of the work dates from early in the next millennium. The King List provides the names of the kings arranged in their dynasties, the length of each reign, and occasional biographical commentary. Unfortunately, much of the information is unreliable, exemplified by the assertion that kingship was lowered from heaven. The document then credits the first ten kings—all mythical—with reigns grossly exaggerated in length. The overriding purpose of the King List was to show that Sumer had always been united under one king. Historical evidence contradicts this assertion, for no ruler managed to extend his dominion beyond his own city-state until the second quarter of the third millennium BCE. Besides listing the mythical kings, the document names those who may have enjoyed a measure of suzerainty over the entire land as well as additional rulers whose authority was merely local and whose reigns overlapped with other Sumerian kings, while failing to mention a number of powerful rulers whose deeds are attested by contemporary inscriptions. Although both the chronology and dating of the text are generally incorrect, the *names* of the later kings are considered historical and trustworthy.

Enmebaragesi and the Dominion of Kish

The history of Sumer in the Early Dynastic period is largely a story of warfare as the rulers sought control over other cities and, later, over the entire region. Apparently the initial city to establish a measure of dominion over the whole of Sumer was Kish, the ruins of which lie some fifty miles south of modern Baghdad. The first Sumerian king whose historicity has been established by contemporary records was a ruler of Kish named Enmebaragesi (or Mebaragesi), who held the proud title King of Kish and probably ruled around 2700 BCE. A number of his deeds are recorded in the Sumerian King List.

Enmebaragesi Battles Elam and Establishes Nippur as a Holy City.   The King List asserts that Enmebaragesi "carried away as spoil the weapons of Elam." Perhaps he actually extended his domain eastward beyond Sumer to include this neighboring kingdom in what is now southwest Iran. The Elamites owed much of their culture to the Sumerians but were caught up in a very long and bitter rivalry with them, perhaps beginning even in prehistoric times. Besides providing military leadership, Enmebaragesi founded the most sacred shrine in Sumer, for he was the first to build a temple in the city of Nippur to the chief Sumerian god Enlil. Located southeast of Kish, Nippur became the Sumerian holy city, the most important religious and cultural center in the land.

GILGAMESH AND THE DOMINION OF URUK

In the meantime the cities of Uruk and Ur began to rival Kish for supremacy. Uruk, about a hundred miles southeast of Kish, is said to have waged war on Kish during the reign of Enmebaragesi's son Agga. The ruler of Uruk at this time was the semilegendary Gilgamesh, the most famous of all the Sumerian kings. According to a possibly exaggerated account, the vigorous Gilgamesh obtained the submission of Agga and put an end to his dynasty. The historicity of Gilgamesh has not been absolutely substantiated, but most scholars regard him as a real person. Thought to have ruled sometime during the twenty-seventh century BCE, the celebrated Gilgamesh is the first person whose name absolutely must appear in a survey of ancient history. He was immortalized both in the cycle called the Gilgamesh Epic—the best-known ancient Mesopotamian literary work—and in scores of myths and legends that grew up around the astounding exploits reported in his name. Gilgamesh became the supreme hero of Mesopotamia, a towering demigod with few peers in the literature of the ancient world.

MESANNEPADDA AND THE DOMINION OF UR

The third contesting power, the great city of Ur (biblical Ur of the Chaldees), flourished southeast of Uruk. Despite the eclipse of the venerable city of Kish by this time, its prestige counted for so much that the title King of Kish had been adopted by rulers of states succeeding to the dominion of Sumer. The title was claimed by a king of Ur named Mesannepadda, who ruled around 2600 BCE or perhaps earlier. The famous royal tombs of Ur may date from time of the dynasty he founded.

EANNATUM AND THE DOMINION OF LAGASH (C. 2450–2360 BCE)

The Use of Commemorative Inscriptions in Reconstructing the History of Lagash.   Sometime after the reign of Mesannepadda, destructive struggles broke out among Kish, Uruk, and Ur for control of Sumer. Elamite bands took advantage of the discord to

Part of the limestone *Stela of King Eannatum* (*Stela of the Vultures*), set up by Eannatum of Lagash to commemorate his victory over the rival city-state of Umma. c. 2450 BCE. Louvre, Paris.

pour into Sumer and disrupt at least parts of southern Mesopotamia. In the meantime the city of Lagash (modern Telloh), located about thirty-five miles northeast of Uruk, assumed an increasingly important role in the affairs of Sumer. Archaeologists have discovered hundreds of commemorative inscriptions at Lagash. Unlike the events of earlier times, known only from accounts written centuries later, details of the history of Lagash come down to us through these contemporary inscriptions, which the archivists of the city seem to have prepared with respect for accuracy.

The Stela of King Eannatum. A ruler of Lagash named Eannatum, who took imposing titles such as He Who Subjects All the Lands, was the most powerful figure of his day. Eannatum expelled the Elamite bands from Sumer and even claims to have safeguarded its eastern frontier by conquering Elam. Around 2450 BCE he managed to extend the sway of Lagash over Sumer. Of the conflicts in this endeavor, we are best informed about Eannatum's successful attack on the nearby city of Umma (modern Tell Jokha) over irrigation rights. The king erected a stela, or carved upright stone monument, to commemorate his victory. The well-known *Stela of King Eannatum* (also called the *Stela of the Vultures*), though surviving only in fragments preserved in the Louvre and the British Museum, tells a story in both words and pictures. The inscription describes the peace terms, while vivid sculptured scenes portray the battle and its grim aftermath, making the limestone slab not only the earliest known diplomatic treaty but also one of the oldest visual accounts of a historical event.

The stela is the most striking early masterpiece of Sumerian stonework in relief (sculpture projecting from a flat background). Scenes on both the face and the back of the stela are arranged in separate registers, a convention continuing into later periods. We learn on the front side that the victory was willed by Ningirsu, the patron god of Lagash, believed by the people to be its real ruler, who is shown bringing his heavy mace down on the head of a prisoner he carries in a net full of defeated, writhing foes. Ningirsu's instrument in victory was King Eannatum, depicted in the upper register of the reverse side wearing a splendid conical helmet as well as a thick cloak worn over his left shoulder. Eannatum leads a solid formation of fast-moving warriors into battle. Wielding leveled spears, the troops are protected by an unbroken wall of huge leather shields covering the body from the neck to the feet. Additional battle equipment includes standardized helmets and flat-headed axes. We see the marching men trampling a shapeless mass of slain naked foes scattered on the ground. In the broken lower register, the king is shown riding in his chariot at the head of his troops on the march, the royal arms including a heavy spear and a large quiver bristling with long darts or arrows. In another fragment, vultures swoop off from the battlefield bearing the severed heads and limbs of the slain in their beaks and talons. The *Stela of King Eannatum* is a grim reminder indeed of the brutality of Sumerian warfare.

Lugalzagesi and the Dominion of Umma (c. 2360–2350 bce)

Although Eannatum succeeded in extending the sway of Lagash over Sumer as a whole, the enemy he had defeated eighteen miles to the north—the city-state of Umma—got its revenge in less than a century. Umma produced an aggressive usurping ruler named Lugalzagesi, who invaded Lagash, slaughtered its people, and put the city to the torch. The voracious Lugalzagesi made extensive conquests, boasting in one of his inscriptions that he controlled all the territory "from the Lower Sea [the Persian Gulf] to the Upper Sea [the Mediterranean]." He claimed that fifty princes bowed to his authority, but his own turn to know the ignominies of defeat came about 2350 bce. The once-mighty Lugalzagesi was then taken as a prisoner to Nippur and displayed in a cage at its main gate, where he was subjected to all manner of abuse by those passing his way. His conqueror, usually referred to as Sargon the Great, spoke a Semitic tongue, not Sumerian. Sargon took control of the country, established a powerful empire, and founded a notable Semitic dynasty. Before considering the achievements of Sargon, we turn to examine some of the salient features of the Sumerian civilization.

CHAPTER IV

SUMERIAN CULTURE THROUGH
THE EARLY DYNASTIC PERIOD

Although Sumerian probably became extinct as a spoken tongue around four thousand years ago, tens of thousands of clay tablets survive in the cuneiform script used to express Sumerian and other ancient Near Eastern languages. Scholars learned to read these texts through a long and painful process. One of the great names in this endeavor was Sir Henry Rawlinson, who developed a keen interest in cuneiform while in the service of the British army in Iran during the 1830s and 1840s. A remarkable and daring individual, Rawlinson took considerable personal risk to copy a trilingual inscription hewn in cuneiform characters on a towering rock face near the ruined town of Bisitun, located east of Mesopotamia in what is now western Iran. He constructed a scaffold for viewing the writing but sometimes had to suspend himself by a rope in front of the rock to make accurate copies of details. The cuneiform inscription—created by command of King Darius I of Persia about 520 BCE—was written in three languages: Old Persian, Akkadian, and Elamite. Rawlinson finally succeeded in deciphering the Old Persian portion, an achievement providing the key to the decipherment of Akkadian. In time, the recovery of Akkadian led to an understanding of Sumerian, though the latter was not correctly recognized as a separate language until after the middle of the nineteenth century. The way was now open for scholars to investigate the extraordinary civilization of ancient Sumer.

RELIGION AND LITERATURE

THE MEANING OF THE UNIVERSE

We have already encountered three Sumerian prototypes profoundly influencing humanity: the concept of the state, the belief in divinely sanctioned kingship, and the invention of writing. The advent of writing led to a host of literary forms such as hymns, myths, epic tales, proverbs, fables, and essays. Sumerian literature is the earliest known, antedating the Homeric epics and the Hebrew Scriptures by close to a millennium. Likewise, the religion of ancient Sumer is the oldest documented by written records. Every aspect of Sumerian civilization from architecture to science was inseparably tied to the divine. Comparable to other people through the ages, the Sumerians speculated about their existence through questions: Who are we?

Where did we come from? Why are we here? What happens when we die? How did good and evil originate? The Sumerian priests, who had the leisure to ponder the great problems of existence, eventually reached a general agreement on basic principles. Their beliefs provided the people with assurances that helped them cope with life.

Cosmology.   The Sumerian thinkers devised a theology (speculations about the nature of divinity) and a cosmology (speculations about the origin and nature of the universe) that became the basic creed of the entire ancient Near East. Not surprisingly, quite a number of biblical stories and motifs have their basis in the literature of Sumer. The Sumerians believed the earth—conceived as Mesopotamia and the neighboring regions—consisted of a flat disk surrounded by a rim of mountains, all floating on a sea of waters. They viewed the entire world as animate, with trees, springs, rocks, and the like being alive and directed by supernatural beings. Above the earth, astral bodies moved across the great sky vault of heaven, which rested on the rim of mountains and was separated from the earth by a moving air substance (called *lil*). A similar hemisphere underneath the earth formed the netherworld— the Land of No Return—where the spirits of the dead resided in a fearsome abode among banished gods and demons. The sun visited this underworld at night, and the moon went below once a month, its *day of rest*. Like a huge bubble, the universe of sky and earth were immersed in an uncreated sea existing from the beginning of time. The primeval sea, regarded as a kind of first cause and prime mover, had given birth both to heaven and to earth.

THE SUMERIAN PANTHEON

The Anthropomorphic Character of the Gods.   The Sumerian religion told of a great pantheon of deities who were anthropomorphic, or human in form and behavior, but were also immortal and endowed with the power to control the universe. Even the most powerful were regarded as human in thought, word, and deed. They required food and drink for nourishment, sometimes became ill to the point of death, and could even be wounded or killed. Apparently this contradictory belief in immortal but perishable gods troubled the Sumerians not in the least, just as other peoples throughout history have ignored fundamental inconsistencies in their own religions.

The Four Creating Deities.   The deities were ranked hierarchically according to their importance and power. Among the most prominent were a triad of gods and a goddess, namely, An, Enlil, Enki, and Ninhursag. These four deities were creators who, through their *Word* alone, had brought the universe into being and placed its components under the charge of one of their offspring. The belief that the *Word* of a god or of gods has the power to create something out of nothingness soon became an accepted article of faith throughout the ancient Near East. Another influential Sumerian religious doctrine was the notion that the gods—to ensure cosmic and cultural continuity—acted as lawgivers. Accordingly, the creating deities had established the *me*, a set of unchangeable laws maintaining the universe in harmonious operation from the beginning of time. Believed to govern everyone and everything, the *me* gave the Sumerians a sense of reassurance in a threatening world.

An and Enki.   The four creating deities represented the four major realms of the Sumerian universe: sky, air, water, and earth. An was the god of the sky, Enlil of the wind, Enki of water, while Ninhursag was a mother-earth goddess. Representing the overpowering vault of the sky, An was the begetter and sovereign of all the other gods. He was a truly majestic being, yet An remained in heaven as a somewhat remote and contemplative figure. Enlil, in a sense, was the national god of Sumer, the one communicating both with the other gods and with humans far more often than An. His chief seat of worship was at Nippur, the most important religious shrine of the land. Enlil's name means Lord Wind, evoking the idea of joining breath with body to create living beings. While all the wind of the earth issued from his mouth, such power could be beneficent and yet possess the terror of the storm. Enlil was also a god of agriculture who had separated heaven from earth with his powerful wind to make room for seeds to grow. In theory, he always remained second to An, but in practice he was called Father of the Gods, even King of Heaven and Earth.

The Rape of Ninlil.   Despite his lofty status, Enlil had strong sexual appetites. One day while walking he spied a beautiful young grain-goddess named Ninlil bathing in the waters of a canal. Enlil became eager with desire and was determined to possess her. According to the *Myth of Enlil and Ninlil*, the goddess expressed great apprehension about having sexual relations with him: "My vagina is too little, it knows not to copulate, / My lips are too small, they know not to kiss. . . ." Impatient, Enlil raped and impregnated Ninlil. The other gods were horrified by this unsavory deed, and even though Enlil was their leader, they banished him to the netherworld. The unfortunate Ninlil, now big with child (the moon-god Nanna), followed Enlil below as his consort. This myth reflects Sumerian beliefs concerning the familiar agricultural cycle of fertilization, ripening, and winter inactivity, viewed as linking life with death.

Enki.   The third-ranking deity in the Sumerian pantheon was Enki, the god providing the fresh waters flowing in rivers to fertilize field and farm, though his liquid was known also for its treacherous allure. In a myth called *Enki and the World Order*, the god performs an act involving the river Tigris that was considered vital to the fertility of Sumer: "He lifts his penis, ejaculates [that is, passes sperm to mate with the river], [and] fills the Tigris with sparkling waters." Yet Enki's province extended far beyond his fertilizing waters, for he was the god of wisdom and the source of all invention, the one who had brought civilization to humanity.

Ninhursag.   A mother-earth goddess, Ninhursag was regarded as the source of all living things. In her role as the goddess of birth, she was called the Mother of All Children. She was also known as the Exalted Lady. Sumerian rulers proclaimed that they were "constantly nourished by the holy milk of Ninhursag." The goddess had probably enjoyed an even loftier status in an earlier day. Her cult, though still influential, was now being gradually overtaken by others more relevant to an urban civilization.

Inanna and Other Deities.   Ranking lower in the hierarchy were the deities in charge of the sun (Utu), the moon (Nanna), and the stars and planets. One of these powerful celestial divinities was the fertility goddess Inanna (the Akkadian Ishtar, the Greek Aphrodite, the Roman Venus). An elusive entity identified with the morning and evening star, Inanna was the goddess of sexual love, storms, and war. Texts tell of her countless lovers and of her ability to engage in incessant sexual intercourse with numerous men without tiring. She often behaved treacherously and was subject to towering rages, traits raising this formidable vehicle of pleasure to the rank of a deity who leads warriors into battle.

Inanna and Dumuzi.   Sumerian texts frequently portray women as vehicles of insatiable sexual appetite. This idea is reflected in the myth called *Inanna and the King,* in which the goddess aggressively employs her lovemaking skills to satisfy her youthful consort, the shepherd-god Dumuzi (the Semitic Tammuz), for "she craves it, she craves it, she craves the bed. . . ." Besides her strong sexual proclivities, Inanna was known for her ambition and cruelty. Although she already held the title Queen of Heaven, she longed for greater power and unsuccessfully schemed to rule the netherworld in disregard for the divine *me*, which we saw was believed to maintain the universe in harmonious operation. Once she had descended to the Land of No Return, however, she found to her dismay that she could not return to the earth without leaving a substitute behind. Thus her consort Dumuzi was taken by force to the underworld, where he would remain forever.

The Sacred Marriage.   Every Sumerian city-state conducted a Sacred Marriage between an important god and goddess associated with the place, a ceremony considered essential to ensure the fertility of its people, animals, and fields. The nuptials took place during the New Year Festival, the most important and joyous religious holiday in the cities of Sumer, celebrated over several days at the time of the spring equinox. The festival culminated on New Year's Day with the Sacred Marriage, enacted by surrogates, in which the two deities were thought to copulate. Inanna and Dumuzi were the divine couple at Uruk, other deities providing the power of procreation elsewhere. At Uruk the king took the role of the deceased Dumuzi, and a specially selected priestess played the part of Inanna, the human surrogates consummating the Sacred Marriage by engaging in sexual intercourse. Such a fertility rite was an essential part of the annual New Year Festival in every Sumerian city-state. Moreover, in emulation of the gods and goddesses, erotic rites involving priests and priestesses were customary in the practice of Sumerian religion, and temple prostitution was universal.

The Divine Assembly.   All the gods met in a divine assembly, always presided over by An or Enlil, to make major decisions. Whenever the assembly agreed to punish a city, its agent was Enlil's wind fashioned into a devastating storm that caused the land to quake and the heavens to tremble. The most exalted group in the assembly was the holy triad of An, Enlil, and Enki. Near this pinnacle of divinity stood the Seven Who Decree Fate, the deities with the power to determine destinies, and, somewhat less eminent, the Fifty Great Gods (who seem to be identical with the Anunnaki, the children of An). All invisible to the human eye, a host of other deities, demons, monsters, ghosts, and the like abounded in the Sumerian pantheon with its three to four thousand supernatural beings. Rabisu, the Croucher, for example, was a dreaded evil figure lurking in doorways and dark corners.

The Centrality of the Temple in Worship

High Priests and Priestesses.   Religion in Sumer centered around the temple, where priests, priestesses, seers, singers, musicians, eunuchs, and hierodules (temple slaves) were all involved in the sacred services. They left the agricultural and economic enterprises to secular officials, workers, and slaves. Generally, female deities required males (that is, priests) for their chief ministrants, while male deities required females (priestesses). Thus a high priest served as the spiritual leader in a city dedicated to a goddess, but a high priestess performed this function in a city dedicated to a god. High priests exercised both religious and political authority, while high priestesses, though religiously influential, were generally subject to secular authority.

Cult Statues and Rites.   Standing inside the temples were images of the great deities, usually made of marble or another form of stone. Here priests and priestesses, who were trained to anticipate every need of the heavenly beings, sheltered and clothed the cult statues because the well-being of the community was thought to depend entirely upon the favor of the gods, especially the patron god of the city. All of the deities could be rather capricious beings, and they required placation through praise, worship, and offerings, or they might send an affliction by means of their *Word*. After all, humanity was created to serve them. Lest clothing convey impurity, the priests of the temple approached the altar nude. The temples witnessed the singing of hymns, the recitation of prayers, and the celebration of special religious festivals. Accompanied by drums, flute, and lyre, hymns usually included expressions of some trouble or calamity as well as words praising the deities as lovers of truth and righteousness.

Sacrifices.   Ministrants sought to propitiate the gods by providing them with food in the form of sacrifices, performed regularly in the temples. A sacrifice is simply an act of offering—or presenting—a material thing to a deity, thereby rendering it holy. Sacrifices were designed to maintain or to restore a proper relationship between the human and the divine. Originally, such acts seem to have been regarded as little more than a method of feeding the gods. Although the deities were thought to be nourished by special food and drink in heaven, they required other refreshment upon coming down to earth. When a liquid was poured on the ground and absorbed, devotees apparently believed that the gods were drinking the offering. Likewise, when meat or grain was burned, worshipers seem to have thought the deities were receiving the offering by inhaling the smoke. When people left food in a sacred place, they must have believed the gods were able to consume the offering. Both deities and humans were thought to benefit from the sacrifices. We noted that the divine world depended on these human acts for sustenance, while the human world regarded them as a means of persuading the deities to use their extraordinary power on behalf of the people coming to their aid. The sacrifices in Sumer consisted of offering the gods drink, bread, dates, vegetables, and, above all, meat. During sacrificial worship, priests poured out water, milk, beer, or wine as a libation in honor of a deity, while burning fragrant spices and perfumed incense. Amidst incantations, a sacrificial beast—often a bull as an embodiment of the cosmic powers of fertility—was led into the temple where it was bound, purified, censed, ritually washed, and slaughtered to make its consecrated life and its vitality and energy available to the deity.

The priests were learned in explaining Sumerian religious practices. Apparently they taught that the essence of animal sacrifices is the recognition of blood as the sacred life force in both human and beast, while the essence of plant and vegetable sacrifices is the acknowledgement of the sacred life force of the deified earth. Libations of wine were related to the notion that wine is the *blood of the grape* and, therefore, the *blood of the earth*, a spiritual beverage to sustain both gods and humans. Libations of water represented the primordial waters of creation, the source for all earthly life and even that of the gods. Water washed away defilement and restored spiritual life. Additionally, water signified the vital liquid of the bountiful rivers, the great Flood that destroyed a disobedient original population, and the flowing life forces of living creatures (blood, sweat, and semen).

Catering to the Needs of the God.   Priests and priestesses served and worshiped the image of the god in the temple as a living being. A divine wardrobe was employed to change its clothes at appointed times and for festivals. Part of the food, beer, bread, and animals offered every day in the temple was earmarked for the deity. Meals were laid out before the sacred statue, one in the morning and another at night, but lighter meals were also served on a regular basis. Whenever the deity was dining, curtains seem to have been drawn round the divine image to block the human gaze from so great a mystery. After the god consumed the food—apparently by looking at the prepared refreshment—the "leftover" portion was removed. Part of this was transferred to the king's table, signifying the strong link between the monarchy and the divine, though most of the food ended up in the stomachs of the priests, priestesses, and other temple personnel. Because several hundred people had to be fed daily, the number of animals sacrificed was proportionally large. The less desirable parts of animals were usually burned on the fires of an altar, the deity receiving this offering by olfaction.

Reverence Statues.   Perhaps ordinary worshipers were able to glimpse the cult statue in the temple from a distance through the doorway of the cella, though they enjoyed

Group of reverence statues. Made of marble with shell and black limestone inlay, these figures were found in the Abu Temple at Eshnunna (modern Tell Asmar). c. 2600 BCE. Iraq Museum, Baghdad, and The Oriental Institute, University of Chicago.

a much better view when the image was taken into a courtyard, which they could approach, during religious festivals. Some devotees arranged to have sculptured stone figures of themselves placed in the temple, their hands clasped in front of the chest in a gesture of devout prayer. To the Sumerians, such reverence statues were not mere representations but potent images with lives of their own. Their enormous eyes staring straight ahead, the reverence statues stood in perpetual adoration facing the deity. People in antiquity feared the power of the eye to beguile and transfix for purposes good or evil. In the case of the reverence statues, the disproportionately large eyes seem related to the ancient belief that the eyes are windows to the soul. The gods, by looking directly into the eyes of a statue, could fathom the spiritual state of the person represented.

SUMERIAN MYTHOLOGY

Creation Stories. Sumerian beliefs concerning human origins were grounded in a number of conflicting traditions. Accordingly to the *Myth of the Creation of the Pickax*, Enlil had fashioned the universe by separating the male *heaven* from the female *earth* with his powerful wind. Then he created the pickax and used the implement to break open the hard crust of the earth, thereby permitting the first people—already produced beneath the surface by the deified earth—to sprout forth like plants. Another tradition stresses that some humans were fashioned from clay and given the breath of life. Whatever their origins, all people were created for one great purpose, to provide the gods with food, drink, and shelter.

The Flood. Eventually the assembly of the gods became displeased with the disobedience of humankind and decided to send a destructive flood to blot out life on earth. Some of the deities were unhappy with this decree, however, and a pious man named Ziusudra (the Sumerian counterpart to the biblical Noah) was forewarned in a dream to build a great boat to save representatives of all living creatures. The Flood and other Sumerian stories became part of the general mythology of the entire ancient Near East, with many of these myths being adopted by the later Hebrews. Because of the heavy Sumerian influence upon the biblical account of Creation and its aftermath in the book of Genesis, numerous religious concepts of ancient Sumer remain quite influential to this day. One Sumerian myth is similar to the Hebrew story of the Fall of humanity from an earlier time of grace and leisure, while another contains parallels to the Exodus story, with the waters of a land being turned into blood as divine punishment for an impious deed. Other myths tell of a tree of knowledge and a lush garden of the deities similar to the Garden of Eden. Believing that they were created in the image of the gods, the Sumerians thought of themselves as a chosen people, a hallowed community with a more intimate relationship with heaven than the rest of humanity.

The Gilgamesh Epic

Turning to another genre, apparently Sumer witnessed the development of the first epic literature, consisting of long narrative poetry celebrating the adventures and feats of a legendary or historical hero. The heroes of Sumerian epics are demigods and kings. The most famous cycle of epic tales was based on King Gilgamesh of Uruk, who probably lived sometime during the twenty-seventh century BCE. The supreme hero of Sumerian story and legend, the great ruler and his exploits were extolled in poems written not only in Sumerian but also in virtually all the other languages of the ancient Near East. About 2000 BCE, or perhaps somewhat later, an unknown Babylonian collected some of the Gilgamesh tales, together with other stories, and wove them into a new whole known as the Gilgamesh Epic.

The Babylonian epic tells us that Gilgamesh was two-thirds god, one-third human, famed for his exploits in war but also for his tyranny. Gilgamesh oppressed the people of Uruk and abducted any woman who took his fancy. His subjects appealed to heaven for help against Gilgamesh, and a huge wild man named Enkidu was created to subdue the king and distract his mind from "the warrior's daughter and the nobleman's spouse." Enkidu was a mortal with flowing hair and untold strength who roamed the countryside with his wild animal companions. Gilgamesh sent a prostitute out to seduce Enkidu, to civilize him, and to bring him to Uruk.

When Enkidu first encountered Gilgamesh, a long and fierce battle raged between them. Yet the two became fast friends after Gilgamesh prevailed. The bulk of the cycle recounts the heroic adventures of Gilgamesh and Enkidu against various monsters. Gilgamesh rejected the love of Ishtar (the Sumerian Inanna) during these exploits, and the insulted goddess dispatched the Bull of Heaven to ravage Uruk. Nevertheless, Gilgamesh and Enkidu managed to destroy the awesome creature. Then Enkidu tore out the bull's right thighbone (perhaps a euphemism for genitals) and rashly threw it in the face of the furious Ishtar. Such impudence did not go unnoticed. Enkidu was seized by a painful, lingering illness that finally killed him.

Stricken with grief and alarmed by the full horror of death, Gilgamesh endeavored to escape the common fate of humanity. His longing for immortality drove Gilgamesh on an odyssey to seek counsel from the elderly survivor of the Flood, Utnapishtim (the Sumerian Ziusudra), who had been metamorphosed into a god with eternal life. Utnapishtim advised Gilgamesh that he could become immortal by eating the *plant of life* growing in the depths of the sea. Although Gilgamesh found the miraculous plant, a snake snatched it away while he was bathing. Gilgamesh learned that his quest for immortality had been in vain. The living are mortal, and the dead cannot be resurrected to life. In the words of the epic, "Mere man, his days are numbered; whatever he may do is but the wind."

THE LAND OF NO RETURN

Haunted by insecurity, the Sumerians addressed their gods with prayers at the temple. They also prayed to their trusted family and personal gods, each being a kind of guardian angel or patron saint. Yet acts of worship were thought to bring only earthly benefits, for Sumerian theology included no concept of the meting out of rewards or punishments after death. The idea of an afterlife embraced neither hope for a heavenlike realm nor fear of a hell. The dead were thought to enter a world below, the Land of No Return, which was "bereft of light" and existed as an altogether dismal abode. The ghostlike spirit of the deceased approached the other world by crossing a "man-devouring river" with the help of a ferryman. The Sumerians buried their dead with food, clothes, tools, weapons, jewelry, game boards, musical instruments, and other grave goods intended to offer some comfort in the gloomy underworld. Some members of the family were interred below the floors of the house, others in cemeteries outside the cities. If the corpse had been improperly buried or inadequately supplied with food, however, the spirit of the dead would haunt the local byways and make vampirelike attacks on luckless travelers for nourishment.

ARCHITECTURE, ART, AND MUSICAL INSTRUMENTS

THE ZIGGURAT

Sumerian architecture and art, much of which was created in the service of religion, shows remarkably high quality. Every major city was dominated by its ziggurat, an architectural form evolving by the Early Dynastic period from the Ubaid tradition of raising temples closer to the heavens on soaring platforms. The ziggurat was a massive staged tower supporting the shrine of the god on its top stage. Scholars have long debated the purpose of these monumental structures, with theories ranging from the idea the ziggurats served as great stairways between heaven and earth for the gods to the proposal they reflected a folk memory of a mountainous region from which the people had originated. The ziggurats were made of a solid mass of sun-dried bricks overlaid with a skin of kiln-dried bricks, originally plastered. The architects avoided the monotony of large uninterrupted walls by incorporating regularly spaced vertical buttresses and recesses, and they perforated the sides with numerous so-called weeper holes, possibly used for drainage. A series of ramplike stairways led to the shrine at the summit.

SCULPTURE AND OTHER ARTS

We saw the Sumerians used reverence statues with disproportionately large eyes in their temples. These and other examples of sculpture show a marked simplification of the human form, clearly a strong artistic convention in Sumer. Archaeologists have discovered a number of small animal statues, which were made of wood and overlaid with gold leaf and lapis lazuli, depicting creatures with symbolic meaning, exemplified by the he-goat as an expression of masculinity. Sculptors also carved splendid figures on stelae and plaques, bowls and vases. Turning to other art forms, scholars suggest artists painted murals on the interior walls of both palaces and temples, though none of these creations survive. We are granted a glimpse of the magnificence of a Sumerian court or temple from excavated musical instruments, decorative inlays, and other sublime finds. In terms of creating objects of personal adornment, the jewelers of Sumer were highly skilled. They generally worked in imported gold and silver, though they also set semiprecious stones such as topaz, carnelian, and lapis lazuli.

CYLINDER SEALS AND SEAL IMPRESSIONS

One exquisite artistic contribution of ancient Mesopotamia was the cylinder seal, a small cylindrical stone cut and drilled with figurative or abstract designs. When rolled over wax or damp clay, a cylinder seal produced a narrow strip of relief. Such an impression might be used to seal containers being shipped from one place to another, to signify ownership, or to serve as a signature in a society that was generally illiterate. An extension of the last function was the validation of a contract or other transaction, the parties involved rolling their seals across the clay tablet upon which the document was written. The artists creating early cylinder seals were ingenious in devising well-executed figurative scenes depicting agricultural, ritual, and warlike activities, though certain other categories show a more decorative and abstract quality. Predominant designs of the Early Dynastic period include elaborate banquets as well as mythological scenes of heroes fighting one another or struggling with wild beasts.

Ceremonial helmet. Found in the royal tombs of Ur, the magnificent piece was beaten from a single sheet of gold and skillfully chased. The holes around the edge were for attachment of inside padding. c. 2500 BCE. Iraq Museum, Baghdad.

MUSICAL INSTRUMENTS

Instrumental and vocal music, likewise dance, played a prominent role in Sumerian life. Excavators have discovered beautifully constructed harps and lyres, percussion instruments such as drums and tambourines, and pipes of reed and metal. Musicians and singers in the temple performed during sacred meals and other temple services. Bards in the palace, accompanied by musical instruments, chanted Sumerian myths and epic tales, all composed in verse. Archaeologists found a superbly crafted harp, dated about 2600 BCE, in the royal tombs of Ur. Now in the collection of the University Museum at the University of Pennsylvania, the harp has been restored to its original magnificence. The top register of its inlaid soundbox shows a naked hero embracing a pair of man-headed bulls, while lower scenes depict real and fantastic animals making preparations for a banquet. A splendid bull's head is attached to the harp, suggesting a ritual function, for the powerful animal was an emblem of strength and fertility. The head is finished in gold leaf, while the beard and details are fashioned of lapis lazuli.

EDUCATION

The Sumerian name for a school was the House of the Tablet (*edubba*), first established to train scribes, their skill necessary chiefly for fulfilling economic and administrative needs of the temple and palace. The sons of wealthy families attended these institutions from sunrise to sunset. The extensive Sumerian literature con-

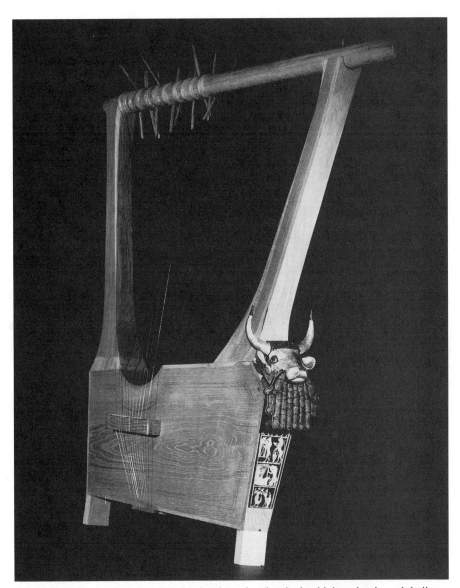

A harp from the royal tombs of Ur. Made of wood with inlaid gold, lapis lazuli, and shell, the magnificent instrument supports the head of a bearded bull, finished in gold leaf. The beard may signify some supernatural expansion of the bull's power. c. 2600 BCE. University Museum, University of Pennsylvania, Philadelphia.

cerning schools never hints at female pupils. Only one known reference mentions a female physician, another a female scribe. Although evidence is lacking, some scholars suggest that perhaps a few exceptional girls from families of great wealth were educated by private tutors. The high priestesses—often of royal blood—must have been literate.

The school boys pursued a basic and an advanced curriculum, which included drawing, reading, writing, mathematics, literature, and biology. The headmaster was called the *school father,* his assistant, the *big brother.* The pupils were known as the *school sons.* Some of the corrections made by teachers when students made mistakes on their clay tablets are still visible. Discipline was extremely strict. One member of the faculty was designated the *man in charge of the whip.* Corporeal punishment was amply provided for anything from wearing untidy clothes and loitering in the street to poor writing habits. Most of the graduates probably became scribes in the service of the palace, the temple, or the rich private estates.

SCIENCE AND TECHNOLOGY

METALLURGY

We know that Near Eastern artisans hammered some implements and ornaments from native copper even during the Neolithic period, when stone was used for making most tools and weapons. True metallurgy did not begin until the discovery of smelting, the high-temperature process of separating pure metal from its ore, first used for copper. The technique such was developed around 4000 BCE, probably in an area of early metalworking extending from eastern Anatolia through northern Syria and Iraq to western Iran, where specialists were soon producing lustrous copper weapons and ornaments. About 3000 BCE they made the notable discovery that copper could be alloyed with smaller quantities of other metals such as arsenic or tin to make bronze, which was not only malleable, like copper, but also flowed easily into molds for casting, while yielding much harder tools and weapons than copper. Archaeologists still use the broad label Bronze Age to denote the period in any area when the major tools and weapons were made of this versatile alloy. Because Sumer lacked deposits of metal, its artisans depended upon imported copper—probably in the form of ingots rather than bulky ore—from the central Iranian plateau and elsewhere. We find evidence of an astonishing range of high quality bronze weapons and farming implements in Sumer in the third millennium BCE. The Sumerians mastered techniques for working in other metals as well, including gold, silver, and lead, which were also imported from the Iranian highlands.

AGRICULTURE

We noted the far-reaching achievements of the Sumerians in irrigation and agriculture. The construction of an intricate system of canals, dikes, and reservoirs required considerable engineering skill, which they demonstrated by utilizing leveling instruments and measuring rods. Their maps aided them in surveying and planning such projects. The Sumerians also developed various horticultural techniques. One of these, shade-tree gardening, protected plants from the drying effects of wind and sun. A famous Sumerian document that historians have entitled the *Farmer's Al-*

manac instructed the farmer in agricultural methods, covering everything from the watering of fields to the harvesting of crops.

MATHEMATICS

Turning to mathematics, the Sumerian system of calculation was based upon the number sixty, which they combined with the decimal system. Although sixty might seem unusual as a base number, the sexagesimal system is quite practical because sixty is divisible by so many other numbers. The system survives in modern reckonings of time and measurement such as dividing the hour into sixty minutes and the minute into sixty seconds. A multiple of sixty divides the circle into degrees, and a factor of sixty divides the year into months and the foot into inches. By the same token, the Sumerian year was divided into twelve lunar months, with an intercalary, or inserted, month added to make up the difference in length between the lunar year and the solar year. The day, which began with sunset, was twelve double-hours in length. Building upon Sumerian mathematical principles, a later Mesopotamian people known as the Amorites discovered the process of multiplication and division, and their teachers compiled tables of square roots, cube roots, and exponential functions for use in schools.

INVENTIONS, TECHNIQUES, MANUFACTURES, AND MEDICINES

The Sumerians are credited with a range of other impressive achievements. They developed the water clock, which measured the passage of time by the amount of water dripping from a vessel. They also invented the sailboat and produced sturdy bronze-bladed plows, some of which were equipped with funnels depositing seed when the ground was broken. Their builders made use of the dome and the true arch, and they created the first known barrel, or tunnel, vaulting by constructing a series of arches side by side. The Sumerians manufactured paints, textile dyes, cosmetics, perfumes, and medicines. Apparently early Sumerian healing arts relied on magic spells and incantations, for illness was attributed to divine displeasure or to possession by demons. By 2500 BCE, however, pharmacists were using elaborate chemical procedures to create prescriptions based on a vast assortment of botanical, zoological, and mineralogical ingredients.

WHEELED VEHICLES

The invention of the wheel represents one of the paramount milestones in the history of humanity. The potter's wheel was already in use by the Uruk period, greatly increasing the ease and efficiency of making clay vessels. Perhaps this invention preceded the application of the wheel to locomotion. Archaeologists unearthed the earliest known pictorial representation of a wheeled vehicle at Uruk, dating from the last centuries of the fourth millennium BCE, though perhaps invented considerably earlier. Much of our knowledge about the construction of early Sumerian wheeled

vehicles is derived from royal burials of the third millennium BCE that contain physical remains of actual chariots as well as models of them. The wheel, which was solid
and formed of two wooden semicircles fastened by struts, was employed on two-
wheeled and four-wheeled carts to transport goods. The advantages for agricultural
workers were incalculable because an ox or an ass hitched to a cart could pull three
times the load the same animal could drag on a sledge or carry on its back. Within a
short time the Sumerians attached the wheel to ass-drawn chariots to run down
enemy forces during times of warfare. As unwieldy as the first wheeled vehicles were,
they rapidly became virtually indispensable for farmers, traders, and warriors.

SOCIAL CLASSES

THE KING AND THE ROYAL FAMILY

The complex urban society of Sumer was characterized by its unequal distribution of
wealth and status. The king stood at the pinnacle of society, drawing untold profits
from his superior position. We noted that the Sumerians believed kingship "was
lowered from heaven by the gods" to guarantee earthly order. The king was entirely
too close to the deities on high to be considered a descendant of a mere mortal, and
divinity extended to the crown prince as well. Born of a sacred "marriage" between
the king and a priestess of an exalted god, the crown prince was regarded as the son
of that deity and subsequently invoked him as his personal patron.

NOBLES, COMMONERS, AND SLAVES

Under the divine kingship, society was divided into three broad, relatively undefined social classes: nobles, commoners, and slaves. In a theological sense, however,
every nonroyal inhabitant of a Sumerian city was considered a servant or even a
slave of its patron god, who enjoyed a claim on all labor and lives. The nobility consisted of a number of wealthy and powerful families supplying the leading priests of
the temple and the high officials of the court. From them, the king drew his coun-
selors, ambassadors, and generals. The power and influence of these exalted families
stemmed from their ownership of large landed estates.

The commoners, by far the largest social class, were free or semifree and represented a broad range of peoples and conditions. They included farmers, cattle breed-
ers, fishers, merchants, traders, scribes, physicians, architects, masons, smiths,
jewelers, sculptors, and potters. Those at the upper end of the strata owned land in
their own right. Although they were free citizens without obligations to the nobles,
they could not hope to rival the nobles in status or power. In the meantime royal
and noble land purchases gradually reduced many commoners at the lower end of
the strata to the status of *clients of the nobility*. The clients included poor peasants,
lesser artisans, and the like. Although they were technically free, the clients depended for their survival on recompense from palace, temple, or noble estates for
their services. They were allotted small plots of cultivable land or given rations of
oil, cereals, fish, milk, wool, and clothing.

Although the vast majority of the Sumerians were free or semifree, slavery was an established institution. Most slaves served on the great estates and in wealthy households. Many were prisoners of war, but representatives of this group were not necessarily foreign-born because a large number of slaves were simply natives of Sumer who had been forcibly taken from defeated cities after battle. Sometimes free citizens were reduced to slavery as punishment for certain offenses, typically for insolvency. Pressed by debt or hunger, a father might sell his children, his wife, or even himself and his entire family into slavery for as long as three years. As any other chattel, slaves were considered the property of the owner and could be branded or flogged, but the need to keep them healthy and strong must have afforded most of them at least some protection against extreme maltreatment.

LEGAL DOCUMENTS

The oldest extant legal documents, though relatively few, are from ancient Sumer. An important example comes from the first reformer known to history, Urukagina, an Early Dynastic ruler of Lagash. Suspected of having been a usurper, Urukagina took the throne of Lagash about 2370 BCE. According to a set of inscriptions from his reign, the king reduced the high fees priests charged for conducting funerals and curbed certain tyrannical practices of the bureaucracy. He claimed his ordinances offered protection for the disadvantaged, the widow, and the orphan, though such phrases may be exaggerations intended to gain support for the politico-social system. One of his inscriptions tells us the patron god of the city, Ningirsu, had entrusted the king with this task of aiding the oppressed, an implication that law was bestowed by heaven for the upholding of the moral order.

PRIVATE HOUSING

Sumerian cities were surrounded by thick, high walls for protection and usually divided into four quarters by broad avenues coming from the outside world through four main gateways. The sprawling temple complex, where a great ziggurat rose toward the heavens, was approached by such an avenue. Yet most streets were narrow, winding, unpaved lanes flanked by whitewashed houses crammed together. The usual house, built of sun-dried bricks and based on a rectangular plan, had several rooms arranged around a central court. The walls of the courtyard were pierced by small windows and doors to provide the interior with light and air. Members of the household and guests entered the house through a narrow hall or chamber leading from the street to the courtyard. Stairs from the courtyard gave access to the flat roof, which provided additional living space during the long days of summer. At night the members of the family could seek relief from the intense heat by sleeping on the rooftop. The dwellings of wealthy Sumerians were larger and better planned, with walls as much as six feet thick to insulate the inhabitants from the scorching heat of the Mesopotamian sun. Some of these houses may have supported a second story.

Reconstructed figure of a woman from a royal tomb at Ur, her elegantly designed headdress and jewelry crafted of gold, lapis lazuli, and carnelian, c. 2600 BCE, Iraq Museum, Baghdad. Excavators found sixty-eight similarly dressed women at the end of passageway to a single tomb and called it the Death Pit.

Archaeologists suggest the rooms of houses, with the possible exception of the paved lavatory, served a variety of purposes in relation to the changing seasons and the shifting size of the family. The kitchen, identified by its hearth or oven, may have functioned also as a living room, sleeping chamber, or workshop. Other rooms may have served as guest rooms, animal shelters, or sleeping quarters for family members and household slaves. Apparently furniture was sparse. An important feature of the house was a burial chamber beneath the floors, though some of the dead were interred in cemeteries. We saw the Sumerians believed in a miserable and ghostly afterlife. To make the other world as bearable as possible, they buried corpses with all manner of grave goods, the quantity and quality depending on wealth and status.

THE ROYAL TOMBS OF UR OF THE EARLY DYNASTIC PERIOD AND THE QUESTION OF HUMAN SACRIFICE

Unlike ordinary mortals, the king and the royal family were expected to enjoy a relatively substantial and blessed afterlife because of their relationship with heaven. When members of the royal family died, their tombs were filled with exquisite treasures made of gold, silver, bronze, and semiprecious stones. The city of Ur is well known for a group of sixteen magnificently furnished royal tombs dating from around 2550 to 2450 BCE. Constructed in huge pits, the royal tombs of Ur were discovered in the 1920s by the renowned British archaeologist Sir Leonard Woolley. The rather elaborate burial chambers were designed with advanced architectural features such as arches, vaults, and domes. These chambers held a seemingly inexhaustible array of material splendors, yet apparently the kings and queens needed far more in death than an abundance of rich objects to preserve their exalted position eternally. Entombed with them were not only ceremonial chariots and the oxen that pulled them but also members of the royal retinue, including guards, musicians, grooms, and ladies-in-waiting. Scores of richly dressed women were buried at Ur holding lyres, their fingers still on the strings. Woolley was convinced the attendants entered the graves willingly and then drank poison, perhaps envisioning preferential treatment while serving the king or queen in the afterlife, though some later investigators suggest the individuals may have been forced into the graves and killed. We do not know if human sacrifice was practiced in other Sumerian cities, for unplundered royal tombs have been found only in Ur.

DRESS, DIET, AND FAMILY RELATIONSHIPS

Priests always shaved their faces and heads, while other men either did likewise or wore long hair and flowing beards. Pictorial art, which does not always correspond with evidence from burials, shows men with bare chests and wearing a fleecy skirt-like garment drawn tightly at the waist. Under this outer garment, most men wore a kind of jockstrap. We know from occasional comments in Sumerian literature that considerable derision was directed at any charioteer whose jockstrap fell off while he was driving his vehicle. Sumerian women usually wore their hair braided and coiled around the head, but on important occasions they displayed elaborate headdresses, one popular form consisting of hair ribbons, pendants, and beads. They fastened their form-covering gowns at the shoulder, leaving the right arm exposed. Again, these garments were frequently made of a fleecy material. Apparently both men and women employed cosmetic paints of red, black, blue, and green.

The staples of the Sumerian diet were dates, fish, unleavened bread made of barley or wheat, and a variety of vegetables and fruits, including chickpeas, cucumbers, onions, turnips, and apples. Lettuce, frequently mentioned in love poems, was a popular food with a sexual association. Cheese supplemented the diet on occasion, and mutton, pork, or duck might be on hand. Apparently the Sumerians made true wine and date wine, but beer—often used to excess—was the universal drink that poets described as bringing "joy to the heart." Brewed from barley and perhaps flavored with dates and honey, beer was consumed from huge communal jugs through long straws or reeds.

The basic social unit of Sumerian society was the patriarchal family. Marriage in Sumer and throughout the ancient Near East was generally a practical matter arranged by the parents. The betrothal became legal when the groom presented a bridal gift of money to the father of the future bride, probably a vestige of an older system of purchase. In the meantime the father put aside a dowry for his daughter to bring to the marriage. Although wedlock was usually arranged, love and desire seems to have intoxicated some couples before marriage, as suggested by sensuous Sumerian songs ringing out with reports of ardent prenuptial lovemaking. The Sumerians found that passion was fleeting, however, and they often lamented marriage and family life as an overwhelming burden. One of their proverbs is revealing: "Who has not supported a wife or child has not borne a leash."

Land was handed down from father to son, though surviving records indicate that some women held land and that the wives of city rulers often administered huge estates. Children were under the absolute authority of their parents, especially the father, and we saw they could be sold into slavery for as long as three years to pay off family debts. Yet they were usually cherished and loved. Indicative of the great importance of blood ties to the Sumerians, one of their proverbs runs: "Friendship lasts a day; kinship endures forever."

CHAPTER V

New Powers and Peoples in Southern Mesopotamia: Agade, Ur, Babylon

Although the Sumerian speakers brought forth the premier urban civilization, which left its mark on virtually every culture of antiquity and even those of today, their unending wars sapped their strength. Conquerors gained control of their land about 2350 BCE, a vivid reminder of the transitory nature of human affairs. The victors were Semites, that is, speakers of one of the Semitic tongues. The Semites in Mesopotamia seem to have originated in territories to the west, north, and possibly east of Sumer, migrating into the area in successive waves. Some Semitic speakers arrived in Sumer, others to the region directly to the north, which became known as Akkad. Historians refer to the population of Semitic speakers as the Akkadians, to their language as Akkadian. The presence of both Semitic and Sumerian names from the time of the earliest written records suggests that the Akkadian speakers (or a Semitic-language group settling before them) and the Sumerian speakers had lived side by side in lower Mesopotamia for centuries.

THE AKKADIAN EMPIRE (c. 2350–2160 BCE)

The Rise and Reign of Sargon of Agade

Apparently the military success of the Akkadians depended largely on the extraordinary ability of one man, Sargon of Agade, who founded a powerful Semitic dynasty. The location and circumstances of Sargon's birth are unknown, but a myriad of legends circulated about him, apparently the oldest of many similar stories of Near Eastern origin concerning the birth and upbringing of a person rising from obscurity to power and fame, exemplified by the Hebrew leader Moses and the Persian king Cyrus the Great. According to one legend, Sargon's mother gave birth to him in secret and then entrusted the infant to a fate of almost certain destruction by launching him on the Euphrates River in a pitch-covered basket. Yet a poor farmer drawing water for his fields saw the basket and pulled Sargon to safety, rearing the foundling as his own son. Another story, possibly containing more than a kernel of truth, reports that Sargon began his political career in the coveted and confidential office of cupbearer—server of beverages—to the king of Kish, eventually overthrowing the royal dynasty of the city. Later, roughly 2350 BCE, Sargon is said to have toppled Lugalzagesi, the Sumerian ruler of the city of Umma, who was then led in a dog collar to the holy city of Nippur and enclosed in a cage at the main gate to be reviled and spat upon by those passing his way. As an added humiliation to the fallen king, Sargon seems to have taken Lugalzagesi's wife as a concubine.

Sargon as Overlord of All Mesopotamia. Sargon then moved energetically and efficiently, consolidating his hold on Sumer, striking out against the troublesome Elamites to the east, and leading victorious military expeditions into what was later called Assyria in northern Mesopotamia. Turning west to capture and sack the fabled city of Mari on the middle Euphrates, Sargon apparently razed a number of cities on the rich plain of northern Syria. By force of arms, Sargon had created an empire extending well beyond the natural frontiers of Mesopotamia. So many legends and stories grew up around his name that the actual extent of his conquests remains unknown. Later traditions credited him with a domain reaching from the Persian Gulf to the Mediterranean Sea. His control, at least along the trade routes, may have extended to central Anatolia, while apparently his influence stretched over a vast area from Egypt and Ethiopia to the Indus Valley. The commanding presence of a magnificent bronze head representing an Akkadian ruler—possibly a portrait of Sargon himself—is preserved in the Iraq Museum at Baghdad. Although the eyes have been gouged out, the head remains an overwhelming mask of serene power.

The City of Agade. Sometime during his rise to power, Sargon founded a new capital at a place usually rendered Agade, though the Semitic spelling is Akkad, the term used for central Mesopotamia as a whole. The inhabitants of the southern half of Mesopotamia knew their entire land as Sumer and Akkad. Archaeologists have not discovered the site of the royal capital of Agade, presumed to have stood on the banks of the Euphrates north of Kish. For a brief period Agade was the wealthiest and most powerful city in the ancient world, its temples and royal palace resplendent with treasures from all parts of the empire.

Trade. Indicative of widespread trade, Akkadian documents mention sailing vessels from other lands, thought to include the Indus Valley and the coasts of Arabia and Persia. All trade in the Akkadian Empire was by barter, the exchange of one commodity for another, for coined money did not come into use in the ancient world for well over a millennium. On the local level, fish might be traded in a marketplace for tools. For international trade, nonperishable staples or manufactured goods could serve as a medium of exchange. Yet because certain commodities were subject to fluctuation in value or were inconvenient to transport, metal had become a more practical medium of exchange. Everyone needed copper, for example, which was easy to trade for other items. Regardless of the medium of exchange, both parties had to agree on the value of a commodity before they struck a bargain. Value in an earlier day had been calculated on the basis of barley, but eventually equivalents were made in copper, silver, and gold. The value of an item was always expressed in terms of weights, the shekel being a customary one. Thus an object, once its value had been established, could be exchanged for another object of like value or for the

Bronze head of an Akkadian king, perhaps Sargon himself. The splendid modeling reflects the metalworking skill of the period. c. 2350–2200 BCE. Iraq Museum, Baghdad.

appropriate weight in metal. Silver served as the normal standard of exchange for larger transactions and for distant trading. Even if the silver had been molded into forms such as ingots or bars, the value of the metal still had to be verified by balances.

Political Changes and Cultural Continuity.   Said by the quasi-historical King List to have ruled for fifty-six years, Sargon founded a Semitic dynasty that dominated Mesopotamia for at least three more generations. He replaced the old dynastic rulers in the cities with Akkadian governors, and he instructed these newly appointed Semitic-speaking officials to pull down the walls of fortified Sumerian cities. For the first time all of Mesopotamia was united under a strong centralized administration, with the kingdom or empire—not the city—serving as the ultimate political unit. In the meantime the Akkadian language, written in cuneiform symbols, began to replace Sumerian almost everywhere except in temple usage. Yet we should keep in mind that the civilization of the Akkadians did not represent a radical break with the past. For centuries the Semites and the Sumerians in lower Mesopotamia—despite their linguistic differences—had been linked by a common culture that can be characterized as essentially Sumero-Akkadian. Sargon wisely paid due respect to the old customs by building a temple at the holy city of Nippur, home of the national god Enlil.

THE REIGN OF NARAM-SIN

Deification of the Ruler.   Sargon's most famous successor was his grandson Naram-Sin, an outstanding figure who was reigning around 2250 BCE. Naram-Sin enhanced the concept of an exalted kingship by taking the title God of Akkad and demanding worship as a living deity, apparently the inauguration of a Mesopotamian religious tradition promoting the cult of both the living ruler and his deceased predecessors. By declaring himself divine, Naram-Sin united the authority of both palace and temple in his own person. His godship was not his only asset, for the king was also a military giant, his conquests ranging far beyond Mesopotamia. He boasts in his inscriptions of having destroyed the prosperous city of Ebla, capital of a powerful north Syrian kingdom. Archaeologists have discovered the official archives at Ebla. Its thousands of cuneiform clay tablets date from the mid-third millennium BCE and offer a valuable source of information about the extraordinary city, which once dominated a wide area extending from northern Syria west to Lebanon and east to parts of northern Mesopotamia.

Now in the Louvre, a famous Akkadian monument in eloquent relief—the *Victory Stela of Naram-Sin*—shows the king wearing the horned helmet of the gods to signify his deification. With mace and bow in hand, Naram-Sin leads his triumphant army up the steep slopes of a wooded mountain while trampling ruthlessly through crushed, dying, and fleeing enemies. In accordance with a convention in ancient art equating size with importance, the army appears on a smaller scale than Naram-Sin. Yet the gods, who dwarfed humans in Early Dynastic sculpture, have been reduced to mere symbols—two stars in the sky. Thus even the depiction of deities reflected the military prowess of the mighty Naram-Sin, who proudly claimed the title King of the Four Quarters [of the World].

THE POST-AKKADIAN PERIOD (c. 2160–2100 BCE)

THE GUTIANS

The empire disintegrated rapidly after Naram-Sin's death, apparently under the impact of internal dissention and foreign assault. Elam declared its independence, revolts broke out in Sumer, and Semitic nomads from Syria attacked. The last of the Akkadian kings was overthrown around 2160 BCE by the aggressive Gutians, who apparently had infiltrated from the Zagros Mountains to the northeast. Although they left few archaeological remains, the Gutians seem to have played an influential or even dominant role in the land for about forty or fifty years. The Sumerians and Akkadians referred to these intruders by unflattering labels such as the "mountain dragons," but historians have insufficient knowledge of the Gutians to make a binding assessment of them or their role.

Victory Stela of Naram-Sin, showing the triumphant king leading his armies up a wooded mountain over the bodies of crushed enemies. c. 2300–2200 BCE. Pink sandstone. Louvre, Paris.

GUDEA OF LAGASH

Evidence suggests the brief Post-Akkadian period was characterized by a return to a pattern of independent rulers in various parts of the land. A few of the old Sumerian cities—notably Uruk and Lagash—revived some of their former traditions. Enjoying extensive trade connections, Lagash flourished under its capable governor, Gudea (c. 2144–2124 BCE), whose face on numerous excavated statues radiates a sense of calm, even wisdom. In addition to his political renown, Gudea's name figures prominently in the history of literature. One widely known extant work takes the form of a long hymn, written exclusively in Sumerian, describing and celebrating Gudea's role in the restoration of the main temple at Lagash. Such noteworthy accomplishments at Lagash and elsewhere laid the foundation for a new flowering of Sumero-Akkadian culture.

THE THIRD DYNASTY OF UR: A SUMERIAN REVIVAL (c. 2100–2000 BCE)

THE REIGN OF UR-NAMMU

Utu-hegal, the ruler of Uruk, succeeded in driving the detested Gutians from the land about 2110 BCE, but he was ousted around a decade later by one of his own officers, the ambitious Ur-Nammu, who had been serving as the governor of Ur. Ur-Nammu elevated the city of Ur to a position of dominance once again. Assuming the title King of Ur, he founded the last predominantly Sumerian dynasty in Mesopotamia, the famed Third Dynasty of Ur. Although all official governmental affairs were conducted in the ancient Sumerian language, the influence of Semitic speakers must have been heavy. This period of Sumerian revival, which lasted about a century under Ur-Nammu and his descendants, was marked not only by great prosperity and military conquests but also by a late flowering of culture, resulting in a brief restoration of much of the old glory. Ur-Nammu was a patron of art and literature. His extensive building activity is exemplified by the great Ziggurat at Ur, now partially restored. Of monumental dimensions, the ziggurat and its crowning shrine originally towered some seventy feet above the ground.

The Code of Ur-Nammu.   The usurper Ur-Nammu turned out to be a strong, able king and an superb administrator. He promulgated the first known "law code" in history, though we should keep in mind that ancient Near Eastern codes were not comprehensive collections of laws regulating virtually every human activity but legal texts concerned with exceptional cases, principally matters of dispute or those requiring reform. In Mesopotamian law, which was essentially unwritten, existing legal tradition prevailed. The Code of Ur-Nammu is known from a later copy surviving only in fragments. The code is preceded by an extensive prologue calling for honest weights and measures, the protection of widows and orphans, some restraint

Reconstruction of the Ziggurat at Ur, by the notable English archaeologist Sir Leonard Woolley, with three receding rectangular platforms and a shrine on top. The form of the summit shrine is hypothetical.

over the economically powerful, and the exile of grafters. The ordinances of the code itself are related to various subjects, including sorcery, adultery by a married woman, false accusation, and the escape of slaves. Perhaps signifying a degree of ethical evolution, crimes of bodily injury were punished by fines for compensation rather than by death or mutilation, as in the later Semitic law codes of Hammurabi or the Hebrews.

THE FALL OF UR AND THE ENTRENCHMENT OF THE AMORITES AND THE ELAMITES (c. 2000–1800 BCE)

Around 2000 BCE the Third Dynasty of Ur began to collapse under the dual impact of declining agricultural yields and new invasions. The nomadic Amurru—usually referred to by the biblical name Amorites—penetrated from the west and, later, the vexatious Elamites from the east. The Amorites were another Semitic-speaking people. They had slowly filtered into southern Mesopotamia from their semiarid homeland on the northern reach of the Syrian Desert. Managing to form local dynasties of kings in cities such as Babylon, a hitherto inconsequential town whose origin is obscure, the Amorites gradually nibbled away the revived Sumerian empire until little remained other than the city of Ur. Then those old enemies of the east, the Elamites, revolted from Sumerian rule and swooped down from their capital at Susa to besiege and destroy Ur. They led its king (the hapless Ibbi-Sin) off to captivity. During the rather chaotic two centuries following the fall of Ur, bitter struggles broke out among local petty kings for supremacy within the traditional borders of Sumer and Akkad, with several city-states growing to prominence, particularly Larsa and Babylon. The Elamites—who had taken control in the south—ruled from Larsa, while the Amorites dominated part of the north from Babylon.

THE OLD BABYLONIAN EMPIRE
(c. 1800–1595 bce)

The Age of Hammurabi

Reunification of Mesopotamia.   Babylon was one of numerous small kingdoms in the Mesopotamian region. Its sixth and unquestionably most important Amorite king was Hammurabi, one of the great figures of world history. Although the dates of his remarkable reign are disputed, a widely accepted calculation suggests 1792 to 1750 bce. Hammurabi was an extraordinary military leader of seemingly inexhaustible energy who forged a large realm many historians call the Old Babylonian Empire. He gobbled up the powerful Elamite city of Larsa to the south. He took control of western Mesopotamia by destroying the celebrated city of Mari—with which he had been allied—lying on the main trade routes between Babylonia and Syria. Long famous as a center of wealth and culture, Mari was the site of a colossal palace with open courtyards and nearly three hundred rooms, its walls beautifully decorated with wall paintings of religious state ceremonies. The voluminous correspondence unearthed at the palace provides considerable information about the politics and diplomacy of the day and remains our chief source of information on Hammurabi's reign. These letters from the royal archives indicate the notable diplomatic skills of Hammurabi, who cunningly played off one ruler against the other, while waiting for the right moment to attack and destroy them one by one.

Hammurabi succeeded in reunifying Mesopotamia almost to its old Sargonic borders, for he carved out an empire stretching from the Persian Gulf in the south to Assyria in the north. The capital of Babylon gave its name to the southern half of Mesopotamia, formerly referred to as Sumer and Akkad, now becoming known as Babylonia. Although Hammurabi's kingdom began to decline and disintegrate soon after his death, the city of Babylon remained the paramount center of civilization for the Semitic-speaking peoples of lower Mesopotamia over the next two thousand years.

Sumerian Becomes a Dead Language.   Sumerian was either dead or rapidly dying as a spoken language by the time of Hammurabi. The tongue enjoyed enormous prestige, however, and Amorite kings continued to use Sumerian for inscriptions on monuments. A dialect of Akkadian was now the predominant spoken language and was used in all diplomatic and business correspondence, but Sumerian literature—

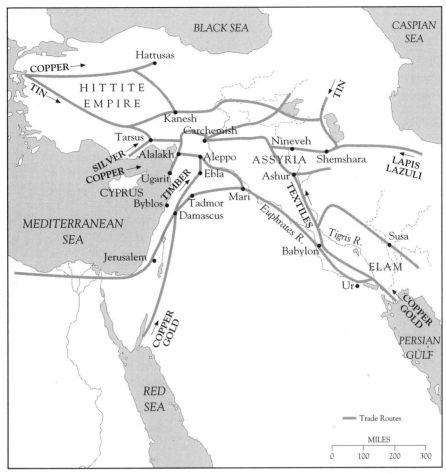

An extensive trading network flourished in the Near East during the second millennium BCE.

copied in Akkadian—provided the basis of the curriculum offered in schools. Exemplified by the Gilgamesh Epic, most known Sumerian literary works are copies rendered in Akkadian during the early centuries of the second millennium BCE.

THE CODE OF HAMMURABI

Collection of Legal Decisions.   The most valuable single document from Hammurabi's reign has been erroneously termed the Code of Hammurabi, though this is not a collection of laws but of legal decisions rendered under royal prerogative to resolve actual cases. We saw that Mesopotamian law was essentially unwritten and adhered to traditional practice. Moreover, ancient Near Eastern codes were not systematic collections of laws regulating nearly all possible contingencies but authoritative directions covering particular legal matters. Apparently Hammurabi promulgated his code—the most comprehensive collection of its kind—as a sort of manual on jurisprudence for the use of judges throughout his extensive realm.

Divine Sanction. After Hammurabi issued his collection of royal verdicts, copies were not only written on clay tablets but also cut in stone and set up in the court-yards of temples for the literate public to consult. The principal source of the code is a magnificent stela of·polished black diorite in the form of an almost eight-foot shaft. Apparently a later raider from Elam carried this copy to the Elamite capital of Susa in what is now southwest Iran. Members of a French expedition unearthed the heavy stela at the site in 1902, hauling the famous monument off to the Louvre as a trophy of archaeology. A relief at the top of the upper part of the front represents the standing Hammurabi paying homage to an enthroned deity, widely regarded as the Babylonian sun-god Shamash (the Sumerian Utu), the guardian and source of law (an alternative view identifies the deity as Marduk, the god of the city of Baby-lon). As the solar deity, Shamash exercised the power of light over darkness and evil. The god's shoulders emit triple flames, and he extends to the king a rod and ring as insignia of royal power. The depiction signifies that the code was authorized by heaven, and the same idea is expressed through words in the prologue and epi-logue. As might be expected, divine sanction made the code much easier to enforce.

The Text. Aside from the sculptured scene at the top, the shaft is taken up by ver-tical columns of beautifully engraved cuneiform characters that form a tripartite text consisting of the code itself, which lists almost three hundred legal decisions, sandwiched between a prologue and epilogue written in highly elevated style. While the prologue celebrates the justice of the king and enumerates the gods of various Mesopotamian cities appointing him for military glory, the epilogue promises divine blessings for future rulers using his royal verdicts as a model and calls down curses on those altering or neglecting the prescriptions.

The Subjects of the Code and the Frequent Use of the Death Penalty. The royal judg-ments of the code were carefully arranged according to subject, including adminis-tration of justice, protection of property, agricultural work, dwelling places, trade and commerce, family and inheritance, assault and injury, various professions, and the sale of slaves. In contrast to the Sumerian penal system, Hammurabi prescribed mutilation for some offenses and death for others regarded as especially dangerous to the well-being of state and society, including bigamy, incest, rape, adultery, abortion, house breaking, certain forms of theft, receiving stolen property, desertion from mil-itary service, brigandage, sorcery, aiding the escape of slaves, malfeasance in public office, kidnapping, and false witness. The death penalty was even applied to the fla-grant extravagance of a wife as well as the adulteration of beer. Curiously, willful murder is not listed as a capital offense, though we can hardly doubt that such a transgressor was executed. Crimes punishable by death required trial before a bench of judges. Parties and witnesses were put under oath. As a last resort when the parties presented clashing evidence or seemed to falsify their oaths, the matter was turned over to the decision of the gods by the ordeal. A speedy deterrent to false testimony, the ordeal was a trial by which the accused was cast into a river to determine divine judgment. A drowning person was judged guilty, but if the accused swam to safety, then the *accuser* was subject to capital punishment. Methods of execution included hanging, burning, drowning, and impaling.

The Threefold Division of Society.   The code indicates Babylonian society was divided into three strata, though these are difficult to define and translate. The highest group seems to correspond roughly to nobles (sometimes rendered as seigneurs, aristocrats, free men of standing, land owners, or gentlemen). Perhaps the second rank should be described as dependents of the palace (sometimes translated as poor men, commoners, tenants, or subordinates). The third strata, the easiest to define, was made up of slaves. Apparently the nobles included palace officials, commanders of the army, wealthy merchants, and priests of the temple, all of whom enjoyed special privileges and owned huge estates that might be divided into small plots and leased to the dependents. The second social division, the dependents, formed the bulk of the population. They lived under many restrictions and were obligated to perform various services in return for using land or enjoying other privileges. The dependents seem to have included small farmers, less affluent merchants and traders, hired laborers, and artisans. Both the nobles and the dependents wore flowing hair and beards, while the slaves were shaven and branded with a distinctive mark.

Of the three social strata, we have the clearest picture of the slaves. Evidently the slave population in Babylonia was much more numerous than in the old Sumerian cities. A large number were imported from abroad, with others being recruited among prisoners of war and their descendants. Some slaves had been free citizens in the past, selling themselves because of debt or hunger. Others had been sold as children by poverty-ridden parents. Enslavement occurred also as punishment for various crimes, including family offenses such as striking an older brother, kicking a mother, or the disowning of parents. Slaves enjoyed few rights but could buy their freedom, if the owner agreed, by accumulating property or borrowing the necessary funds from the temple.

Penalties for Bodily Injuries Differed According to Social Standing.   One of the most striking characteristics of the code is that bodily injuries inflicted upon nobles were punished differently from those against other members of society. The dependents received monetary compensation for such injuries, and offenses directed at another person's slave entailed a payment to the owner, but the code usually applied the *lex talionis* for acts of physical violence against nobles. The Latin expression *lex talionis* (law of retaliation) refers to the policy of revenge and vengeance by which punishment corresponded in degree and kind to the offense. Stated another way, this meant "an eye for an eye and a tooth for a tooth," a familiar principle in biblical texts. Under the Code of Hammurabi, any bodily injury sustained by a noble was inflicted in the same degree on the guilty person or a relative of the offender, and public administration of the penalty was expressly ordered. The *lex talionis* is discernible throughout the code for assaulting a noble, with penalties such as the cutting off of a hand that struck a father, the loss of a tongue that denied a parent, the removal of a surgeon's hand that caused the loss of life or limb, and the putting out of an eye that pried into forbidden secrets. Scholars debate whether this harsh principle is a regression or an advance in the history of law. Those favoring the latter view argue that the *lex talionis* curbed private revenge by providing public punishment for offenses.

Although the code applied the *lex talionis* when nobles suffered from acts of physical violence, they were expected to live by a higher standard of conduct and were liable to heavier punishment for inflicting bodily injuries on members of their own social rank. A noble who broke the bone of another noble, for example, was punished by having his own bone broken, but he paid only a monetary fine if he inflicted the same injury on a dependent.

The code recognized the importance of intention. Individuals causing accidents or injuries beyond reasonable possibility of prevention were usually only fined, though the *lex talionis* was applied for cases of carelessness or neglect, with punishment based strictly on deeds rather than intentions. If the house of a noble had been poorly constructed and collapsed, killing his son, for example, then the son of the builder was put to death. Such cases reflect the belief, which is expressed in other Semitic codes, that punishment is effective as a deterrent only when applied swiftly and without hope of mercy.

Women.   Many provisions of the code pertain to marriage and the relationships between men and women. Marriage was arranged by parents. The groom's father paid the bride price, which varied according to the status of the parties, and the father of the bride paid the dowry she brought into the marriage. In this very patriarchal society, the woman left her own family to live in that of her husband. By the standards of time, however, women enjoyed certain rights. The dowry remained hers after marriage and descended to her children or, if she died childless, returned to her family. Marriage was customarily for life, but wives who suffered from abuse or neglect could divorce their husbands and return to their fathers. Although a husband could divorce his wife at will, she retained her dowry in this situation, and he was required to give her money equal to the full amount of the bride price and also to provide for the support of their children. Yet the wife was viewed essentially as a possession of her husband. If she failed in her duties, he could send her away without compensation, keeping both the dowry and the children. If she went about the city belittling him, she would be drowned. If he fell into debt, she could be sold to satisfy the financial obligations. Monogamy was not always practiced. If she bore no children, he might arrange for a concubine to live in their house to bear them herself. If she engaged in business without his permission, he could marry again and compel her to serve his second wife as a servant. Moreover, a strong double standard existed between husband and wife in terms of sexual permissiveness. An unfaithful husband was not penalized. If a wife and her lover were caught in the act of sexual intercourse, however, the pair would be bound together and drowned, though the deceived husband could pardon his wife, and the king in turn might spare the guilty man.

RELIGION

Headship of Pantheon Transferred to Marduk. Hammurabi elevated Marduk—originally the rather obscure patron god of the city of Babylon—to the head of the official pantheon, but the king tactfully proclaimed this divine preeminence had been conferred by An and Enlil. In reality, most of the functions and exploits of Enlil were simply transferred to the usurping Marduk, who had become a god of fertility, vegetation, and magic. Although each city continued to worship its own god, all now owed allegiance to Marduk as the highest deity of the empire. The Babylonian priests obligingly substituted Marduk for Enlil in the story of creation. The traditional Sumero-Akkadian beliefs were not fundamentally altered, however, and the Amorites of Babylonia continued paying homage to the familiar Sumerian deities worshiped in Mesopotamia from time immemorial, though now usually calling them by Akkadian names: Anu for An, Ea for Enki, Belit-ili for Ninhursag, Belit for Ninlil, and Ishtar for Inanna. Earlier, the Akkadians had bestowed the designation Bel upon Enlil. Derived from the Semitic word *baal* (lord), Bel was more of an exalted title than a personal name. The supreme Marduk had acquired all the attributes of the Akkadian Bel by the time of the Old Babylonian period and was frequently called simply Bel, or Lord. He seems to have enjoyed wide popular support.

Marduk Battles and Defeats Tiamat. A representative of order in the universe, Marduk shows up in art wearing a tunic adorned with stars, and he carries a scepter as well as a thunderbolt, bow, spear, or net. Old Babylonian mythology relates that Marduk rose to preeminence among the gods after conquering Tiamat, the enormous and monstrous goddess of primeval chaos. An annual New Year Festival—usually observed in the spring—celebrated the battle between Marduk and Tiamat and was thought to promote fertility for the forthcoming year. As the priests in the temples recited mythological accounts of the great combat between Marduk and Tiamat, mock battles were fought in the streets. In the meantime the king and a sacred prostitute engaged in ritual sexual intercourse within the precincts of the temple, for their act was thought to provide a magical aid to plant, animal, and human fertility.

Temple and Secular Prostitution. Apparently the Amorite Babylonians greatly valued temple prostitution as an essential hallmark of their civilization. The sacred prostitutes were recruited from both females and males, the latter providing homosexual lovemaking in the temples. We find no evidence from documents that either heterosexual or homosexual relations with the prostitutes was discouraged in the least. The ordinary temple prostitutes ministered to travelers and local residents. During religious festivals they were extremely busy playing their professional role with the many worshipers flocking to the cities. Sacred prostitution was viewed as a lofty calling imparting far more than sensual pleasure, for its practice was thought to provide worshipers with a holy and mysterious means of achieving physical union with the divine. Besides the ordinary officiants, special temple prostitutes served the pleasures of their individual deity each night.

Not all prostitutes were holy. Secular prostitutes of both sexes sold sexual favors from the taverns, which served virtually as brothels. They could be seen making love in public streets and squares as well, for open sexual displays were not considered scandalous. Many of the female tavern prostitutes were so well rewarded for their calling that they amassed considerable dowries and made respectable marriages upon retirement from public service. Yet under no circumstances could a female temple prostitute lower her lofty standards by entering a tavern to have a drink of wine. The penalty—death by burning—must have checked any possible temptation to do so.

THE END OF THE OLD BABYLONIAN PERIOD (C. 1595 BCE)

After the reign of Hammurabi, the Old Babylonian Empire gradually weakened and lost control over the south, though the diminished state continued to exist until a powerful people known as the Hittites swept out of Anatolia in a devastating invasion that reached Babylonia about 1595 BCE. The Hittites plundered and burnt Babylon, bringing the reign of the last of Hammurabi's successors to an abrupt end. One crucial reason for the fall of the kingdom was the characteristic openness of Mesopotamia to invasion, a feature contributing to the ruin of both Sumer and Akkad. Soon an aggressive people of obscure origin known as the Kassites, discussed in chapter 12, seized control and ruled Babylonia for centuries. We now turn to the grandeur of ancient Egypt, whose civilization rivaled Mesopotamia in its impact upon humanity.

CHAPTER VI

LIFE AND DEATH ALONG THE NILE: EGYPT THROUGH THE OLD KINGDOM

The civilization of Egypt developed in a vast expanse of desert. Normally such an arid land did not permit the existence of a flourishing, well-populated country. Yet the ancient Egyptians created a remarkable civilization that has both baffled and inspired the human imagination through the ages. What set Egypt apart? Much of the answer comes from the remarkable Greek historian Herodotus, who made a grand tour of Egypt in the fifth century BCE and called the country "the gift of the Nile." No other geographical feature exercised such critical impact upon ancient Egypt as the great Nile River, the source of its celebrated riches.

The Nile arises in lakes Victoria and Albert in East Africa, where the river is known as the White Nile. From Lake Victoria the river courses nearly 3500 winding miles northward to the Mediterranean Sea, a journey taking about ninety days. The White Nile has a principal tributary, the Blue Nile, originating near Lake Tana in the mountains of Ethiopia. The two Niles merge at modern Khartoum in the Republic of Sudan to become the Nile proper, though the united waters are joined farther north by one final tributary, the Atbara, also rising in the Ethiopian highlands. Of great importance for ancient history, the Blue Nile and the Atbara carry an abundance of rich silt.

What the ancient world knew as Egypt was a narrow band of land along the final 700 miles of the Nile. The turbid river crossed this long stretch by running northward through virtually rainless deserts until reaching the deltaic plain providing its outlet on the Mediterranean. The Nile made a noisy entry into ancient Egypt a few miles south of the modern city of Aswan. Here a massive obstruction of red granite known as the First Cataract impeded its flow, resulting in a system of broken rapids. Over time the rushing river not only carved many intricate passages through the stone but also sculptured a string of rocky islands, the most northerly and important being Elephantine. Ancient chroniclers report that the gushing waters squeezing through the cluster of islands and rocks of the First Cataract made a deafening roar.

Six cataracts were visible on Nile waters between Khartoum and Aswan prior to the construction of modern dams. Because these rocky obstructions were named by explorers advancing upstream, the First Cataract was the most northerly, the Sixth Cataract—about a hundred miles above Khartoum—the most southerly. The cataracts were of fundamental importance to the fertility of ancient Egypt, for they stirred up the river and kept its rich silt suspended until the water reached Egypt.

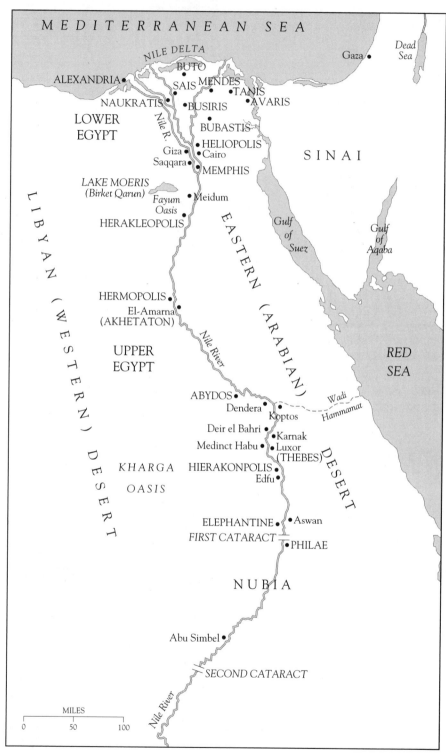

MEDITERRANEAN SEA

NILE DELTA

Dead
Sea

Gaza •

BUTO •

ALEXANDRIA •

SAIS •

MENDES •

• TANIS

NAUKRATIS •

• BUSIRIS

• AVARIS

LOWER
EGYPT

Nile R.

• BUBASTIS

SINAI

Giza •

• HELIOPOLIS

Saqqara •

• Cairo

• MEMPHIS

LAKE MOERIS
(Birket Qarun)

• Meidum

Fayum
Oasis

HERAKLEOPOLIS

Gulf
of
Suez

Gulf
of
Aqaba

L I B Y A N   (W E S T E R N)

HERMOPOLIS •

El-Amarna •
(AKHETATON)

Nile River

EASTERN (ARABIAN)

RED
SEA

UPPER
EGYPT

D E S E R T

ABYDOS •

Dendera •

Wadi
Hammamat

Koptos •

Deir el Bahri •

• Karnak

KHARGA

OASIS

Medinct Habu •

• Luxor
(THEBES)

HIERAKONPOLIS •

Edfu •

DESERT

ELEPHANTINE •

• Aswan

FIRST CATARACT

• PHILAE

N U B I A

Abu Simbel •

SECOND CATARACT

Nile River

MILES

0   50   100

Nile River

Ancient Egypt and the principal sites mentioned in the text (Greek place names are printed
in capital letters, modern Arabic names in small letters).

Although the First Cataract formed the natural frontier of the country in antiquity, the Egyptians sometimes managed to extend their boundaries to the Second, Third, and even Fourth Cataracts. Today the Second Cataract lies hidden below the waters of Lake Nasser, produced after the construction of the Aswan High Dam in the 1960s. The dam has not caused an inundation of the First Cataract, located a few miles north, but has greatly reduced the flow of water here.

Along the distance from the First Cataract northward to modern Cairo, about 550 miles, the river has dug in the stone desert plateau a sometimes deep gorge known as the Nile Valley, a narrow winding ribbon consisting of the river and the fertile alluvial soil lining its banks. Varying from about three to thirteen miles in width, the Valley is flanked on the west by the Libyan Desert, a fearsome wasteland that the ancient Egyptians identified with death and terror. The Eastern (or Arabian) Desert on the opposite side is a dry mountainous region that provided artisans with minerals and hard stones.

A short distance north of Cairo the river divides into smaller branches to form a huge fan-shaped plain of alluvial deposit more than one hundred miles long and nearly two hundred miles wide. After passing through this lowland of marsh and meadowland known as the Delta—so termed by the ancient Greeks because its triangular shape reminded them of their capital alphabetic character of the same name—the tributaries empty into the Mediterranean. About sixty miles south of the Delta and a few miles west of the Nile is a vast natural depression now known as the Fayum, a veritable oasis fed by Nile waters and noted from early days as a remarkably fertile region. A large lake that the Greeks called Lake Moeris (now Birket Qarun) filled much of the Fayum in antiquity but is considerably smaller today. The Egyptians also exploited a string of more westerly oases in the Libyan Desert, though viewing these lush spots more as frontier areas than integral components of their country.

The edges of the Nile Valley stretch away to an abrupt and arid horizon or rise sharply as steep sandstone or limestone cliffs. Visitors to ancient Egypt discovered the inhabitants were usually confined near the banks of the Nile. Today we still find a striking contrast between a long, narrow strip of productive soil and the flanking desert sands. Not surprisingly, the Egyptians called their country the Black Land—*Kemet*—and they called the surrounding desolate area the Red Land—*Deshret*—an apt description of the characteristic color of the sand and rocks in the sterile desert.

THE INUNDATION

Clearly, only the presence of the great Nile permitted a flourishing civilization to develop in arid Egypt. In antiquity the Nile Valley was noted for its proverbial agricultural richness, a fertility clearly tied to the annual overflowing of the Nile, which has ceased since the building of the Aswan High Dam. Each year melting snows and torrential spring rains near the sources of the Nile sent water surging northward, thrashing by the cataracts, but gently swelling through the stone-walled Valley of southern Egypt, where the rising waters began to overflow their banks in July. Is it any wonder that, according to our reckoning, the Egyptian New Year began in July?

The waters reached their peak in September or October, when the Valley was flooded up to the towns and villages built on rising ground at the edge of the desert. Herodotus observed that "all of Egypt becomes a sea, and only the towns remain above water, looking rather like the islands of the Aegean." When the waters gradually retreated in late October and in November, a layer of rich black mud was left behind. Crops were then sown, and the dry warm climate ripened them by March or April. This beneficent cycle was reflected in the names the Egyptians gave the seasons of the year: Flood Time, Planting Time, and Harvest Time. With its approximately 12,000 square miles of fertile soil, Egypt was the most favored agricultural land in the ancient world.

COMMUNICATIONS AND NATURAL RESOURCES

Besides providing fertile soil through the unfailing regularity of its inundation, the Nile also served as an easy transportation route. Egyptians traveling north on a boat proceeded with the current. For the return voyage south, they merely unfurled their sail to catch the prevailing wind blowing from the north, rarely having to use oars. Additionally, the country was nearly self-sufficient. Unlike Mesopotamia, Egypt possessed enormous quantities of stone that facilitated the creation of sculpture and enduring monumental architecture. The Egyptians used the black mud deposited by the Nile for making sun-dried bricks. An abundance of clay was available for pottery. Extensive gold mines flourished in the Eastern Desert, a copper-bearing region as well. Here the Egyptians also obtained plentiful supplies of such semiprecious stones such as amethyst, garnet, onyx, and turquoise. The few raw materials they lacked were close at hand. When the Egyptians required additional gold, for example, they obtained great quantities of the lustrous metal from the land of Nubia to the south, and they imported some copper from Cyprus. They traded with Lebanon for its stately tree of fragrant hard wood known as cedar of Lebanon, and with a distant land they called Punt—probably located along the African shores of the southern Red Sea—for incense and hard tropical woods such as ebony. Thus the Egyptians had little cause to look far away for their needs, which helps to explain the insular quality of their civilization.

The physical setting also encouraged Egyptian isolation by shielding the country from invasion. While the grim deserts stretching away on both sides of the Nile Valley provided formidable barriers against incursion from the east or the west, the Nubian Desert and the cataracts of the Nile River discouraged penetration from the south. Only in the north, where the Delta faced the Mediterranean Sea, was Egypt relatively exposed. Thus the Egyptians, unlike the Mesopotamians, who lived in constant danger of assault by hostile neighbors, enjoyed centuries of relative peace and tranquility. Egypt soon became a unified kingdom, whereas ancient Mesopotamia remained a land of city-states and short-lived empires throughout its long history. The unpredictable deadly floods and storms of Mesopotamia, coupled with the unhealthy climate, encouraged additional gloom and pessimism. The Egyptians, on the other hand, were blessed with the unfailing rhythm of the life-giving Nile and were usually protected from outside danger and pestilence. Not surprisingly, they seem to have been generally optimistic and cheerful in their secure home.

THE PREDYNASTIC PERIOD (c. 5000–3000 BCE)

In general, civilization emerged earlier in Mesopotamia than in Egypt, where the early steps are obscure and difficult to trace. River movement and the accumulation of silt has obliterated most of the earliest traces of human activity along the Nile, but archaeologists have discovered Paleolithic tools dating to around 200,000 years ago. Before the ending of the last Ice Age—about 8000 BCE—a diverse population of nomadic hunter-gatherers roamed extensively over northeast Africa, crossing the Nile in both directions seeking game. At that time the entire region was relatively moist. The retreat of the ice caused a gradual desiccation of the land, eventually turning grasslands into desert, though cycles of higher and lower rainfall prevailed in the areas adjacent to the Nile Valley until an extreme level of aridity was reached around the middle of the third millennium BCE. As the plains dried up, the nomadic hunter-gatherers and many of the animals they preyed upon moved into the Nile Valley and its fringes.

THE EARLIER CULTURES (c. 5000–3500 BCE)

Although precise dating is impossible, Egyptologists conventionally refer to the long prehistory in Egypt from roughly 5000 to 3000 BCE as the Predynastic period, which spans the centuries from the emergence of the first distinct villages on the banks of the Nile to the unification of the country. The Predynastic period is conveniently divided into two broad phases, the earlier from around 5000 to 3500 BCE, the later from about 3500 to 3000 BCE. Inhabitants in Egypt had reached a Neolithic stage of development by the beginning of the earlier phase, exemplified both by their use of finely worked tools and their combination of hunting with the domestication of plants and animals. Prehistorians debate whether the change from food gathering to food production was an indigenous development or was introduced from outside through contacts with Syria-Palestine or perhaps neighboring regions in Africa.

During this earlier phase a number of different groups of people inhabited Egypt. Although those living south of the Delta exhibit some physical variation, for the most part they were a small, delicate people with long, narrow skulls, brown skin, and black wavy hair. Their physical characteristics still appear among the Ethiopians, the Berbers in northern Africa, and the southern Egyptians. The inhabitants of the Delta were taller and had broader skulls and sturdier bodies. Perhaps settlers from southeast Asia had begun to enter the Delta and mingle with the native population, as in later times, when immigrants gradually drifted into southern Egypt.

The Delta and Valley also varied in terms of environment, which helped to give rise to different economic traditions, burial customs, and pottery designs. The earliest traceable farming settlements in northern Egypt were located at Merimda on the southwestern edge of the Delta, dated roughly 5000 BCE, and later at sites around the Fayum. By about 4000 BCE, we find an important culture in southern Egypt: the Badarian (named for the representative sites of Badari). The next cultural manifestation of this earlier phase in southern Egypt, dating about 4000 to 3500 BCE, is known as Naqada I, or Amratian (after the sites of Naqada and Amra).

The early Neolithic farmers in southern and northern Egypt buried their dead with grave goods, indicating they had already come to believe in a continued existence after death. They had learned to build simple reed dwellings and to make pottery for cooking and storage. Farmers in the Nile Valley retained floodwater by modifying natural basins in order to provide water for their fields. The two most important crops in the Valley and Delta were barley and emmer wheat, both of which have been identified with species grown in the earliest farming villages of southwest Asia. Grain was stored in pits lined with straw matting. Other chief crops included various vegetables as well as fruits such as dates and figs. The Egyptians also cultivated flax and flowers. From flax came linen for clothing. Flowery meadows nourished domesticated bees. Apparently the practice of beekeeping originated in Egypt, where farmers collected much honey from their long cylindrical beehives.

Wild game and fish supplemented the diet. Fish was plentiful in the Nile Valley, which supported large numbers of animals, including the antelope, elephant, giraffe, rhinoceros, gazelle, ibex, deer, and ostrich. Wildlife was attracted to the marshes and sand banks of the river, the domain of fierce creatures such as the crocodile and the hippopotamus. Bountiful game flourished on the fringe of the desert, and both geese and ducks were successfully domesticated, along with sheep, pigs, goats, dogs, donkeys, and cattle.

Evidence of metalworking appears during this phase. From sites of the Badarian culture of southern Egypt, we find copper artifacts in the form of small rings and beads and a few simple tools. Although the Egyptians had not yet developed efficient techniques for the smelting of ore, they had learned to cover steatite beads with a blue-green glaze colored with the copper ore malachite, the beginning of an Egyptian artistic tradition that would lead much later to the invention of superb glass vessels and ornaments. Finds of slate palettes for grinding raw lumps of malachite into eye paint show the Egyptians were already developing the cosmetic arts.

THE NAQADA II (OR GERZEAN) CULTURE (C. 3500–3000 BCE)

Egypt rapidly evolved toward civilization in the final phase of the Predynastic period, which is termed Naqada II (or Gerzean, after the site of Gerza) and dated about 3500 to 3000 BCE. Naqada II was a culture of southern Egypt that apparently reached to the Delta and was crucial to the development of a unified Egyptian state. Copper was now worked with increasing skill and cast into numerous tools and weapons. Artisans made stone vessels, animal-shaped slate palettes, flint implements with rippled blades, glazed vessels and jewelry, and distinctive pottery. By this time a number of larger settlements had emerged, some reaching five thousand inhabitants, with people living in rectangular houses of sun-dried brick and wood.

There are increasing signs of social stratification, exemplified by great differences in the size of tombs. Perhaps the largest towns had evolved into competing principalities by this period, for some palettes show rulers—they are depicted as fierce animals—trampling over foes.

We saw that the funerary customs of the Predynastic Egyptians indicate belief in an afterlife. In the absence of a developed writing system, other religious beliefs of the Nile dwellers cannot be verified by archaeological findings and are open to different interpretations. In historic times many of the numerous gods and goddesses in the Egyptian pantheon were either linked to animals or personified by them, a tradition perhaps originating before Naqada II. Although the prehistoric Egyptians trapped and killed animals and birds for food, apparently they beheld them with great awe and reverence, using representations of creatures such as the crocodile or the hippopotamus for their tribal emblems. Several thousand years later many Egyptian deities retained animal or bird heads on human bodies.

Probable Egyptian Contact with Mesopotamia.   Although maintaining its essential African character, Naqada II exhibits a number of features and forms having the earmarks of sudden introduction from the late Uruk culture of Mesopotamia, including the presence of cylinder seals, advanced techniques in copper working, carved stone vessels, niched brick building façades, and new artistic motifs such as entwined snakes, fantastic animals with long necks intertwined, a hero flanked by felines, and predators tearing their prey. Apparently these innovations coincided with the arrival of newcomers from Mesopotamia.

LANGUAGE AND WRITING

Modern Egyptians speak Arabic, a legacy of the Arab conquest of 642 CE, yet Egyptian was their traditional tongue. Although Egyptian is now a dead language, its final form (Coptic) survives in the liturgy of the Coptic Church. The ancient Egyptian language belongs to a wide linguistic family, Afro-Asiatic, extending from North Africa to southwest Asia. In most cases, the African branch of this group is non-Semitic (represented today by tongues such as Berber and Chad), while the Asian branch is Semitic (represented by Hebrew and Arabic). Words from both the African and Asian sides have been identified in the language of ancient Egypt, often taken as evidence that Egyptian took form before the branches of Afro-Asiatic became separate from one another.

THE DEVELOPMENT OF EGYPTIAN WRITING

Hieroglyphic Writing.   Before 3000 BCE, the Egyptians developed their first form of writing, now called hieroglyphs. This term is derived from Greek and means "sacred carvings," probably because later travelers from Greece first saw such writing on the walls of Egyptian temples. Although the Egyptians may have borrowed the idea of writing from Mesopotamia, they developed a distinctive system of their own. Their hieroglyphs were small picturelike symbols whose pictorial character was never lost, in contrast to the highly stylized signs of cuneiform.

We saw in chapter 3 that Sumerian cuneiform developed through several stages, beginning with the use of simple pictures known as pictograms, which designated the objects depicted, later advancing to the use of phonograms, which expressed speech sounds. The theory that hieroglyphic writing experienced a parallel development cannot be shown, for the earliest examples that can be read include phonograms representing vocal sounds. Although the Sumerian phonograms expressed both consonants and vowels, the Egyptian signs were restricted to consonantal sound values. Both the Sumerian and Egyptian scripts employed determinatives, signs with no sound value that were added to words to make the meaning clearer.

In time the Egyptians used three kinds of phonograms, representing one, two, and occasionally three consonants. The most important phonograms were the alphabetic signs, twenty-four in number, expressing single consonants. The Egyptians never developed their embryonic alphabetic signs into a true alphabet, for they continued to write their hieroglyphs in a complex manner. On the basis of the uses noted here, hieroglyphs could be employed as pictograms to represent the object shown, as ideograms to stand for an idea associated with the object, as phonograms to express one to three consonants, and as determinatives. Hieroglyphs were usually written from right to left, though sometimes from left to right or top to bottom. The signs are always read in the opposite direction from which the human and animal figures in the script are facing.

Hieratic and Demotic Writing.   Hieroglyphic writing was in use for more than three thousand years, though the script was employed in later times largely for carved or painted inscriptions intended to last for eternity on Egyptian monuments, whether royal, religious, or funerary. Because this form of writing was entirely too time-consuming for the efficient production of ordinary documents, the Egyptians developed two simplified scripts from hieroglyphic known as hieratic and demotic. Hieratic, which was already in sporadic use by the early third millennium BCE, was more cursive and less detailed than hieroglyphic. Employed at first for both secular and sacred documents, hieratic came to be used only for religious texts. Hieratic could be written either in vertical columns or horizontal lines, but the direction was always right to left. Demotic, a standardized shorthand, was an even more highly cursive script. Developed from hieratic about 700 BCE, demotic was employed for business documents and private letters. Demotic was written in horizontal lines and from left to right.

Paperlike Material Made from Papyrus.   The Greek word papyrus, probably derived from an Egyptian term, is the origin of our word paper. Hieratic and demotic were usually written on a flexible paperlike material made from the inner pith of the stalks of the papyrus plant. The Egyptians first peeled away the hard outer rind of the stalk to fashion necessities such as baskets, sails, sandals, and rope. Then they cut the pith into thin strips and arranged them side by side, placing a second layer

HIEROGLYPHIC C. 1900	HIERATIC C. 1900 BCE	DEMONTIC C. 400 BCE	MEANING
			Bundle of fox skins
			Whip
			Stone jug
			Papyrus roll

These examples, from left to right, show the formal Egyptian writing (hieroglyphic), an abbreviated, cursive script (hieratic), and a rapidly written shorthand (demotic).

crosswise over the first. This double layer was pressed together and dried, resulting in a smooth and durable light-colored writing surface. Scribes wrote on papyri with pen and ink, black and red being most commonly used.

Coptic. A dramatic change in the writing system occurred during the early centuries of the Christian era. The Egyptian Christians of the time exhibited considerable hostility to their non-Christian heritage. Viewing hieroglyphic writing and its derivative demotic as idolatrous and thus completely unsuitable for expressing Christian texts, they wrote their language in a script composed primarily of Greek capital letters. Egyptian in this form came to be known as Coptic. With the conversion of the majority of Egyptians to Christianity in the fourth century CE, the new religion banned the old scripts. The literate now wrote Egyptian only in Coptic and soon lost the ability to read and write the ancient hieroglyphs.

JEAN FRANÇOIS CHAMPOLLION AND THE DECIPHERMENT OF HIEROGLYPHIC WRITING

A clue to the decipherment of hieroglyphic writing was discovered in 1799, when a French officer in Napoleon's famous military expedition to Egypt unearthed the so-called Rosetta Stone near the western Delta town of Rashid (known to Europeans as Rosetta). Now in the British Museum, the Rosetta Stone is a large broken slab of black basalt that was inscribed in the early second century BCE with parallel texts in hieroglyphic, demotic, and Greek. Using the Greek part of the inscription, which was easily read, scholars made some halting steps toward the colossal task of deciphering the Egyptian scripts. The Rosetta Stone finally surrendered its secrets to the French scholar Jean François Champollion in 1822, when he succeeded in working out the fundamental principles for the accurate decipherment of hieroglyphs, the basis for all subsequent Egyptology.

EARLY DYNASTIC PERIOD (FIRST AND SECOND DYNASTIES, c. 3000–2647 bce)

Unification (c. 3000 bce)

Egypt became the first unified country in history, though the process took centuries to complete. Apparently the early Predynastic farming villages gradually coalesced into a number of small provinces or principalities, perhaps equivalent to the later Egyptian administrative districts that the classical Greeks and modern historians call nomes, of which in historic times there were twenty-two in the Nile Valley and twenty in the Delta. Each prehistoric principality seems to have included a major town where the ruler of the territory lived. Eventually confederations of principalities arose, the antecedent to the consolidation of Egypt. Later historical sources suggest that by late Predynastic times two major countries had emerged, a kingdom of Upper Egypt in the south and a kingdom of Lower Egypt in the north, both so named because the Nile flows from south to north. Accordingly, Upper Egypt would have encompassed the Nile Valley and Lower Egypt the Delta. The king of each land is said to have worn a crown, a white one in Upper Egypt and a red one in Lower Egypt. Yet many Egyptologists doubt that a united prehistoric kingdom ever existed in the Delta. Although the extent of territory governed by early shadowy kings remains uncertain, apparently one of their successors ruled a unified Egypt around 3000 bce. This was roughly the time Egyptian writing was invented. Thus the ending of the prehistoric age and the Predynastic period virtually coincided.

The Chronological System Adopted by Egyptologists for the Historic Period

Most of the more than three-thousand-year span of ancient Egyptian history is traditionally divided into thirty royal dynasties, beginning with the unification of Egypt and continuing down to the conquest of the country by Alexander the Great. This was the scheme of an early third-century bce Egyptian priest named Manetho, who compiled a chronology of Egyptian history in Greek, a work preserved only in garbled fragments through writers of much later date. Broadly speaking, the thirty dynasties represent ruling families (to which a thirty-first was subsequently added), generally grouped according to the cities of royal residence. We should keep in mind that the textual corruption of the surviving fragments, the unreliability of the specified lengths of reigns, and other flaws pose difficulties in reconstructing accurate chronologies without additional evidence. Moreover, Manetho's system was never systematically updated in antiquity to provide for the period after Alexander the Great. Regrettably perhaps, his use of Greek versions of proper Egyptian names (thus Amenophis rather than Amenhotep) has been almost universally adopted by Egyptologists, a system not followed here.

Although modern scholars retain Manetho's dynastic division as a convenient framework, they further arrange the tangled chronicle of Egyptian history into larger blocks of time: the Early Dynastic period (First and Second Dynasties, c. 3000–2647 BCE), the Old Kingdom (Third through Eighth Dynasties, c. 2647–2124 BCE), the First Intermediate period (Ninth through mid-Eleventh Dynasties, c. 2124–2040 BCE), the Middle Kingdom (mid-Eleventh through Thirteenth Dynasties, c. 2040–1648 BCE), the Second Intermediate period (Fourteenth through Seventeenth Dynasties, c. 1648–1540 BCE), the New Kingdom (Eighteenth through Twentieth Dynasties, c. 1540–1069 BCE), the Late period (Twenty-first through Thirty-first Dynasties, c. 1069–332 BCE), and the Greco-Roman period (332 BCE–642 CE).

NARMER (FL. C. 3000 BCE)

According to Manetho, Upper and Lower Egypt were unified by a powerful monarch called Menes, the traditional founder of the First Dynasty. Although a number of modern scholars regard him as a purely legendary figure, others suggest Menes may have been the alternative name for an early Egyptian ruler named Narmer, who clearly claimed kingship over a united Egyptian state.

The Palette of King Narmer (c. 3000 BCE). One of the earliest historical monuments from Egypt, known as the *Palette of King Narmer*, probably commemorates a victory of Narmer over the Delta. The ceremonial slate palette—shield shaped and about twenty-four inches high—served originally as a tablet for the grinding of eye-paint. This masterpiece is now in the collection of the Egyptian Museum in Cairo. On both sides of the palette a story is told in relief to memorialize Narmer. Many Egyptologists suggest the palette depicts the conquest of all Egypt by the king and the unification of the country under his rule. The various scenes are carved on registers, that is, horizontal bands placed one above the other, with most figures placed on baselines. Beginning with the reverse, the upper register shows a pair of human-faced cow heads, usually conceived as Hathor, the goddess of sexual love and joy. The images of Hathor flank the representation of an important building, perhaps a temple or the royal palace, used to frame one of the king's names—Narmer—written in hieroglyphic script. The other figures are also identified by hieroglyphs, though some of the signs are difficult to interpret at this early stage in the development of the writing system. The middle register depicts Narmer wearing the conical-like White Crown, appearing thereafter in Egyptian art as the emblematic headgear of the kings as ruler of Upper Egypt. The crown is held in place by straps, at the end of which is a false beard. Although the men of all classes along the Nile were clean shaven, the Egyptians equated hair with power, as did the later Hebrews.

Drawing of the *Palette of King Narmer* (reverse). Found at Hierakon-polis, this image-rich slate slab was used for preparing eye makeup. c. 3000 BCE. Egyptian Museum, Cairo.

Hanging from Narmer's waist is another symbol of his authority—a dried bull's tail—associating the king with an animal of immense power, one probably thought to enjoy a special relationship with heaven. Clutching with his left hand the hair knot of a kneeling enemy, perhaps a Delta prince or king, Narmer brandishes a mace with his right and is about to sacrifice the hapless man by bringing the instrument crashing down on his skull. The human sacrifice takes place before the sky-god and solar deity Horus, of whom the king was considered an incarnation. Horus, repre-

Drawing of the *Pallette of King Narmer* (obverse).

sented here as a falcon with a human arm, uses a piece of rope to hold captive a personified papyrus thicket, perhaps symbolizing foreign prisoners or the Delta, where
the plant grew in great abundance. To the Egyptians and other ancient people, size
denoted importance. Thus Narmer is more than twice the size of the courtier standing behind him on a separate baseline. This attendant bears the king's sandals, probably an indication that the sanctity of the moment has made the ground holy.
According to the biblical book of Exodus, begun considerably later, the Hebrew
prophet and lawgiver Moses removed his shoes when he saw the burning bush—

interpreted as a divine appearance—because he was standing on holy ground (Exod. 3:5). In the bottom register, below Narmer's feet, his foes flee in terror.

The Obverse.   Four registers appear on the obverse of the palette. Again, the top register exhibits two images conceived as Hathor flanking the representation of an important building, within which appears the king's name. On the second register Narmer visits a battlefield while wearing the hatlike Red Crown, appearing thereafter in Egyptian art as the emblematic headgear of the kings as the ruler of Lower Egypt. Narmer strides forth, followed by his sandal bearer and preceded by both a high court official—possibly the queen or the crown prince—and warriors bearing standards to indicate the sovereign presence of the great king. We see a grisly scene rising up starkly on the right, ten decapitated corpses whose heads have been placed between their legs so they could be collected and counted, a practice from which the expression "head count" arose. The third register contains the depression used for grinding the eye paint, a circular area formed by the intertwining of the long, serpentlike necks of two felines, each of which is held fast by an attendant. Here Mesopotamian influence is evident, for such fantastic animals often appeared on Sumerian cylinder seals. Possibly symbolizing the union of Egypt, the beasts seem to be lionesses or panthers. We see in the lower register that Narmer—now in the guise of a bull—has broken down a fortified city, its walls and towers represented in the earliest known architectural plan. Meanwhile the bull is preparing to mount a helplessly prostate man shown utterly naked and terrified in the moment before the victor's brutal sexual assault.

The paramount significance of the *Palette of King Narmer* is the depiction of the king as a deified figure—whether under the appearance of a man, hawk, or bull—majestically isolated from all ordinary people and alone responsible for his conquest. Even in this Early Dynastic period the Egyptians believed kingship was intrinsically united with the divine.

Artistic Conventions Already Present.   King Narmer's body, as depicted on the palette, exhibits the artistic conventions that governed Egyptian figurative portrayal for the next three thousand years. Apparently in an attempt to show every part of the body in the way most recognizable, the Egyptians represented the eyes and the shoulders frontally but the head, legs, and hips in profile. Exceptions were made only when both hands were engaged in the same action, in which case the shoulders were rendered in profile. Another characteristic device employed on the palette, superimposed registers, also became conventional for ancient Egyptian art, particularly in carved or painted decoration, as on the walls of a tomb.

The Two Lands after Unification

Distinct Realms.   The ancient Egyptians regarded the unification of their country as one of the pivotal events of their history, though the inhabitants of the Nile Valley and those of the Delta never lost a sense of the two lands of Upper and Lower Egypt. The northerners in the Delta, looking outward upon the maritime civilizations of the

Mediterranean, often came under the influence of new ideas, but the southerners of the Nile Valley were more isolated and insulated, less susceptible to the adoption of new techniques, more inclined to resist new philosophies. Reflecting the distinctiveness of the two realms, the king was always officially styled King of Upper and Lower Egypt. Another of his titles was Lord of the Two Lands. As such, he was crowned twice—once with the tall, conical-like White Crown of the south, which was made of felt and white clay, and also with the hatlike Red Crown of the north, the rear of which included a high peak and an attached metal strip projecting toward the front and terminating in a spiral. Following his dual coronation, the king often wore the Double Crown combining the designs of the northern and southern crowns.

The Founding of Memphis.   Sometime in the early First Dynasty a capital for newly united Egypt was founded in the strategic boundary region where Nile Valley meets Delta. The Egyptians called this administrative center White Wall because the sun-dried brick walls around the royal palace were whitewashed, but the great city is more familiar to us under its later name of Memphis. The capital was deliberately established near the juncture of Lower and Upper Egypt, from which point the king could more easily exercise control over both parts of the kingdom.

THE OLD KINGDOM (THIRD THROUGH EIGHTH DYNASTIES, c. 2647–2124 BCE)

The Third through the Eighth Dynasties constitute the Old Kingdom, a period of internal stability and remarkable prosperity lasting about five hundred years. The Old Kingdom witnessed a glorious efflorescence of civilization built upon the formative base established during the Early Dynastic period. The king, regarded as a god, built a centralized bureaucracy focused on Memphis but with branches in the nomes. While irrigation works were extended and improved, copper mines and stone quarries were developed, all resulting in increased prosperity. Artisans produced splendid jewelry, stonework, and furniture. Boats made of wood or papyrus and caravans of donkeys provided transportation for trading expeditions to the Eastern Desert, Nubia, Punt, Lebanon, Syria, and even Anatolia. About 2500 BCE, the Egyptians built the world's oldest known paved road, constructed mainly of stone slabs, which crossed nearly eight miles of desert to connect several quarries with loading docks on the shores of Lake Moeris. In the meantime they pushed the southern frontier to the First Cataract and beyond, gaining some control over Nubia.

RELIGION

Herodotus noted that the Egyptians were the most religious of all people. Their religion—not easy to define with its changing concepts—developed through various stages, from simple polytheism in the Predynastic period, to the world's earliest known tendencies toward monotheism in the Eighteenth Dynasty, and then back to polytheism again.

Archaeological evidence from the Predynastic period suggests the prehistoric Egyptians venerated insects such as scarabs, all animals, certain plants, manifestations of nature, and heavenly bodies. On the basis of such reverence, local deities arose in the villages along the Nile, with those of animal form predominating. In time these animal gods were anthropomorphized, or partially humanized, and they were frequently represented as a composite of human and beast. Anubis, one of the gods of the dead, for example, was originally depicted as a jackal, but later he shows up with the body of a man and the head of a jackal.

Following the political unification of Egypt, the old gods were to some extent fused with one another into a state pantheon. Such a fusion hardly posed a theological problem because the ancient peoples of the time regarded no god as all-encompassing. Thought to possess one or more of the attributes of divinity, each deity provided worshipers with another approach to the infinite. In short, the supernatural beings tended to intertwine and meld together. Thus the Egyptians, through their many gods, created a series of superimposed holy images, none effacing another. Meanwhile the practice had arisen of offering daily animal sacrifices in the temples for the nourishment of the gods, though the deities were thought to feed only upon the *essence* of the sacrifice, leaving the *material* of the sacrifice intact.

The Great Deities

Re and the Chief Center of Sun Worship, Heliopolis.   Religious beliefs often seem to reflect the state of life on earth. The abundance along the Nile may help to explain why the Egyptians created rather beneficent deities. Perhaps not surprising in a country with almost constant sunshine in the daytime and a truly bountiful river, their solar and riverine gods were among the most prominent in the pantheon. The Egyptians held the sun in special awe and worshiped the great orb under various names and manifestations. Under the name Re, for example, the sun became the supreme god of the Old Kingdom. The center for the worship of Re was a city north of Memphis known in Egyptian as Iwnw (the biblical On), which the Greeks called Heliopolis, meaning city of the sun. At Heliopolis other solar deities such as Atum and Horus were identified with Re.

Represented as a falcon-headed man crowned with the solar disk, Re personified the power of the sun. He was among the first of the gods to receive kingdom-wide recognition, and throughout Egyptian history Re remained one of the most important deities in the land. The Egyptians believed that each day he crossed the celestial ocean in a barque as helmsman of the world. Then he changed to another sacred boat for the return trip through the netherworld at night. Called the Father of the Gods, Re was also the king of the other deities and the father of humankind. Both people and creatures were said to have arisen from his sweat and from the tears shed by Re's eye, itself thought to possess an intellect of its own and the ability to separate from him.

Atum.   An even older Heliopolitan theogony identified the creator-god as Atum, another manifestation of the sun. Through a holy mystery, Atum was self-created. Perhaps the Egyptians' concern for fertility had prompted them to develop a concept of divine sexuality. Yet creator deities generally required no sexual partner, nor were they confined to one sex, and they impregnated themselves to give birth. Sometimes called the Great-He-She, Atum was one of these deities who was essentially bisexual in the sense of uniting the attributes of both sexes. Atum brought forth the first pair of divine children through masturbation, ejaculating out of himself brother and sister, Shu (the air) and Tefnut (moisture), whose children were Geb (the earth) and Nut (the sky). Geb and Nut gave birth to numerous gods and goddesses, including Osiris, Isis, and Seth, all of whom in turn created a multitude of heavenly beings and inanimate objects. Usually represented as an aged, bearded man, Atum and the hand he used for creative masturbation appeared together at times as a divine couple on coffins.

Ptah. The Egyptian pantheon included additional creator-gods besides Re and Atum. In the rival religious center at nearby Memphis, the new capital, the creator-god was Ptah, who was represented as a man holding a long scepter and clad in mummy's apparel. The priests of Ptah taught that the god conceived the idea of the universe and brought it into being by the authority of his *Word* alone, merely speaking the names of all things to spring them into existence. By thought and utterance, therefore, he had brought forth all gods, all spirits, all humans, and the entire physical universe from nothingness, a possible antecedent of the belief of the ancient Hebrews that their god created merely by speaking. The exalted Ptah came closer to theological transcendence than any other Egyptian divinity during the Old Kingdom. We saw that creator deities generally were bisexual beings who impregnated themselves. Regarded as both male and female, Ptah was frequently shown with female breasts. He was not only the creator of the universe but also the patron of artisans, and the Greeks identified him with the divine blacksmith Hephaestus.

Apis. Ptah was thought to be incarnated in the sacred bull Apis, a living beast installed in the great temple of Ptah at Memphis and bearing special markings on forehead, tongue, and flank. Each Apis—considered an intermediary between humanity and Ptah—was conceived when Ptah miraculously came down from heaven in the shape of a flame and impregnated the mother cow. When one Apis died, the people mourned his death, and his mummified body was placed in a huge sarcophagus alongside those of his predecessors. The priests immediately searched the fields until they found the divine successor bull bearing the same markings. For forty days after the enthronement of the new Apis in the temple, only women were admitted to his sacred presence and, as an act of homage, they raised their long dresses to give him pleasure by revealing their genitalia.

Min. We saw the Egyptians recognized divine creativity under many guises. One of these was Min, a god of virility and fertility, who was regarded as a bestower of male sexual potency and thus a creator-god. He was thought to generate growth in grain as well and was closely associated with important fertility and harvest festivals. He was also the guardian deity of nomads and hunters. Min was depicted as a standing male figure wearing a tall plumed crown and brandishing a flail, while his prominent and erect penis proudly announced his readiness for sexual union.

Anubis.   Several other Egyptian deities are worthy of mention. Anubis, represented as a jackal-headed man, was the god of embalming, the guardian of tombs, and the protector of the dead. One of his duties was to weigh the heart of the deceased—the Egyptians believed the heart was the seat of intelligence—against a feather representing the goddess of truth and orderly conduct (Ma`at). If lifetime virtues were in excess of faults, the deceased was entitled to life and happiness in the netherworld, but whenever the weighing of a heart indicated an excess of unsavory deeds, the organ was immediately consumed by the repugnant Devourer of the Dead—a composite monster who was part lion, part hippopotamus, part crocodile—crouching hungrily by the side of the balance.

Hathor.   One of the oldest and most notable deities in the pantheon was Hathor, the goddess of sexual love, joy, gold, music, dancing, drunkenness, beauty, fertility, and childbirth. Because she presided over the toilet of females and offered divine protection to both women and children, all Egyptian women worshiped her as a universal mother. Hathor was also a great cosmic power in her role as goddess of the starry sky. The identification of the sky with the cow was widespread in the Delta, which helps to explain why Hathor was given bovine features. She was represented in art in several different forms, usually as a cow with a solar disk between her horns, a cow-headed woman with the solar disk, or as a woman with the horns and solar disk. Hathor was said to suckle the king, and she also suckled the newly dead to sustain them during their mummification, their journey to the judgment hall, and the weighing of their hearts. The solar disk between her horns symbolized a masculine and bisexual component. We should not be surprised that the eye of Re sometimes took the form of Hathor. The Greeks identified her with their goddess of sexual love, Aphrodite, while the Romans identified her with Venus. These later goddesses, having been created by fathers without mothers, also had unusual masculine attributes.

Thoth.   The god of wisdom, Thoth was in charge of learning and magic and was held to be the inventor of language, mathematics, and writing. The Egyptians, like other ancient peoples, thought written words were literally permeated with power. They believed Thoth, who was considered the scribe and messenger of the gods, exercised great magical powers through his unrivaled command of language and thus frequently invoked him in illness. When Anubis weighed the heart of the dead, Thoth stood near the scales to record the innocence or guilt of the deceased. Thoth was represented most often as an ibis-headed man, an ibis, or a baboon. On occasion he appeared wearing the horns of the crescent moon on his head, a reflection of his function as a lunar deity with the power to dispel darkness during the hours of night. The Greeks venerated Thoth and identified him with Hermes, their messenger of the gods.

The Osiris-Isis-Horus Myth.   Egyptian gods were frequently grouped by twos (husband and wife) or threes (husband, wife, and child). Heavenly triads have enjoyed a prominent place in the history of religion, exemplified by the famous Egyptian family of Osiris, his wife Isis, and their son Horus. According to one version of the Osiris-Isis-Horus myth, Osiris was a god-king who not only persuaded the Egyptians to give up cannibalism but also introduced them to civilization. We are told his subjects were devoted to him, but his jealous brother Seth—deciding to supplant him—slew Osiris, dismembered his body into fourteen pieces, and scattered them over the land, except the penis, which he threw into the river. Then Osiris' faithful sister and wife Isis made a grief-stricken pilgrimage throughout Egypt searching for the parts, collecting all but the penis, which had been devoured by fish. After using her magical powers to reassemble and partially resurrect Osiris, Isis presented the king with a substitute for his penis, a golden magic phallus that she had made from nothing. With the magic phallus Osiris and Isis had an incestuous union (brother-sister marriages were commonly practiced in the Egyptian royal family). In due course and after many dangers, their son Horus was born and was hidden in the Delta marshes from the wrath of Seth, now ruling Egypt. Horus, who was usually represented as a falcon, was determined to avenge his father's murder and to challenge Seth for the kingdom. In a bloody struggle, Horus castrated Seth, who in turn managed to pluck out one of his nephew's eyes, later restored by Thoth. The injured eye—signifying the moon—became a prominent feature on many Egyptian monuments as a symbol of sacrifice.

In one episode, as reported in a Middle Kingdom papyrus, Seth made sexual advances to Horus and copulated between his buttocks, thinking this would make his nephew appear powerless to the other gods. Yet Horus outwitted Seth by putting his hand between his buttocks and catching his uncle's semen. Isis then decided to retaliate against Seth for his deed. She sprinkled a sample of Horus' own semen on lettuce growing in the garden of Seth, who ate the leafy plant shortly afterward and was unknowingly impregnated. Later, when Seth was in the presence of the other gods, the consumed semen emerged from his forehead in the form of a gold sun disk, apparently connected with the myth of the birth of Thoth from his head. Seth was furious, for his own trickery had rebounded on himself.

The dispute between Horus and Seth was finally settled before a tribunal of divine judges, who decided that Osiris—having lost his true reproductive powers—could no longer rule the living and would become the king and judge of the dead in the underworld, while Horus would become the new king of Egypt. The murderer Seth, on the other hand, became a reviled outcast for eternity. Represented as a big-eared composite animal with a tufted or forked tail, Seth symbolized discord, and he became the god of storms, confusion, drought, and warfare, ostracized by the Egyptians as the embodiment of all evil.

Osiris was represented as a green mummy holding a crook and a flail, symbolizing the dual benefits of protection and discipline offered by Egyptian kings. He was worshiped not only as the god of the dead but also as the personification of the inundated Nile and as the god of vegetation. His green color identified him with plant life and fertility, and his phallus became a symbol for life overcoming death. Unlike most dying fertility gods, however, he was not resurrected to life on earth. We saw that he served as king of the underworld, while his son Horus lived and ruled in his place on earth.

Isis was represented as a woman with a throne on her head. Of all the Egyptian goddesses, she was the most popular. Her husband Osiris was identified with the rising waters of the Nile, and she was regarded as the land awaiting the flooding. Gifted with exceptional powers transcending those of most other deities, Isis was the supreme mother-goddess. She was the perfect mother and the perfect wife. She cured the sick and brought the dead to life. Through her, good triumphed over evil. Her many divine functions included her role as a great female creator. Isis re-created her brother and consort Osiris. She made the phallic instrument through which she impregnated herself. She was like so many other chaste goddesses bearing children without normal copulation, such as Mary, the mother of Jesus. In a sense, Isis was a lineal ancestor of Mary. Representations of this sacred Egyptian mother with the divine child Horus on her lap became the deliberate model for the Madonna of Christianity, and hymns of praise to Isis were adapted by the early Christians to honor Mary.

THE INTERTWINED POLITICAL AND RELIGIOUS FUNCTIONS OF THE KING

An Incarnate God.   The Osiris-Isis-Horus myth tells of deities who combine human and divine qualities and demonstrate both secular and religious concerns. A parallel existed in ancient Egypt where, in a sense, government and religion were hardly distinguishable because of the dual role of the king as head of state and a living god. At the beginning of the Old Kingdom the king was regarded as the animating principle of the country, not as a mortal but as a powerful divine force, the sky-god Horus incarnate. In early Egyptian art the falcon, a symbol of Horus, is often shown hovering behind the head of the king in a protective manner. By the reign of King Narmer, Horus had become identified with the sun cult. Thus the living king was regarded as the heavenly sent son of the supreme manifestation of divinity—the sun—but upon dying became Osiris, while his successor was identified with Horus. The king thereby linked two hallowed cults, that of the sun through Horus and that of fertility through Osiris. Because the king's sacred powers combined heavenly-solar and netherworld-fertility characteristics, he exercised authority in both divine realms.

The King's Titles and Names.   The royal titles and names clearly reflected the belief that the king was a god. By the Fifth Dynasty the ruler generally bore five titles—they expressed his divine nature or his power—and each was followed by either an epithet or a name. The first title was Horus, which was followed by the Horus name, the official name of the king as the earthly manifestation of a god exercising power in the skies. The fourth name and the fifth name were each enclosed in a cartouche, an oval probably signifying the course of the sun across the heavens and conveying the idea that the king ruled all within this vast solar circuit. During most periods the king was best known by his fourth name (his throne name assumed at his accession), which was employed on his monuments and in his documents, and by his fifth name (usually his personal name from birth). Yet at different times the Egyptians favored different choices from the range of names. Moreover, while foreign rulers re-

Drawing of a limestone funerary stela of King Djet of the First Dynasty, from his tomb at Abydos. Each king of the First Dynasty is best known by his Horus name, which was inscribed within a rectangular frame (*serekh*) representing the royal palace. King Djet's Horus name was Cobra (*djet*), written with the hieroglyphic sign for cobra. Standing above is a falcon representing Horus, of whom each king was an embodiment. The crisply carved original, dating c. 2900 BCE, is now in the Louvre, Paris.

ferred to an Egyptian king by his fourth name, Manetho most often used a Greek version of the fifth name in his chronology. Is there any wonder that identification of Egyptian rulers is sometimes uncertain? For convenience, modern historians assign numbers—about which they often disagree—to the various kings with the same fifth name, exemplified by the New Kingdom rulers Thutmose I through Thutmose IV.

The Term Pharaoh.　The center of the kingdom was the royal complex at Memphis, where the king and his family lived in splendor. The custom eventually arose of applying the term *pr-ʿo*, originally meaning "great house," to the palace and court of the king. Not until the middle of the Eighteenth Dynasty was *pr-ʿo* employed as a deferential expression referring to the king himself, and only in the tenth century BCE was the term used as a title in conjunction with the royal name. The Hebrews had their own version of the word *pr-ʿo*, rendered in the Bible as *Pharaoh*, the title commonly—though illogically and anachronistically—prefixed today to the names of all Egyptian kings, even those living two thousand years before the tenth century BCE.

The King as the Maintainer of Maʿat.　The Egyptians believed their god-king provided them with a link to a set of eternal and powerful principles known as *maʿat*—representing wisdom, harmony, justice, and truth—which ensured a state of righteousness and order in human society. This concept, clearly fundamental in Egyptian thought and behavior, was personified as Ma`at, the goddess of such an exalted standard that no single word or phrase can express her domain, although for convenience she is often called the goddess of truth and justice. Usually represented as a woman with an ostrich feather on her head, Ma`at is just one example of the strong feminine element in the Egyptian religion, a presence that was far less prominent at the highest level of the masculine-dominated religion of Sumer. The rich treasury of gifts from *ma`at* was thought to include cosmic harmony, as expressed in the cycle of seasons, the rising and setting of the sun, the flooding of the Nile, the yield of the soil, and the like. The belief in *ma`at* gave the Egyptians a sense of security and engendered devotion to their king as its guardian and provider.

Royal Power. Clearly, the Egyptians considered their divine king essential for the survival of a safe, ordered society. Prudent kings exhibited a careful balance between exerting authority over their subjects and showing them loving care. Each king was regarded as the soul of the state, a god bringing about the prosperity of commerce, the success of the army, and the endurance of peace. He directed the energies of the people, declared the law, headed the state religion, commanded the army, and controlled the economic life of the country. The basis of wealth in ancient Egypt was land, and in principle the king owned all the land. Much of his power stemmed from the control of agriculture and the right to levy taxes. The king was nearly absolute during the Old Kingdom, when the Egyptians believed a ruler of superhuman authority was required to maintain harmony and prosperity.

The Vizier and Other State Officials. Every king employed deputies drawn from his relatives and the nobility to advise him, dispense his justice, perform his religious functions, supervise his public works, and serve in his military expeditions, though in theory his officials had no power in their own right but merely voiced his divine commands. The most important official was the vizier, or superintendent, usually a close relative of the king. In time the viziership and other offices of state became hereditary, the men handing their posts on to their sons. Exercising considerable administrative and judicial powers, the vizier carried out royal orders through a vast hierarchy of officials and scribes. This extensive bureaucracy—operating through departments at Memphis—conducted censuses of land and people, estimated the size of the harvest, collected taxes in kind, ran the treasuries, and supervised the vital irrigation system. Moreover, a number of nobles won royal appointments as governors of the nomes. In some cases, especially in the Fifth and Sixth Dynasties, we know far more about the nobles than the king. The role of the rulers as omnipotent gods was so lofty that scant information remains about their personal feelings or thoughts.

TOMBS AND FUNERARY CUSTOMS

The Egyptians were far less concerned about their earthly dwellings, meant merely for temporary lodging, than about their graves, or houses for eternity. The devel-

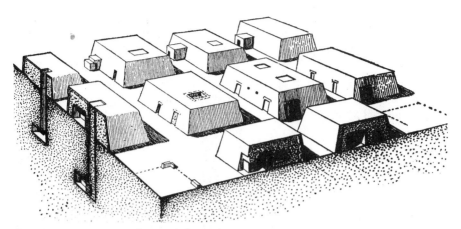

Cutaway reconstruction of a group of mastabas.

oped ancient Egyptian culture centered on a *denial of death*, the pivotal concept of their civilization. Accordingly, much more effort was put forth in preparing a necropolis than in maintaining a living city. A parallel tendency shows up in Egyptian art, much of which was created not to enrich ephemeral life but to grace eternity through burial. We noted that a large part of the art of antiquity focuses on belief, and the Egyptian tombs provide the best artistic record of religious concepts from the ancient world.

The Mastaba.   The two primary functions of tombs were to house the dead body and to provide everything necessary for the hereafter, notably food and drink, funerary equipment, and the most valuable belongings of the deceased, the last constantly luring grave robbers. Prehistoric Egyptian graves were covered with mounds of sand or heaps of loose stones, but the persistent desert winds often blew away the sand, and jackals regularly foraged among the stones. Spurred by the need for more substantial grave coverings, the Egyptians learned by the end of the Predynastic period to construct great tombs now called mastabas for royal and noble burials. The word *mastaba* is modern Arabic for "bench," for these tombs faintly resemble the low benches standing outside many Egyptian houses today. The early mastaba was a solid, rectangular structure of sun-dried bricks, with sloping sides and probably a flat roof. The sides were relieved with deep niches, later reduced to two that functioned as false doors on the eastern side, thought to permit the deceased to enter and leave at will. Although the concept of the afterlife was originally limited to the king and the royal family, the nobility soon came to have hope of attaining eternal existence. Reflecting the belief in a hereafter, one of the recesses of the mastaba gradually became deeper to serve as a funerary chapel, in which offerings were made for the sustenance of the deceased. The offering chapel eventually developed into a complex of many chambers, the walls of which were decorated with vivid scenes from daily life that focused on food to sustain the deceased with magical power. By this stage, stone had been adapted in the construction of the superstructure. Opening from the top of each mastaba was a deep shaft running below ground to the burial chamber, itself gradually increasing in size and complexity. The shaft was filled with rubble after the burial and sealed with a heavy stone slab.

Early Royal Tombs and Evidence of Human Sacrifice.   The tombs of the king and the royal family were much more elaborate than other mastabas. Although only the king was assured of an afterlife in the Predynastic period, anyone he required to serve him in the hereafter might be granted eternal existence as well. Thus immortality was extended to the king's family and to those nobles required as courtiers in the royal court of the netherworld. We saw in chapter 4 that the royal tombs of Ur, dated to a period not long after Early Dynastic Egypt, contain kings and queens buried with sacrificed retainers. In Egypt, we find clear evidence by the Early Dynastic period of mass human sacrifice, probably by poison, of numerous retainers—exemplified by courtiers, scribes, artisans, concubines, court dwarfs, guards, and herders—as well as royal animals, all buried near the king at the time of his death to provide him with eternal services. The best chance of a blessed immortality came in association with the god-king, and the sacrificed servants may have given their lives willingly and without hesitation. The practice did not survive the Early Dynastic period, however, after which vast quantities of magic statues were substituted for flesh and blood.

Imhotep and the Step Pyramid of King Djoser (c. 2620 BCE).   The world's first colossal structure made entirely of cut stone was erected during the Third Dynasty at Saqqara, a high bluff on the desert west of the capital at Memphis and serving as its necropolis (city of the dead). This was the Step Pyramid, built to preserve for all eternity the body of King Djoser (or Netjerikhet, c. 2628–2609 BCE), the second king of the dynasty, in one of its underground chambers. Such a great tomb reflects the belief that the god-king, if properly cared for, would live forever to aid and protect his people. Egyptian civilization came of age in Djoser's reign, which inaugurated a long period of prosperity and tranquility. For the first time we can identify individuals other than the king by name. Imhotep, one of the preeminent geniuses of Egyptian creativity, served as Djoser's vizier as well as his architect, the first of recorded history. So great was Imhotep's renown as an innovator and sage—he was celebrated by later writers as an architect, physician, priest, magician, and scribe—that the later Egyptians deified him as a son of Ptah, and the Greeks identified him with their god of medicine Asclepius. By creating the first royal pyramid, another word derived from Greek, Imhotep brought about a major change in royal tomb design and produced a wonder that inspired Egyptian architects of later periods. He employed small blocks of local limestone rather than brick to construct the Step Pyramid, whose ruins still tower above the desert floor in majestic grandeur. Although Imhotep seems to have planned this tomb as a single great mastaba, he made dramatic modifications in the design during construction by piling a series of mastabas of decreasing size on top of one another, thereby creating six enormous steps, each faced with polished white limestone. Rising like a stairway and attaining

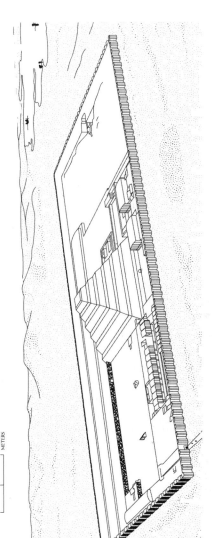

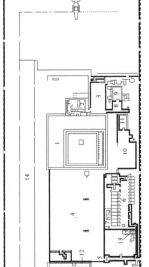

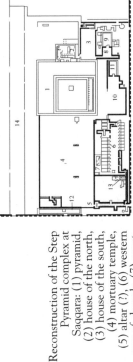

1. Stepped pyramid derived from square-plan mastaba
2. Funerary temple of Zoser
3. Court with serdab
4. Large court with altar and two B-shaped stones
5. Entrance portico
6. Heb-Sed court flanked by sham chapels
7. Small temple
8. Court before North Palace
9. North Palace
10. Court before South Palace
11. South Palace
12. South tomb
13. Royal Pavilion
14. Magazines

Reconstruction of the Step Pyramid complex at Saqqara: (1) pyramid, (2) house of the north, (3) house of the south, (4) mortuary temple, (5) altar (?), (6) western row of chapels, (7) courtyard with two sets of hoof-shaped markers, (8) south tomb with adjacent chapel, (9) enclosure wall, and (10) entrance portal and passage. The various structures surrounding the Step Pyramid were connected with ceremonies designed to glorify Djoser in the afterlife, including the *sed* festival, a jubilee celebrated by the king in both life and death. His spirit was thought to run a ritual race in the central courtyard during this celebration of royal authority, the two prominent stones marking the course.

a height of more than two hundred feet, the pyramid resembles a ziggurat without a temple at the summit. The stupendous size of the Step Pyramid proclaimed the celestial godhead of the king, while its external structure provided a monumental staircase upon which he ascended into heaven to join the other gods.

The massive enclosure wall of the pyramid complex was more than a mile in length, another indication of King Djoser's transcendent authority. Unlike the later pyramids, the Step Pyramid was surrounded by various courtyards and dummy buildings—they are completely solid with immovable doors—constructed so the deceased king might continue his ritual activities in the afterlife. These erections seem to be stone imitations of his sun-dried brick palace and temples in Memphis. The entrance passage of the complex was decorated with the earliest known columns, which are not freestanding but engaged into projecting walls that bear most of the great weight of the stone ceiling. The columns were carefully sculptured in the form of a bundle of reeds, probably inspired by the tied bundles of papyrus stalks employed to support the roofs of sun-dried brick buildings at the time.

A mortuary temple used for the cult of the deceased king was constructed on the north side of the pyramid. Priests brought food offerings to the mortuary temple, where eye holes in one wall permitted a statue of Djoser that was sealed in a small adjoining chamber to look at the food, consuming its essence through the medium of his statue. The original statue is now in the Egyptian Museum in Cairo. The pyramid complex also included various underground burial chambers. Some of the solid stone walls of these rooms were decorated with fine low reliefs of King Djoser engaged in certain religious ceremonies as well as ornamental panels made of exquisite blue-green glazed tiles and forming false doors in imitation of the reed matting rolls suspended over the doorways of palaces and houses. The false doors, impenetrable by mortals, permitted the king's spirit to enter and leave at will.

THE AFTERLIFE

The Step Pyramid and the later pyramids can be understood only in the context of the religious background of the Old Kingdom. We saw that from early times the Egyptians believed their ruler and royalty enjoyed eternal life, and the concept was later extended to include the nobles and privileged classes. By the New Kingdom such access was thought to be available to the ordinary dead who had lived an exemplary life on earth. Only the king was a god in death, of course, but others did retain their human personalities. The hereafter was regarded as similar to life on earth, though far more elaborate and comfortable, an altogether delightful abode. Thus the utmost effort was made to preserve the bodies of the dead, conceived as virtual living corpses.

The Ka.   The Egyptians believed that safeguarding the bodies of the dead was essential to provide for the well-being of the *ka*, an otherworldly form of human existence. The ancient Egyptian word *ka*, though an extremely elusive concept, suggests a combination of the intellectual and spiritual properties of life, a sort of personality double giving the deceased the individuality enjoyed in life. Yet the *ka* was far more than this, for the entity required offerings of both food and drink in the tomb for survival. The tomb itself was known as the house of the *ka*. Symbolized by a pair of raised arms, the *ka* was born with a person as an integral but distinct aspect of being and was united with the individual's body at the moment of death.

Mummification.   Believing the *ka* might die if the body deteriorated, those Egyptians who could afford the expense employed undertakers to provide for their mummification. At first only the king and the other members of the royal family were embalmed, but the practice was gradually extended to the nobles and later to others. The process took about seventy days. The initial steps involved removing the liver, lungs, stomach, and intestines from the body through an incision in the side of the abdomen and, during one period, placing these entrails in four vessels called Canopic jars. Next the brain was softened with chemicals and carefully extracted through the nostrils with a metal hook and discarded, but the heart was regularly left in the body because this organ was considered the seat of the intellect and emotions. The corpse was packed with various materials to retain its shape and then rapidly dehydrated in a naturally occurring dry salt compound known as natron. The next step involved wrapping the body tightly in strips of fine linen, upon which artists painted the features of the deceased to ensure that the *ka* would recognize the individual. Amulets were placed between the strips to protect the body. The climax of the process was a magic ceremony known as the Opening of the Mouth—designed to restore consciousness and the use of limbs to the dead person—which included censing the mummy, baptizing it with Nile water, and touching its lips with a ceremonial metal instrument. The process of mummification became more elaborate over the centuries, with more attention paid to sarcophagi and coffins than body preservation. After the Old Kingdom the head was frequently covered with a painted mask representing the deceased. In the meantime anthropoid coffins were introduced, their appearance imitating a mummy wearing a mask, another provision to help the *ka* identify the body.

Ka *Statues.*   Even if the mummy deteriorated or fell victim to mutilation, the *ka* could still live through the *ka* statues, sculptured likenesses of the deceased that were housed in the tomb. To make certain that the *ka* recognized the *ka* statues, each was made to resemble the dead individual as closely as possible. By the beginning of the Fourth Dynasty sculptors were fashioning such portrait statues with an unprecedented naturalism. Other measures required to keep the *ka* alive included rendering prayers on its behalf. We saw that the *ka* needed sustenance above all to enjoy continued existence, and food offerings were left at the time of burial and thereafter. Skilled artisans painted or carved representations of food on the tomb walls to serve as magic substitutes if the real food ran short or spoiled. To give joy to the *ka*, artists covered the walls with scenes of ordinary life such as banquets, religious festivals, hunting parties, and lush gardens. An ample supply of furniture—sometimes covered with sheet gold or inlaid with gold and ebony—was placed in

A magnificent pair of painted limestone tomb statues of Prince Rahotep and his wife Princess Nofret (Fourth Dynasty), found in a mastaba at Meidum. In Egyptian art women were depicted with lighter complexions than men. c. 2560 BCE. Egyptian Museum, Cairo.

the tomb to make the *ka* comfortable. The surviving pieces of furniture are remarkable for their precise elegance and the simple refinement of their lines. Many other treasures were left in the tombs for the *ka*, such as translucent stone vases and exquisite jewelry consisting of turquoise, carnelian, and lapis lazuli set in gold and silver.

The Ba and the Akh.   The *ba*—sometimes loosely referred to as a sort of external soul—was another manifestation of the person surviving into the afterlife. In the Old Kingdom only the kings possessed a *ba,* but eventually the concept was extended to all. Represented as a bird or as a human-headed bird, the *ba* was thought to embody vital powers giving the deceased mobility. The *ba* could transform itself into any form and, as such, was able to revisit haunts of the dead person in the mortal world. These roamings began at sunrise, but the *ba* needed to return to the tomb at dusk for water and rest. On occasion the *ba* journeyed to the realm of the gods to maintain association with the third personal entity in the afterlife, the *akh.* Entirely remote from this world, the *akh*—usually represented as a bird—allowed the presence of the deceased to exist in the celestial or heavenly abode.

The Pyramids at Giza (c. 2549–2460 bce)

The most imposing monuments of the Old Kingdom and the universal wonder of humankind to this day are the three great pyramids erected a few miles north of Saqqara at Giza on the west bank of the Nile during the Fourth Dynasty. Tombs were always built on the west bank toward the setting sun, while temples were constructed on the east bank. Countless travelers to Giza have been astonished by these mammoth pyramids built by three Fourth-Dynasty kings: Khufu (or Cheops, as the Greeks called him), Khafre (Chephren), and Menkaure (Mycerinus). Reminding the viewer of huge royal reliquaries, the pyramids at Giza seem to have served not merely as tombs but also as temples associated with the solar cult.

The Shape of the Pyramids Probably Influenced by the Benben *of Heliopolis.*   Apparently the change from a step pyramid to a true pyramid was partly related to the increasing influence of the solar cult at Heliopolis. When worshipers entered an open court of the principal temple here, they came into the presence of a sacred stone known as the *benben,* itself regarded as an avenue by which the divine sun manifested itself. A primeval form of the obelisk, the *benben* was topped with a pyramidal and probably gilded tip that was emblematic of the slanting rays of the sun pouring down upon the earth. The Egyptians thought the tip of the *benben,* which caught the first solar rays in the morning and the last at night, was endowed with magical potency. Apparently their belief that a model of an object could enjoy the same properties as the original inspired them to fashion the true pyramids as representations of the pyramidal tip of the *benben.* The king used the rays of the sun as a ramp in his ascent to the gods, according to the so-called *Pyramid Texts,* the magico-religious spells and prayers that were inscribed on the internal chambers of the royal tombs of the Fifth and Sixth Dynasties to ensure a safe transition to the next life. In short, the true pyramid seems to have been conceived as a colossal *benben* aiding the king in his ascension to the heavens.

THE GREAT PYRAMID (C. 2530 BCE)

Nothing better illustrates the extent of royal power in the Old Kingdom than the three unforgettable pyramids at Giza. The statistics are staggering. The Great Pyramid, erected by Khufu (or Cheops, c. 2549–2526 BCE), was originally 481 feet high—more than twice the height of the Step Pyramid—and 756 feet long on each side. Built of approximately 2.3 million blocks of limestone, some weighing more than fifteen tons, the Great Pyramid is the largest in Egypt and one of the most immense buildings ever erected. This apogee of pyramid construction covers more than thirteen acres, encloses a volume of eighty-five million cubic feet, and is completely solid except for corridors, passageways, air shafts, and two relatively small burial chambers. If masons cut all its stone into blocks one foot square and then laid them end to end at the equator, the resulting low wall would extend approximately two-thirds of the way around the earth.

The Workers.   The notable Greek historian Herodotus, who visited Egypt around 450 BCE and wrote the earliest surviving full account of the country, tells us 100,000 men spent twenty years building the Great Pyramid. This number, clearly a gross exaggeration, must represent misinformation supplied to Herodotus by the guides of his day, for the ancient Egyptian authorities could not have effectively organized more than a few thousand people at one time. Regardless of the size of the workforce, an average of 315 heavy stones were quarried, dressed, and put in place each day, assuming the project was completed in the reported twenty years. We can hardly grasp the enormousness of such a task. The feat was carried out within King Khufu's twenty-three-year reign by workers employing the simplest tools and lacking the wheel. The lurid accounts by Greek and Roman writers of the Egyptian use of forced labor to construct the pyramids are now regarded as fanciful. Most of the workforce was made up of peasants—they were paid with food and clothing and provided with shelter—laboring during the months of inundation, a period when agricultural activities could not be undertaken on the land. Apparently each village sent its quota of workers to the quarries and the construction site. The builders must have willingly participated in erecting the pyramids, regarding the king as a living god who sustained their lives, safety, and prosperity.

The Quarrying and Moving of the Limestone Blocks.   Many questions remain concerning construction, though we can safely ignore a number of ludicrous theories. Workers quarried the core blocks of limestone on the spot. They cut the casings of unblemished limestone at a quarry on the east bank of the Nile, ferrying the stone by raft or barge to the construction site via the river and then perhaps over land flooded by the annual inundation. The majority of scholars dismiss Herodotus' statement that the Egyptians raised the stones with wooden levers. According to the most widely accepted theory, gangs of laborers used wooden sledges to drag the blocks up a temporary, carefully lubricated ramp system made of clay and stone debris. While a number of Egyptologists suggest a single straight ramp, others propose a system arranged in spiraling tiers around the four sides of the pyramid, and some theorize a combination of the two. The workers would have extended the ramp system in length as the structure rose course by course.

The Casing and Capstone.   Finally, the entire pyramid, including the sealed entrance, was faced with a casing of gleaming white limestone cut with such unerring precision the eye could scarcely detect the joinings. Unfortunately, this finely dressed limestone was stripped off for building projects in medieval Cairo, about eight miles away. The capstones of the pyramids were sometimes gilded. Those at Giza were probably sheathed in gold or a natural alloy of gold and silver called electrum. Towering above the ground, the capstones caught the first rays of sun at daybreak and the last at nightfall. Thus, while all the land was darkened below, the gilded capstones shone with the sun's holy light.

The Interior Chambers and Passageways.   For its colossal size alone, the ancient Greeks included the Great Pyramid among the Seven Wonders of the World. Soaring above the desert plain and visible for miles in any direction, the structure was a constant reminder of the might and glory of the god-king. Yet the interior spaces, withstanding the immense weight of the stone above, must also be regarded as an architectural marvel. A passageway was cut through the lower masonry of the pyramid and the solid bedrock below, descending at an angle and terminating in a subterranean burial chamber nearly a hundred feet under ground level, though this crypt was abandoned before completion. Then a second main chamber—erroneously called the Queen's Chamber—was constructed high in the superstructure of the monument, perhaps originally intended as the place of burial for the king, but this room also was abandoned before completion. Another room, the celebrated King's Chamber, was prepared at a higher level and approached at an angle through the magnificent Grand Gallery, itself graced with polished limestone walls. The King's Chamber was constructed of rose granite and provided with air shafts passing through the great mass of the pyramid to the outside. The chamber was roofed with great beams of granite weighing fifty to sixty tons each. Its ceiling was relieved of the tremendous weight pressing down by the incorporation of five compartments located immediately above, the topmost provided with a pitched roof redirecting the force of the crushing load to the walls. The King's Chamber is entirely empty today except for a granite sarcophagus, which originally must have contained a wooden coffin holding the body of Khufu.

Funerary Barks.   We frequently encounter long royal ships, or barks, buried in sealed pits near the entombed kings of the Old Kingdom. Two dismantled barks were found in pits alongside the Great Pyramid. Elegant, slender, and beautiful, these cedar-timbered vessels seem to have been intended for the king's celestial journeys in the next world.

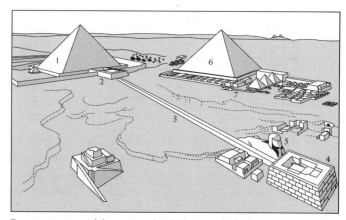

Reconstruction of the pyramids of Khufu and Khafre at Giza: (1) pyramid of Khafre, (2) mortuary temple, (3) covered causeway, (4) valley temple, (5) Great Sphinx, (6) pyramid of Khufu, (7) pyramids of the royal family and mastabas of nobles.

THE PYRAMID COMPLEX

A high boundary wall enclosed each pyramid complex, restricting entry to anyone but priests and ranking officials. Every pyramid was the center of an intricate network of subsidiary tombs, temples, and other elements thought to provide the god-king with all he required for continued existence in the afterlife. The pyramids of the three kings at Giza, for example, are surrounded by smaller pyramids for the queens and members of the royal family as well as neat rows of mastabas for the notables of the court, who would serve the ruler in the next world.

The Valley Temple and the Mortuary Temple.   One of the important buildings of a pyramid complex was the valley temple. After the death of a king, a funerary ship transported his body up the Nile and, upon reaching the site of the complex, entered an artificial canal leading to the valley temple. Apparently the king's body was embalmed in this building. Then the coffined royal mummy was taken along a long covered causeway, or ceremonial way, to a mortuary temple flanking the king's pyramid. The mortuary temple was the scene of important preburial ceremonies such as the Opening of the Mouth. Following the entombment of the mummy, priests at the mortuary temple practiced the funerary cult of the deceased king with daily prayers and offerings to ensure his eternal afterlife.

THE GREAT SPHINX OF GIZA (c. 2500 BCE)

Alongside the valley temple of Khafre rises the Great Sphinx, the earliest surviving statue of colossal size and the first known version of this form of mythical creature. Fashioned from a huge natural outcrop of limestone remaining in a local quarry, the Great Sphinx has the body of a recumbent lion and the head of a king wearing a

Reconstruction of the Great Sphinx at Giza (as restored in the fifteenth century BCE), based on surviving fragments in the British Museum and on other sphinxes and royal statues. The Great Sphinx, dating c. 2500 BCE, was carved from limestone bedrock as a guardian figure with the body of a recumbent lion and the head of a ruling king, identified in the New Kingdom as Khafre. The figure was brightly painted and a royal statue may have stood against the chest.

royal headdress, probably intended as a portrait of Khafre (c. 2518–2493 BCE), who built the second pyramid at Giza. The Egyptians believed their kings adopted this guise to protect sacred precincts from intruders. Thus the Great Sphinx was acting as a powerful sentinel of his pyramid. Perhaps the colossus was also intended to represent the king as a manifestation of the divine sun. Even though badly damaged, its inscrutable face remains an almost terrifying mask of regal power. The Greeks, who were awed by visits to the Sphinx, regarded the immense head as a smoldering symbol of Egyptian enigma.

TECHNOLOGICAL, EDUCATIONAL, AND LITERARY ACCOMPLISHMENT

Irrigation.   Although the Egyptians strongly influenced the entire ancient world through the excellence of their visual arts, the Mesopotamians were generally more advanced not only in literary achievement but also technology and mathematics. Partly because the Nile provided an admirable highway, the Egyptians did not adopt the wheel until the close of the Second Intermediate period. Yet we should not overlook their many skills and accomplishments. As a matter of survival, they succeeded in controlling the waters of the Nile by employing a complex system of ditches, canals, embankments, and catch basins, all of which had to be kept in perfect repair for taming the river and storing some of its water for use in the dry season.

Calendars and Devices for Measuring Hours.   Unlike most people in antiquity, the Egyptians devised a form of solar calendar (theirs was pegged to a heliacal observation), which modern scholars call the civil calendar. This Egyptian system of time reckoning was more accurate than the Sumerian calendar based on those beguiling but inaccurate lunar cycles. The civil calendar had twelve months of thirty days each, to which was added five festival days at the end of the year, giving a total of 365 days. Although this calendar made no allowance for leap years and thus lost one whole day every four years, the discrepancy was too gradual to affect life adversely, and every 1460 years the cycle was completed. The civil calendar of the Egyptians—the direct ancestor of our own—was far superior to any other of the period, and thousands of years later Julius Caesar used their system of time reckoning as the model for his famous Julian Calendar.

   The Egyptians employed other calendars for determining the dates of the great religious festivals of the kingdom. Popular belief attached magical and religious significance to the days of the year, and such calendars indicate lucky and unlucky days. Magico-religious concerns, as well as the need for a reliable calendar, encouraged the Egyptians to study astronomy. Through their astronomical observations, they devised star charts for telling the time of night, first attested on coffin lids of the First Intermediate period for the use of the deceased. In the meantime they measured hours by fashioning both water clocks—devices providing time by the flow of water—and sundials.

Education.   Children remained under their mother's care until they were around four years of age, learning basic rules of behavior and good manners. Thereafter the various social classes were educated differently. The royal princes and the sons of great noble families—the latter being groomed for top administrative posts—were tutored privately in an elite palace school. Perhaps the princesses and a number of the daughters of the nobles joined them, or were at least taught the rudiments of reading and writing. Some upper-class boys, occasionally girls as well, attended specialized schools to acquire proficiency in the art of writing, a prelude to becoming a scribe. An individual with scribal training was much in demand for prestigious posts in the highly centralized bureaucracy. Other boys were educated to become architects, engineers, or priests. Because the Egyptians believed the gods were responsible for many cases of illness, the medical profession was closely tied to the priesthood. The most important subjects in schools were reading and writing, though other fields were not neglected. Lower-class children were generally trained by their mothers and fathers. A boy of humble origins usually followed the trade of the father—perhaps a small-scale farmer, baker, or artisan—though a truly gifted individual might rise to a position of great authority.

Literature.   Few works of Egyptian literature have come down to us from the Old Kingdom. Some official documents and the like survive on papyrus, but inscriptions on the walls of tombs supply the greater part of the material, exemplified by boastful accounts highlighting the virtues and career of the deceased. Near the end of the Old Kingdom we find magic spells to ensure a safe passage of the king to the afterlife inscribed on the chamber walls within royal pyramids. Egyptologists call this famous corpus the *Pyramid Texts*.

Social Classes and Daily Life

The King and Royal Family.   The long stability of ancient Egyptian society seems to have been due, in substantial part, to the strong belief in the benevolence of the divine ruler. Because each king wanted to keep his sacred line as pure as possible, brother-sister marriages were common in the royal family. The queens and princesses of Egypt—sharing in the king's divine blood—played a far more prominent role in the affairs of state than the obscure royal females of Mesopotamia.

The Nobles. The next lower rung in the social structure was occupied by the great noble families. Their substantial estates included relatively spacious villas built of sun-dried bricks and provided with beds, tables, chairs, stools, cushioned long seats, and other furniture. Set amidst lush gardens with lily ponds, these rich dwellings were pleasant settings for entertainment provided by musicians playing harps, lutes, oboes, and pairs of clappers, accompanying twisting young female dancers, naked except for short skirts and bejeweled collars. The nobles kept dogs and monkeys for pets, and they enjoyed various activities involving boating, fishing, and hunting. They brought birds down with throwing sticks—a weapon in the form of a curved stick thrown by hand—and hunted lions and other large game animals with spears. We saw that the nobles held the great posts of authority under the king, including the senior priestly offices, and they served as governors of the nomes.

Artisans, Peasants, and Slaves.   Most people were poor, living in sun-dried brick huts crowded together along crooked, narrow lanes, though we saw that an occasional ambitious and talented male from this background rose in rank to hold a position of influence and power. The vast majority of men served in the labor force as artisans, unskilled laborers, peasants, or slaves. The top social rung of this population was occupied by artisans and other skilled workers. The court and the nobility had need of specialists such as cabinetmakers, goldsmiths, and jewelers. Some skilled workers—exemplified by quarriers, masons, carpenters, bricklayers, sculptors, and painters—spent their workdays erecting and decorating palaces, temples, and tombs. In the meantime other men pursued occupations such as millers, bakers, potters, weavers, dyers, fullers, merchants, traders, and school teachers. These specialists enjoyed a higher standard of living than either the peasants toiling in the fields or the huge gangs of unskilled laborers (generally conscripted peasants) building pyramids and other structures during the annual inundation. The lowest rung on the social ladder was occupied by slaves. Apparently slavery was rare in all periods and generally restricted to foreign war captives, who worked in temples and on the great estates. Slaves were not without rights and could own and bequeath property.

Diet.   In terms of the lower classes, the favorite drink was beer, made by fermenting barley bread. Simple food sufficed, usually nothing more than a few loaves of bread and perhaps some vegetables or an occasional serving of fish, eggs, or meat. The nobles enjoyed a bountiful diet. Beer and wine were popular beverages, and the daily fare included bread made of emmer wheat or barley and spread with honey, supplemented by vegetables such as lettuce, onions, beans, leeks, chickpeas, lentils, carrots, turnips, radishes, cucumbers, and spinach. The nobles consumed great piles of dates, melons, figs, grapes, and other fruits. Flocks of geese and ducks were plentiful on farms and important in their diet. Sheep, goats, and cattle were fattened both for temple sacrifice and dining. The nobles gained additional sources of protein from hunted game such as gazelle and ibex and from milk, cheese, and butter. The devout among them avoided pork, regarded as an abomination because pigs were identified with Horus' detested enemy Seth. Although the Nile abounded with fish, one of them was said to have eaten the penis of Osiris after his body was cut into pieces and scattered by Seth. Accordingly, those who were faithful in observing ritual prohibitions eschewed fish as well as pork.

Dress.   Egyptian children of all classes and both sexes ran about naked into adolescence, and they are depicted in art with their heads shaven, except for a long lock left on one side. Men normally kept their heads shaven, while women usually had short hair. Although prehistoric Egyptian men frequently wore only a penis sheath, which survived into the historic period, by the Old Kingdom men usually dressed in white linen loincloths resembling short kilts. Women wore formfitting dresses held up by straps over the shoulders and reaching to the ankles. Both men and women of the upper classes adorned themselves with jewelry and wigs, used scented unguents, and applied black and green eye paint. Elite women also employed red lip paint and rouge.

Marriage, the Harem, and the Role of Women.   Marriage usually took place just after puberty, youths being enjoined to move out of the parental home in order to found a separate household. Egyptians seem to have preferred monogamy, but some wealthy houses included a harem, that is, quarters reserved for lesser wives, concubines, and female slaves. Although women enjoyed many rights in Egypt, the country remained a patriarchal society, for a husband was free not only to keep concubines, with whom he maintained a continuing sexual relationship, but also to engage in sexual liaisons outside the household without fear of penalty, whereas a wife involved in an extramarital affair was subject to punishment, as in Mesopotamia. Yet even when the household included concubines, the chief wife generally acted as the husband's companion and confidant. A wife was especially esteemed in her role as mother. Because only a minority of offspring survived to adulthood, wives attempted to increase their childbearing ability by using fertility charms in the form of naked women, often portrayed with unusually large genitalia. The mother nursed her children for three years and provided them with their initial training. Each day the upper-class mother brought her older male children beer and bread in school.

The legal and economic position of Egyptian women approached that of men, though they were excluded from holding state office and were barred from activities involving the wielding of blades, such as reaping. Women had the right to own property, bring lawsuits, and divorce their husbands. Although few upper-class girls were formally educated and most became wives and mothers, some were prepared for the influential scribal profession. A number of other elite women—even daughters of the royal family—were trained to become priestesses in the temples, where they danced, sang, and played musical instruments to accompany religious ceremonies. Women from a somewhat lower social register might become temple prostitutes, midwives, or professional mourners. The duties of the professional mourners included beating their brows and wailing to heaven during funerals.

Turning to the lower social rung, peasant woman worked in the fields during harvests. She and other nonelite wives carried out seemingly endless tasks in managing the household, spending much of the day nurturing the younger children and baking bread in hot ashes, first grinding the necessary meal between stones. Another of their obligations was doing laundry by pounding clothes on stones in a nearby canal or in the Nile. They also faced a constant round of spinning, sewing, and weaving. Female workers predominated in the Egyptian textile industry, known for its fine linen, though a male-operated loom was introduced after the mid-second millennium BCE, and men largely took over the task of weaving.

EROSION OF ROYAL POWER DURING THE FIFTH AND SIXTH DYNASTIES (C. 2454–2140 BCE)

Advancement of the Nobility and the Cult of Re. The Egyptian king lost a measure of his overwhelming power during the Fifth and Sixth Dynasties. This development stemmed not only from the growing independence of the nobility—they no longer regarded the kings as absolute divinities—but also from the ascendancy of the priesthood of the powerful solar cult of Re at Heliopolis. Although each monarch remained officially the incarnation of Horus, the early stress on the god was now replaced by an emphasis on the sun. With this unfolding, the kings become subordinate to Re, taking the additional title Son of Re. When they visited temples, the kings still treated all deities—except Re—as their equals, but signs abounded of the royal eclipse. New royal pyramids were built on a much smaller scale than those at Giza, and the edifices also betrayed rather shoddy construction techniques. Moreover, the distance between the monarch and the nobles began to lessen as the governors of the nomes and other provincial nobles aspired to an afterlife apart from service to the king, another development undermining royal prestige and authority. The power and wealth of the nobles was clearly demonstrated by the rich tombs they constructed in the nomes during the late Fifth Dynasty. Egypt experienced a period of gradual decline under a series of shadowy kings in the Sixth Dynasty, when resources were siphoned off into a costly funerary culture, with far greater sums expended on the royal and noble dead than the living. Apparently Manetho's Seventh and Eighth Dynasties (c. 2140–2124 BCE) were marked by confusion and weakness.

FIRST INTERMEDIATE PERIOD (NINTH THROUGH MID-ELEVENTH DYNASTIES, c. 2124–2040 BCE)

For circumstances that remain poorly understood, perhaps compounded by unfavorable climatic changes in Africa and the Near East, the Old Kingdom suddenly collapsed about 2124 BCE and was succeeded by the First Intermediate period, a chaotic era lasting almost a century and marked by famine and widespread disorder. The eclipse of a strong centralized government was reflected in a return to the state Egypt had known before unification, with nobles ruling nomes functioning virtually as independent principalities. Although some local rulers claimed the titles and prerogatives of the kings of a unified Egypt, they were merely transitory figures with only local recognition. In the absence of effective central authority, foreign trade declined sharply, while temples were damaged and royal tombs looted. Tribes infiltrated the country from Nubia to the south and from Palestine and Syria to the east. Surviving texts tell of marauding thieves and overwhelming discontent. Under the force of such calamities, the old Egyptian optimism and confidence vanished.

CHAPTER VII

EGYPT IN THE MIDDLE
AND NEW KINGDOMS

Several rival families contended for supremacy at the close of the First Intermediate period, especially those of Herakleopolis and Thebes, and the governors of both cities took the title of king. Finally the rulers of Thebes, formerly a relatively insignificant provincial town in Upper Egypt nearly 450 miles south of Memphis, managed to extend their authority over several neighboring nomes. One of the vigorous Theban rulers, Mentuhotep II of the Eleventh Dynasty, asserted his rule over the whole of Egypt around 2040 BCE, and the period that followed is now known as the Middle Kingdom. This chapter traces the millennium of Egyptian history from the opening of the Middle Kingdom through the New Kingdom, briefly concluding with the Late period, the conquest of Alexander the Great, and the subsequent Greco-Roman period. The Middle Kingdom was characterized by its effective royal government, aggressive policies abroad, and artistic achievement. Following the Second Intermediate period, a time of domination by outsiders, Egypt embarked upon the brilliant New Kingdom, creating a great Asian empire and enjoying prosperity and extensive building projects at home.

THE MIDDLE KINGDOM (MID-ELEVENTH THROUGH THIRTEENTH DYNASTIES, c. 2040–1648 BCE)

MENTUHOTEP II (C. 2040–1999 BCE)

During his long reign after reunification, Mentuhotep II directed Egyptian affairs from the royal capital at Thebes. His great military campaigns—intended to secure his borders and to reestablish safe trade routes—penetrated Sinai to the northeast, Libya to the west, and Nubia to the south. In the beautiful bay of towering cliffs at Deir el-Bahri, located on the west bank of the Nile opposite Thebes, Mentuhotep erected for himself a unique mortuary temple designed as a stepped mastaba rising in three stages, the lower two adorned with graceful colonnades. The burial chamber—hewn into the rock beneath the cliffs—was provided with a seated sandstone statue of Mentuhotep, its flesh painted black, its expression seemingly to reflect brutal power.

Amenemhet I (c. 1980–1951 bce)

Mentuhotep II's second successor was deposed about 1980 bce in a palace revolution led by a certain Amenemhet (Ammenemes in Greek), who may have been the vizier. Amenemhet I was the first king of the powerful Twelfth Dynasty, whose brilliant and determined rulers promoted a reinvigorated Egypt. Amenemhet built fortresses near the Second Cataract in Nubia to protect trade routes, and he constructed a line of strongholds known as the Walls of the Ruler on the eastern edge of the Delta to curtail infiltrations from Asia. Despite his many accomplishments, Amenemhet lacked royal blood and wore an uneasy crown in the face of jealous nobles. He needed to safeguard his reign and the future of his dynasty. To govern all of his kingdom more effectively and securely, Amenemhet moved his residence to a yet undiscovered fortified site to the north—Itj-tawy (meaning Seizing the Two Lands)—located some thirty miles south of Memphis, though the old capital of Thebes remained a great religious center. He spearheaded a revival of pyramid building for royal burials. To ensure the continuity of his dynasty, Amenemhet made his son Senusret (Sesostris) I coruler with him about 1971 bce. The practice of co-regency contributed to the stability of Egypt throughout the Twelfth Dynasty and would be resumed in the New Kingdom.

Religion in the Middle Kingdom

Amon-Re.   Amenemhet I took his name after Amon, a prominent local god of Thebes having sovereignty over air and light. Amon's name means the Unseen One, and his image was painted blue to denote invisibility. An omnipresent force, Amon became identified with the sun-god Re of Heliopolis. The Twelfth Dynasty kings promoted Amon, and the priests obliged by grafting the deity onto Re as Amon-Re. In the meantime the kings took the title Son of Amon-Re in lieu of the old designation Son of Re. Under the name Amon-Re, Amon became the supreme national god of Egypt, ultimately becoming a great imperial deity with a universal nature whose powerful rays were said to reach to the ends of the earth. He bore the proud title King of the Gods and was worshiped in numerous temples. Amon-Re offered divine inspiration to his devotees at the site of the modern village of Karnak, which has given its name to the northern half of the ruins of ancient Thebes on the east bank of the Nile. Karnak was the location of Amon-Re's state temple, the largest ever built on Egyptian soil, its vast array of structures dating from the Middle Kingdom down to Roman times.

Funerary Texts.   Although the concept of the afterlife was originally restricted to royalty, we noted that the nobles gradually began to aspire after eternal existence. By the end of the Old Kingdom high local officials were being buried in their own districts rather than in the vicinity of the royal pyramid, their lavishly furnished tombs and exalted funerary customs rivaling privileges of the king himself. The nobles believed they could conquer death by fervently and sincerely worshiping the god Osiris and by leading virtuous lives. We saw that the verdict concerning the afterlife was rendered by a divine tribunal weighing the heart of the deceased against the feather of truth representing Ma`at. As a precaution against the frailties of human conduct, however, these privileged Egyptians tried to outflank the judgment of the dead by preserving the body of the deceased and resorting to magic. Thus the funerary usurpations of the nobles extended to a set of ancient ritual spells originally designed to ensure the king a safe passage to the afterlife. Because these magic formulas were inscribed on the chamber walls of certain royal pyramids of the Fifth and Sixth Dynasties, Egyptologists call them *Pyramid Texts*. As early as the Old Kingdom, some of the funerary spells were revised to secure a pleasant afterlife for the upper classes and were painted on the inside of their wooden coffins. These revised spells, most of which survive from Middle Kingdom burials, are published under the title *Coffin Texts*. An even larger part of the population began to aspire for eternal bliss around the beginning of the New Kingdom, and the funerary spells were again revised. These later texts—known today as the *Book of the Dead*—were recorded mainly on papyrus scrolls and deposited in the tombs of the deceased.

MIDDLE KINGDOM PROSPERITY AND TRADE

The coregency of Amenemhet I and his son Senusret I lasted for around ten years. Amenemhet died suddenly about 1962 BCE—Manetho reports he was murdered by one of his own subordinates—and Senusret I became the sole king. Middle Kingdom Egypt rose to a peak of prosperity and power under Senusret I (c. 1960–1916 BCE), Senusret III (c. 1878–1859 BCE), and Amenemhet III (c. 1859–1814 BCE), forceful kings in the tradition of Amenemhet I. Senusret III, for example, a contemporary of Hammurabi, was a tough military leader who led his army into Palestine, but his most vigorous thrusts were reserved for Nubia to the south. The wealth of Nubia was essential to the Egyptian civilization, and eventually the Nubians were reduced to submission.

Senusret III and the other Twelfth Dynasty kings took various steps to curb the independence of great nobles in the nomes. This was no mean task because some of the provincial nobles maintained their own armed forces and fleets of ships. To counter the power of the nobility, the kings aided merchants, traders, and artisans. They also promoted the welfare of the entire population by improving the irrigation system and ordering land reclamation. Although the great oasis now known as the Fayum was fed by the Nile during the annual flood via a natural channel in the desert hills, much of the water drained away. The kings built dams and canals at the Fayum, thereby creating a huge catch basin that retained the overflow and provided for irrigation throughout the year, even during the driest months. The Fayum with its new permanent body of water—called Lake Moeris in late antiquity—and its vast tracts of reclaimed land became one of the most agriculturally productive regions of Egypt. The Middle Kingdom kings completed many additional public works, exemplified by a channel cut through the granite of the First Cataract to facilitate access via the Nile to mineral-rich Nubia and regions farther south. They obtained copper ores and turquoise through trade with Sinai and also sent trading expeditions to Palestine, Syria, Phoenicia, Cyprus, Crete, and Punt.

ART AND FUNERARY MONUMENTS

Amulets.   The Middle Kingdom witnessed a revival of art. The wealth and cultural restoration of the period were symbolized by the jewelry of the royal court, which was superbly executed and worn not only for adornment but also for religious and magical attributes. The king embellished his crown and other headdresses with an essential symbol of royalty, the uraeus. Regarded as a manifestation of Re, the uraeus took the form of a rearing cobra and was said to spit fire at the king's enemies from its place on the royal forehead. Another amulet thought to provide magical protective force for the bearer was the ankh, a cross with a loop at the top, which was a sacred emblem signifying life. The figure was a recurrent attribute of the gods, who are frequently depicted on temple and tomb walls handing the ankh to a king. Many Egyptians of the Middle Kingdom wore and were buried with ornamental scarabs, powerful tokens denoting the eternal renewal of life. The scarab belongs to a family of beetles. Female scarabs lay their eggs in a ball of dung, which they roll before them on the sand until the young hatch. The Egyptians observed this phenomenon and concluded that sacred dung beetles were spontaneously created from their own substance.

Sculpture and Tombs.   Although statues of Middle Kingdom kings remain colossal and majestically eternal in bearing, sometimes the heads appear lined with a brooding concern or even a hint of frailty, typified by several surviving portraits of Senusret III. These prudent, cautious rulers usually erected modest pyramids for their funerary monuments. In the meantime the provincial nobility were abandoning the traditional mastabas for fine rock-cut tombs. Originating in the Old Kingdom, rock-cut tombs were usually set in steep cliffs at remote sites on the west bank of the Nile. No superstructure was built, for the entire complex was simply hewn from the living rock. Fronted by a shallow columned portico or by a terraced courtyard, each rock-cut tomb also contained a funerary chapel, where offerings were presented for the sustenance of the deceased, as well as the burial chamber itself.

LITERATURE

The Middle Kingdom enjoyed a rich literary tradition, with examples ranging from entertaining tales of travelers to homilies exhorting loyalty to the king. The Egyptians still considered their king divine, though hymns sung in praise of Middle Kingdom rulers mention monarchal responsibility to the people, an unthinkable concept in the Old Kingdom. An immensely popular work of the period was a dazzling fictional tale known as *The Story of Sinuhe*, telling how a political exile achieves fame and wealth in an Asian kingdom but still longs for his homeland and is permitted by a gracious Egyptian king to return to the royal court in his old age. Such remarkable works helped to sustain the prestige of the kings during the Middle Kingdom, the golden age of Egyptian literature.

Other genres include proverbs, mythologies, love poems, advice on etiquette, and medical treatises. Surviving medical texts indicate the Egyptians believed some

Rock-cut tombs at Beni Hasan, dating c. 2030–1850 BCE. Thirty-nine tombs stand side by side on a cliff face on the east bank of the Nile, built for powerful provincial families. A number of the entrances are noted for their fluted columns carved from the face of the rock. Twelve of the tombs contain magnificent mural paintings on plastered surfaces.

ailments stemmed from natural causes, others being the work of demons. Treatment relied on a combination of remedies ranging from exorcisms and spells to the prescription of drugs, some of which were medically efficacious. Apparently the Egyptians inaugurated the surgical procedure of circumcision, cutting away the foreskin sheathing the head of the penis. Egyptian circumcision was performed at the onset of puberty, perhaps at first as a rite of initiation but later for cleanliness and the prevention of disease. Much later, the Greek historian Herodotus expressed strong aesthetic disapproval of the practice, criticizing the Egyptians for "choosing to be clean rather than of seemly appearance." A procedure with a different consequence was commonly performed on pubescent Egyptian females. This was clitoridectomy, or the removal of the clitoris (sometimes other external vaginal tissues were also cut away), an effective means of reducing female sexual pleasure and activity, whereas circumcision has little consequence on male sexual enjoyment.

THE SECOND INTERMEDIATE PERIOD (FOURTEENTH THROUGH SEVENTEENTH DYNASTIES, c. 1648–1540 BCE)

Within a decade of the death of Amenemhet III about 1814 BCE, the great Twelfth Dynasty began to decline. Amenemhet's son seems to have been followed by a daughter, Queen Sobekneferu (c. 1805–1801 BCE), whose short rule brought the dynasty to a close. The next phase of the Middle Kingdom—the Thirteenth Dynasty (c. 1801–1648 BCE)—was characterized by a lessening of prosperity and a growing enfeeblement of central authority. This poorly understood century and a half was followed by the Second Intermediate period—Fourteenth through Seventeenth Dynasties—a time of profound changes in the entire fabric of Egyptian life.

The Hyksos

The weakening grip of the central government during the late Middle Kingdom had permitted an increasing influx of Semitic-speaking immigrants from the Palestinian region into the Delta. They produced a ruling class of tribal chiefs or petty princes traditionally known by the Manethonian term Hyksos (a word probably derived from an Egyptian designation meaning "rulers of foreign countries"), who took advantage of the chaotic conditions to establish a separate kingdom in the Delta by the seventeenth century BCE. The Hyksos slowly expanded their sphere of influence and gained rule over much of Egypt by about the middle of the century. Six powerful Hyksos kings, reigning from around 1648 until 1540 BCE, resided at their northeastern Delta capital of Avaris. They adopted the external trappings of Egyptian kingship and oversaw a lively trade with a number of foreign lands but lost control over Nubia. Apparently part of southern Egypt maintained a degree of uneasy autonomy at this time under the rule of native vassal princes at Thebes, who paid taxes to the Hyksos kings and were united to them through marriage ties.

Later generations of Egyptians vilified the Hyksos as destructive invaders and merciless tyrants, but apparently these foreign kings governed in the manner of native rulers by promoting Egyptian culture, taking Egyptian names, and employing Egyptian officials. One reason for their success in establishing themselves as overlords over much of Egypt was technical innovation, especially in the military field, for they introduced the horse-drawn chariot (and with it the spoked wheel), body armor, a composite bow with metal arrowheads, and bronze tools and weapons. Their bronze implements were far superior to the copper tools and weapons of the Egyptians.

THE NEW KINGDOM (EIGHTEENTH THROUGH TWENTIETH DYNASTIES, c. 1540–1069 BCE)

Ahmose (c. 1540–1525 BCE)

The Expulsion of the Hyksos at the Beginning of the Eighteenth Dynasty. The native princes of Thebes had yielded only a resentful obedience to the overlordship of the Hyksos, whose presence was probably despised by the general population. Adopting Hyksos innovations such as bronze weapons, the horse-drawn war chariot, and the deadly composite bow, the rulers at Thebes began a campaign to expel the foreigners from their land. The struggle reached a turning point around 1550 BCE, when the Theban ruler Kamose succeeded in carrying the campaign for Egyptian independence to the very gates of Avaris, though he failed to take the city. Kamose's younger brother and successor Ahmose (Amosis in Greek) defeated the Hyksos and expelled them from Egypt about 1540 BCE. Although there was no change in family, Ahmose was honored by later generations as the founder of a new dynasty—the Eighteenth—because he reunited all of Egypt under native control. The great Eighteenth Dynasty (c. 1540–1296 BCE), which marked the beginning of the New Kingdom, was a time of military expansion, tightly centralized royal rule, Egyptian nationalism, and artistic renaissance.

Tightly Centralized Rule.   To deter any further influx of Asians into Egypt, Ahmose pursued the Hyksos into southwestern Palestine, finally subduing them after a three-year siege of their stronghold at Sharuhen. After conquering southern Palestine, Ahmose recovered Nubia, vital to Egypt for supplying luxury goods such as gold, ivory, ebony, carnelian, amethyst, and ostrich plumes. Ahmose ensured that Egyptian policy was followed in Nubia and that its tribute was sent to him at the great capital of Thebes by placing the entire region under the strict control of a royal deputy, commonly called the viceroy, a high office surviving throughout the New Kingdom. Because the Hyksos had emasculated the nobility and thus the hereditary governors of the nomes, Ahmose was able to bring these districts under the rigid control of a large and complex royal bureaucracy. The only source of potential opposition to the king lay in the priests, and their cooperation was bought with lavish gifts. Ahmose now functioned as the absolute ruler of a militarized state.

Thutmose I (c. 1504–1492 bce)

Imperialism.   The shock of foreign domination had deeply affronted Egyptian pride, fostering a determination to extend the frontiers of Egypt as far as possible by creating an Asian empire to complement the traditional African dominion to the south. Yet the new attitude was to some extent forced upon the kingdom by the rise of western Asian powers such as the Mitannians, Hittites, and Assyrians, all of whom pursued obtrusive policies in Syria and Palestine.

Ahmose had initiated the process of Egyptian expansion into Asia by attacking southern Palestine. The new imperialistic policy was followed by his immediate successors, particularly Thutmose (Tuthmosis) I, who became king about 1504 bce. Referring to himself as "he who opens the valleys which his forebears did not know," Thutmose mounted great military thrusts at the head of a splendid army equipped with the horse and war chariot. His fighting men consisted of native soldiers and some foreign mercenaries, all led by Egyptian noble officers. Each soldier served when needed for campaigns but lived rent-free the rest of the time on an approximately eight-acre parcel of land provided by the government. Using the swift chariot tactics introduced by the Hyksos, Thutmose pushed the southern boundary well below the Third Cataract in Nubia. He also marched his army northeast to the banks of the Euphrates in Syria and even crossed the great river to raid the kingdom of Mitanni stretching across the northern reaches of Mesopotamia. The king conquered many territories in Syria-Palestine, turning their control over to local princes, who demonstrated their submission by sending tribute. As a result of tribute pouring into the kingdom from many foreign lands, the Egyptian temple establishment became increasingly wealthy.

The Valley of the Kings.   From the reign of Thutmose I until the end of the New Kingdom, Egyptian rulers built rock-cut tombs of subterranean chambers in the necropolis now known as the Valley of the Kings in the barren desert hills on the west bank of the Nile opposite Thebes. The resources that monarchs had formerly employed in erecting pyramid complexes now went into immense mortuary temples. Perhaps because the pyramids of their predecessors had been plundered, the kings separated their actual burial places from their mortuary temples, with the hope that the latter would not betray the location of their richly decorated and arrayed funerary chambers tunneled up to five hundred feet into the cliffside. Almost without exception, these attempts to defeat grave robbers would prove to be unsuccessful.

The Joint Reign of Hatshepsut and Thutmose III (c. 1479–1457 bce)

Thutmose I's successor, Thutmose II, married his half sister Hatshepsut and died at a comparatively young age around 1479 bce. The king left as his legitimate successor his only son, Thutmose III, a boy aged about ten or twelve and born of a minor wife. Because of the youth of the new king, his stepmother Hatshepsut assumed the position of regent. She seems to have discharged her office with appropriate restraint for a brief period, leaving Thutmose theoretically in control of the kingdom, but then Hatshepsut boldly had herself proclaimed *king*—not ruling queen—and acted as the dominant partner in a joint reign lasting roughly twenty years. The era of Hatshepsut shows female succession was possible in Egypt, though the practice was unusual and probably considered a poor substitute for male occupation of the throne. Hatshepsut styled herself king in order to reign with the full authority of a god, and she took all the royal titles except Mighty Bull. Depicted in reliefs and much of her statuary as a male, she was referred to in typical kingly fashion as Son of Amon-Re. Most of her attention was devoted to peaceful enterprises such as building projects and the expansion of trade, but apparently she personally led a military expedition south to Nubia.

Mortuary Temple of Hatshepsut at Deir el-Bahri (c. 1470 bce). Hatshepsut heaped offices and favors upon a powerful and gifted official named Senmut, possibly her lover, who has been credited with the design of her mortuary temple nestled against the splendid semicircular bay of towering cliffs at Deir el-Bahri on the west bank of the Nile opposite the capital at Thebes. Her monument was built beside and inspired by the mortuary temple of Mentuhotep II, built about five and one-half centuries earlier. A three-mile walled avenue extended from the river bank to Hatshepsut's temple in antiquity and was flanked along its entire course by statues of her in the guise of brightly colored sphinxes with false beards. Attempting to justify her usurpation of supreme power, Hatshepsut had the temple walls adorned with painted reliefs immortalizing the story of her purported divine birth as a child of Amon-Re—the result of a depicted union between the god and her mother—and recording her major achievements as a ruler. One extraordinary group of reliefs commemorates a great seaborne trading expedition Hatshepsut dispatched to the distant land of Punt, where the ancient Egyptians obtained processed myrrh, used as incense. We saw that Punt was probably located on the African shores of the southern Red Sea. The artist provides detailed scenes of the inhabitants of Punt and their surroundings on the African coast, the oldest known anthropological study of a foreign culture. The pictorial record includes a representation of the departing Egyptian ships being laden with goods such as gold, baboons, processed myrrh, and myrrh trees.

Mortuary temple of Hatshepsut, Deir el-Bahri. c. 1470 BCE.

Hatshepsut's mortuary temple remains one of the great architectural master-pieces of all times. The white Theban limestone structure rises from the valley floor in three spacious retreating steps, which take the form of magnificent colonnaded terraces connected by central processional ramps. The austere rhythm of the pillars and columns reflects in a striking manner the configuration of the lofty cliffs be-hind, thus uniting architectural and natural forms. Although the terraces appear somewhat stark today, originally they were enhanced by some two hundred painted statues of Hatshepsut, including twenty-eight colossal statues of the "king" in the guise of Osiris standing before the pillars of the uppermost terrace. The terraces were additionally enlivened by bountiful gardens planted with fragrant myrrh trees and rare plants brought back from the trading venture to Punt.

The main sanctuary for the cult of Hatshepsut was cut into the sheer wall of the cliff and approached by a corridor from the uppermost terrace. This terrace was de-signed with subsidiary sanctuaries as well as an altar for the worship of Amon-Re. Hatshepsut's actual burial chamber was tunneled into the cliffside of the nearby Val-ley of the Kings, only to be emptied by grave robbers sometime in the distant past.

THE INDEPENDENT REIGN OF THUTMOSE III (C. 1457–1426 BCE)

The Defacement of Hatshepsut's Monuments.   Although the ultimate fate of Hat-shepsut remains unknown, most scholars assume she died peacefully of natural causes. She had given Thutmose III considerable military authority during her life-time, but he must have chafed to be free of her dominance and continued presence.

Thutmose took vigorous control of the kingdom as sole ruler about 1457 BCE. Apparently his reorganized government was not at first openly antagonistic to the memory and achievements of Hatshepsut. Yet about midway in Thutmose's independent reign, his agents hacked her name from monuments, deliberately damaged or erased her reliefs, and mutilated her statues, as though she had never reigned. The reason for these defacements remains unclear.

Brilliant Military Campaigns.   Thutmose built up a devastating military machine, a marked change in Egyptian policy from the relatively pacific regime of Hatshepsut. The disappearance of Hatshepsut from the records coincides with a dangerous revolt of the subject princes ruling Palestinian and Syrian towns. Thutmose III acted swiftly to meet this threat and crushed the resistance of the rebels about 1456 BCE at Megiddo. Now an archaeological site in Israel, Megiddo was then a strategic fortress town commanding the coastal trade route from Egypt to Syria. The engagement at Megiddo was the first in a series of seventeen brilliantly executed campaigns Thutmose fought in western Asia over a period of some twenty years, pushing Egyptian rule to the east beyond the Euphrates and to the north as far as the borders of the empire of the Hittites, who had expanded from Anatolia southward along the Mediterranean coast. Thutmose's thrusts brought him into conflict with the kingdom of Mitanni, which had extended its domination from the middle Euphrates in Mesopotamia westward into north Syria. Inflicting devastating defeats on the Mitannian forces in north Syria, Thutmose III pushed the Egyptian empire in western Asia to its maximum extent. His second successor, Thutmose IV (c. 1401–1391 BCE), adopted the strategy of establishing a coalition of the two powers against a common enemy, the Hittites of Anatolia. After an alliance was concluded, a Mitannian princess entered the Egyptian royal harem as a diplomatic seal to the bargain.

Egyptian control in Syria-Palestine, which was based on garrisons located at strategic points, gave the region a period of relative peace and stability. The government of each subject territory was in the hands of a local prince, who was expected to send tribute to Egypt and to promote Egyptian interests. Thutmose III removed the male children of the local princes to Egypt as hostages for their fathers' good behavior. He gave them an Egyptian education at the royal court and managed to instill a remarkable loyalty in the young men that proved quite useful when they returned home to succeed their fathers as rulers. These activities in Asia led to a spectacular increase in Egyptian trade and prosperity, fostering an epoch of new richness in artistic expression.

AMENHOTEP III (c. 1391–1353 BCE)

The immediate successors of the military genius Thutmose III—Amenhotep II (c. 1426–1401 BCE) and Thutmose IV (c. 1401–1391 BCE)—ruled a relatively calm and secure empire. When Thutmose III's great-grandson Amenhotep III began his long reign about 1391 BCE, the kingdom was immensely wealthy. The royal harem contained large numbers of foreign princesses whose presence was designed to cement diplomatic ties. Amenhotep chose for his principal wife an Egyptian com-

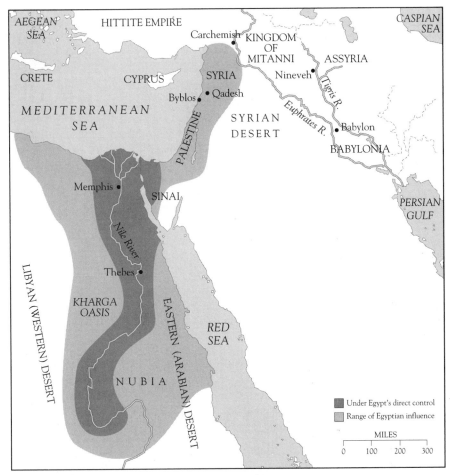

The Empire at its height, under Thutmose III, c. 1450 BCE.

moner from a military family, the remarkable and energetic Queen Tiy, while his own daughter became one of his minor wives.

NEW KINGDOM TEMPLES

Arrangement and Architectural Features.   The Egyptian temple evolved into its definitive form during the Eighteenth Dynasty. Devotees approached such an edifice along a broad, sphinx-lined processional avenue leading from the edge of the Nile or from a road. Entrance to the temple was gained through a monumental gateway consisting of two immense sloping rectangular towers called pylons, each fronted by great flagstaffs bearing long distinctive banners, a feature derived from the scrap of cloth flying from a pole attached to the prehistoric Egyptian reed shrine to show the place was taboo. Temples were built along a central axis with a succession of

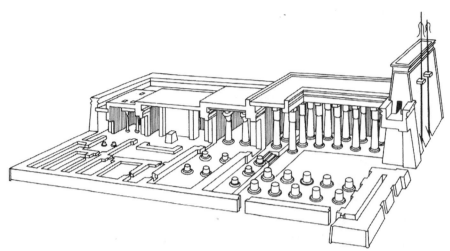

Cutaway reconstruction of a typical pylon temple of the New Kingdom, the design reflecting the processional character of its ceremonies.

enclosed spaces of increasing exclusiveness and sanctity, progressing from airy columned forecourts accommodating crowds of worshipers attending religious festivals, through dimly lit hypostyle halls and intermediate rooms accessible only to the elite and those in divine service, and finally to the inner sanctuary—the smallest and darkest of the chambers—where the priests conducted their most sacred and mysterious rituals.

Several architectural features of the elongated temples were innovative. Egyptian architects inaugurated the hypostyle hall, characterized its overpowering forest of columns bearing the weight of the roof. The columns in the central section of the hypostyle hall were elevated over those on the sides to permit some lighting and ventilation through a row of upper windows known as a clerestory, a feature adopted by the architects of the later Roman world as well as the designers of medieval cathedrals.

The Island of Creation and the Priesthood.   The plan of the Egyptian temple was determined by underlying mythological and ritual requirements. According to a well-known Egyptian creation legend, a hallowed mound of dry land had risen above the primordial waters covering the face of the earth prior to the creation of living things. This Island of Creation was regarded as the place of origin of both Egypt and its inhabitants. From the days of the simple prehistoric reed shrines, the Egyptians believed every temple contained a magical and powerful manifestation of the Island of Creation. Accordingly, the floor level of the temple rose gradually, almost imperceptibly, from the great entrance to the inner sanctuary, its Island of Creation, which housed the cult statue. The gods belonged to an invisible holy world and normally appeared on earth only through their images in reliefs or statues. The sanctuary and the adjoining private chambers served as earthly living quarters of the god,

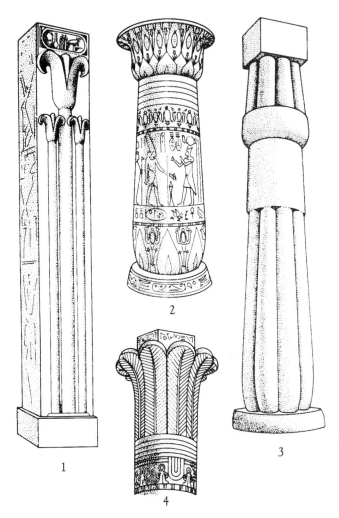

1

2

3

4

The typical Egyptian columns and their crowning capitals were carved and painted to reproduce in stone the forms of earlier plant building materials, which continued in use for lesser buildings. The examples above show a pillar ornamented with a lotus (1), a column and capital suggesting a papyrus (2), a column and capital in the form of a tied bundle of papyri (3), and a capital shaped like palm leaves (4). The Egyptians made the first stone capitals in the world. Their columns and capitals were both functional and symbolic, for the lotus signified Upper Egypt, the papyrus Lower Egypt.

who was anointed, fed, and worshiped by priests. In theory, the deified king was the sole officiant of the temple, but he was unable to be everywhere at once and delegated priests—ranged in a hierarchy—to act on his behalf. During religious festivals they paraded the cult statues in the public areas of the temple for worship and adoration. The priesthood was hereditary but functioned as a secondary profession, for priests attended to sacred duties only one month in every four, spending the rest of their time pursuing careers as scribes, physicians, and the like. We saw the temples were additionally staffed not only with priestesses, whose duties were generally confined to providing music and dancing during festivals, but also with temple prostitutes.

The Temple of Luxor. The southern end of the modern town called Luxor—part of the site of ancient Thebes on the east bank of the Nile—is famous for a notable

Reconstruction of the Temple of Luxor, built chiefly by two kings, Amenhotep III (c. 1391–1353 BCE) and Ramses II (c. 1279–1213 BCE).

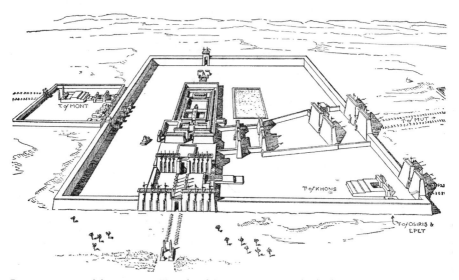

Reconstruction of the immense Temple of Amon-Re at Karnak, the largest ever erected, begun c. 2000 BCE and extended eastward for twenty centuries. This bird's-eye view provides some idea of the complexity of the sacred precinct.

New Kingdom temple begun by Amenhotep III about 1390 BCE and extended by subsequent rulers until completed over a century later. Known today as the Temple of Luxor, this beautiful complex stands across the river from Hatshepsut's mortuary temple at Deir el-Bahri. Thebes was the sacred city of Amon-Re, thus a focus of pilgrimage, and the Temple of Luxor was dedicated to the Theban holy family, namely, Amon-Re, his divine wife Mut, and their son, the moon-god Khonsu (or Khons). The Amon of Luxor was associated with inexhaustible fertility, while the Amon of nearby Karnak, the great national shrine, was more closely identified with the sun.

Additions to the Temple of Amon-Re at Karnak.   The Temple of Luxor was connected with the Temple of Amon-Re at Karnak to the north by a paved processional avenue extending well over a mile and flanked by sphinxes, hundreds of which still survive in place at the beginning and end of the way. Although Karnak was under the sovereignty of Amon-Re, smaller temples were erected nearby to Mut, Khonsu,

Model of the famous Hypostyle Hall, Temple of Amon-Re at Karnak. Completed c. 1280 BCE, the beautifully columned Hypostyle Hall was a triumph of Egyptian architecture. A clerestory fixed between the taller central columns and the shorter side columns provided shaded light, thereby furnishing a pleasing transition from the sunlight of the open court to the darkness of the inner sanctum. Metropolitan Museum of Art, New York.

and other deities. The overwhelming and confusing complex at Karnak, which lacks the graceful proportions of the Temple of Luxor, is the most massive temple of all times and was constructed over an incredible two-thousand-year period from the Middle Kingdom to Roman times. Kings never seemed to tire of trying to rival their predecessors by erecting, adding, demolishing, and rebuilding at Karnak. The great temple complex was divided into stupendous sections by six massive pylons and adorned with miles of painted reliefs. The most important constructions are from the Eighteenth and Nineteenth Dynasties. The preeminent structure from the Nineteenth Dynasty is the huge Hypostyle Hall, its 134 gigantic columns capped by papyrus buds. The sheer size of the hall is overpowering, sufficiently spacious to encompass the entire cathedral of Notre Dame of Paris.

The Festival of Opet.   The most important festival of Thebes was that of Opet, an annual celebration of great rejoicing involving large bands of priests and lasting several weeks during the second month of the inundation season. In the dramatic opening event, attendants carried the statues of Amon, Mut, and Khonsu in resplendent boat-shaped receptacles, or barks, from the maze of pylons and obelisks at Karnak to visit the statue of Amon in Luxor. Apparently the festival was thought not only to enhance the fertility of Amon-Re from Karnak but also to rejuvenate the potency of the reigning king. When the celebration was graced by monarchal

Fragment of a wall painting from a New Kingdom noble's tomb at Thebes. Accompanied by his family, the owner stands in a small papyrus boat and practices the traditional pastime of fowling in the marshes, hurling his throw-stick into a flock of birds. c. 1450 BCE. British Museum, London.

attendance, the king entered the incense-laden atmosphere of the restricted chambers of the temple to participate in a miraculous rite in the presence of the statues of the Karnak Amon and the Luxor Amon, the latter having a prominent erect penis. The colorful ceremony may have included some sort of sacred marriage or union of the inscrutable Amon-Re, the creator par excellence, and his consort Mut.

THE INTERLUDE OF AKHENATON (AMENHOTEP IV, C. 1353–1337 BCE)

Promotion of Atonism.   Amenhotep III was succeeded by his son Amenhotep IV, about whom more has been written than any other Egyptian king. His chief queen was the mysterious and evidently powerful Nefertiti, though her origin remains obscure. Perhaps like Queen Tiy, the young king's mother, the stunning Nefertiti came from a military family. Amenhotep IV is famous for departing from the traditional Egyptian religion, which provided for a multiplicity of deities but acknowledged the essential unity and oneness of divinity, as expressed by the power of the sun uphold-ing the cosmos. Amenhotep was especially devoted to a transcendent solar-god re-ferred to by scholars as the Aton, though the term is not an actual name but signifies the visible disk of the sun, the seat but not the being of the deity. The Aton was thought to manifest the sheer creative life force and power emanating from the solar orb. In short, the god was the creator of all life and the nourisher of the universe.

The cult had enjoyed some prominence under Thutmose IV and Amenhotep III. Early in the reign, Amenhotep IV constructed several temples dedicated to the Aton—only vestigial remains survive—in the vicinity of the Temple of Amon-Re at Karnak. Outwardly, he still recognized Amon-Re and the other deities, but the king increasingly focused his attention on the Aton. After ruling several years, Amenhotep openly embarked upon a radical simplification of the Egyptian religion by fervently promoting the Aton at the expense of the ancient religious tradition. The king publicly disclaimed any allegiance to Amon-Re by changing his name from Amenhotep (meaning Amon is Content) to Akhenaton (He Who Serves the Aton). The underlying reasons for Akhenaton's major modification of the Egyptian religion remain controversial. Perhaps he was partly motivated by fear of the ever more powerful priesthood of the old state religion of Amon-Re centered at Thebes, wielding political, financial, and religious force in the kingdom. Yet we should not overlook the real possibility of sincere conviction.

The New Capital of Akhetaton (Amarna).   Whatever the impetus for promoting his god, the king initiated decisive changes in the Egyptian religion. To mark his loy-alty to the Aton, Akhenaton founded a new capital almost three hundred miles north of Thebes at an unsettled site he selected and named Akhetaton (the Hori-zon of the Aton), the modern village of Tell el-Amarna, which has given its name to the entire period of the reign and its characteristic culture, the so-called Amarna age. At Akhetaton, the king built a huge roofless temple open to the sun's rays as the main shrine of the new religion. The Great Temple of the Aton contrasted sharply with the covered darkness of the halls and rooms of most older sacred edi-fices in Egypt.

Monotheistic Tendencies.   Akhenaton gave his officials orders not only to hack out every reference to Amon-Re and other deities on Egyptian temples and monuments but also to destroy their images wherever possible. More significantly, the full devel-opment of the doctrine of a singular divinity came later in the reign, with a painstaking suppression of the plural form "the gods" in earlier texts. Akhenaton's actions were aimed at nothing less than the elimination of traditional polytheism in favor of his sole god. By removing rivals to the Aton, the king approached the con-cept now called monotheism—the doctrine that only one deity exists—more closely than any previous historical figure. Atonism quickly took on the intolerance peculiar to religions focusing on one god. The royal government disbanded the priesthoods of other deities and even suppressed the popular funerary cult of the res-urrected god Osiris. In the meantime the king prohibited the use of cult statues of

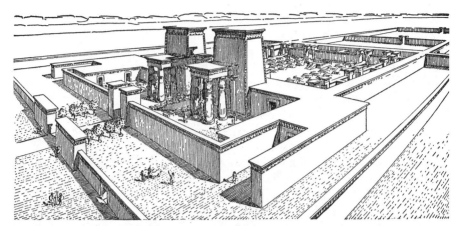

Reconstruction of the Great Temple of the Aton in Akhenaton's capital of Akhetaton (modern Tell el-Amarna). The sacred complex was open to the beneficent rays of the Aton and lacked the enclosed sanctuary of the traditional Egyptian temple. The rows of squat pillars were offering tables that were piled high with food, drink, and flowers and flanked by incense burners.

the Aton, the only tolerated image becoming the sun disk with rays terminating in protective and life-giving hands, for a depiction in human form would insult the eternal majesty and glory of this abstract being, said to be the one god of people everywhere.

The King as the Son of the Aton.   Atonism proclaimed the Aton was incarnate in his beloved son—the king—a belief comparable to the Christian doctrine of the incarnation of God the Father in God the Son. Certain funerary texts identify the Aton and the king as virtually a single being. Now mortuary prayers—no longer addressed to Osiris—were directed to Akhenaton and, through him, to the Aton. Only the king, sharing in the Aton's divinity as his son, and the royal family were authorized to worship the Aton directly. The rest of the population was expected to worship the king as the son of the sole god.

The Great Hymn to the Aton.   The spirit of Atonism is clearly reflected in the hauntingly beautiful hymns that are said to have been composed by Akhenaton himself. Scholars find one of these, the famous *Great Hymn to the Aton,* striking similar in both imagery and structure to the Hebrew Psalm 104, composed some six or seven centuries later. The *Great Hymn* extols the Aton as the "Sole God" and "Creator," the fashioner of a beautiful earth and the bestower of manifold blessings upon humanity.

Radical Royal Imagery.   Akhenaton regularly described himself in inscriptions as King Who Lives in Truth, or Ma`at, once an epithet confined to the gods. Some scholars suggest the emphasis on truth in religion was extended to the radical art of the reign. Although Egyptian art had been almost unchanging in its austere restraint since the Old Kingdom, with idealized statues of the kings emphasizing their might and invincibility, Akhenaton encouraged artists to adopt a novel style, often interpreted as an extreme form of naturalism. The king is depicted with an androgynous physiognomy—fleshy thighs, wide hips, pronounced belly and buttocks, swelling breasts, elongated neck—in addition to gaunt face, narrowed eyes, prominent nose, and rubbery lips. This exceptional physiognomy also became the norm for representing the members of the royal family and, to a lesser extent, courtiers and officials identifying themselves with the king. The unique physique is most clearly seen on the colossal statues of Akhenaton made for the largest of the new temples of the Aton at Karnak. Scholars warmly debate whether the revolutionary blend of male and female features stemmed from the actual physical appearance of the king—possibly the result of a serious disease—or had some other meaning.

As long as the king lived, artists created paintings and reliefs in the capital portraying the royal family in scenes of relaxed informality, with the seemingly jubilant members expressing tender affection for one another while the Aton radiates light upon them. A famous sculpture of supreme elegance was produced during the reign. This is the portrait bust of Nefertiti—now in Berlin—characterized by flowing lines, elongated neck, and dreamy expression, all combining to form an image of untouchable, precariously balanced female beauty.

The Amarna Letters.   The site of Amarna became famous in 1887, the year natives unearthed part of the international diplomatic correspondence of Akhenaton and his father from the ruined royal palace. The Amarna Letters, as they are called, contain considerable information about the empire of Egypt on the eve of its decline. Written on clay tablets in Akkadian cuneiform, then the language of international correspondence, the collection includes letters from dependent princelings and from Mitannian, Kassite, Assyrian, and Hittite kings, who refer to the Egyptian ruler as their brother. Egyptian influence was now maintained over the empire as much by gifts as by garrisons, for all of the subject princes ask for gold. Although the correspondence indicates that Egyptian control over Palestine and Syria was beginning to weaken, the tablets also reveal extensive trade with faraway lands such as Mycenae, Crete, and Punt.

The Empire.   To a limited degree, Akhenaton preserved the traditional role of the king as a war lord, initiating a campaign in Nubia and keeping garrisons in Asia. Although he seems to have governed with the support of the army during his seventeen-year reign, apparently he was far more concerned with Atonism than the fate of the empire. His reign witnessed the fall of the Mitannian kingdom before the expanding Hittites. Many of the Amarna letters contain frantic pleas for assistance from vassal princes threatened by the Hittites, but Akhenaton responded only occasionally with military assistance. By the last years of the king's life, the Egyptian hold on Syria was on the verge of collapse and was gravely threatened in Palestine.

The Confused Succession.   Having neither cult statues to parade during festivals nor a colorful mythology, Atonism must have offered scant appeal to ordinary Egyptians, probably deeply resentful at the tampering with their cherished beliefs and customs. Even so, had Akhenaton been succeeded by an adult son with the will to continue promoting the new faith, Atonism might have survived and eventually become popular. Yet Akhenaton and Nefertiti produced six daughters—no male heir—and apparently the chief queen died three years before the end of the reign. Two of the daughters seem to have been advanced, in turn, as their father's consort, but only additional daughters were forthcoming from these unions. Around this time the king brought two young princes forward—Smenkhkare and Tutankhaton—who apparently were sons of Amenhotep III. Akhenaton married them to two of his daughters. The older prince, Smenkhkare, was elevated as coregent upon reaching manhood, but he lived only a few months after Akhenaton himself died about 1337 BCE. Smenkhkare was succeeded by his brother Tutankhaton, a child scarcely more than eight years old.

TUTANKHAMON (TUTANKHATON, C. 1336–1327 BCE)

Tutankhaton and his wife Ankhesenpaaton (the daughter and widow of Akhenaton) lived at Akhetaton for two years, worshiping the Aton. Yet Tutankhaton's extreme youth prevented him from promoting Atonism, even if he had so wished, and his advisers reinstated the traditional deities. The king and queen finally marked their capitulation by moving to Thebes and altering their names to Tutankh*amon* (Living Image of Amon) and Ankhesen*amon* (She Lives in Amon), indicative of the restoration of the traditional religion of Amon-Re at Thebes. Tutankhamon fell to an untimely death in his late teens. His sumptuous small tomb of four chambers in the Valley of the Kings opposite Thebes—miraculously discovered essentially intact by Howard Carter in 1922—staggers the imagination, though the richness of the funerary equipment must have paled beside that of a great king. Most of the contents are now in the Egyptian Museum in Cairo.

AY (C. 1327–1323 BCE)

Tutankhamon's reign had been dominated by two powerful individuals, the priest Ay, serving as vizier and regent, and a young general called Horemheb, who rose to power and enjoyed high civil and military rank. Tutankhamon left no living heirs, and at his death an internal conflict arose concerning the succession. Ankhesenamon desperately tried to assert her authority against Ay. She wrote to the Hittite king Suppiluliumas, pleading with him to send one of his many sons to become her husband and the next king of Egypt, frantically trying to maintain her position through a risky foreign alliance. The Hittite ruler delayed, and when he eventually dispatched a son, the prince was murdered on the way, presumably by agents of those with alternate plans, though we cannot rule out bandits. The queen was forced to wed the aged Ay, a marriage alliance giving him the throne, and she is never heard of again. During his brief reign of four or five years, Ay continued the restoration of traditional policies and completed a rock-cut tomb in the royal style on the west bank, opposite Thebes, in the Valley of the Kings.

Horemheb (c. 1323–1295 BCE)

Before Ay died, he presumably chose as his successor the experienced general Horemheb, a man of unknown origin, who enjoyed a long and stable reign as the last ruler of the notable Eighteenth Dynasty. Horemheb was strongly backed by the army and the priests of Amon-Re. Although he had risen to power through his professed loyalty to Tutankhamon, perhaps Horemheb was an opportunist. He now headed the Theban party and presided over the systematic destruction of all traces of Atonism. While members of the old royal family were branded as heretics, Horemheb was recognized as the only legitimate king since the reign of Amenhotep III. The names Akhenaton, Tutankhamon, and Ay, were hacked off monuments and erased from texts. In the meantime Horemheb repaired traditional temples and built extensively himself, exemplified by his rock-cut tomb in the Valley of the Kings. He dismantled the town of Akhetaton as well as many buildings associated with Atonism. Yet Akhenaton's haunting idea of focusing on one deity survived him and found later expression in the religions of Zoroastrianism, Judaism, Christianity, and Islam.

Ramses I (c. 1295–1294 BCE): The First of the Ramesside Kings

Having no son to follow him, the aged Horemheb groomed the vizier Ramses as his successor. Thus about 1295 BCE the kingdom passed to Ramses (Ramesses) I, descending from a military family lacking royal lineage, who inaugurated the Nineteenth Dynasty. The kings of the Nineteenth and Twentieth Dynasties (c. 1295–1069 BCE) are known today as the Ramessides because the majority of them bore the name Ramses. Ramses I came from the Delta, and he shifted the royal residence to the north, though Thebes remained the administrative capital. He and his successors of the Nineteenth Dynasty made heroic efforts to revitalize Egypt.

Seti I (c. 1294–1279 BCE)

When Ramses' brief reign ended about 1294 BCE, his son Seti (Sethos) I succeed him as king and continued the policy of promoting the old religion and systematically removing all visible traces of Atonism. His military campaigns restored the authority of Egypt in Nubia and western Asia. Seti even found time for numerous building projects such as his mortuary temple on the west bank opposite Thebes. His greatest architectural achievement was realized at the holy city of Abydos—a place of pilgrimage long associated with the cult of Osiris—about a hundred miles north of Thebes as the Nile flows. Here the king constructed the celebrated Temple of Seti I in fine limestone. Dedicated to the Osirian triad and other deities, the structure included special chambers for the enactment of the resurrection of Osiris

A lithograph of the facade of the Great Temple of Ramses II at Abu Simbel, based on a drawing by the British artist David Roberts in 1838, when a vast drift of sand covered much of the site.

and, behind the temple, a massive subterranean complex apparently designed as a cenotaph (an empty, commemorative tomb) of the king.

RAMSES II (C. 1279–1212 BCE)

The Battle of Qadesh (c. 1274 BCE).   About 1279 BCE, Seti I was succeeded by his son Ramses II, the greatest king of the Nineteenth Dynasty, whose long and extravagant reign of sixty-seven years represented a stunning quest for monarchal glory. Ramses advanced into Syria. He boasted of victory following a desperate battle with the Hittites, the prime Egyptian adversary, near the city of Qadesh on the Orontes River about 1274 BCE, though in actuality he made only a narrow escape from the encircling trap laid by the opposing armies. Thereafter the Egyptians failed to offer any serious challenge to the Hittite hold on northern Syria. Although Ramses had barely escaped alive, he always represented the battle of Qadesh as a great Egyptian victory.

The Peace Treaty between the Egyptian and Hittite Empires (c. 1258 BCE).   Sixteen years later, about 1258 BCE, when each of the old opposing sides was faced with a dangerous expansion of Assyrian power, the Hittite king Hattusilis III proposed a defensive alliance with Egypt. Ramses proved willing, and a pact was concluded. Both Egyptian and Hittite versions of this notable international peace treaty sur-

A lithograph of the interior of the Great Temple of Ramses II at Abu Simbel, based on a drawing of 1817 by the Italian excavator Giovanni Battista Belzoni, the first explorer to clear the entrance and enter the rock-cut chambers of the monumental Nubian shrine.

vive. The terms were prudent, even humane. Each king pledged to renounce further hostilities, to refrain from attacking the lands of the other, and to provide assistance in the event of attack by a third party. The treaty was "witnessed" by a thousand Egyptian and Hittite gods, and the alliance was later cemented by a brilliant dynastic marriage between Ramses II and the richly dowered eldest daughter of the Hittite king.

The New Capital of Pi-Ramses and Monumental Building Projects at Abu Simbel and Elsewhere.   During the second half of the reign, Egypt enjoyed relative peace and flourished. We saw that Ramses' ancestors sprang from the Delta, and he created a new capital called Pi-Ramses (the Domain of Ramses) in the northeastern part of the region. Pi-Ramses alternated with Memphis as the chief royal residence during the Nineteenth and early Twentieth Dynasties. Although Ramses II was the most vigorous builder to occupy the Egyptian throne, many of his stupendous monuments were more impressive in terms of overwhelming size than refinement. The king often usurped previous buildings, replacing the names of the royal builders with his own. Moreover, Ramses obtained much of the stone for his prolific new constructions by pulling down the monuments of his predecessors. His famous building legacy includes two temples at Abu Simbel in Nubia. Hacked out of the rugged sandstone cliffs overhanging the river, the temples were majestically impressive but offered scant useable space behind their gigantic pylonlike façades. The larger accorded divine honors to Ramses himself along with other deities and was cut 185 feet into the solid rock through a series of interior halls. Four 67-foot seated figures of the king—these colossal images lack the grace and precision of earlier Egyptian statuary—were hewn out of the soft Nubian sandstone to adorn the façade. The second shrine was built a few hundred feet away in honor of the goddess Hathor, along with Ramses' favorite wife Queen Nefertari, and was enhanced with 35-foot statues of the king and queen. In the 1960s both temples were moved to a nearby plateau high above their former sites to protect them from the waters of Lake Nasser, created by the building of the Aswan High Dam. Ramses also completed the Great Hypostyle Hall of the Temple of Amon-Re at Karnak. One of the supreme wonders of antiquity, the hall was supported by a thick cluster of soaring columns having plant-form capitals. While Ramses exalted Amon-Re at Karnak, he glorified himself through his great funerary temple—popularly known as the Ramesseum—on the west bank opposite Thebes. His constructed his rock-cut tomb in the nearby Valley of the Kings.

Mammoth Sons' Tomb in the Valley of the Kings.   Ramses sired more than one hundred children by numerous wives during his long reign. Inscriptions and other evidence suggest that fifty of his fifty-two sons may have been buried in the largest rock-cut tomb ever discovered in Egypt. Recently uncovered and mostly unexcavated, this elaborate funerary complex in the Valley of the Kings contains a pillared central hall, a passage to a statue of Osiris, and other corridors leading to at least sixty-seven chambers, many decorated with wall paintings. This enormous tomb contrasts with others in the Valley of the Kings, most of which contain fewer than a dozen chambers built along a single passage. Archaeologists think excavation will reveal a lower level with additional rooms, perhaps the actual burial chambers.

MERNEPTAH (C. 1212–1203 BCE)

The Coming of the Sea Peoples.   By the time Ramses died around 1212 BCE, he had already outlived his first dozen male offspring. His successor, his thirteenth son Merneptah, was well advanced in years. An inscription on a stela of Merneptah's reign is the only known Egyptian text mentioning a tribal group called Israel, a key for determining that this population was present in part of the land of Canaan (an ancient name for western Palestine) in the late thirteenth century BCE. Several of Merneptah's other inscriptions refer to an invasion of the western Delta in the fifth year of his reign by Libyan tribes allied with the elusive Sea Peoples, a varied group of migrating maritime raiders surging along the eastern Mediterranean at the close of the Bronze Age and violently disrupting its old settled lands. While the origin of the Sea Peoples remains sketchy, the Aegean and western Anatolia are usually identified as their homeland. They created havoc in their attacks on eastern Anatolia, Syria, Palestine, and Egypt. Although Merneptah repulsed the Sea Peoples from his kingdom, they would return with even greater ferocity a generation later.

Ramses III (c. 1184–1153 bce)

Repulse of the Sea Peoples.   A dynastic change about 1186 bce inaugurated the Twentieth Dynasty, whose second ruler—Ramses III—was the last great king of the New Kingdom. Ramses pushed back two invasions of Libyan tribes. He was also faced with a new wave of the dreaded Sea Peoples. They had already inflicted death blows on the great Hittite Empire, which dissolved into separate kingdoms, and were rapidly approaching Egypt over both land and sea along the coasts of Syria and Palestine. Ramses managed to repulse them from the borders of Egypt shortly after 1180 bce. Some of the Sea Peoples fled to Syria and Anatolia, while others may have sailed westward to Sicily and Sardinia. One group, the biblical Philistines (the Egyptians called them the Peleset), settled in coastal towns along the southern strip of the Levant, which derives its designation Palestine from their name. The decoration and shapes of Philistine pottery suggests that at least some members of the group originated in the Aegean world. Although Egypt retained certain strongholds in Palestine for a while, control over the remnants of its Asian domains steadily weakened under the rule of Ramses' immediate successors.

The Mortuary Temple at Medinet Habu.   One of the great monuments of Ramses III was his enormous mortuary temple at Medinet Habu on the west bank at Thebes, though its overall quality betrays a continuing decline in Egyptian art. Ramses' achievement in overcoming the Libyans and Sea Peoples is immortalized in the somewhat mechanical and uninspired reliefs adorning the outer walls of the structure.

Rapid Decline under the Later Ramessides (c. 1153–1069 bce)

The eight kings reigning from the death of Ramses III until the end of the Twentieth Dynasty about 1069 bce all tried to bask in the name Ramses, but they presided over a rapidly eroding New Kingdom marked by growing weakness, impoverishment, and internal disorganization. The destruction of the Hittite Empire and the ravaging of the Levant by the Sea Peoples had drastically curtailed Egyptian trade with parts of Anatolia having abundant deposits of silver and iron, this coming not too long before these metals would assume vital importance in the enrichment of state treasures and the manufacture of arms. Meanwhile the remnants of the Asian domains were gradually slipping away, leading to even more serious economic consequences at home. The army, now composed largely of foreign mercenaries, often proved difficult to manage. At the end of the Twentieth Dynasty, the capital seems to have been shifted from Pi-Ramses to Tanis, another city in the northeastern Delta. By the last years of the reign of Ramses XI (c. 1099–1069 bce)—the last king of the Ramesside line—the crown had lost much of its power to the high priest of Amon-Re at Thebes. This led to a territorial division of the country, the king presiding over Lower Egypt from the capital of Tanis, while the high priest governed Upper Egypt with virtual kingly power from Thebes. Despite the shocking disintegration of traditional government, Ramses XI remained titular head of all Egypt until his death about 1069 BCE, bringing to a close the period we know as the New Kingdom.

THE LATE PERIOD (TWENTY-FIRST THROUGH THIRTY-FIRST DYNASTIES, c. 1069–332 BCE)

During the Twenty-first Dynasty (c. 1069–945 BCE), which marked the beginning of the Late period, northern Egypt was governed by a line of kings at Tanis, while the high priests of Amon-Re, in hereditary succession, continued to rule the south from Thebes. Thereafter, despite occasional interludes of prosperity and native rule, Egypt generally fell victim to unrest, divided authority, and foreign conquest. The confused Twenty-second Dynasty (c. 945–715 BCE) was Libyan—its thoroughly Egyptianized rulers descending from people who had originated west of Egypt but had managed to settle in the kingdom at an earlier time—and the Twenty-fifth (c. 715–656 BCE) was Nubian. The Nubian rulers brought decades of stability to the country, but they were driven south into their home territory after the Assyrians penetrated Egypt from the east in the seventh century BCE. Assyria was now the dominant power in western Asia, its empire extending from Mesopotamia to the shores of the Mediterranean. The Assyrians appointed governors to administer the subjugated areas in Egypt, yet Assyrian power was waning, and the Egyptians briefly regained their independence and produced a brilliant renaissance of Egyptian culture during the Twenty-sixth Dynasty, commonly called the Saite period (664–525 BCE). This revival ended abruptly in 525 BCE, when the Persians overran the whole of Egypt and incorporated the country into their expanding empire as a satrapy, or province. The generally efficient Persian rule was interrupted by a period of Egyptian independence embracing the first half of the fourth century BCE, made possible by internal disarray in the Persian Empire. Although the Persians managed to reoccupy Egypt in 342 BCE, they lost the country a decade later.

THE GRECO-ROMAN PERIOD (MACEDONIAN-PTOLEMAIC KINGS AND ROMAN EMPERORS, 332 BCE–642 CE)

The Persians now faced the military genius of that most celebrated of all conquerors, Alexander the Great, king of Macedonia. After gaining ascendancy over all of Greece, Alexander began capturing the vast Persian Empire piece by piece. He made a triumphal entry into Egypt in 332 BCE, inaugurating there the era of Macedonian-Ptolemaic rule. His turbulent successors—the Greek-speaking Ptolemies—stood at the head of an Egyptian state characterized not only by intellectual and artistic ferment but also by rapacious exploitation of the indigenous population. During this period both Greek and Asian deities were incorporated in the state pantheon, though the age-old religious practices of Egypt were still accorded honor.

Ptolemaic rule lasted a little more than three centuries, ending when the Romans seized the country in 30 BCE. From that date until the seventh century—by then the country had become predominantly Christian—Egypt was a province of the Roman Empire and was administered by a prefect appointed by the emperor. After the collapse of the western part of the Empire in the fifth century, the surviving eastern half, governed from Constantinople, continued to hold Egypt. Then a powerful tide of Arab armies, inspired by Islam, began attacking the contracted form of the old Roman Empire in the seventh century. The Arabs made phenomenal conquests, including Egypt in 642. The spectacular ancient Egyptian civilization had decayed centuries earlier. The country was now linked politically, religiously, and culturally with the Asian heartland of Islam, a change signaling the rapid decline of Egyptian Christianity and the replacement of the final form of Egyptian—Coptic—with Arabic as the official language. Under the impact of the Arab conquest, the surviving vestiges of the ancient Egyptian culture faded, while knowledge of its history dwindled into a vague but glorious memory of a seemingly timeless legend.

CHAPTER VIII

THE HITTITES OF ANATOLIA AND THEIR NEIGHBORS

We saw in chapters 3 through 5 that the early part of the third millennium BCE witnessed considerable fluctuation in the fortunes of the Sumerian city-states of southern Mesopotamia as they struggled with one another for land and political dominance, until they finally fell under the successive control of the Semitic-speaking Akkadians and the fierce Gutians. Then the Sumerians gained ascendancy once again about 2100 BCE and founded the brilliant Third Dynasty of Ur, though its sway ended around the close of the millennium at the hands of the Semitic-speaking Amorites, whose sixth and most important king was Hammurabi. Meanwhile, as noted in chapter 6, the Egyptians were developing their distinctive civilization along the Nile during the third millennium BCE, the bulk of which forms the Early Dynastic period and the Old Kingdom. High civilization also permeated the expanse of land lying between Mesopotamia and Egypt during the same time frame, illustrated by an ancient city in northwestern Syria called Elba, whose Semitic-speaking inhabitants dominated a far-flung region stretching from Syria to northern Mesopotamia.

We focus in this and the next three chapters on developments in Anatolia and Syria-Palestine during the second and first millennia BCE, while turning in the final chapters to the unfolding events in Mesopotamia and Persia down to the era of Alexander the Great, though we should keep in mind that the various regions of eastern Europe and western Asia exerted considerable influence upon one another. Much of the second millennium BCE witnessed the flourishing of great states in a vast area extending from the Aegean region to Egypt and to Mesopotamia, including Mycenaean Greece, Minoan Crete, the Hittite Empire, New Kingdom Egypt, Mitanni, Assyria, Amorite Babylonia, and Kassite Babylonia. The advent of several of these powers was related to a signal development at the opening of the millennium: the remarkable spread of the various Indo-European-speaking peoples in Europe and Asia. They were the linguistic ancestors of the current speakers of the widely distributed Indo-European languages. One group of Indo-Europeans, the Hittites, ensconced themselves among the native population of Anatolia, creating a great state that often successfully challenged Egyptian ascendancy over Syria. Additional Indo-European speakers settled in Greece, Italy, and the rest of Europe. Others penetrated Iran and subsequently India. The second millennium BCE was also the era of the elusive Hurrians—their tongue was neither Indo-European nor Semitic—who exerted considerable influence in western Asia. A Hurrian popula-

154

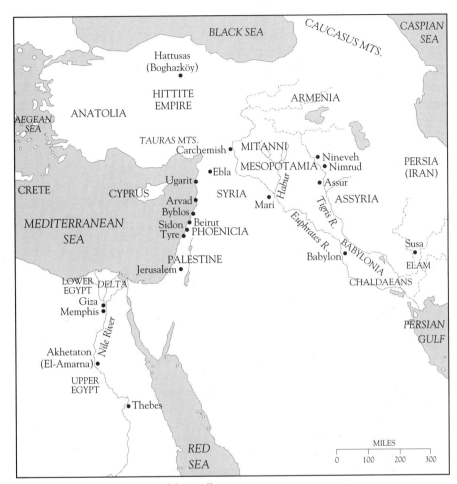

The Near East in the second and first millennia BCE.

tion predominated in the powerful kingdom of Mitanni, which was formed in the sixteenth century BCE and reached its height in the next, stretching from its heartland in northern Mesopotamia to the coast of Syria.

For much of the period from roughly 1600 to 1200 BCE, the history of Anatolia and Syria-Palestine was closely linked to the three powerful empires of the region, all contending for dominance through military and diplomatic maneuvers: New Kingdom Egypt in the south, Mitanni in the east, and the Hittite Empire in the north. The Hittites broke the power of Mitanni about the middle of the fourteenth century BCE. Yet the Hittites' great empire disappeared shortly after 1200 BCE, the result of a series of violent invasions by the elusive Sea Peoples at the end of the Bronze Age, and was succeeded by a mosaic of new political units in Anatolia. The disruptions relating to the Sea Peoples also weakened the grasp of the Egyptians on their Asian domains, ultimately pushing them back to the Nile. Not until the coming of Alexander the Great nearly nine centuries later would any other single development make the same impact on the ancient world as the surge of the dreaded Sea Peoples. In the vacuum left by the eclipse of Egypt and the fall of the Hittite Empire, the largely Semitic population of Syria-Palestine—most notably the Phoenicians and the Hebrews—soon carved out small independent states for themselves. In the meantime a development of the highest consequence was taking place in western Asia: the first significant use of iron as a functional rather than an ornamental material, ushering in a new phase of ancient history known as the Early Iron Age, dating from around 1200 to 1000 BCE.

Although we encounter many diverse cultures and peoples in this and the following three chapters, the two most important historical developments in Anatolia and Syria-Palestine are the rise and fall in the north of the great realm of the Hittites during the period from about 1650 to 1180 BCE and the establishment in the south of small Semitic states, which flourished from around 1180 to 700 BCE.

THE MIGRATIONS OF THE INDO-EUROPEAN-SPEAKING PEOPLES

An Indo-European is simply a person whose native tongue is one of the Indo-European languages. Thus the term is essentially a linguistic concept rather than a reference to an ethnic type or material culture. Although disagreeing about details, linguists suggest that an unrecorded language, usually labeled Proto-Indo-European, evolved more than 6000 years ago somewhere in an area extending from southeast Europe to the northern foothills of the Caucasus, its existence known only from surviving traces in the vocabularies of descendant tongues. Apparently by the third millennium BCE, Proto-Indo-European had split into a number of dialects. These dialects, spread by nonliterate peoples migrating in Europe and Asia, eventually developed into a great family of Indo-European languages, now spoken on every continent and by fully half of the population of the planet.

The Indo-European speakers began moving across Europe and western Asia before 2000 BCE, acquiring skills from the civilized peoples they encountered along the way. Some penetrated Anatolia, the most notable of whom are known to history as the Hittites. Indo-European speakers also settled on the mainland of Greece, fusing with the natives to give rise to the famous Mycenaean civilization, while others migrated into Italy and the rest of Europe. The Basque language in the Pyrenees is a last remnant of the ancient tongues spoken in southwest Europe before their arrival. Some Indo-Europeans entered what is now Iran, the forebears of the Medes and the Persians, and subsequently a part of them swept eastward with their horse-driven chariots into northern India and established the Sanskrit language. Although scholars used to blame those migrating to northern India for the destruction of the venerable Indus civilization, the earliest known urban culture on the Indian subcontinent, many investigators now suggest other causes for the collapse, particularly natural disasters or social and economic problems.

English and nearly all the other tongues of modern Europe—the most important exceptions are Hungarian, Finnish, Estonian, and Basque—have an

Indo-European ancestry, along with most of the languages of Iran, the Indian subcontinent, and other parts of Asia, as well as extinct tongues such as Latin, Old Persian, and Sanskrit. The Indo-European languages fall into ten main subfamilies,
which may be divided for convenience into eastern and western groups. The eastern
group consists of the Albanian, Armenian, Balto-Slavic, Indo-Iranian, Anatolian,
and Tocharian subfamilies, of which the last two are extinct. The western group
consists of the Celtic, Germanic, Greek, and Italic subfamilies. The Germanic subfamily includes English, while the Italic embraces Latin and its modern descendants
known as the Romance languages. Linguists attempt to group the Indo-European
subfamilies together by varying degrees of affinity based on the time of their diver-
gence, though the relationships remain disputed. Despite the lack of agreement for
a model of the linguistic family tree, the common origin of the various Indo-
European tongues is apparent in numerous words, exemplified by the similarity of
the Modern English *new* to the Armenian *nor*, Sanskrit *návas*, Hittite *newas*,
Tocharian *ñuwe*, Old Irish *nue*, and Latin *novus*.

THE ESTABLISHMENT OF HURRIAN KINGDOMS
(c. 1800–1550 BCE)

Among the most elusive of the migrating peoples in the ancient Near East during
the early second millennium BCE were the Hurrians, speakers of a distinctive language, neither Indo-European nor Semitic, which they learned to write in the
cuneiform script. Archaeologists have found cuneiform texts of their extinct tongue
in several places, including the famous palace at Mari on the middle Euphrates, from
which a dynasty of Amorite kings ruled until Hammurabi destroyed the great city.
The Hurrians are generally believed to have started trickling down from the mountains north and northwest of Mesopotamia by the mid-third millennium BCE, pene-
trating both northern Mesopotamia and southeastern Anatolia. They were scattered
throughout Mesopotamia and Syria by the first quarter of the next millennium. Establishing a number of kingdoms in the lands they occupied, the Hurrians played a
crucial role in transmitting certain religious and cultural ideas they had borrowed
from the Mesopotamians to the Hittites, Phoenicians, Hebrews, and, indirectly, to
the Greeks and the Western world. Their mythological literature made a profound
impact on the Hittites, whose own religious texts betray a heavy Hurrian influence.

THE HURRI-MITANNIAN KINGDOM
(FL. c. 1550–1350 BCE)

Apparently various Hurrian states in the area from the northern reaches of
Mesopotamia to the Syrian coast were brought together in the new kingdom of Mitanni around 1550 BCE. The undiscovered capital of Mitanni—Wassukanni—is
generally thought to have been in the vicinity of the Khabur River region of northeastern Syria. Certain Indo-European words in surviving Mitannian documents
provide clues for a widely accepted theory that the Hurrians themselves had come

under the rule of a small Indo-European-speaking warrior aristocracy—historians often label them the Mitannians—who had migrated into Hurrian-occupied lands. The Mitannians adopted the Hurrian language, but they took personal names akin to those of the Indo-European invaders of India. They invoked deities such as Mitra, Varuna, and Indra—later familiar in northern India—though calling these divine figures Mitrasil, Arunasil, and Indar. The Mitannians also acknowledged the Hurrian weather-god Teshub and his consort Hebat, a mother-goddess bearing the impressive title Queen of Heaven.

A major force in western Asia until about 1350 BCE, the Syro-Mesopotamian kingdom of Mitanni checked the ambitions of the Hittites to the west, the Egyptians to the south, and the Assyrians to the east, even forcing the formerly powerful Assyrian kingdom into vassalage. The exceptional military ability of Mitanni partly rested on new skills in horse training. The Hurrians wrote handbooks on the subject, using Indo-European technical terms they had learned from the Mitannians. Said to have been masters of chariot warfare, the Mitannians seem to have been pioneers in introducing the light horse-drawn chariot with spoked wheels to the Near East. The Hurri-Mitannians employed their two-wheeled chariots as highly mobile firing platforms for archers. Yet the effectiveness of these mobile firing platforms was counteracted when the opponents of Mitanni responded by inaugurating scale armor for both warriors and horses.

Egyptian-Mitannian Coalition

We saw in chapter 7 that Egyptian pride had been deeply stung by the long period of Hyksos domination. After overthrowing and expelling the Hyksos in the sixteenth century BCE, the Egyptians adopted an aggressive policy of carving out an Asian empire. These forays soon brought Egypt into rivalry with expansionist western Asian powers, most notably, the Mitannians and Hittites. Undertaking the conquest of Syria, Egyptian kings came into conflict with the Hurri-Mitannians, and Thutmose III (sole reign, c. 1457–1426 BCE) defeated them in battle. The strategy of his second successor, Thutmose IV (c. 1401–1391 BCE), was based on a coalition of Egypt and Mitanni against a common enemy, the Hittites of Anatolia. The alliance he concluded was cemented when a Mitannian princess entered the Egyptian royal harem.

The Fall of Mitanni

Despite the diplomatic and matrimonial links between Egypt and Mitanni, the latter fell prey to Hittite designs in the reign of the Egyptian king Akhenaton (c. 1353–1337 BCE), who seems to have been more concerned with his religious revolution than the fate of the Asian empire. During this period Mitanni was beset by power struggles. Its king, Tushratta, was challenged for the throne by several members of the royal family, a dangerous division seriously weakening the state. About 1350 BCE the Hittites broke the power of Mitanni and annexed all its Syrian possessions, while allowing a diminished Mitannian state to survive in northern Mesopotamia as a buffer to the Assyrians. With the collapse of the empire of Mitanni, however, Assyria was reborn as a major military power and demonstrated steely resolve in expanding westward from its heartland on the middle course of the river Tigris. The Assyrians conquered and annexed what was left of the Mitannian kingdom in the thirteenth century BCE, gradually absorbing the Hurri-Mitannians. By 1200 BCE the Hurrian language had vanished from the records.

EARLY ANATOLIA

Geography and Climate

The large peninsula called Anatolia, constituting the greater part of what is now Turkey, has served through the ages as a great two-way land bridge linking Asia and Europe, the route used by numerous migrating and conquering peoples. Alexander the Great came this way to invade Asia in the fourth century BCE. Few areas of comparable size present such a wide variety of landscapes and climates. The southern and western coasts enjoy a Mediterranean climate, with dry summers and rainy winters. The southern coast on the Mediterranean produces citrus fruit, while the western, facing the Aegean Sea, is noted for fine olive groves and vineyards and reminds visitors of the southern shore of Greece. The deeply indented Aegean coast throws out long rocky promontories toward southeast Europe and has many offshore islands.

The peninsula is dominated by a huge central region, the Anatolian Plateau, lying between the Black Sea to the north and the Mediterranean to the south. Dotted with shallow salt lakes, the central region experiences meager rainfall and is associated with herding and the growing of grain. The plateau is rimmed on the north and south by coastal mountains, which exceed 10,000 feet and obstruct rain-bearing winds but contain rich deposits of iron, copper, and silver. The Pontic Mountains in the north follow the southern coast of the Black Sea, while the Taurus Mountains in the south run parallel to the Mediterranean in a broken, irregular line. These Anatolian ranges impeded, though not entirely blocked, access to the Mediterranean and Black seas in antiquity. To the west the plateau descends more gently to the well-watered and fertile valleys of the Aegean coast. Although the central region lacks navigable rivers, a long shallow stream known in ancient times as the Halys River (modern Kizil Irmak) crosses the rugged eastern part. The Halys rises in the mountainous east, flows southwest, and then swings northward in a great crescent-shaped bend, finally cutting through lofty mountains and emptying into the Black Sea.

The Neolithic Period and the Early Bronze Age (c. 7000–2000 BCE)

Çatal Hüyük.   Archaeologists have uncovered a number of prehistoric agricultural sites in Anatolia. One of the largest and most complex of these communities has been partially excavated at Çatal Hüyük in the Konya Plain of southwest-central Anatolia. Occupied from before 7000 to about 5600 BCE, Çatal Hüyük developed into a bustling town enjoying a high level of Neolithic culture. At the height of its prosperity, beginning around 6000 BCE, the settlement dominated trade over large parts of the central region. Smiths in the community produced copper and lead beads as well as other small metal objects.

Troy II and Alaca Hüyük.   Evidence suggests that bronze technology was practiced in Anatolia from around 3000 BCE. During the third millennium BCE—the Anatolian Early Bronze Age—the peninsula supported numerous city-states ruled by kings from their heavily fortified citadels. Much of the importance of these small independent kingdoms was tied to their metals and metal products. Archaeologists have made notable discoveries of precious objects, many fashioned from metal, in Anatolian treasuries and royal tombs. These troves reflect both the considerable wealth of the kings and the material achievements of their states. One of the most spectacular finds came from the second settlement of ancient Troy (known to archaeologists as Troy II), which flourished in the distant northwest about 2300 BCE. The site was first occupied about 3500 BCE, and each of the several successive settlements was built on the ruins of its predecessor, slowly creating a high mound now called Hissarlik. The German Heinrich Schliemann, famous for his pioneering archaeological activity in Anatolia and Greece, excavated Troy II from Hissarlik in the late nineteenth century. His efforts yielded an amazing cache of gold and bronze ornaments, their beautiful designs indicating a long tradition of metalworking. Schliemann called the find the Treasure of Priam, after the famous legendary king of Troy. Later investigators discovered remarkable royal tombs dating from the third millennium BCE at a site called Alaca Hüyük, located in north-central Anatolia. These famous tombs housed several generations of corpses of the ruling class buried with their funerary paraphernalia and private possessions, including domestic vessels, weapons, and finely executed metal ornaments and figurines. Such finds suggest widespread trade and an active exchange of traditions.

ARRIVAL OF INDO-EUROPEAN-SPEAKING PEOPLES (C. 2400–1900 BCE)

The closing centuries of the third millennium BCE probably witnessed a great influx of speakers of an Indo-European language, Luwian, who established themselves in much of western and southern Anatolia. The area the Luwian speakers occupied experienced a century or so of political unrest and declining prosperity, though the northern and central parts of the peninsula were less affected. Eventually settled conditions returned, marked by a profitable trade among the various regions of Anatolia and beyond. By 1900 BCE Assyrian merchants, attracted by the wealth of Anatolia, had established flourishing trading posts at several towns in the eastern region, the most important being at Kanesh (modern Kültepe). Apparently the Assyrians were the first literate population in Anatolia. Archaeologists have unearthed clay tablets at Kanesh and at several other sites providing valuable information about the long-distance trading practices of the time as well as the illiterate population of the region. Written in a dialect of Akkadian known as Old Assyrian, the documents mention native rulers of various city-states, with some personal names being recognizably Indo-European. Linguists studying the period of the Assyrian trading posts have detected the presence in the central plateau of a second Indo-European-speaking people—they are now conventionally labeled Hittites—who seem to have appeared on the scene by the end of the third millennium BCE.

THE HITTITES

THE LANGUAGES OF ANATOLIA IN THE SECOND MILLENNIUM BCE

The Hittites seem to have originated somewhere in the area extending from southeast Europe along the upper shore of the Black Sea to the northern foothills of the Caucasus. They must have intruded into Anatolia either from the northwest via the Balkans or from the northeast through the passes of the Caucasus, ultimately settling on the central plateau. At this time the plateau was occupied by a population who called their land Hatti—the origin of the later designation Hittite—and spoke a non-Indo-European language, now conventionally labeled Hattic. Apparently the arriving Hittites gradually imposed themselves upon the Hattic speakers as a ruling elite, while borrowing much from the indigenous culture. As a language, Hittite was far more flexible than Hattic and by degrees replaced the latter as the predominant spoken tongue in the central region, though Hattic continued to be employed in religious ceremonies.

The Hittites were not the only Indo-Europeans who had migrated to Anatolia. Linguists have determined that an Anatolian subfamily of closely related Indo-European languages—all now extinct—were spoken in what is now Asian Turkey and northern Syria during the second millennium BCE. Luwian was in general use in much of the west and the south, the more obscure Palaic in the northwest, and Hittite in central Anatolia. Some scholars have offered the intriguing suggestion that northwest Anatolia—the area of ancient Troy—was occupied by speakers of an early form of Greek, also Indo-European but belonging to another branch of the family. If ever substantially verified by archaeological findings, this theory would help to explain why Troy played such an important part in later Greek tradition.

The Hittites eventually learned to write in the cuneiform script, no doubt having borrowed the principle from Mesopotamia. Excavators have uncovered more than 25,000 of their clay tablets written during the period from around 1650 to 1200 BCE, most inscribed in Hittite, with others in the closely related Luwian and Palaic. Additionally, the Hittites wrote a number of tablets in tongues completely different in structure from Indo-European, namely Hattic, Hurrian, and the Semitic language Akkadian, the last being employed by the states of the ancient Near East for official letters and treaties during most of the second millennium BCE.

CONSOLIDATION AND EXPANSION OF HITTITE POWER (C. 2000–1650 BCE)

After the Hittites penetrated the central plateau by the close of the third millennium BCE, encountering a flourishing Early Bronze Age culture, they gradually established

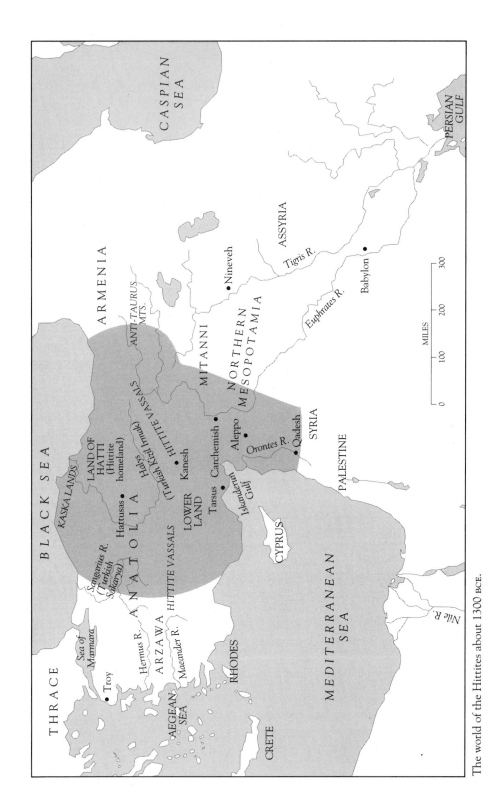

The world of the Hittites about 1300 BCE.

themselves as a ruling minority. Yet they assimilated many of the ways of the indigenous population. Accordingly, the Hittites eventually prohibited their old custom of engaging in sexual relations with domesticated animals—a common practice among nomads—and imposed the death penalty to discourage potential transgressors. They were organized at first in a number of city-states, but around 1700 BCE one of their kings fused these units into a larger kingdom. A later Hittite ruler organized the might of his warrior nobles and extended the kingdom about 1650 BCE, taking for his capital the storm-swept mountain stronghold of Hattusas, now known as Bogazköy, in the great bend of the Halys. He then changed his name to Hattusilis, "the man from Hattusas." Excavators at the site have unearthed from the official archives thousands of cuneiform tablets dating back to about the mid-seventeenth century BCE. Most of these texts concern history, politics, diplomacy, law, social structure, literature, and religion—a valuable source of information about the civilization of the Anatolian kingdom.

THE OLD KINGDOM (C. 1650–1500 BCE)

Hattusilis I (c. 1650–1620 BCE) and Mursilis I (c. 1620–1590 BCE).   Borrowing from the usage of the old Hattic speakers, the Hittites called their kingdom Hatti Land, while their neighbors referred to them simply as the Hatti. The two principal periods of Hittite history are conventionally labeled the Old Kingdom and the New Kingdom, or Empire. The former constitutes a span of about one hundred and fifty years, roughly 1650 to 1500 BCE, and opens with the reign of Hattusilis I. He and his immediate successors sought to maintain the security of their realm and to control trade through Syria into Mesopotamia. These early kings assaulted Cilicia in southeast Anatolia and then penetrated northern Syria. Hattusilis' grandson and energetic successor, Mursilis I, began his reign around 1620 BCE. Mursilis thrust deeply into Mesopotamia in a lightning campaign resulting in the capture of the city of Babylon about 1595 BCE. Mursilis' startling attack led to the rapid contraction of the Old Babylonian Empire that Hammurabi had forged and permitted the powerful Kassites, discussed in chapter 12, to occupy and rule Babylonia for half a millennium. Soon after Mursilis returned home laden with booty, he was murdered in a palace conspiracy. This marked the beginning of a generally catastrophic period lasting about two centuries and characterized by a series of royal assassinations and the loss of Hittite territory in northern Syria, devoured by the expanding Mitannian power.

THE NEW KINGDOM, OR EMPIRE (C. 1370–1180 BCE)

Suppiluliumas I (c. 1370–1326 BCE).   Following the interlude of almost unrelieved Hittite decline, a reinvigorated monarchy inaugurated the period called the New Kingdom, or Empire, dating from roughly 1370 to 1180 BCE, and pushed its control westward almost to the Aegean Sea and southward over the Taurus Mountains into Cilicia and northern Syria. This period—the zenith of Hittite power—began when a vigorous young prince named Suppiluliumas ascended the throne about 1370 BCE. Suppiluliumas I proved during his long reign to be the most brilliant military strategist in the Near East since the days of Thutmose III of Egypt. He enjoyed a successful campaign against Arzawa, a powerful state in western Anatolia, but most of his time was spent combating Mitanni, the main adversary of his immediate predecessors. He broke the power of Mitanni and ruled its former northern Syrian possessions through subject states centered on Carchemish, thereby increasing tension between the Hittites and the Egyptians, though the latter were then preoccupied with the religious revolution of Akhenaton. Passions were later excited on both sides when young Tutankhamon of Egypt died without a son to follow him on the throne about 1327 BCE. His widow Ankhesenamon sent a frantic plea to Suppiluliumas seeking a marriage alliance with one of his many sons, promising to make the prince the next king of Egypt. In her appeal the queen imperiously vowed, "I will on no account take one of my subjects and make him my husband" but then frantically cries, "I am very much afraid." Because the unprecedented request aroused his suspicions, the Hittite king hesitated until determining that the proposal was genuine. He then dispatched a son to Egypt, but he had moved too late. As noted in chapter 7, Suppiluliumas' son was murdered at the borders of Egypt, and the queen was obliged to marry one of her subjects, the elderly royal adviser Ay, who secured the throne in this manner. The murder was never avenged, for the great Hittite king died shortly thereafter of a pestilence that his warriors had brought back from a Syrian campaign, though hatred of Egypt smoldered for decades.

The Battle of Qadesh (c. 1274 bce) and the Peace Treaty between the Hittite and Egyptian Empires Empires (c. 1258 bce). A decisive military showdown between the Hittites and Egyptians over northern Syria seemed inevitable with the emergence of a resurgent Egypt under Seti I (c. 1294–1279 BCE) and his ambitious successor Ramses II (c. 1279–1213 BCE). Ramses II set out to push the frontier of his kingdom from southern Syria up to the Euphrates during the reign of the Hittite king Muwatallis (c. 1295–1269 BCE). This was the final serious Egyptian attempt to wrest northern Syria from Hittite control. The plan collapsed when Ramses fought a desperate but indecisive battle with Muwatallis near the Syrian city of Qadesh on the Orontes River about 1274 BCE. Although Ramses marched back to Egypt empty-handed, the triumph of his foes was hollow because Assyria began to advance from the east toward the Euphrates. This Assyrian aggression prompted the next Hittite king Hattusilis III (c. 1262–1238 BCE) to propose a defensive alliance with Egypt. Apparently Ramses realized the two kings had a mutual interest in protecting themselves from Assyria, and the historic pact was successfully concluded around 1258 BCE. A few years later the new Egyptian-Hittite bond was cemented by the marriage of Hattusilis' eldest daughter to Ramses II. Before long a second Hittite princess entered the royal harem, accompanied, like the first, by a fabulous dowry.

The Sea Peoples and the Destruction of the Hittite Empire (c. 1180 bce). The Hittite Empire was already in a state of serious decline. The Assyrians had absorbed Mitannian territory as far as the Euphrates. The Syrian vassals were becoming lax in meeting their obligations. Western Anatolia was shaking off Hittite control, though the Hittites continued to maintain their grip on the states along the northwestern trade route leading through the Balkans. Presumably this important avenue was a source of tin, which was alloyed with copper to manufacture bronze and was thus vital to a Bronze Age economy.

Beset by both internal and external forces, the Hittites were unable to withstand a varied throng of migrating maritime raiders, the Sea Peoples, as the Egyptians called them, who were surging along the eastern Mediterranean at the end of the thirteenth century and the beginning of the twelfth. Although the origin of these fierce invaders is a matter of controversy, both Aegean and western Anatolian groups may have been involved by the time they were finally stopped at the borders of Egypt shortly after 1180 BCE. Earlier, about 1180 BCE, a wave of Sea Peoples had ravaged coastal Anatolia and northern Syria, thereby severing the lifelines of Hittite trade and leaving the weakened center of the empire easy prey for annihilation by additional enemies swooping down from the northern hills. With its abrupt destruction, the once-powerful Hittite Empire faded from memory.

ARCHAEOLOGICAL DISCOVERIES

Historians at work before the late nineteenth century regarded the Hittites as a rather insignificant tribe, known only from records compiled by the Egyptians and Assyrians and from scattered references in the Hebrew Bible. Then in 1879 a gifted thirty-four-year-old scholar named Archibald Henry Sayce, deputy professor of comparative philology and later professor of Assyriology at Oxford, traveled to Anatolia and observed numerous monuments and inscriptions of a similar form. "Suddenly the truth flashed upon me," Sayce later recalled, for all the monuments displayed "the same characteristic features, the same head-dresses and shoes, the same tunics, the same clumsy massiveness of design and characteristic attitude." Returning to England, he reported to his colleagues that the remains were Hittite, evidence of a powerful Hittite domain in the distant past. Although conventional scholarship immediately rebuked Sayce's valuable insights, later investigators discovered abundant confirming evidence.

In 1906 a German expedition led by the irascible Hugo Winckler began excavating at the Anatolian site of Hattusas (modern Bogazköy) near the great bend of the Halys and uncovered a city of majestic plan with a state archives of some 25,000 cuneiform tablets, many of which were written in the Akkadian language, easily read, whereas the documents in Hittite were not accessible. Unfortunately the excavation was conducted in a such a helter-skelter fashion that the order of the tablets was disrupted, though Winckler's work yielded considerable knowledge concerning Hittite history and culture. Finally in 1915 the brilliant Czech scholar Bedrich Hrozný deciphered Hittite, showing the language belongs to the Indo-European family.

HITTITE CIVILIZATION

SOCIETY AND KINGSHIP

The Hittites generally assimilated elements of other cultures, especially from Mesopotamia through Hurrian influence, to form a distinctive civilization of their own. Hittite society may be characterized as multilingual and ethnically mixed, and this diverse social order was regulated by a relatively humane code of law. With few towns of any size in Anatolia, most people lived in agricultural villages surrounded by cultivable territory. Theirs was a patriarchal society, with women and children subject to men. The population included slaves, of which a large number—those captured in foreign warfare—served as agricultural laborers, thereby freeing Hittite citizens for military duties.

The aristocracy consisted of a limited number of rich and powerful families. The most prominent of these was the Great Family—the relatives of the king—whose members provided the highest officers of state and governors for important provinces and towns. The wealth of the Great Family was anchored in its vast estates and large herds, for agriculture was the mainstay of the economy. Unlike the Egyptians and Mesopotamians, the Hittites were prevented by the cold winters of the central region from producing two or three harvests a year, yet they grew ample crops of barley and wheat on their valley estates and cultivated grapes on the hillsides.

The king functioned as an absolute figure during the imperial period, combining the functions of ruler, military commander, supreme judge, and chief priest. He supported a substantial harem, for dynastic marriages had become a characteristic feature of international relations by the opening of the New Kingdom, but only his consort bore the title of queen (*tawanannas*). She enjoyed remarkable prestige and played an important role in both religious and political matters. The king distributed state-owned land to the aristocracy in return for services to the crown. Local governors and other high officials were bound by oaths of loyalty to him. This system of swearing fidelity to the king was extended to the vassal rulers of conquered foreign states, and they bore the additional obligations of sending him a yearly tribute and fighting on his behalf during wartime. The Hittites regarded their monarch as the viceroy on earth of a great deity known as the Weather-God of Hatti. The king's sacred nature was symbolized by the winged sun disk, borrowed from the Egyptians. Although not regarded as a god during his lifetime in the fashion of the Egyptian kings, the Hittite ruler was deified at death, with offerings made to his divine spirit.

TECHNOLOGY AND MILITARY EFFICIENCY

Anatolia was rich in metals, especially silver, gold, copper, and iron. The Hittites— or at least people they ruled—had developed improved techniques in Anatolia for the smelting of iron by 1200 BCE, thus laying the foundation for the Early Iron Age in the region. Yet these advances did not offer substantial benefits to the Hittites because the smelted iron of the period was no better than good bronze and was so costly to process that manufactured iron implements were more valuable than gold. Although iron was being employed as a functional—not merely ornamental—material for a few tools and weapons by the onset of the Early Iron Age, the complexity of iron technology prevented the metal from coming into general use in the ancient Near East until the opening of the first millennium BCE.

Hittite towns were strongly fortified and enclosed by massive walls crowned with battlements and provided with projecting defensive towers. Many of the monumental gateways piercing the walls were designed with hidden exits, presumably permitting Hittite warriors to make surprise counterattacks on besieging enemies. Much of the success of the Hittites in carving out their great empire resulted from their remarkable military prowess, which was tied in large measure to their chariots. The powerful class of Hittite charioteers, commanded by nobles, rode three to a chariot. Although the vehicles were relatively heavy and lacked maneuverability, they made excellent assault weapons for demolishing enemy lines during organized charges. Two strong horses would sweep them through the lines, while one of the warriors on board made deadly attacks on the opposing side with a javelin or bow. Hittite foot soldiers were armed with battle axes, daggers, and swords, the last sometimes designed in a terrifying curved shape, its cutting edge on the outside of the blade. Disciplined by harsh training, the members of the infantry concealed themselves under cover of natural features or darkness to move over long distances and make surprise attacks.

RELIGION

The incompletely known Hittite religion was a tolerant polytheism based on the worship of anthropomorphic deities. In Anatolia, as in Mesopotamia, temples played both an economic and religious role. The main temple complex in the Hittite capital included extensive storerooms as well as a cult building containing the divine statue. Reflecting the diverse cultural inheritance of the Hittite Empire, the population worshiped Anatolian and Syro-Mesopotamian divinities. The Hurrian influence was especially strong. The Hittites adopted many members of the pantheon from conquered territories and towns, while also incorporating numerous Mesopotamian beliefs concerning magic, omens, and demons. They eventually fused all these elements into a complex amalgam.

Their leading deities were linked to the great powers of nature. The Hittites retained an old Anatolian mother-goddess known to them as the Sun-Goddess of Arinna, the chief figure in the pantheon. The Sun-Goddess was exalted as the patroness of the state, and the king and queen served as her high priest and priestess. Among the goddesses' majestic titles were Queen of the Land of Hatti and Queen of Heaven and Earth. Yet without the fertilizing waters of her consort, the Weather-God of Hatti, the Sun-Goddess could not conceive. The Weather-God was a powerful deity of the storm, the source of lightning and thunder. Bearing the title King of Heaven and enjoying attributes similar to Zeus of the Greeks, the Weather-God often shows up in sculpture grasping a bolt of lightning in one hand and an axe in the other. Sometimes he appears mounted upon his sacred animal, the bull. The

Sun-Goddess and the Weather-God united to produce a son named Telepinu, another survivor of a pre-Hittite pantheon. Telepinu was responsible for a good harvest, but Hittite mythology tells us he disappeared at times, thereby bringing drought and famine to the land. The great deities were worshiped under Hurrian names by the end of the New Kingdom, a development suggesting strong cultural continuity. Accordingly, the Sun-Goddess of Arinna and the Weather-God of Hatti became known as Hebat and Teshub, the two supreme figures of the Hurrian pantheon.

The Hittites invoked a multitude of lesser deities described collectively as the Thousand Gods of the Hittites. Reflecting their devotion to a vast and unspecified number of divinities, the Hittites referred to themselves as the People of a Thousand Gods. Their deities were consumed by overpowering lust and deadly feuds, a rowdy lot endowed with all manner of humanlike frailties, but they provided protection for humanity in return for the performance of sacrifices and other acts of worship. Thus the goal of Hittite religion was to acquire and retain the favor of the gods by fulfilling ritual duties. The position of the king was paramount in achieving that end. As the chief priest and the principal deputy of the gods, the king was responsible for appeasing all the deities through various ritual observances and by making an annual pilgrimage to their great shrines during the thirty-eight-day spring festival.

LITERATURE

The Kumarbi Myth and Other Texts.   Although Hittite religious texts are often permeated with elements agreeable to local taste, they are generally derived from Mesopotamian literature. The Hittites made numerous translations of Babylonian and Hurrian epics. The best preserved Hittite literature derived from Hurrian sources is the story of Kumarbi, a god who seized the kingship of heaven but was overthrown and castrated by his son Teshub. Such myths were transmitted to the Greeks. The Kumarbi compositions reached Greece through Phoenicia and probably served as the kernel of the story of Zeus' overthrow of his father Cronus. The Hittites also borrowed literary forms such as letters, treaties, and laws. Their most absorbing literary texts are the semilegendary annals of the Hittite kings, which scribes composed in a vivid literary style. These narratives show the Hittites minimized explaining some disaster as divine retribution for human offense—the usual Mesopotamian interpretation of historical calamities—instead frequently finding the cause in human misdeeds or mismanagement. Although the Hittite royal records often make truly extravagant claims, minor episodes are sometimes described with objective detachment, telling what had happened in a rather forthright manner in contrast to the pious justifications of Mesopotamian royal inscriptions.

ART AND ARCHITECTURE

Palaces and Massive Walls.   Hittite palaces and temples were imposing but far less sumptuously decorated than similar structures in Egypt, the Aegean world, and Mesopotamia. The capital at Hattusas was the site of the most important palace of all: the residence of the rulers of the Hittite Empire, strategically perched on a towering rocky hill and designed with a central colonnaded courtyard opening onto the

The ruins of the Lion Gate, Bogazköy (ancient Hattusas), c. 1400 BCE. One of the four entrances to the city, the massive gate was provided with double arches—the lions ornamented the outer arch—and was flanked by lofty watchtowers and set in walls twenty-five feet thick.

royal apartments. Enormous defensive walls at Hattusas and elsewhere gave settlements an impression of invulnerability, heightened by the use of projecting towers and intricate entrance systems bringing attackers under cross fire. The vast mountain city of Hattusas was protected by two massive walls. The outer circuit was about four miles long. The inner and stronger wall was constructed upon a rampart of earth faced with dressed stone. Both walls were built of huge irregular stones, many over six feet long. Anyone approaching the Hittite capital must have been struck by the grim majesty of its gigantic fortifications.

Sculpture in Relief. Hittite sculpture is known for its characteristic solidity and great size. Much of our knowledge of this art comes from the surviving portal sculpture adorning the sides of city gates. These creations take the form of relief, that is, sculpture whose figures are not freestanding but project from the background on which they are carved. The huge reliefs on city gates are immediately recognizable as lions, sphinxes, or warriors. The well-known Lion Gate of ancient Hattusas is just one of the many surviving gates testifying to the Hittites' ability to fashion remarkable portal sculpture. Its sturdy lions with gaping jaws seem to be emerging from the naked stone to guard the entrance, a startling display of animal presence.

Yazilikaya. Much additional knowledge of Hittite sculpture comes from figures carved on rock walls. A spectacular group survives near the site of ancient Hattusas at a remarkable shrine now called Yazilikaya. Here an outcrop of rock forms two natural chambers that served as a dramatic place of worship in the days of Hittite

Figure from the King's Gate, Bogazköy (ancient Hattusas). Carved in high relief and dating c. 1400 BCE, the sculpture represents a Hittite warrior wearing a characteristic kiltlike garment and conical helmet with ear guards.

power. Sculptors at Yazilikaya—a Turkish word meaning *inscribed rock*—cut many figures in low relief on the vertical faces of its rocky cliffs, though numerous problems concerning the interpretation of the images remain to be solved. The larger chamber depicts ranks of male and female deities advancing in procession to a central scene showing the principal god and goddess, Teshub and his consort Hebat, facing one another. The figures of the smaller chamber evoke the intensity of religious fervor and are considered the finest examples of Hittite pictorial artistry. The composition includes the figure of a dead Hittite king (Tudhaliyas IV) in the protective embrace of a god (identified as Sharruma). Nearby an enormous sword ap-

Drawing of the central group of figures in Chamber A at Yazilikaya, showing the god Teshub, who stands on two lesser deities, facing his consort Hebat, who stands on a lion. c. 1320 BCE.

pears to have been thrust into the rock, for the pointed end of its blade is not represented. The sword is surmounted by the head of a god, and its elaborate hilt takes the form of lions. The smaller chamber may have served as a shrine for praying to the underworld deities and as a mortuary chamber for the ashes of kings. We know that Hittite rulers were cremated, while burials of ordinary people consisted of cremations or simple inhumations.

Dress.   Judging from reliefs on monuments, Hittite warriors donned kiltlike garments for battle. In terms of daily dress, men and women wore tunics as well as shoes or boots with pointed, upturned toes offering protection against heavy winter snows. Both sexes adorned themselves with jewelry such as rings, bracelets, necklaces, and earrings. Most men were clean-shaven, and Hittite men and women usually wore long hair, often arranged in pigtails. Kings and priests dressed in long gowns and special headdress for religious ceremonies. On certain state occasions the king may have also put on the high conical hat, a symbol of divinity on the heads of gods in Hittite reliefs.

THE SUCCESSORS OF THE HITTITES IN ANATOLIA TO ABOUT 600 BCE: PHRYGIANS, CIMMERIANS, NEO-HITTITES, URARTIANS

THE PHRYGIANS (C. 1180–700 BCE)

With the disappearance of the Hittite Empire around 1180 BCE in the wake of the onslaughts of the Sea Peoples, contending states struggled to control the agricultural

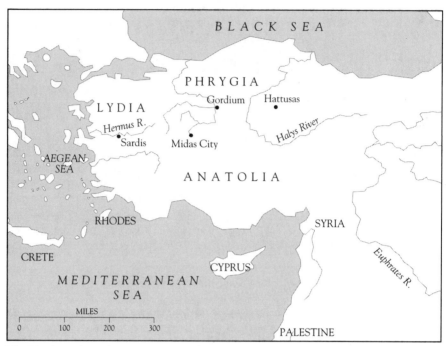

The Phrygians formed an important kingdom in central Anatolia after the collapse of the Hittite Empire, ruling from their capital of Gordium. The site known as Midas City was a principal shrine.

and mineral wealth of Anatolia as well as its valuable trade routes. The nonliterate Phrygians, who had settled in northwest Anatolia late in the second millennium BCE, immediately swept into the vacuum left by the political collapse of the Hittites and formed a kingdom in the highlands of central Anatolia, the heartland of the old Hittite Empire. They wore the famous conical Phrygian cap, a soft felt or wool headdress with a pointed crown curling forward. These people spoke another Indo-European language, Phrygian, a tongue probably standing outside the Anatolian subfamily. Greek tradition—often the best available source for information about the Phrygians—may be correct in reporting they had crossed into Anatolia from an earlier homeland in southeast Europe.

The Phrygians dominated much of Anatolia from their holdings in the central highlands until the beginning of the seventh century BCE. Their tradition as a pastoral people notwithstanding, the Phrygians built fortress cities in the ninth and eight centuries BCE that were characteristic of their kingdom at its height. Ruling from their capital of Gordium, the Phrygians constructed a system of serviceable roads later utilized by the ancient Persians. They covered the tombs of the elite with huge mounds of artificial earth, thereby creating conspicuous monuments. Archaeologists excavating the royal tombs lying under the colossal burial mounds at Gordium discovered considerable painted pottery, metalwork, and inlaid wooden furniture, a trove reflecting both the skill of Phrygian artisans and the wealth of the rulers. Traditionally, the largest of the tombs has been associated with the name Midas.

An actual King Midas (or Mita) is said to have brought Phrygia to the apex of its power in the late eighth century BCE. Far more famous is the Midas of Greek legend, about whom we hear riveting tales of his power to turn objects to gold by touch and of his suicide by drinking bull's blood. Thus the Greeks gave the Phrygians a place in their legends as a wealthy population living in a distant country to the east. Greek and Phrygian contact influenced both people. Around the middle of the eighth century BCE the Phrygians learned to write their language in a linear alphabet closely resembling that of the early Greeks, though linguists debate which alphabet developed first. The rise of Phrygia was cut short around 700 BCE by a devastating Cimmerian invasion marked by the plundering and burning of Gordium and other important centers. Although a number of Phrygian settlements escaped major damage or revived, Phrygia no longer exerted major political influence in the region. In the sixth century BCE the kingdom fell in succession to Lydia, Media, and Persia, three ascending Near Eastern states encountered in chapters 13 and 14.

THE CIMMERIANS (C. 700–625 BCE)

The Cimmerians were a warlike people who were driven from southern Russia into the Caucasus by their kindred, the Scythians. Breaking through that formidable mountain range at the end of the eighth century BCE, the Cimmerians embarked on a ferocious rampage in Anatolia. The historic King Midas, who disappears from the records during these fearsome days, seems to have made a hasty alliance with the Assyrians in a desperate attempt to stop the invasion. In 705 BCE the Cimmerians crushed an Assyrian army somewhere in central Anatolia, a battle claiming the life of the Assyrian ruler Sargon II. Soon the horde plundered and burnt Gordium and other Phrygian settlements. The Cimmerians remained formidable until they were finally defeated by a rising power in western Anatolia—the Kingdom of Lydia—in the late seventh century BCE. The Cimmerians then withdrew to the countryside of western Anatolia near the Black Sea, where they lived an essentially nomadic existence and were gradually absorbed into the indigenous population.

THE NEO-HITTITE STATES (C. 1180–750 BCE)

After the collapse of the Hittite Empire under attacks from migrating tribes around 1180 BCE, some of its domains stretching from central and southeastern Anatolia into northern Syria continued to retain a measure of the Hittite cultural legacy for more than four centuries. These entities evolved into a multitude of independent city-states and principalities that historians term the Neo-Hittite states, all of which feared subjugation by the growing power of Assyria. The rulers of the Neo-Hittite states inscribed their monuments not in Hittite but in a dialect of closely related Luwian, using a distinctive style of pictographs (commonly called Anatolian Hieroglyphs) rather than cuneiform. Apparently the population of the Neo-Hittite states was made up of local peoples and Luwian speakers. The latter had gained political dominance after being driven from their old strongholds in western and southern Anatolia by the advance of tribes from the north (the Gasga and the Muski).

The center of each Neo-Hittite state was a heavily fortified city, such as Carchemish, which defended the crossing of the Euphrates into northern Syria and played a principal political and cultural role in the region. These cities enjoyed flourishing economies, partly resulting from their practice of collecting tolls on the major trade routes from northern Mesopotamia to Syria and Anatolia. At Carchemish and elsewhere royal palaces were adorned with heavy stone reliefs and stelae, many exhibiting an air of stark ferocity in their scenes of hunting activities, military exploits, and chariot fighting.

Outside pressure gradually undermined the Neo-Hittite states. By the tenth century BCE the nomadic Arameans were making serious incursions from east of the Euphrates, ultimately gaining control over several of the principalities. The ninth and eighth centuries BCE witnessed repeated thrusts by the aggressive Assyrians, who overwhelmed the Neo-Hittite states and absorbed them piecemeal, thus obliterating the last vestiges of their political independence.

THE KINGDOM OF URARTU (c. 850–600 BCE)

In response to strong Assyrian pressure from the south, a number of hitherto independent peoples of the Armenian mountains unified in the ninth century BCE, forming a kingdom known as Urartu that centered on Lake Van in what is now the eastern extremity of Turkey. The language of the Urartians was written in cuneiform and was closely related to Hurrian, the important non-Indo-European tongue disappearing from the records centuries earlier. Apparently both Urartian and Hurrian descended from a common mother tongue. The able Urartian kings resisted Assyrian aggression through an entrenched network of mountain fortresses. They also developed a powerful army rivaling that of the Assyrians and began expanding far afield, soon threatening the northern border of Assyria and exerting considerable influence over a number of the Neo-Hittite states of northern Syria. At the same time they interrupted the vital trade routes of the Assyrians. The eighth century BCE witnessed Assyria launching a succession of deadly military campaigns against the powerful kingdom, now its chief rival, and finally emerging victorious from a decisive battle in 743. One by one the Neo-Hittite states of northern Syria began to offer their submission to Assyria. Thereafter Urartu survived under considerably reduced circumstances until taken over by the Medes of what is now Iran in the early sixth century BCE. The Urartians soon disappeared from history, absorbed by an Indo-European-speaking people known as the Armenians, whose language is still spoken as the mother tongue of the Armenians of both Turkey and the ancient state of Armenia.

The Urartians, though much influenced at first by the older tradition of Assyria, had developed a distinctive hybrid culture known chiefly for its advances in stone architecture and metalworking. They improved Mesopotamian architectural designs by creating stone towers with battlements and buttresses that blended harmoniously with the rocky landscape. Their chief cities were enclosed by massive walls and dominated by huge citadels offering adequate capacity for the storage of wine, oil, and food in anticipation of sudden Assyrian attacks. Numerous rock inscriptions and stelae throughout the northeastern expanse of modern Turkey still proclaim the valor of Urartian kings, whose extensive royal estates were worked by warriors, prisoners of war, and slaves. Urartian artisans drew from bountiful supplies of gold, silver, and copper to achieve a new standard of excellence in metalworking. They decorated military helmets with repoussé reliefs, for example, and they worked the rims of their great cauldrons with heads of sirens, griffins, and bulls, orientalizing motifs highly influencing early Greek art. Their rich cultural tradition exerted an even greater impact on the Medes and the Persians.

CHAPTER IX

THE PHOENICIANS AND OTHER EARLY SEMITIC SPEAKERS OF SYRIA-PALESTINE

The adjoining regions known in antiquity as Syria and Palestine became home to many Semitic-speaking peoples. Among those we encounter in this chapter are the notable Phoenicians, the greatest seafarers of the ancient world in the early first millennium BCE. We turn in the next two chapters to the Hebrews, whose Scriptures made an incalculable impact on both Christianity and Islam. Syria-Palestine, though of widely fluctuating dimensions in antiquity, generally embraced all of what is now the states of Lebanon and Israel and the western portions of Syria and Jordan. With an average width of fewer than a hundred miles, the combined lands of ancient Syria and Palestine stretched along the eastern coast of the Mediterranean for about four hundred miles. This important area was hemmed in on three sides by natural boundaries: the Taurus Mountains and the upper Euphrates River in the north, the Syrian Desert in the east, and the arid heights of the Sinai Peninsula in the south, yet these barriers failed to offer substantial protection against invasion.

Largely mountainous and inhospitable, Syria-Palestine was not particularly rich in natural resources or fertility. Although a narrow coastal strip—its expanse wider in Palestine than Syria—extended along the length of the Mediterranean shore, this lowland was separated from the interior by the snow-covered Lebanon Mountains in Syria and by rugged hill country in Palestine. Such ridges and uplands served not only to compress the inhabitants of both regions near the coast but also to obstruct the westerly winter winds from the Mediterranean. The latter circumstance produced arid conditions on the eastern slopes but rainfall on the western, thereby permitting the growing of crops on that side without artificial irrigation. Yet even here precipitation was unpredictable and rather scanty, especially in the extreme south.

A characteristic feature of the hilly country of ancient Palestine was its deep fractures. The greatest of these ran from north to south to form the Jordan Valley, with its famous Jordan River linking the Sea of Galilee and the Dead Sea. This usual north-south orientation was interrupted by the Jezreel (or Esdraelon) Valley extending from the Mediterranean to the Jordan Valley and flanked by the Mount Carmel range. Turning to the northern part of Syria-Palestine, this stretch was blessed with a profusion of natural harbors as well as vast stands of the famous cedar of Lebanon, a highly valued wood for shipbuilding and construction. Many of its people became highly skilled maritime traders and shrewd timber merchants.

The settlements of Syria-Palestine were as varied as the landscape. A number on the coast developed into wealthy seaports. Others flourished as mountain

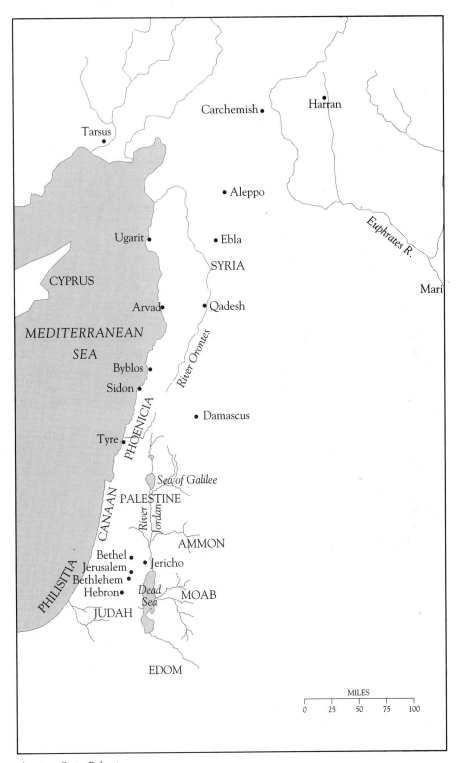

Ancient Syria-Palestine.

fortresses guarding vital valleys and passes, while some stood on the fringe of the desert to command valuable caravan routes. Yet the mountainous character of the country tended to keep the settlements divided and small, a ready target for conquest. Alien kings repeatedly invaded this terrain, for they desired its valuable timber and sought control over its seafaring coast and vital caravan routes. We saw that Syria-Palestine lay between and attracted two formidable rivals in the Late Bronze Age, the Egyptians and the Hittites. During the height of the Egyptian and Hittite empires, the former held Palestine, whereas Syria became painfully entangled first in the rivalry between Egypt and Mitanni and then between Egypt and the Hittite state. These conflicts were followed by a seemingly endless series of invasions and conquests of Syria-Palestine by neighboring peoples.

SEMITIC LANGUAGES IN SYRIA-PALESTINE

We noted in chapter 3 that Semites are people whose native tongue is one of the closely related Semitic languages, all assumed to be derived from a common unrecorded ancestor we now label Proto-Semitic. Thus any reference to Semites in general should be construed as a linguistic rather than an ethnic concept. We are uncertain where the members of this language family originated, though suggestions include territories to the north, west, and east of southern Mesopotamia. In early historical times Semitic speakers inhabited vast expanses in the Near East and formed the greater part of the population of Syria-Palestine.

Living Semitic languages are exemplified by Arabic and Hebrew, the latter revived as a vernacular only in the late nineteenth century. Such tongues have undergone many alterations through centuries of contact with other linguistic families. The ancient Semitic languages had several principal characteristics. They lacked both a neuter gender and a form for the definite article. Tense usage for expressing the time of an action was relatively undeveloped. Most verbs, nouns, and adjectives were derived from roots of three consonants. Linguists also point out that the characters of ancient Semitic alphabets denoted consonants only, though readers mentally supplied the proper vowel sounds as they read a text, as readers of Arabic script do today. The use of subordinate clauses with conjunctions being rare, all the Semitic languages tended to avoid synthesizing thoughts sharply and were characterized by a simplicity of sentence structure. From the standpoint of modern European literature, however, ancient texts in Semitic tongues seem to pulsate with a poetic and symbolic vigor.

EBLA (c. 2900–1800 BCE)

The population of the ancient city of Ebla (modern Tell Mardik) in northwest Syria spoke a Semitic language now called Eblaite. The early inhabitants of the place may have been the first substantial group of Semitic speakers in Syria. Situated on a rich agricultural plain, Ebla was already prospering by the early third millennium BCE and experienced its height from about 2600 to 2250 BCE. Archaeologists working at the site have unearthed roughly 20,000 cuneiform tablets and fragments that date from as early as about 2500 BCE, a rich source of information about the handsome city and neighboring territories. Ebla served as the capital of a remarkable northern Syrian kingdom and grew rich as an important trade center, controlling caravan routes from all points of the compass. The kingdom gained dominance over a number of city-states in north Syria and apparently even reduced large tracts of northern Mesopotamia to vassalage. Thus Ebla became a dangerous rival to the powerful Akkadian Empire centered in southern Mesopotamia. Archaeological evidence shows the city was destroyed about 2250 BCE, probably the work of the Akkadian king named Naram-Sin, who boasts of this very deed in his inscriptions. Ebla was later rebuilt and prospered until about 1800, though never regaining its former prestige and power.

THE AMORITES (c. 1800–1600 BCE)

Biblical writers speak of a number of early Semitic-speaking peoples inhabiting Syria-Palestine, though often using terms with blurred meanings. Among these groups are the seminomadic Amorites, elements of a larger population that apparently had originated on the northern fringes of the Syrian Desert and had come under the influence of the Sumero-Akkadian culture. The Akkadians sometimes mention the Amorites in their texts, calling them the Amurru. We noted in chapter 5 that the Amorite capital was the city of Babylon. The famous Amorite ruler named Hammurabi, reigning during the first half of the eighteenth century BCE, subdued the whole of Mesopotamia and forged a powerful domain that many historians call the Old Babylonian Empire. Besides dominating the history of Mesopotamia from about 1800 to 1595 BCE, the Amorites were a major force in Syria-Palestine during the same period. They spoke a tongue linguists call Amorite, one of the northwest Semitic groups of languages.

THE CANAANITES (c. 1500–1200 BCE)

Ancient texts mention a fluctuating geographical area called Canaan, generally embracing the coastal lands of Syria-Palestine and occupied today by Lebanon and Israel. The origin of the name remains obscure, possibly derived from a term referring to the rich purple or crimson dye produced from a sea snail common to the waters of the region. Biblical writers sometimes employ the designation Canaanites as a general term for the Semitic speakers forming the greater part of the population of Palestine before the period of Hebrew ascendancy in the late second millennium BCE. The people inhabiting what is now Lebanon also referred to themselves as Canaanites, though they are better known today as Phoenicians, the name the Greeks gave them at a later time. Although somewhat vague, the term Canaanites is convenient for designating the inhabitants of the entire Syro-Palestinian coast during much of the latter half of the second millennium BCE. Canaanite also has a linguistic meaning, referring not only to a family of the northwest Semitic group of languages but also a specific tongue within the family. The Canaanite family of languages developed over several millennia to include Canaanite, Phoenician, Hebrew, and Moabite.

THE PEOPLE OF UGARIT (c. 1450–1200 BCE)

Considerable information about Canaanite culture in Syria comes from the small kingdom and city-state of Ugarit, which was located near the shore in the northwestern part of the country. Excavations indicate the site—now called Ras Shamra—was occupied before 3500 BCE and flourished from about 1450 BCE until its destruction by the Sea Peoples shortly after 1200 BCE. Although ruled by a native Canaanite dynasty, Ugarit was successively a vassal state of the Hurri-Mitannians, the Egyptians, and the Hittites.

The inhabitants of Ugarit spoke with pride of their splendid harbor, and the settlement grew enormously wealthy as an international trading center lying on the crossroads of numerous caravan and sea routes. The profitable trade helped to pay for magnificent royal palaces, temples, and libraries on the acropolis. Ugarit enjoyed commercial links to Mycenaean Greece and served as the main port of entry for copper ore from the nearby island of Cyprus. Ugarit also enjoyed a profitable trade with Egypt, the venerable city of Aleppo in northern Syria on the vital route between the Orontes and the Euphrates valleys, and the major cities bordering the Euphrates River. The people of Ugarit were noted for their fine ornaments of silver and their excellent bronze work, the latter made from Cypriot copper. They also manufactured and exported cosmetics, ivories, jewelry, wooden objects, and their famous purple textiles.

The Ugaritic Alphabet.   The local scribes of Ugarit were trained in the various languages of the Near East. About 1400 BCE they learned to write their own native Canaanite dialect, now called Ugaritic, by impressing unique cuneiform symbols on clay tablets. They had devised one of the first alphabets in history, though linguists find evidence of earlier experimental forms conventionally referred to as Proto-Canaanite. In the alphabetic system, each sign represents a sound rather than an idea or a word. The cuneiform alphabet of Ugarit employed thirty signs and was read from right to left. Archaeologists have unearthed dictionaries and grammars in several languages at the site, indicative that the city was a center of learning.

Religion.   Many texts discovered at Ugarit reveal a rich Canaanite mythology anchored in more than thirty anthropomorphically conceived deities with remarkably fluctuating relationships and roles. The beliefs of Ugarit profoundly influenced the earliest religious ideas and cult practices of the Hebrews. Thus the twentieth-century decipherment of the Ugaritic cuneiform alphabet has contributed significantly to our understanding of passages in the Hebrew Bible. The supreme deity was

Sign	Equivalent	Sign	Equivalent
	ʾa		ž
	b		n
	g		ẓ
	ḫ		s
	d		ʿ
	h		p
	w		ṣ
	z		q
	ḥ		r
	ṭ		ṯ
	y		ġ
	k		t
	š		ʾi
	l		ʾu
	m		ś

The signs of the Ugaritic cuneiform alphabet and equivalents.

the wise and elderly El, the king of the gods, who presided in cosmic majesty over the world he had created. A being of inexpressible strength, El is often symbolized as a bull. His main consort was the mother-goddess Asherah, symbolized by a stylized tree near the altar at Canaanite high places, which were hills or elevated platforms used for sacrifice. Another great deity was El's youthful and vigorous son Baal, regarded not only as a fertility-god promoting agricultural life but also as a violent storm-god of the mountains.

El being a rather remote figure, Baal was the most prominent and popular deity in the pantheon. Like his father, Baal was often worshiped in the guise of a bull of unfathomable strength. The mythology of the god revolves around his death and resurrection. The people of Ugarit believed Baal, or the Lord, fought annually with his ancient opponent Mot, or Death, a god associated with parched summer soil. Baal met his death when the vegetation perished every year and was made to descend into the underworld with the clouds, wind, and rain that he dispensed, though he emerged from below at the conclusion of winter to battle furiously with Mot, forcing his enemy to enter the earth. Baal was associated in these struggles with the warlike fertility-goddess Anat. With the restoration of Baal's powers, fertility was thought to be restored on earth. Such supernatural struggles correspond to the agricultural cycle and reflect an overriding concern with the fruitfulness of flock and field upon which the very existence of the people depended. Beside such religious myths, the inhabitants of Ugarit also developed mythic hero legends. The best example is the *Legend of Keret*, the story of mythical King Keret's meditation on his fortunes and misfortunes.

THE PHOENICIANS (c. 1400–300 bce)

The Phoenicians were coastal Canaanites related both in language and culture to the people of Ugarit. For centuries they were the greatest seafarers of the ancient world. Homer sang of them, as did the prophets Isaiah and Ezekiel. They sailed the most advanced ships of the day, setting forth from their handful of tiny city-states along the eastern Mediterranean to reach the limits of the known world and perhaps even beyond. Their ancient maritime land of Phoenicia, about 160 miles long and seldom more than twenty miles wide, formed a narrow strip between sea and mountains that corresponded roughly to modern Lebanon plus an extension to the south. Although sometimes referring to themselves as Canaanites, after the whole region, these Semitic speakers usually went by the names of their cities. An inhabitant of Sidon, for example, was generally called a Sidonian. The Greeks knew these people and the other Canaanites as the *Phoinikes*, one connotation being the *reddish purple folk*, possibly a reference to the prized dye for which Phoenicia was famous throughout the ancient world. Modern historians use the term Phoenicians, derived from Greek, as a general designation for the indigenous coastal inhabitants of what is now Lebanon.

The Rise of Phoenicia as a Trading Power

Never developing a united political structure, Phoenicia remained divided into a number of autonomous city-states, each vulnerable to neighboring powers. Phoenician cities were dominated by Egypt during much of the second millennium bce. Then waves of the dreaded Sea Peoples invaded the eastern Mediterranean at the end of the thirteenth century bce and the beginning of the twelfth. Although the city of Ugarit was destroyed during these onslaughts, the Phoenicians' population centers survived and began to revive. Their city-states attained complete independence from Egyptian control by about 1100 bce, ushering in a golden age. Phoeni-

cian sailors and merchants outstripped all competitors in the sea trade of the
Mediterranean world for the next 350 years.

Phoenician Cities.   Offshore islands dotted the sea, and deep gorges hacked the
Phoenician coast into natural enclaves. All the cites of Phoenicia—among the most
famous in the ancient world—were seaports. From north to south the chief settle-
ments were Arvad (Greek Arados, Latin Aradus, modern Arwad), Gubla (biblical
Gebal, Greek Byblos, Latin Byblus, modern Jubayl), Berot (Greek Berytos, Latin
Berytus, modern Beirut or Bayrūt), Sidon (modern Saydā), and Tyre (Greek Tyros,
Latin Tyrus, modern Es Sur). The names of this scintillating cluster of ancient city-
states—conventionally known as Arvad, Byblos, Beirut (or Berytos), Sidon, and
Tyre—are liberally sprinkled on the pages of Homer and the Hebrew Scriptures.
Whenever feasible, these cities were built on land jutting into the sea or on offshore
islands. The inhabitants, who were protected by lofty stone walls and towers, lived
in tightly packed houses of several stories with balconies. Apparently kingship was
the oldest form of government in the various Phoenician city-states. The kings and
their families claimed divine descent, though monarchal power was limited by the
powerful merchant class.

Byblos.   Having a profitable trade with both Cyprus and Egypt, Gubla (the Greek
Byblos) remained the preeminent Phoenician city-state until the beginning of the
first millennium BCE. Egypt exported papyrus to the city in exchange for Phoenician
products such as the highly valued cedar of Lebanon. Apparently papyrus came to
Greece through Phoenician intermediaries. The Greek word for papyrus was *byblos.*
So closely did the Greeks identify Gubla with the writing material that they began
calling the city Byblos around the end of the second millennium BCE. From the
word *byblos* came the later Greek word *biblion* (book). When the stormy pronouncements of the Hebrew prophets were translated into Greek, papyrus gave its name to
the sacred texts. Thus the English word Bible is derived from the Greek *biblia*
(books).

Egypt exercised considerable control over Byblos during much of the second
millennium BCE. The city served as a distribution center for Egyptian goods, and
countless vessels plying the Nile were hewn from the durable cedars of Lebanon. We
saw that the influence of Egypt in Phoenician affairs increasingly weakened after
the invasions of the Sea Peoples. The Egyptian narrative work called *The Adventures of Wenamon* tells of the ill-starred mission of an Egyptian priest named Wenamon to Byblos to buy timber for a ceremonial barge about 1100 BCE. The
Phoenicians treated him with scorn and contempt, an indication of how far New
Kingdom Egypt had declined in the eyes of its former vassals.

Tyre and Sidon.   By this time Sidon and especially Tyre had risen above Byblos in
terms of commercial power. King Hiram I of Tyre (c. 970–936 BCE) was the leading
monarch in the Phoenician cities of his day. He built an almost impregnable port at
Tyre by using boulders and rubble to join together two offshore islands, creating a

citadel on the sea. On the north and south shores of the newly unified island, majestic sea walls went up to serve as shields for two grand harbors within the protective embrace of the unique isle.

The Hebrew kings David (c. 1000–961 BCE) and Solomon (c. 961–922 BCE) entered into treaties with Hiram, who provided the latter with building materials and artisans for the construction of his Temple at Jerusalem dedicated to Yahweh, the god of the Hebrews. Solomon's Temple and its lavish trappings were influenced, no doubt, by Phoenician models. The willingness of Hiram to provide Solomon with assistance of this scope probably stemmed from a Phoenician deficiency in agriculture. The biblical account reports that Solomon gave the Tyrian king an annual payment of wheat and oil in exchange for providing the building materials and skilled workers (I Kings 5:11).

PHOENICIAN CULTURE AND MARITIME VENTURES

For centuries the Phoenicians borrowed from the cultures of neighboring lands such as Egypt, Cyprus, Greece, Anatolia, and Mesopotamia, though without relinquishing their own creative genius. Sailing ever westward, they made a profound contribution to the ancient world by transmitting elements of their eclectic and cosmopolitan culture to the western Mediterranean.

The Phoenician Alphabet.   One of the greatest achievements of the Phoenicians was their famous alphabet of twenty-two letters, which had gradually evolved from earlier Semitic alphabets such as that of Ugarit. Linguists find evidence that this writing system had become standardized into the form we know as Phoenician shortly before 1000 BCE. Each of the Phoenician signs, written from right to left, stood for a consonantal sound. Spread by Phoenician seafarers over the Mediterranean world, the Phoenician alphabet (*aleph, beth, gimel. . .*) was almost certainly borrowed, in modified form, by the Greeks to fashion their own writing system (*alpha, beta, gamma. . .*). The Greeks took the final great step in the development of alphabetic writing by employing specific symbols for vowels, and they carried their alphabet throughout the European world. All modern western alphabets are Greek derived and thus are probable descendants of the Phoenician writing system.

Religion.   The Phoenicians inherited the essentials of their religion from their Canaanite neighbors, with cultic practices revolving around the interwoven concerns of death and fertility. One of the ways that Phoenician men encountered the divine was through sexual relations with female or male temple prostitutes. Moreover, Phoenician worshipers offered incense, fruit, wine, and live animals in their many temples to bribe or appease heaven. Each animal was killed and dismembered, and at least some part of the victim was burned on an altar. Apparently children also were sacrificed in Phoenicia, though possibly only during times of extreme calamity. The Phoenician colony of Carthage, whose inhabitants had a reputation for extreme cruelty, has yielded thousands of urns containing the charred bones of sacrificed children. The Hebrews, occupying the area south of Phoenicia, also practiced

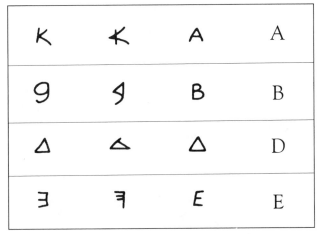

K	⟨	A	A
9	⟨	B	B
△	△	△	D
⅃	⅂	E	E

Early alphabetic writing originated in the Levant about 1600 BCE and gradually evolved into fully alphabetic systems and modern alphabets. Some important stages in this development are represented above. The first column shows four letters of the Canaanite script, as written in the late second millennium BCE, which evolved in various phases, including Early Phoenician and Greek, represented in the second and third columns, to the Roman letters employed in most modern western scripts.

some form of human sacrifice in early times and even occasionally at a relatively late date, at least until the prophet Jeremiah and others strongly condemned the rites in the seventh century BCE (Jer. 7:31, 19:5, cf. Lev. 18:21, Judg. 12:31, 2 Kings 23:10, 2 Chron. 33:6).

Reluctant to employ statues of their deities, the Phoenicians preferred to represent them with amorphous cult stones and empty thrones. El stood at the head of their pantheon, though Baal was a more important figure because he produced the storms bringing the annual revival of vegetation. Baal assumed numerous manifestations, under slightly changing names. His powerful consort is usually referred to by her Greek name Astarte (Phoenician Ashtart, biblical Ashtoreth). She bore the title Queen of Heaven and functioned primarily as a goddess of sexual love, fertility, and war. Quite natural in a goddess of fertility, promiscuity was central to her being, and Astarte and her cult prostitution was popular throughout much of the ancient Near East. The potent fertility-goddess Ishtar was her Mesopotamian equivalent. The later Greeks identified Astarte with powerful goddesses such as Aphrodite and Artemis. The Hebrew king Solomon was criticized in the biblical account for glorifying and worshiping Astarte (1 Kings 11:5, 33). She was seldom worshiped alone, however, because a young male deity that the Phoenicians called Adon—another manifestation of Baal—was usually by her side. Of the sundry local variations of this god, the most notable is the Babylonian deity Tammuz (the Sumerian Dumuzi).

Adon was a god of fertility and vegetation who died at the beginning of the summer from wounds inflicted by a wild boar, but Astarte descended to the netherworld

Stamped with Phoenician influence, this gold pendant from Tell el-Ajjul represents a fertility goddess (possibly Astarte), the schematic design showing her head, breasts, belly, and vulva. c. 1600 BCE. The Israel Museum, Jerusalem.

to rescue him from the hands of death. His yearly death and resurrection reflected the Near Eastern preoccupation with the vital agricultural cycle. The Adon River (modern Nahr Ibrahim) near Byblos was sacred to the god. The river takes on a red color every spring when prevailing winds blow a great quantity of dust from the red earth of the region into its tributary mountain streams. Ancient worshipers believed the waters had undergone a miraculous transformation into Adon's sacred blood. Devotees came from Byblos and elsewhere to the shrine of the god near the source of the river to celebrate his death and springtime resurrection with various rites, including orgiastic ceremonies, which took place during an annual summer festival known as the Adonia. From the fifth century BCE, festivals in his honor were held also in Greece, where he was known as Adonis.

Technology and Art.   Although much of their trade was in products manufactured by others, the Phoenicians adapted numerous techniques and artistic styles from

Egypt, Mesopotamia, and the Aegean world to achieve a very high level in their own industries, especially shipbuilding, cloth dying, weaving, jeweling, metalworking, ivory carving, and glassmaking. Many of their products were true masterpieces and in great demand over a wide area stretching from Mesopotamia to Spain. Archaeological exploration has uncovered a large assortment of their coveted ivory carvings at modern Nimrud, the site of an ancient capital of Assyria. Acquiring the art of glassmaking from the Egyptians, the Phoenicians excelled in making glass bowls and bottles as well as necklaces of glass beads. They fashioned textiles—woven from flax, cotton, and wool—into their customary clothing of pointed caps, close-fitting tunics, and long flowing robes. Extracting dye from a local sea snail, the murex, the Phoenicians were famous for a dying process that yielded textiles in brilliant colors ranging from pink to a lustrous deep purple. So valued was the deepest shade of purple that for centuries the color was called *royal purple* and was reserved in many places for monarchs and others of high rank, thus the expression "born to the purple."

Trade and Colonization.   With minimal land to exploit, the Phoenicians turned to seaborne trade at an early period. A steady stream of ships passed between Byblos and Egypt in the third and second millennia BCE. We saw that by the beginning of the first millennium BCE the Phoenicians had become extremely prosperous by outstripping all others in the maritime trade of the Mediterranean. Their political and commercial influence along the coasts of the Levant in the tenth century BCE is exemplified by the naval assistance that Hiram of Tyre gave Solomon, notably seamen and pilots to operate a fledgling Hebrew commercial fleet operating from the Gulf of Aqaba.

Phoenician warships, which escorted merchant vessels, were a hundred feet or more in length and provided with high sterns and bows. Heavy and broad, driven by both sails and oars, these ships had two banks of rowers—one above another—and served as a model for certain early Greek warships. The Phoenicians made incredible voyages on their strong ships to explore increasingly distant routes. The Greek historian Herodotus even attributes them with circumnavigating Africa. They managed to sail at night by observing the North Star, probably the first seafarers to navigate in such a fashion. Aside from these feats, the Phoenicians are deservedly famous for the colonies and trading stations they established in Cyprus, Rhodes, Anatolia, Crete, Egypt, Sicily, Malta, Sardinia, the Balearic Islands, Marseilles, southern Spain, North Africa, the Atlantic coast of Africa, and possibly even Cornwall in Britain.

Carthage.   The most famous of all Phoenician colonies was Carthage on the coast of North Africa, traditionally founded by settlers from Tyre in 814 BCE. Originally a trading station and city—its name means New City—employed by Phoenician ships bound for faraway Spain, Carthage grew into a great metropolitan port. Phoenicia had already come under the domination of Assyria, whose kings were determined to control the trade routes from Mesopotamia to the Mediterranean, and Carthage increasingly took on the role of protector of the Phoenician colonies, ultimately welding them together into an extremely powerful empire that challenged the Greeks and later the Romans for control of the western Mediterranean.

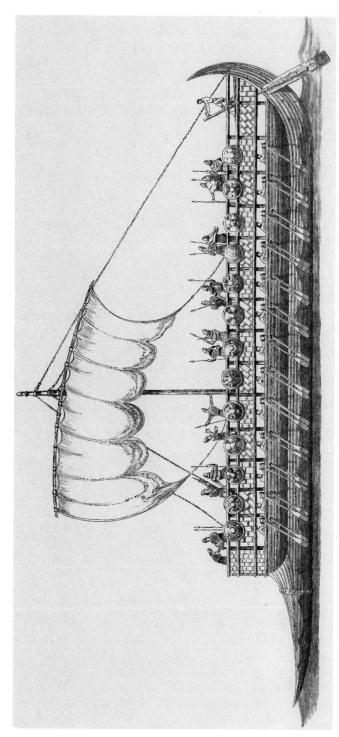

The Phoenician warship, based on an Assyrian relief. These vessels escorted merchant ships and were known for their speed, afforded by a combination of sail and two banks of rowers, one of which was hidden from outside view.

THE DECLINE OF THE PHOENICIAN CITY-STATES

As for the city-states of Phoenicia, Assyrian kings forced them to pay tribute from the ninth century until 612 BCE, when the heartland of Assyria was invaded and destroyed. Phoenicia soon came under the yoke of Neo-Babylonia, though Tyre withstood a siege of thirteen years before its capture in 572 BCE. The fall of Tyre was a final blow to Phoenician power, and the old trading preeminence was gradually lost to neighboring countries, though the Phoenicians themselves remained famous and active as seafarers for centuries. The Phoenician cities continued in a state of vassalage to Babylonia until they were captured by the Persians in the sixth century BCE. Thereafter Phoenicia fell successively to Alexander the Great in the fourth century BCE and to the Romans in the first century BCE. Long before the advent of Roman rule, however, Phoenicia had lost a large measure of its distinctive stamp to the Greek-tinctured culture known as Hellenistic, diffused throughout the territories conquered by Alexander.

THE ARAMEANS (c. 1200–720 BCE)

We first hear of the Arameans, another Semitic-speaking people, as nomads roaming the Syrian Desert and marauding neighboring territories. Taking advantage of the destruction of the Hittite Empire in the early twelfth century BCE and the relative weakness of Assyria and Babylonia at the time, they began seizing large parts of Syria and Mesopotamia, gradually forming a network of city-state kingdoms as they advanced. Their most important holdings fell on the eastern side of the Lebanon Mountains and extended from Damascus northward to the great bend of the Euphrates River. Damascus, believed by many scholars to be the oldest continuously inhabited city in the world, was a valuable caravan center.

Their nomadic origins served the Arameans well in trading ventures. They became the principal traders of the entire region stretching from the Persian Gulf to the Mediterranean, thereby creating a great commercial empire. Yet the aggressive Assyrians were now marshaling their military might and reaching for a new pinnacle of power. After 900 BCE determined Assyrian armies routed the Arameans and again extended the Assyrian reach to northern Syria and the mountains of Anatolia. The Assyrians gradually absorbed the western Aramean cities, though Damascus did not fall until 732 BCE. Notwithstanding the loss of political independence, the Arameans continued their vital trading activities, carrying their system of weights and measures—adopted in the Assyrian and Persian empires—as well as their language over much of the ancient Near East.

Aramaic.   By the time of the fall of Damascus to the Assyrians, the language of the Arameans— Aramaic—had been widely disseminated from Egypt to Babylonia. Aramaic is a northwest Semitic language closely related to Phoenician and Hebrew and was usually written in the twenty-two letters of the Phoenician alphabet. The cumbersome cuneiform scripts could not compete with its flexibility, and the seventh and sixth centuries BCE witnessed Aramaic in its various dialects gradually

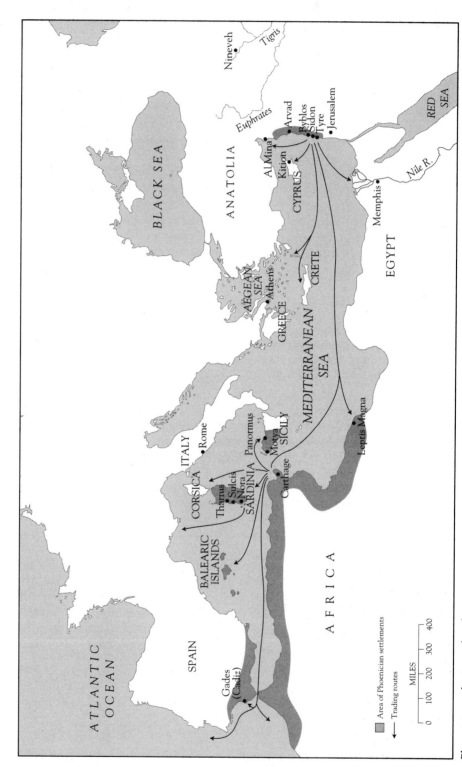

Phoenician colonies and trade routes.

supplanting Akkadian as the lingua franca—or international language—of the Near East. Aramaic became the administrative language of the Persian Empire, founded in the second half of the sixth century BCE, though replaced there by Greek after the conquests of Alexander the Great. Greek later served as the lingua franca of the eastern half of the Roman Empire. Yet Aramaic-speaking groups continued to circulate as merchants and traders as well as soldiers and slaves. Apparently Aramaic was the dominant spoken language in Palestine by the first century BCE, though Greek had made serious inroads, and Hebrew survived both as a vernacular and a sacred language. Presumably, Aramaic in various dialects was the everyday language of Jesus and most of the earliest Christians, who were Palestinian Jews.

THE PHILISTINES (c. 1190–700 BCE)

Among the elusive Sea Peoples that Ramses III repulsed from the Nile Delta in the early twelfth century BCE were the Peleset. The Egyptian king acquiesced in their settlement on the southern coastal strip of Palestine, apparently hoping the Peleset would serve as vassals protecting his valuable trade routes to the north, but his successors proved incapable of maintaining control over the area. Remaining a distinct group for many centuries, the Peleset eventually gave their name to the whole of the land—Palestine—while they became known to history by their biblical name of Philistines. Historians refer to the coastal district where they settled as Philistia.

The Philistines established five city-states: Ashdod, Ashkelon, and Gaza on the coast, and Ekron and Gath inland. Each was ruled by its own lord, but all combined into an Aegean-style confederacy during wartime. Although virtually nothing is known of the Philistine's non-Semitic language, which gradually died out because they adopted a local Canaanite dialect, archaeological investigation points to an extremely rich and highly developed Philistine culture. Early styles of dress, pottery, and armor seem to suggest an Aegean origin. The Philistines enjoyed an extensive knowledge of agriculture and may have introduced the vine and olive to the region. They fashioned olive presses and established an extremely profitable oil industry. The effectiveness of their powerful army, trained by a warrior overlord class, stemmed partly from their monopoly on the iron now arriving in the country for the first time in any quantity. The Philistines also maintained a virtual monopoly on the smithing and use of the metal, denying iron weapons and tools to their neighbors. Their storied fighting ability and their control of iron permitted them to dominate all of Palestine during the twelfth and eleventh centuries BCE.

Their inland expansion soon led to conflicts with the Hebrews, who occupied the hills of Palestine beyond the coastal plain. The Hebrews held the Philistines in utter contempt, partly because the latter did not practice circumcision, the removal of the foreskin of the penis. The sagas of Samson and Delilah and of David and Goliath in the Hebrew Bible represent colorful accounts of the early struggles of the two groups, as told from the Hebrew viewpoint. The Hebrews finally organized a monarchy in the late eleventh century BCE in an effort to counter the enemy. Calling upon their superior arms and military organization, the Philistines prevailed until the

The Assyrians, under King Sargon II, besiege the Philistine city of Ekron in 712 BCE. This nineteenth-century engraving is based on a wall relief from Sargon's palace at Khorsabad.

famous Hebrew king named David overwhelmed them in battle and confined them to their narrow coastal strip in the early tenth century BCE. Philistia came under the loose hegemony of Egypt in the same century and was conquered by Assyria in the eighth. The Babylonian king Nebuchadnezzar utterly destroyed the Philistine cities at the close of the next century, and the Philistines suddenly disappear from the historical record, virtually without a trace. Later centuries would witness Philistia itself falling successively under the domination of Persia, Greece, and Rome.

CHAPTER X

THE HEBREWS

The derivation of the word Hebrew remains uncertain. Although the Hebrews generally referred to themselves as the Israelites, or the Children of Israel, they also applied the alternative designation Hebrews, especially in earlier times. They abandoned the term Israelites as a general name for themselves after the division of their kingdom in the second half of the tenth century BCE. Thus the designation Hebrews is a convenient appellation to distinguish them from the other peoples of the ancient Near East until the late sixth century BCE, when they became known as the Jews. In many respects the Hebrews were unique among the inhabitants of the earth. They wrote the sacred classic called the Hebrew Bible, one of the most influential works of all time. Incorporated in the Christian Scriptures as the Old Testament, the Hebrew Bible left an indelible imprint upon both Christianity and Islam.

By around the tenth century BCE some members of the Hebrew elite had learned to write their language, Hebrew, which belongs to the Canaanite family of the northwest Semitic group of languages. We read of "the language of Canaan" in the Hebrew Bible (Isa. 19:18), for the word *Hebrew* was not applied to the tongue until the Hellenistic period beginning hundreds of years later. About the time the Hebrews learned to write, they began to record their oral ancestor traditions—which they supplemented by a considerable amount of historical material—thereby creating texts that gradually evolved into the Hebrew Bible. Their history, from a secular viewpoint, is that of a people inhabiting a minor country overshadowed by the more powerful and brilliant states of antiquity. Their Bible is not primarily concerned about secular history, however, for the Hebrews regarded their Scriptures as a record of *sacred* history, a narrative of events providing revelations of the ultimate meaning of human existence. They believed their deity was the lord and ruler of the universe and that he operated through history to set forth and disclose his grand design for humanity.

ORIGIN AND HISTORY OF THE HEBREWS

THE LEGENDARY BIBLICAL STORY

The book of Genesis contains many legendary narratives, appearing sometimes in duplicate or even triplicate form, which provide the only direct source for the origin of the Hebrews. The earliest nonbiblical reference to the Hebrews occurs on a triumphal stela, dated about 1200 BCE, from the reign of the Egyptian king Merneptah. The Merneptah inscription indicates that a people known as Israel inhabited

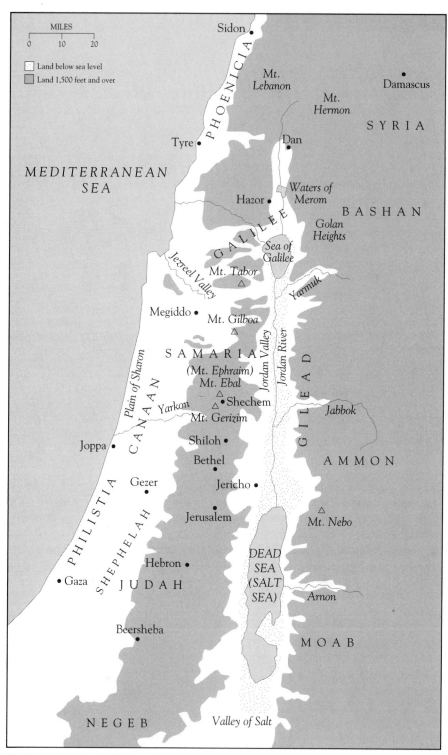

The land of ancient Palestine.

Palestine at the time. Given the uncertainties that arise from the biblical narrative and the dearth of extrabiblical documentary evidence, scholars hold a range of theories regarding the history of the Hebrews.

The Patriarchs and Matriarchs.   A widely supported view regards most of the early Hebrews, though of diverse origin, as indigenous to Canaan, but the book of Genesis presents them as foreigners originating in Mesopotamia. Genesis contains well-known legends about their reputed ancestors, frequently called the patriarchs (Abraham, Isaac, and Jacob) and the matriarchs (Sarah, Rebekah, Leah, Rachel, and others), but we do not know if these stories are based on the lives of actual historical individuals. The Hebrews' own folklore traces their origin as an identifiable ethnic group back to the elusive Abraham (originally known as Abram). The Abraham saga, a rich mosaic of peoples and individuals, tells us that Abraham was a pastoralist with substantial herds and flocks who departed from his homeland in Mesopotamia (Genesis 11:28–12:5 seems to suggest two widely separated places—Ur in southern Mesopotamia or Haran in the northern region). Accompanied by his wife Sarah (originally known as Sarai) and his nephew Lot, Abraham is said to have eventually led a clan of the Hebrews to Canaan, an ancient name for the part of Palestine lying west of the Jordan River. One of the stories in Genesis relates that a divine being bestowed the name Israel on the patriarch Jacob, Abraham's grandson, after wrestling with him. The biblical narrative also depicts the Hebrews as descendants of Jacob's twelve sons, each being an ancestor of a tribe named after him. We are told that during a severe famine the family of Jacob left Canaan and settled in Egypt, where their kinsman Joseph had risen to a position of importance in the government. Scholars regard these colorful biblical stories as generally legendary accounts that were subject to considerable variation and embroidery during their oral transmission.

The Exodus.   Subsequently, according to the biblical narrative, the Hebrews were reduced to performing burdensome tasks in the Goshen district until they made their great escape from Egypt—the Exodus—under the leadership of Moses. No existing Egyptian source even hints at an Exodus, though the biblical account reports the Egyptians suffered such cataclysmic afflictions associated with the event that their king, who is unnamed, was forced to allow the Hebrews to leave the country. Apparently the biblical narrative of a long sojourn in Egypt followed by a dramatic escape is a late Hebrew adaptation of an earlier story in wide circulation throughout Egypt and the Levant. In short, the biblical account is replete with complexities and raises serious credibility problems. Yet the Exodus remains the central event of the Hebrew Scriptures, a national epic that left a deep psychological impression on the Hebrews, gave them a sense of national consciousness, and endowed them with a belief they had been chosen by the deity to whom they committed themselves. Commemorated to this day by the spring festival of the Passover, the Exodus provided the Hebrews with the cornerstone of their religion.

Moses.   The second biblical book, Exodus, tells the story of the Hebrews' deliverance from Egyptian bondage and their stay at Sinai. The biblical narrative relates that they made their escape under the leadership of a man with an Egyptian name, rendered in English as Moses (Hebrew *Moseh*), a Hebrew who had grown up in the Egyptian royal court after being rescued as a babe from the Nile. We are told that Moses led the Hebrews into the wilderness. After nearly three months of wandering, according to the biblical account, they came to Mount Sinai (also called Horeb), traditionally located somewhere on the peninsula of the same name, where they encamped and worshiped a deity who used the peaks of the mountain for meetings with humans.

THE YAHWEH CULT

The Sacred Name Yahweh.   The Hebrews and other peoples of the ancient Near East believed that a name revealed the intrinsic nature of a person or a deity, an idea reflected in biblical accounts of an individual's name being changed in response to a critical alteration in status or personality. One name of the god of Mount Sinai, as rendered in English, must have been Yh. Because vowels were nor written in early Semitic alphabets, we can only guess that the name was pronounced Yah (yäh). The English word hallelujah (hallelu-yah), of Hebrew derivation, means *praise Yah* and was frequently employed in its Hebrew form as a shout of praise—a solemn cultic cry—to Yah. The Hebrews spoke this personal name of their god until they learned to write around the tenth century BCE, thereafter prohibiting its utterance, reflecting a fear that vocalizing the sacred name might give humans power over the deity. By this time the name was rendered by four letters, transliterated in English as YHWH. Vowels were not used in the spelling until the Christian era, when the name was written Yahweh.

The divine name was explained in the biblical book of Exodus to mean "I am who [or what] I am" (Exod. 3:14), though that was not its original meaning, a subject about which scholars disagree. One interpretation regards the sacred name itself—like the word hallelujah—as originally a cultic cry denoting religious fervor. Other suggestions include the possibility that the name is not of Hebrew origin and may be derived from the Aramaic *to fall* or the Arabic *to blow*, the latter supporting a view that Yahweh was originally a storm-god. When reading the Bible aloud, later Jews substituted the title of honor Adonai (my Lord) for the personal name Yahweh.

The Covenant at Sinai.   The biblical account relates the Hebrews made a covenant with Yahweh at Mount Sinai, that is, a binding relationship with the deity based on their promises and obligations. This was similar to the political treaties of vassalage in the ancient Near East, with a suzerain offering protection to vassals in return for their loyalty. Thus the relationship of Yahweh to the Hebrews was to be patterned on the model of a king to his subjects. We read that with Moses acting as their mediator, the Hebrews promised Yahweh to obey his laws in return for his protection and for being his "own possession among all peoples" of the earth (Exod. 19:5). In short, Yahweh set the Hebrews completely apart from others in exchange for a commitment to honor a collection of laws embracing many aspects of life, the so-called Book of the Covenant, which biblical scholars have identified as an independent unit inserted into the Sinai tradition of the book of Exodus (Exod. 20:22–23:33). For the most part, the Covenant Code betrays the interests of an agricultural rather than a wilderness setting and reflects a later adaptation of Canaanite and other laws to the covenant tradition.

The Ten Commandments.   The core of Yahweh's demands is concisely formulated as the Ten Commandments (also called the Decalogue). Through linguistic analysis, scholars have determined the Commandments have undergone a lengthy development. Moreover, the Hebrew Bible contains two versions, one in Exodus (Exod. 20:1–17) and another in the fifth book, Deuteronomy (Deut. 5:6–21). Originally each commandment seems to have been in the form of a short unconditional demand that lacked the explanatory comments some of them gained through a later expansion of the text. To take but one example reflecting the lengthy development of the Commandments, Exodus 20:8–11 links the Sabbath obligation to Yahweh's rest on the seventh day, whereas Deuteronomy 5:12–15 links the same commandment to the escape from Egypt.

THE "CONQUEST" OF CANAAN

The biblical narrative tells us that after the Hebrews wandered for a while in the desert, Yahweh gave them permission to conquer the land of Canaan, specifically promised to Abraham, the promise reaffirmed to his descendants, and renewed in the time of Moses. Lying between the Mediterranean coast and the Jordan Valley, ancient Canaan generally enjoyed a Mediterranean climate of hot, dry summers and rainy winters, subject to considerable modification as the result of varying altitudes. Its topography included four main zones: the coastal plain in the east, the central hill country farther inland, the Jordan Valley in the west, and the mountainous desert region called the Negeb in the south. The Jordan Valley, the result of a deep fracture parting the land lengthwise from north to south, was furrowed by the famous river of the same name linking the Sea of Galilee and the Dead Sea. An important secondary fracture—the Jezreel Valley—extended from the Mediterranean to the Jordan Valley and provided a ready avenue for both traders and warriors. Much of the country was better suited to pasturage than to farming, but the coastal plain, the Jezreel Valley, and the northern part of the Jordan Valley—the vicinity of the Sea of Galilee—were relatively fertile. Although the seaboard was dotted with several harbors, they could not match the exceptional Phoenician ports to the north.

Contrasting stories of the conquest of the Promised Land of Canaan appear in the biblical books of Joshua and Judges. The account in Joshua 1–11 relates that after the death of Moses, his former disciple Joshua led the united Hebrew tribes across the Jordan River. They captured the city of Jericho, their trumpets blaring, and subjugated the rest of Canaan through a ruthless extermination of the inhabitants, a campaign taking only five years and witnessing the easy fall of many massively fortified cities. Judges 1, however, attributes the conquest of Canaan to the actions of separate tribes or small groups of tribes over an extended period, their efforts frequently producing inconclusive results.

Many scholars seriously challenge the familiar biblical stories of nomads fresh off the desert conquering the Promised Land, instead regarding the Hebrews themselves as essentially Canaanites. Archaeological findings show the onset of a period in the thirteenth century BCE marked by famine and plague as well as the destructive activities of the Sea Peoples, afflictions marking the end of the Bronze Age. The archaeological record suggests some Canaanite survivors of these calamities, possibly augmented by a small number of refugees from Egypt, fled from the coastal plain and established scattered villages in the central hill country shortly after 1250 BCE, becoming what archaeologists might term early Hebrews, mainly a society of farmers and herders.

EARLY HEBREW RELIGION ANCHORED IN THE CANAANITE FERTILITY CULT

The culture and religion of the early Hebrews was closely tied to the Canaanite traditions. We saw that the Canaanite pantheon was headed by the senior god El. His prolific chief consort Asherah bore seventy deities, including the mighty storm-god Baal, or the Lord, the most prominent figure in the fertility cult of Canaan. A typical Near Eastern god of death, resurrection, and fertility, Baal frequently took the form of a bull—a powerful symbol of reproduction—and was considered the creator of humankind. His chief consort Astarte, a great Canaanite goddess of fertility, was often referred to as Baalat, or his Lady. The Canaanites also acknowledged local manifestations of Baal, known collectively as the Baalim. The Baal of each locality was thought to possess a specific area of ground and control its fertility.

The Canaanite religion was highly erotic in the sense of interpreting the rhythms of agriculture in terms of human sexuality, the age-old fertility principle of the ancient Near East. One of the religious obligations of the Canaanites was the ritual enactment in their temples of Baal's lovemaking activities as a magical aid to promote fruitfulness. Thus sacred prostitution played a prominent role in the fertility cult, with worshipers accepting the ancient principle that ritual sexual practices provided access to the divine. When a male participant and a female prostitute were joined in sexual intercourse in the temple, the former identified with Baal and the latter with Astarte, each believing their imitation of the copulation of the god and his consort might bring the divine Lord and his Lady together in a fertilizing union. Another variety gave male participants sexual access to male prostitutes. In short, temple prostitution was regarded as both an avenue for sensual pleasure and a magical rite promoting the fertility of nature.

The early Hebrews shared in the Canaanite agricultural cult and worshiped both El and Baal. Biblical writers frequently identify Yahweh with El (e.g., Gen. 14:18–20, 22, 33:20, Exod. 6:3). Cumulative scriptural and archaeological evidence suggests a pairing of El's chief consort Asherah with Yahweh. The biblical narrative tells us the sacred symbol of the goddess—a stylized tree (asherah)—sometimes stood in Yahweh's Temple at Jerusalem (2 Kings 18:4, 21:7, 23:6), as did vessels dedicated to her (2 Kings 23:4). Many Hebrews seem to have been devoted to her, perhaps even worshiping the goddess as a consort of Yahweh. Archaeologists discovered startling evidence from the eighth century BCE at the remote site of Kun-tillet Ajrud southwest of the Dead Sea, a storage jar bearing the inscription "Yah-weh and his Asherah." Below the inscription is a painting of three figures, two of which are thought to represent Yahweh and Asherah.

In this early period the Hebrews seem to have regarded the worship of both Yahweh and Baal as entirely legitimate. They appealed to the Baalim to provide them with grain and wine, herds and flocks. They even addressed Yahweh as Baal on occasion, continuing this practice at least until the eighth century BCE (Hos. 2:16). Altars dedicated to Baal stood in Yahweh's Temple at Jerusalem as late as the seventh century BCE (2 Kings 21:2–4). The Hebrews frequently named their chil-dren after Baal. Their famous kings Saul (c. 1026–1004 BCE) and David (c. 1000–961 BCE) had sons with Baal names (1 Chron. 8:33, 14:7).

Strictly speaking, belief in more than one deity was not in conflict with the Ten Commandments. The First Commandment instructs the Hebrews to put Yahweh first among the gods, nowhere denying their existence. The Commandment simply makes a demand: "You shall have no other gods before me" because "I . . . am a jeal-ous God. . . ." (Exod. 20:3–4). The biblical book of Deuteronomy, probably com-posed in the seventh century BCE, asserts that Yahweh has allotted the worship of other deities "to all the peoples under the whole heaven," with the exception of the Hebrews, who have been set aside as "a people of his own possession. . . ." (Deut. 4:19–20). We find here a clear expression of Yahweh's suzerainty over his chosen people, but certainly not a belief in monotheism.

THE BOOK OF JUDGES

The biblical book of Judges continues the Genesis-Joshua narrative and purports to cover the history of the Hebrew tribes from the time of the "conquest" of Canaan until just before the establishment of the monarchy in the second half of the eleventh century BCE. Although the later Hebrews looked upon this era as a heroic age, the book is robbed of credence by its countless anachronisms, contradictions, and incredible details. Specifically, the book tells stories of certain deliverers, who were called judges by the English translators of the Hebrew Bible, though the office was not primarily one of administering justice. Instead, the judges are portrayed as tribal heroes or charismatic military leaders in times of war, with authority generally limited to the duration of a crisis. The reader is left to suppose they exercised lead-ership over a unified coalition of twelve tribes, yet closer examination shows the biblical stories involve local rather than national events.

We are told that one of the great military leaders during this period was a woman named Deborah, a judge and a prophet who formed a coalition of tribes to defeat a superior Canaanite army in the Jezreel Valley. The poetic account of her victory, known as the Song of Deborah, which comprises all of Judges 5, may be the oldest extant biblical poem. Possibly dating from the later twelfth century BCE, the composition echoes the rhythmic pulse and poetic parallelism of Ugaritic verse. Other individuals mentioned as judges—exemplified by Gideon (also called Jerub-baal) and the herculean Sampson—were extolled in prose and verse. Gideon is said to have triumphed over the elusive Midianites, while the legendary stories about Samson tell of a hero whose undisciplined sexual passions curtailed his exploits over the Philistines.

THE HEBREWS AND THE PHILISTINES

The Philistines—originating as one of the marauding Sea Peoples—posed a serious threat to the Hebrews. After being repulsed from Egypt shortly after 1180 BCE, the Philistines settled on the Canaanite coast. Their celebrated fighting ability and their advanced weapons, both in bronze and iron, permitted them to dominate Canaan during the twelfth and eleventh centuries BCE. Their expansion led to conflicts with the Hebrews occupying the central hills. The Philistines embarked upon a major offensive against the Hebrews in the eleventh century and crushed them about 1050 BCE in two battles near a place called Ebenezer, where the foothills met the coastal plain. The Philistines then established garrisons in the Hebrew hill country and dominated the region.

The biblical narrative tells us the Philistines, in the second battle of Ebenezer, captured the Ark of the Covenant, the most venerated of all Hebrew sacred objects. We read that the Hebrews had carried the Ark from the time of the Exodus until they crossed the Jordan into the land of Canaan. The biblical account portrays the Ark as a wooden chest serving as a dwelling of Yahweh, a parallel to the Egyptian belief that gods reside in portable shrines. The Hebrews also regarded the Ark as a portable throne upon which Yahweh sat and led his people into battle as their monarch. We hear the sacred chest contained two stone tablets—holy objects Yahweh reputedly presented to Moses on Mount Sinai—inscribed with the Ten Commandments. The Ark was thought to be of such sacredness that were an unauthorized individual to touch it, even accidently, this sacrilege demanded instant punishment by death (2 Sam. 6:6–7). Yet the Philistines are said to have safely carried the Ark of the Covenant off to their city of Ashdod as a trophy of war after defeating the Hebrews at Ebenezer.

THE EARLY MONARCHY: SAUL AND ISHBAAL (C. 1026–1000 BCE)

Saul (c. 1026–1004 BCE).   The iron-wielding Philistines were so successful in dominating the central hill country that the need for Hebrew political unity became increasingly imperative in the late eleventh century BCE. According to one of the conflicting accounts in the book of 1 Samuel, a soothsayer-priest-prophet named Samuel, the last of the judges, reluctantly gave his blessing to the election of a king. We read he anointed Saul—a proven fighter from the warlike but small tribe of Benjamin—to become the first national monarch. Anointing, or the application of oil as a sign of consecration, was part of the ceremonial of enthronement in the ancient Near East. The Hebrew rite was thought to convey power from Yahweh for exercising royal authority and to render the king's person sacrosanct.

The authority of the warrior-king Saul did not extend far beyond the central hill country. His own tribe of Judah in the south was considered on the fringe of his kingdom. Saul devoted much of his reign to fighting the Philistines in the west and various desert tribes in the east. Apparently he was generally successful when he confined his military endeavors to the hills but was unable to win battles fought on the open plain. The king was burdened, moreover, by both the displeasure of Samuel and the ambition of a young charismatic warrior named David, the latter constantly maneuvering to draw popular support away from him and eventually becoming a deadly rival. The plot was complicated by the intimate friendship of David and the crown prince Jonathan and by the marriage of David and Michal, the king's daughter, whose hand was bought with the foreskins of two hundred slaughtered Philistines. Saul finally declared David an outlaw, and his youthful adversary fled to the Philistines for refuge, becoming a mercenary in their army. The situation became hopeless for the king when his forces were crushed attacking the Philistines holding the Jezreel Valley. Despairing in the face of catastrophic defeat and the death of Jonathan and two other sons in battle, Saul ended his tumultuous life by falling upon his own sword.

Ishbaal (c. 1004–1000 BCE).   Saul was succeeded by his fourth son, Ishbaal, whose name indicates that the fallen king had worshiped—in addition to Yahweh—the Canaanite gods. The name Ishbaal, meaning man of Baal, was distorted by later editors to Ishbosheth, man of shame, because they wished to avoid names compounded with Baal, a deity made odious by that time through vigorous prophetic attacks (the correct name appears in 1 Chron. 8:33 and 9:39, the caricature in 2 Sam. 4:1). Ishbaal inherited a kingdom greatly diminished in size, for the Philistines again took control of most of the land, and he was plagued by their recognition of David as vassal king over Judah in the south. For several years David contested the throne with his rival. Eventually Ishbaal was murdered by two of his officers, possibly on secret orders from David, who denied complicity and took over the remnants of Saul's kingdom.

THE UNITED KINGDOM: DAVID AND SOLOMON (C. 1000–924 BCE)

David (c. 1000–962 BCE).   The triumphant David—celebrated as a warrior, poet, and musician—now ruled a kingdom uniting the northern and southern tribes for the first time. Although the embellished exploits of his youth became the subject of legend and romance, in reality David had played the unsavory role of a brigand chieftain willing to throw his support alternatively to Saul or to the Philistines to advance his personal interests. Such ethical shortcomings marked his entire reign, exemplified by the sordid story of his adultery with Bathsheba and the murder of her husband, Uriah the Hittite, whose death the king arranged. Bathsheba was then transferred to David's own harem and became his favorite wife.

Capturing Jerusalem from the Jebusites, David made the ancient Canaanite city the capital of his united kingdom. Well-fortified Jerusalem stood outside traditional Hebrew territory, and thus the old tribal animosities and influences would be minimized. David housed his court and harem in the palace he built at the new capital, and the dynasty he founded ruled from the storied city for four centuries. David also exalted Jerusalem as a religious center, reorganizing the priesthood on a splendid scale to oversee sacrifices and other rites. Some twenty years earlier, according to the biblical account, the Philistines had attributed an outbreak of plague to the presence of the Ark of the Covenant in their territory, prompting them to return the sacred chest to the Hebrews. We are told that David brought the Ark to Jerusalem with much singing and celebration and enshrined it in a tentlike sanctuary. Such an act must have reflected, in part, a policy of employing the religion of Yahweh to strengthen the fragile bond between the southern and northern tribes.

Apparently David took advantage of the eclipse of Egypt at the time to build up a fairly strong kingdom. The biblical account relates that David employed shrewd cunning and a series of decisive battles to crush his old allies the Philistines, relentlessly pushing them back to a narrow strip along the coast of southern Palestine. We read he subjected the Canaanite cities and also extended his dominance over Ammon, Moab, and Edom, three small kingdoms east and southeast of the Jordan River and the Dead Sea. The king is said to have conquered Aramean territories stretching northward toward Syria and to have gained control over the arid southern regions of the Negeb and the Sinai. In the meantime David imposed burdensome taxes and a highly unpopular system of forced labor to provide workers for a great building program at Jerusalem. Discontent among his subjects became rampant. Moreover, the old king's last years were much embittered by the intrigue and treachery of two of his sons, each plotting for the crown.

Solomon (c. 962–924 BCE). When David was advanced in age, Bathsheba and others persuaded him to name her son Solomon as coruler and successor, which meant passing over an older son of the king. Not long after David's death, Solomon seized the opportunity to slaughter his potential rivals. Biblical tradition attributes brilliant mental powers to this monarch, yet his rule often bordered on despotism and brutality. Desiring to reign in the grandiose style of a potentate, Solomon maintained a huge harem of 700 wives and 300 concubines, many of whom sealed diplomatic or mercantile bargains. He also inaugurated a vast building program that included a great palace complex, which was built in thirteen years and lavishly decorated with wood, ivory, bronze, and gold by Phoenician artisans provided by the king's ally Hiram of Tyre. The principal feature of the palace complex was its costly Temple, undoubtedly influenced by Phoenician models. The integration of the palace and Temple was inspired by the Near Eastern view of the king as an incarnation of deity. Solomon's Temple, built to enshrine the Ark of the Covenant, became the center of the official cult. He erected additional temples to honor the divinities of his numerous wives and sometimes joined the women in celebrating their rites. Such foreign gods would be worshiped in Jerusalem for some three hundred years.

Surrounded by his wives and concubines, eunuchs, bureaucrats, and ministers, Solomon developed a vigorous trading and commercial policy. Caravan trade over long distances had become practical by this time, thanks to the earlier domestication of the camel, an animal superbly able to carry heavy burdens over vast stretches without food or water. The government sponsored profitable trading ventures to neighboring states. Solomon, as David before him, also collected customs on goods

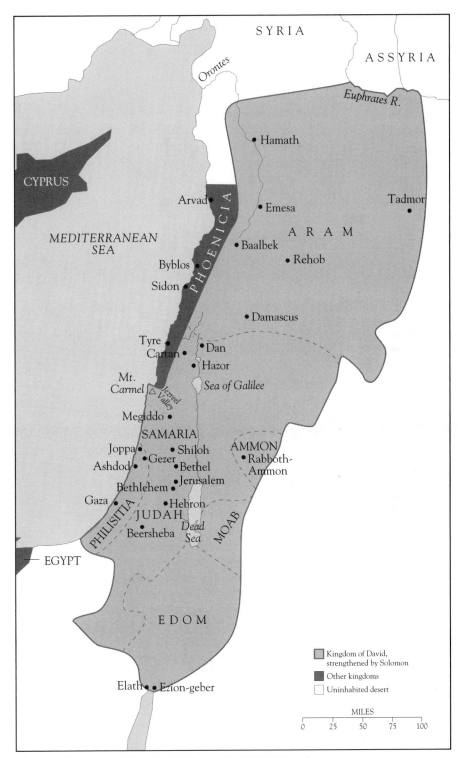

The united kingdom of David and Solomon (c. 1000–924 BCE).

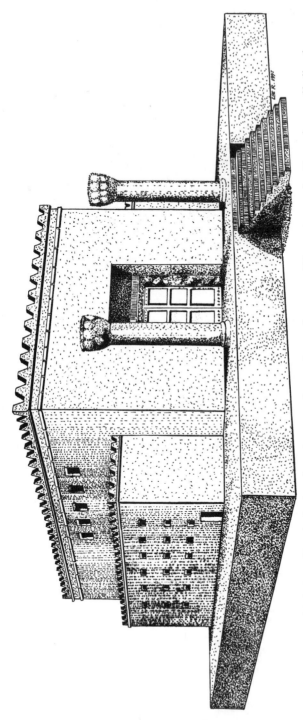

A reconstruction of Solomon's Temple, built in Jerusalem according to the usual pattern of Canaanite temples. Two columns of hollow bronze flanked the entrance, while the interior, containing numerous pieces of sacred furniture, was paneled with cedar and carved by Phoenician artisans with flowers, palm trees, and cherubim, overlaid with gold.

passing through his kingdom on the valuable trade routes from Egypt to Arabia and from Egypt to Mesopotamia. With assistance from Hiram of Tyre, he constructed a fledgling fleet of trading ships at the ancient town of Ezion-geber near the head of the Gulf of Aqaba. Hebrew fleets, operated by Phoenician crews and consisting of the small coast-hugging vessels of the day, sailed from Ezion-geber to ports along the Red Sea and beyond. The archaeological record shows that both copper and iron were mined—undoubtedly by slaves—in the neighborhood of Ezion-geber. Meanwhile an elaborate foundry operated at the site by Phoenician metallurgists produced both copper and iron ingots as objects of trade.

Solomon also fortified many cities, divided the realm into twelve administrative districts to mute the old tribal frontiers, and imposed ruinous taxes to pay for his excessive building projects. He conscripted many subjects into his standing army, which was furnished with large numbers of chariots and horses purchased abroad. The king also made countless individuals perform forced labor four months every year. His extravagant schemes imposed undue sacrifices upon his people, especially in the agricultural north, now seething with resentment against the southern capital of Jerusalem.

The Divided Monarchy: The Northern Kingdom of Israel (c. 924–722 bce)

Jeroboam I and His Weak Successors (c. 924–885 bce). Solomon's despotic rule had devastating consequences for the united Hebrew kingdom after his death around 924 bce. The northern tribes petitioned Rehoboam (c. 924–907 bce), the dead king's son and designated successor, for relief from their excessive tax burdens and forced labor. Rehoboam's response to a delegation from the north was both disdainful and arrogant: "My father made your yoke heavy, but I will add to your yoke; my father chastised you with whips, but I will chastise you with scorpions" (1 Kings 12:14). The king seriously erred in attempting to browbeat the discontented northern tribes into submission. Led by Jeroboam, who had found refuge in Egypt after unsuccessfully plotting against Solomon, they rebelled and tore the Hebrew kingdom into two rival kingdoms. Jeroboam I was acclaimed king of the ten northern tribes, now constituted as the kingdom of Israel, and he chose Shechem as his first capital. The Davidic dynasty, represented by Rehoboam, was left with only the southern tribes of Judah and Benjamin, known as the kingdom of Judah, which centered on its capital of Jerusalem.

Separation left both kingdoms weak, though Israel in the north, which survived approximately two centuries, enjoyed a much larger population than Judah and its land was more fertile. The first king of Israel, Jeroboam I (c. 924–904 bce), inaugurated a number of measures to strengthen his hand. He asserted his complete independence from Judah by severing all ties with the Temple at Jerusalem and reactivating two old sanctuaries at Dan and Bethel, located at the southern and northern extremities of the kingdom. Jeroboam is said to have set up gilded statues of bulls (the "calves of gold" mentioned in 1 Kings 12:28) in honor of Yahweh at both Dan and Bethel in place of the cherubim adorning the Temple at Jerusalem.

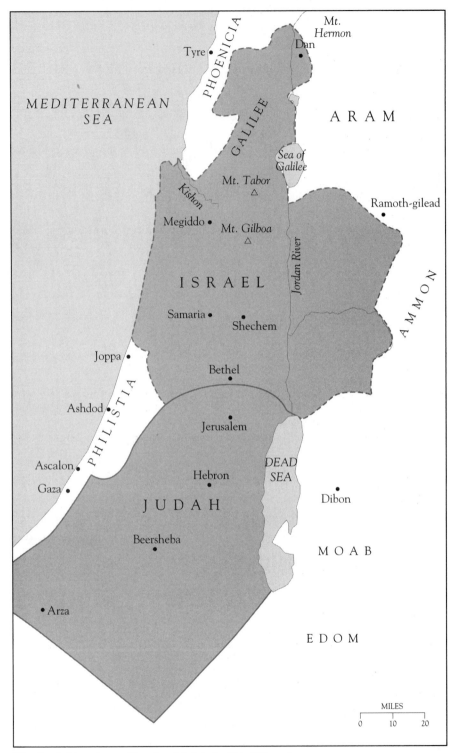

The divided kingdoms of Israel and Judah (c. 924–722 BCE).

No doubt the king hoped the powerful figure of the bull—a symbol for Baal—would appeal to his subjects and wean them away from making pilgrimages to Jerusalem, a custom enriching the coffers of Judah but draining financial resources from Israel. Although Judean tirades against Jeroboam as a promoter of Canaanite religious practices color the biblical account, ample archaeological evidence shows that popular religion at the time in both Israel and Judah was characterized by syncretism and polytheism. We should keep in mind that the references in 1–2 Kings to the sinful ways of the kings of Israel reflect the attitude of a much later age when the official Yahweh cult extolled a rigorous obedience to the national deity.

The Omride Dynasty (c. 885–843 BCE).   Israel was plagued with dynastic instability. The biblical narrative relates that Jeroboam's son was assassinated, the beginning of a series of bloody endings for the kings of Israel, the result of chronic plots for the throne. Years of civil war finally ended when a military commander named Omri gained the upper hand and established the Omride dynasty about 885 BCE. The most prosperous period for the northern kingdom came during the reigns of Omri (c. 885–873 BCE) and his son Ahab (c. 873–851 BCE). Omri established a new and permanent capital called Samaria, where he and Ahab erected a magnificent palace and fortifications. Omri also ended a fifty-year period of almost continuous border clashes with Judah. Israel flourished under his leadership, though the new prosperity was confined almost exclusively to the upper tier of society. Omri made an alliance with the king of Tyre and sealed the agreement by obtaining the king's famous daughter Jezebel as a bride for his son Ahab.

After the death of Omri about 873 BCE, Ahab and Jezebel presided over a brilliant court at Samaria. Many historians regard Ahab as the greatest king of Israel, though his reputation was badly maligned by biblical writers. When confronted with an Assyrian advance into the center of Syria, Ahab contributed ten thousand infantry and two thousand chariots to a united force from Israel, Tyre, and Damascus. With almost seventy thousand troops, the formidable Syro-Palestinian coalition fought the invaders to a standstill about 853 BCE at Qarqar on the lower Orontes.

Ahab's successes were completely outweighed, in the eyes of strict Yahwists, by his policy of sanctioning the worship of both Yahweh and Baal, the same course followed by his father. The king was confronted by the strong venom of the prophets Elijah and Elisha, who detested his Phoenician wife Jezebel because she worshiped Baal-Melkart, the official protective deity of Tyre. Although Ahab built a temple of Baal for the queen and sometimes worshiped the god himself, he had no intention of personally rejecting Yahweh and gave his children names compounded with the sacred element Yah. The biblical narrative condemns Jezebel for her fervent commitment to her religion, however, and relates that her unrelenting proselytizing brought her into increasingly heated conflicts with the prophets of Yahweh. We read that Elijah even predicted the Omri dynasty would be utterly wiped out in the next generation (1 Kings 21:21–29).

The Jehu Dynasty (c. 843–745 BCE).   After Ahab's death, according to the biblical narrative, the politically powerful Yahwist prophet Elisha continued his unswerving hostility toward the Omride rulers. The cycle of Elisha stories preserved in 2 Kings emphasizes the miraculous and indicates the prophet was ready to cast terrible afflictions upon anyone crossing him. When a group of small boys mocked Elisha at Bethel, he is said to have called down a curse of Yahweh upon them, resulting in bears running out of the woods to tear the children apart. We also read that Elisha inspired an army commander and adventurer named Jehu to overthrow the prestigious Omri dynasty. The biblical account relates that Jehu immediately engineered a thoroughgoing blood bath, thought to have taken place about 843 BCE. Jehu began the carnage by murdering the fleeing King Jehoram, Ahab's son, with an arrow in the back. He had Jezebel hurled from a window and then mangled the dead queen mother beyond recognition under the feet of his horses, leaving her body to be devoured by dogs. Jehu even slew the new king of Judah, Ahaziah, who had picked an unfortunate time to visit his uncle Jehoram, king of Israel. We read the butchery extended to the seventy sons of Ahab—thereby removing every legitimate claimant to the throne of Israel—and included many princes of Judah as well.

Jehu (c. 843–816 BCE) sanctioned an oppressive and zealous obedience to the Yahweh cult as well as the slaughter of Baal worshipers. This was a time of steady decline for Israel, now completely dominated by the powerful Aramean kingdom of Damascus. Yet the long reign of Jehu's great-grandson Jeroboam II (c. 785–745 BCE) witnessed a spectacular, if temporary, restoration of prosperity and territory to the northern kingdom. His son Zechariah reigned only months before falling victim to a murderous plot marking the end of Jehu's dynasty. This assassination was followed by a rapid succession of kings, with an attendant series of coups and counter-coups, leaving a tottering Israel easy prey to attack by a reinvigorated Assyria.

Assyrian Conquest and Annexation (c. 745–722 BCE). Assyria had menaced Syria-Palestine in the Omride period, though its fortunes declined during the first half of the eighth century BCE. Then enjoying an extraordinary revival under the vigorous rule of Tiglath-pileser III (c. 745–727 BCE), Assyria began a massive western thrust, reducing Israel to a small territory surrounding Samaria and requiring payment of a huge tribute. After Tiglath-pileser's death, Hoshea of Israel (c. 732–724 BCE) vainly attempted to throw off the Assyrian domination, a disastrous blunder bringing the enemy to the very gates of Samaria. Following a three-year siege, Samaria fell about 722 BCE and was burnt to the ground. Assyria abolished what was left of the kingdom of Israel, annexed its territory, exiled many thousands of its leading citizens to northern Mesopotamia, and replaced them with colonists from other subjugated lands. The scattered Israelites probably became assimilated with the local populations. They soon vanish from the historical record and have been known ever since as the Ten Lost Tribes of Israel.

The Southern Kingdom of Judah (c. 924–586 BCE)

The Early Rulers (c. 924–798 BCE). We noted that the division creating the rival kingdoms of Judah and Israel came when Solomon's son Rehoboam (c. 924–907 BCE) refused to grant the northern tribes relief from excessive tax burdens and forced labor. Rehoboam, like his father, promoted the worship of deities besides Yahweh, the policy also followed in Israel. His small and weak kingdom of Judah, stubbornly loyal to the dynasty of David, managed to survive until about 586 BCE, though frequently falling under the control of Egypt, Assyria, and other states. We read in 1 Kings 14 that the fifth year of the reign of Rehoboam witnessed a major invasion of Judah by Egyptian king Sheshonk I (c. 945–924 BCE), though many scholars suggest this event occurred late in the time of Solomon. Sheshonk (the biblical Shishak) is said to have plundered Jerusalem, carrying away many splendid treasures from the Temple and royal palace. Sheshonk was a Libyan mercenary commander who had usurped the Egyptian throne and established the Twenty-second Dynasty. Under his rule, a revitalized Egypt temporarily reestablished its influence in Palestine, subduing both Judah and Israel.

We noted that under the Omride dynasty, ruling Israel from about 885 to 843 BCE, the northern kingdom grew strong and completely overshadowed Judah. Then the bloodthirsty Jehu massacred all the Omrides around 843 BCE. He also butchered Ahaziah, king of Judah, who was visiting his Omride relatives in the northern kingdom at the time, and next struck down forty-two Judean princes. The queen mother Athaliah (c. 843–837 BCE), daughter of Jezebel, seized power in Judah. The first woman to rule the country, and the last for almost eight centuries, Athaliah exterminated the successors of David to maintain her hold on the throne, though the Jerusalem priests hid the infant prince Joash, supposedly a son of Ahaziah, in the Temple for six years. The priests placed Joash (c. 837–798 BCE) on the throne at the end of that period and put the queen to death.

Foreign Domination and Decline (843–639 BCE). Jehu's usurpation of the northern kingdom about 843 BCE marked the beginning of a period of steady decline in Israel and Judah, both of which were apparently dominated for the next four decades by the powerful Aramean kingdom of Damascus. We saw that during the second half of the eighth century BCE, the Assyrians marched westward to dominate all of Syria-Palestine. When Israel rose in revolt against Assyria, the Judeans prudently made an act of submission. Although losing every real semblance of independence, they escaped the terrible fate of the northern kingdom, whose political existence ended with the famous Assyrian invasion about 722 BCE. Later, King Hezekiah (c. 727–698 BCE) entangled Judah in an anti-Assyrian coalition. After the angry Assyrian ruler Sennacherib crushed his opponents one by one, Hezekiah and his son Manasseh (c. 697–642 BCE) remained chastened and loyal vassals.

The Reign of Josiah (c. 639–609 BCE) and his Cultic Purification. King Josiah, the grandson of Manasseh, was able to promote the interests of Judah, partly because Assyrian might was crumbling under the combined weight of challenges from its powerful neighbors and civil strife at home. Josiah effected a sweeping cultic purification marked by rigorous attempts to eliminate all non-Yahwistic practices and all deities except Yahweh. One result was the slaying of priests touched by other religious traditions, while another was the abolition of every Yahwistic shrine except the Temple at Jerusalem. The inspiration of this movement was a scroll—perhaps written in the reign of Manasseh—discovered while the Temple was being repaired about 622 BCE. Referred to in the biblical narrative as a "book of the law" (2 Kings 22:8), the work almost certainly forms the core of the book known to us as Deuteronomy. A widely accepted scholarly insight suggests that an early edition of the biblical books Deuteronomy through Kings was composed in conjunction with Josiah's cultic purification to express the official history of the Hebrews down to that period, later rewritten to incorporate events taking place after the king's reign. Scholars use the term Deuteronomic history for this supposed work because of the common viewpoint expressed in the Deuteronomy-Kings books, namely, the elimination of all deities except Yahweh and the centralization of the Yahwistic cult at Jerusalem.

In the final quarter of the seventh century BCE, the Assyrians, their empire in serious decline, had established an alliance with Egypt. Although the specific circumstances remain poorly understood, apparently the Egyptians were seeking not only to preserve Assyria as a buffer against the rising power of Neo-Babylonia but also to assert their own dominance over Syria-Palestine. Josiah exploited the eclipse of Assyrian power by inaugurating a dangerous effort to restore the united monarchy of David and Solomon. Taking advantage of the fall of the Assyrian capital of Nineveh before a combined assault in 612 BCE—an event celebrated with rapturous boasting in the biblical book of Nahum—Josiah aligned Judah with the Babylonians. When the Egyptians, under King Necho II (c. 610–595 BCE), rushed northward about 609 BCE to aid a small, surviving group of Assyrians regrouped near Carchemish on the upper Euphrates, Josiah attempted to intercept the Egyptian army at the strategic mountain pass near the city of Megiddo. His forces met a crushing defeat and Josiah himself died of his wounds.

Babylonian Domination and the Fall of the Kingdom of Judah (605–586 BCE). Under the leadership of their renowned ruler Nebuchadnezzar, the Babylonians shattered the Assyrians and their Egyptian allies at the battle of Carchemish in 605 BCE, becoming the new overlords of western Asia. Unfortunately, and against the reported advice of the prophet Jeremiah, the Judean monarchy became involved in ill-conceived plots with Egypt against Babylon, prompting Nebuchadnezzar to begin the long march west to strike Jerusalem. The city fell in 597 BCE, and Nebuchadnezzar replaced the frightened eighteen-year-old king, Jehoiachin, with a puppet monarch named Zedekiah (c. 597–587 BCE), an uncle of the deposed ruler. We read that Nebuchadnezzar stripped the Temple and palace of innumerable treasures and uprooted many members of the Judean nobility from their homes, carrying them and young Jehoiachin off to Babylon as captives.

Before long, Zedekiah blundered into fresh plots with Egypt against Babylon, and the winter of 588–587 BCE witnessed Nebuchadnezzaar's forces suddenly appearing before the walls of Jerusalem. Famine had devastated the city by the time the Babylonians breached its walls in 586 BCE. After his sons and chief ministers were butchered before his eyes, the unfortunate Zedekiah was blinded and sent in chains to Babylon, where he spent the rest of his days as a prisoner. The hallowed Temple and other principal buildings of Jerusalem went up in flames, their remaining treasures carted away. Most of the wealthy and influential Judeans were led off as captives to Babylonia, though some of the rural population remained behind. Nebuchadnezzar's deportations of Judeans to Babylonia, coupled with the flight of many others to Egypt, meant that many Judeans now lived outside Palestine.

THE BABYLONIAN EXILE AND RETURN (597–537 BCE)

The Judeans—customarily called the Jews from this time—developed farmlands, embarked upon commercial ventures, and enjoyed a measure of freedom during the Babylonian exile. They maintained identity as a religious community, their corporate life centering around sacred observances of prayer and public fasting. Perhaps the Jews gained permission to erect places of public worship in Babylonia, though clear documentation is lacking. Certainly, many of them longed to return to their homeland and rebuild the Temple of Yahweh at Jerusalem.

When Cyrus the Great, founder of the Persian Empire, conquered Babylonia and its extensive holdings in 539 BCE, the balance of power in the ancient world shifted to Persia. In an edict of 537 BCE, Cyrus allowed the Jews to return to Judah (known by the Greco-Roman equivalent of Judea after the exile) for the rebuilding of the Temple. The prosperity that the Jews had enjoyed in Babylonia prompted the majority to remain behind. Those returning to their homeland were markedly different both culturally and religiously from the Judeans carried to Babylonia half a century earlier.

THE PERSIAN, HELLENISTIC, AND HASMONEAN PERIODS (539–63 BCE)

Constituting a small vassal state of the vast Persian Empire, Judea was now administered politically by a governor—usually Jewish—and functioned as a theocracy in matters religious under a high priest at Jerusalem. For more than two centuries Palestine and the Jewish community in Judea remained under Persian hegemony. Then in 332 BCE the Greek-speaking Alexander the Great of Macedonia absorbed Palestine, including Judea, in the process of conquering the immense Persian realm. The invading Macedonians imported a brilliant but diluted Greek cultural heritage, which coexisted with native cultures within the boundaries established by the conquests of Alexander. This is the origin of the Hellenistic period that flourished for three hundred years after Alexander.

Following Alexander's death in 323 BCE, his generals embarked on tortuous struggles over the succession, with both Ptolemy and Seleucus claiming rights over eastern Mediterranean territories. Judea was governed at first by the Ptolemies of Egypt, under whom there was considerable intellectual development. Some Jews, particularly those from the upper ranks of society, became considerably Hellenized, speaking and dressing in the Greek manner. Judea then fell under the control of the Seleucids of Syria around 200 BCE. The Seleucid rulers attempted to unify the peoples of their realm, including Judea, by imposing a thoroughgoing Hellenization, prompting great resistance from the traditionalist group within Judaism. A Seleucid ruler named Antiochus IV Epiphanes is remembered for his insistent opposition to

Jewish traditions such as sacrifices in the Temple and circumcision. In his determination to stamp out Judaism and enforce Hellenization, Antiochus even desecrated the Temple in 168 BCE, thereby provoking a Jewish uprising—the Maccabean Revolt—led by the ruthless fighter Judas Maccabeus, member of a family of country priests. After several years of intense hostilities, the Jews finally liberated Jerusalem in 165 BCE. They immediately rededicated the Temple, an event still commemorated in the eight-day festival known as Hanukkah (meaning dedication), which is observed in late December and distinguished chiefly by the lighting of an eight-branched candelabrum known as a menorah each evening of the celebration.

Eventually the Jews gained complete independence from the Greek-speaking Seleucids, and for nearly a century Judea remained an independent kingdom ruled by the Hasmonean dynasty, the descendants of Judas Maccabeus. We saw that the Hasmoneans were a priestly house, and the later successors of Judas combined the offices of high priest and ruler, except when the sovereign was a woman.

ROMAN DOMINATION (63 BCE–135 CE)

A struggle for power was raging within the Hasmonean dynasty during the fourth decade of the first century BCE, providing the Romans with a convenient excuse for intervention. The Roman general Pompey stormed Jerusalem in 63 BCE, and a vastly reduced Judea was converted into a Roman protectorate. Although a Hasmonean revolt in 40 BCE temporarily reestablished the political independence of Judea, the Romans soon hopelessly defeated the Hasmoneans and supplanted them with Herod the Great (37–4 BCE), a loyal Roman vassal from Judean territory in the south known as Idumea. In many respects Herod served the Jews well, exemplified by his magnificent rebuilding of the Temple, but his Jewish subjects regarded him an alien and detested his senseless brutality and mass killings. After Herod's death in 4 BCE, his kingdom was divided among three of his sons. Judea itself, following a decade of chaotic misrule, was brought under direct Roman rule in 6 CE.

The first century CE was a period of intense religious and social discord among the Jews, resulting in a highly variegated Judaism. The Romans, who struggled to keep the ferment in check, administered Judea by officials in their civil service known as prefects, later procurators, whose rule proved to be burdensome. Judea seethed with discontent as fanatical Jewish factions preached revolution. In 66 CE a revolt broke out in Palestine. One party, the belligerent Zealots, attracted the poor and many adventurers to their camp, which was dedicated to eradicating Roman rule and punishing the wealthy Jews backing the foreigners. Yet rival Jewish factions embarked on a campaign of massacring one another, thereby diluting the resistance to the Roman overlords. In the meantime the able Roman general Vespasian and his legions arrived to quell the uprising, but he was proclaimed emperor while besieging Jerusalem. Thus Vespasian returned to Rome, leaving the campaign to his son Titus, who finally managed to take Jerusalem in the year 70. The Romans destroyed the old city. They burned and razed the venerable Temple, first carting off its treasures, though the Western Wall—popularly known as the Wailing Wall—was

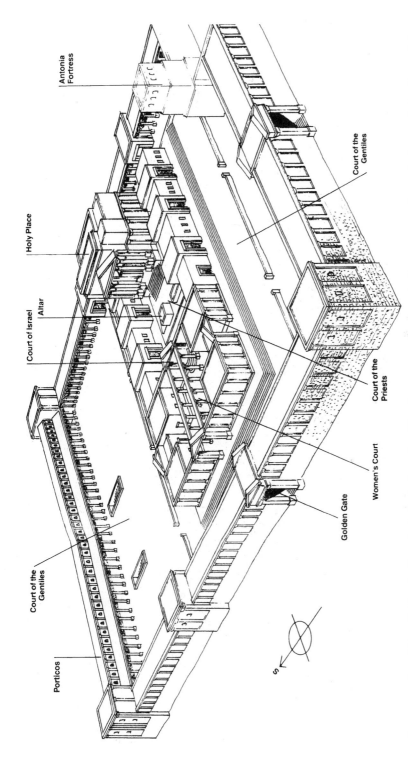

Antonia
Fortress

Holy Place

Court of Israel

Altar

Court of the
Gentiles

Porticos

Court of the
Gentiles

Court of the
Priests

Women's Court

Golden Gate

S

Reconstruction of Herod's Temple. Herod rebuilt the Jerusalem Temple on a magnificent scale. Its courts were increasingly sacred: the Court of the Gentiles (people not Jewish), the Court of the Women, the Court of the Israelites (restricted to males), and the Court of the Priests. Only priests could enter the Temple itself. The innermost chamber, or holy of holies, was restricted to the high priest, who enjoyed access only on the Day of Atonement, Yom Kippur, a solemn festival celebrated with elaborate rites to purify the people from sin.

MEDITERRANEAN
SEA

ROMAN PROVINCE
OF SYRIA

• Chalcis

• Damascus

• Tyre

• Caesarea
Philippi

• Gischala

Capernaum

Golan Heights

KEDAR

Beth
Shearim •

• Jotapata

GALILEE

*Sea of
Galilee*

Usha •

• Sepphoris

• Hippos

• Nazareth

• Gadara

Dora •

SAMARIA

• Pella   DECAPOLIS

Caesarea
Maritima •

Plain of Sharon

Samaria
(Sebaste) •

• Shechem

Jordan

Joppa •

• Modein

Lydda •

• Beth-horon

Jericho •

• Philadelphia

Jamnia • Gazara

Jerusalem •

Qumran •

PERAEA

• Ascalon
(free city)

Bethlehem •

Herodium •

• Machaerus

Hebron •

*DEAD
SEA*

IDUMAEA

Masada •

NABATAEAN KINGDOM

▢ Kingdom of Herod the Great

MILES

0   10   20

Kingdom of Herod the Great (37–4 BCE).

Triumphant Romans marching with the seven-branched candelabrum (menorah) and other spoils from the Temple after the fall of Jerusalem in 70 CE. This relief, representing the victory procession when the Romans returned home the following year, adorns the marble Arch of Titus, erected in Rome c. 81 CE.

left standing and serves to this day as the most sacred place of prayer and an object of pilgrimage for Jews. The Jewish fortresses in the vicinity of Jerusalem were soon taken. The last holdout, Masada, was perched on lofty cliffs near the Dead Sea and considered impregnable. Yet Masada fell in the year 73, and we hear from the famous first-century Jewish historian Josephus that the Zealots holding this stronghold committed mass suicide to avoid Roman capture. Following the Jewish revolt, the Romans tightly controlled Palestine. They abolished the high priesthood and allowed non-Jewish immigrants to settle in the region. Although the Jews had suffered appalling casualties, a remnant survived in Palestine.

The last great Jewish revolt against Rome broke out during the reign of the emperor Hadrian (117–138) and seems to have been partly precipitated by a law he promulgated against circumcision, a practice he regarded as a horrible mutilation. This uprising, occurring between the years 132 and 135, was under the vigorous leadership of Simon Bar Cochba. After the Romans quashed the rebellion, Hadrian built a Roman city upon the ruins of Jerusalem and adorned the new settlement with statues of Jupiter and other Roman deities. A large foreign population was imported to the walled city—renamed Aelia Capitolina in honor of Hadrian (Publius Aelius Hadrianus) and the god Jupiter Capitolinus—but Jews were generally forbidden entrance. The traditional name Judea was now changed to Syria Palestina, named for the Philistines, an attempt to weaken the link between the land and the Jewish people. Many of the remaining Jews migrated from the area. Over the next centuries this scattering, or Diaspora, brought them to many places and was characteristic of Jewish existence until the establishment of an independent Jewish state in the twentieth century.

CHAPTER XI

The Religion-Centered Hebrew Culture

The political history of the Hebrews is dwarfed in importance by their culture, which focused on key religious concepts and gradually evolved into Judaism, the fountainhead of two other major world religions, Christianity and Islam. We should not forget, however, that the religious doctrines of the Hebrews were anchored in the beliefs of their Canaanite relatives and other neighbors in the ancient Near East. The same is true of the Hebrew Bible, the most important documentary evidence for studying the religious evolution of Judaism. The texts of the Hebrew Bible were written during many centuries by numerous authors and have several levels of dependability. Scientific statements are often inaccurate or even contradictory. The first biblical book, Genesis, for example, asserts that plants and animals were created before human beings (Gen. 1:1–2:3), but the next passage reports that human beings were created first (Gen. 2:4–3:24). Such irreconcilable statements support the widely held scholarly theory that ancient editors combined documents from several sources of different dates to compile the first four books (and certain other passages) of the Hebrew Bible. These problems notwithstanding, the course of history would be tied indelibly to its message.

HEBREW DAILY LIFE AND SOCIETY

MEALS AND DIETARY LAWS

During meals Hebrew families drank wine and ate bread made from barley or wheat. This fare was supplemented with fruit, vegetables, and occasional pieces of meat. Most scholarship on Hebrew meals focuses on the strict dietary laws, which are detailed in Leviticus 11 and Deuteronomy 14:3–20, mandating the consumption of clean animals and prohibiting unclean ones, regulations also extending to the sacrificial system. Generally, clean land animals, exemplified by sheep and cattle, had cloven hoofs and chewed their cud. The pig, which does not chew its cud, was regarded as particularly unclean. Other rules governed the slaughter of animals and the preparation of meat, a luxury reserved for special guests and religious festivals. Cooking was absolutely prohibited on the Sabbath, the seventh and holy day of the Hebrew week, its observance sanctified by complete abstinence from work.

SOCIAL ORGANIZATION AND MARRIAGE AND THE FAMILY

Growing scholarly agreement views the Hebrews, from the mid-thirteenth century BCE, as settled farmers inhabiting villages of the central highlands of Canaan, where they were loosely associated as tribes. Perhaps these units functioned as simple chiefdoms ruled by powerful heads of dominant families who arbitrated disputes. We noted in the previous chapter that the Hebrews were without a central political organization until economic conditions and external political pressure forced their local leaders to accept a monarchy in the second half of the eleventh century BCE.

The primary social institution of the Hebrews was the extended family headed by a father and made up of numerous sets of childbearing adults and their dependants. The concept of family also embraced wider circles of kinship, the clan, the tribe, and the nation. The father exercised central authority within the family, with the power to divorce his wife without explanation and to put disobedient children to death. Yet the mother enjoyed great influence and played a vital role in managing the household, teaching the children, and diffusing family conflicts.

Hebrew families viewed marriage as both a business transaction and an important social event. Although most marriages were monogamous, polygamy was an accepted practice and was common among the upper ranks of society. Wealthy men might have several wives, enlarging the scope of the family but sometimes producing households ridden by jealousy and strife. Males and females were rarely allowed to choose their own sexual partners, for the father of the household was responsible for arranging the marriages of his children. Usually a written or oral contract was involved, stipulating a marriage present to be given to the bride's father in compensation for the loss of her work and services. The marriage present ordinarily took the form of money, but goods or services were occasionally substituted. The making of the marriage agreement marked the beginning of the betrothal—a period lasting about twelve months—when the couple was legally bound to a future marriage.

The bride and groom, frequently first cousins, were commonly married when they were little more than children. As in Mesopotamia, marriage involved no special religious ceremonies. The bride simply left her family and joined that of her husband. The evening of the wedding day witnessed the groom wearing a crown and setting out with his friends for the bride's home, the members of his entourage providing music on tambourines and other instruments. When he arrived, the bride would be dressed in her finest array of clothing and jewels, her face covered with a veil, removed only after the couple found themselves alone later in the evening. The bride and her attendants joined the procession and went on to the groom's house. Carrying torches to light the way, the members of the wedding procession sang, danced, and played musical instruments. Although the wedding feast at the house of the groom lasted at least seven days, the couple consummated their marriage the first night. Bloodstained linen was displayed the next day to attest the bride's virginity. Females were enjoined to enter marriage as virgins—the penalty was stoning when a husband brought a substantiated charge of premarital sexual intercourse against his wife—though such chastity was not required of males.

The Hebrews were strongly encouraged to direct their sexual behavior toward the production of legitimate offspring. Levitical laws not only prohibit adultery, incest, homosexuality, and bestiality but also assign the penalty of death to these practices (Lev. 20:10–16). Children were regarded as blessings from Yahweh, yet they were also considered property and could be sold as slaves in times of need. Families particularly desired male children, in part because sons kept ancestral property within the family. All boys were circumcised eight days after birth to signify their initiation into the covenant community of the Hebrew nation. The firstborn son usually enjoyed special honors and rights such as taking control of the household at his father's death and receiving a larger inheritance than his younger brothers. The birth of a girl was less highly valued than that of a boy, partly because she would eventually marry and join another family.

EVOLUTION OF THE FOUR FUNDAMENTAL CONVICTIONS OF THE YAHWEH CULT

The Hebrews adopted many religious customs and beliefs of neighboring peoples, modifying what they acquired from others in accordance with their own traditions. Thus one of the paramount Hebrew legacies to the West is a system of ancient Near Eastern religious doctrines and practices, albeit fashioned into a distinctive complex of faith and conduct. Over many centuries the Hebrews developed four fundamental convictions that provided the central teaching of their religion: (1) Yahweh demands their exclusive loyalty, (2) Yahweh is perpetually bound to them through a covenant relationship, (3) Yahweh commands them to obey his law, and (4) Yahweh is a spiritual rather than a material being, the last not fully developed until the completion of their Bible.

1. YAHWEH DEMANDS THE EXCLUSIVE LOYALTY OF THE HEBREWS

THE HEBREW PANTHEON

The Yahweh Cult Was Monarchic, not Monotheistic.   Scholars have traditionally regarded the first conviction—Yahweh demands exclusive loyalty—as an expression of monotheism, the belief in the existence of only one god. Yet we should be careful not to make an absolute distinction between polytheism and monotheism in the religious systems of either the ancient or the modern world. Indeed, the so-called monotheistic religions of today—Zoroastrianism, Judaism, Christianity, and Islam—all recognize lesser divinities such as angels and demons. The early Near Eastern pantheons, including that of the Canaanites, were headed by a high god, under whom subordinate deities functioned. We noted that the Canaanite high god was El, whose attributes of mercy and virtue greatly influenced the Hebrew concept of Yahweh. Scholars point out that an intellectual belief in one god was never central to the Hebrews' faith. The early Hebrews practiced a polytheistic religion akin to that of their neighbors and worshiped the Baalim and other deities in addition to their national god Yahweh, conceived as a king.

Yahweh as a High God Assisted by a Divine Assembly.   The Hebrews believed Yahweh was aided in his rule by a divine assembly. Many biblical texts from the twelfth century BCE down to the Babylonian exile tell stories of Yahweh presiding over a council of subordinate gods whose duties include reporting to and proposing strategy to him as well as praising him (1 Kings 22:19–23, Ps. 82:1, 6, Job 1:6–2:10, Isa. 6).

The Sons of God.   A variety of terms and titles found their way into the Hebrew Bible to denote the members of Yahweh's divine assembly. Members of one group, the sons of God, show up in many roles. We read they angered Yahweh by having sexual intercourse with earthly women and producing offspring, demigods of gigantic statue and superhuman strength called the Nephilim. To prevent humanity from becoming permanently semidivine, Yahweh is said to have limited the span of human life to a maximum of 120 years (Gen. 6:1–4).

The Host of Heaven.   Yahweh's heavenly assembly also included astral gods—the sun, moon, and stars—referred to in the biblical narrative as the host of heaven. We read that the host of heaven, who were regarded as an organized military force in the celestial sphere, were marshaled to fight as Yahweh's army against the Canaanites (Judges 5:20).

Angels and Other Celestial Beings.   The Hebrew Bible also mentions the presence of angels in the heavenly assembly. Typically anthropomorphic, angels played a prominent role in the Yahweh cult as divine messengers and were thought to descend to earth by means of a ladder (Gen. 28:12). All the Near Eastern religions included divine messengers, a class of supernatural beings patterned after the courtly retinue surrounding earthly rulers. We read also of celestial beings of bizarre appearance— the seraphim (winged fiery serpents) and cherubim (winged sphinxlike creatures)— both derived from older Near Eastern lore. Associated with the presence of Yahweh, the cherubim and seraphim were said to stand near the throne of Yahweh and sing his praises, among other duties. The biblical narrative relates that Yahweh was able to fly through the heavens by riding on a cherub (2 Sam. 22:11, Ps. 18:10), while the visions in Ezekiel 1 and 10 portray cherubim furnishing power for the flight of Yahweh's chariot-throne.

THE PROPHETS ELEVATE THE CONCEPT OF YAHWEH

Prophetic activity had long been familiar in the ancient Near East. The eighth, seventh, and sixth centuries BCE witnessed the emergence of a series of influential Hebrew prophets seeking to elevate and dignify the concept of Yahweh by distinguishing him starkly him from his subordinate deities. This movement promoting the concept of Yahweh's sovereignty was strongly resisted by popular practice, with its devotion to the subordinate deities—the Baalim and others—whose worship had deeply pervaded Hebrew life.

The Hebrew prophets claimed to be Yahweh's divine messengers. Perceiving the past as an ideal age of truth and righteousness, they struggled for the restoration

Reconstruction of cherubim carved on the walls of the Temple, based on numerous carved ivory plaques of Phoenician manufacture. Apparently the hybrid supernatural creature known as the sphinx—familiar in ancient Near Eastern art—was the precursor of the Hebrew cherub.

of its principles. Largely legendary stories about the prophets in the biblical narrative indicate they exhibited considerable diversity of character and function, including telling the future, working miracles, advising and castigating kings, and delivering messages from Yahweh, often in a state of ecstasy, that is, a trance involving loss of control over both emotions and physical movements. Thus their oracles were often frenzied and veiled in colorful imagery. In general, the authority of the prophets depended upon the belief that Yahweh spoke through them. An important class of these divine messengers was attached to the royal court and preached to the kings of both Israel and Judah, while others lived alone or in solitary communities, but all seem to have boldly condemned countless religious and social practices of their day.

The "Major" Prophets.   Many of the prophets lived during the period from about 750 to 539 BCE, troubled times witnessing the destruction of the northern kingdom of Israel by the Assyrians, the fall of the southern kingdom of Judah to the Babylonians, and the exile of the Judeans in Babylon. The Hebrews recognized three "major" prophets—Isaiah, Jeremiah, and Ezekiel—whose purported utterances were collected in the biblical books of Isaiah, Jeremiah, and Ezekiel, though all three works became repositories of much additional and later material. Isaiah, a prophet of Judah, seems to have been active in the traumatic years of the second half of the eighth century BCE. He proclaimed that Judah, like Israel, was on the road to destruction. Stylistic and theological differences indicate that only the first thirty-nine chapters of the book bearing his name can be assigned to Isaiah's time. Chapters forty through fifty-five represent the outpourings of a later prophet—conventionally called Second Isaiah—who presented his message during the exile, while the remaining chapters of the book were completed after the return to Jerusalem from Babylon. Another Judean, Jeremiah was active in the late seventh and early sixth centuries BCE. His oracles, which portray Yahweh weeping over the disobedience of the Hebrews, cover the period down to the destruction of Jerusalem. The learned priest-prophet Ezekiel exercised the most important part of his career in Babylon during the first half of the sixth century BCE. Condemning Judah for its crimes, Ezekiel foresees a coming catastrophe.

The Twelve.   The purported utterances of the twelve other prophets—Hosea, Joel, Amos, Obadiah, Jonah, Micah, Nahum, Habakkuk, Zephaniah, Haggai, Zechariah, and Malachi—were also subject to drastic editing and countless interpolations. In the Hebrew Bible they appear together as one book known as the Book of the Twelve, though they are separated into small independent books in the Christian Scriptures. The Christian tradition designates this group of divine messengers the Minor Prophets because of the brevity of the books bearing their names.

Partial Separation of Yahweh from the Subordinate Deities.   The prophet Hosea's ministry to his native Israel in the eighth century BCE came during a period of near anarchy shortly before the fall of the northern kingdom to Assyria about 722 BCE. Hosea condemns both the worship of the Baalim and the fertility rites associated with Baalism as unfaithfulness to Yahweh. By attacking the subordinate deities associated with Yahweh, however, Hosea is assaulting the traditional Yahweh cult itself. Several Hebrew writers of the seventh and sixth centuries BCE express strong disapproval of the subordinate deities as intruders from other lands. The prophets Jeremiah and Zephaniah, for example, depict the host of heaven as foreign deities allotted to other peoples, not the Hebrews, from whom Yahweh demands exclusive loyalty.

The Survival of Multiple Divinities.   Despite such expressions of exclusive loyalty to the state god, the Hebrews continued to assume the existence of other divinities. The later texts of the Hebrew Bible still depict Yahweh dispatching angels from his divine assembly with messages for humans. The postexilic Jews developed an elaborate angelology, often attributed to the infiltration of ideas from the Zoroastrian religion of Persia (discussed in chapter 12). Angels are now portrayed as a hierarchy, headed by seven (or four or three) archangels, the counterpart of the Amesha Spentas (the Holy Immortal Ones) of Zoroastrianism. The Persian religion also seems to have influenced the Jews to begin depicting angels and archangels as powerful spiritual beings waiting to serve as Yahweh's warriors in the final battle against Satan.

Satan as the Archenemy of Yahweh.   By this time Satan was conceived as the great adversary of Yahweh. Prior to the Babylonian exile, however, the Hebrews regarded Satan as an honored member of Yahweh's divine assembly with the duty of accusing evildoers (Job 1:6–12, 2:1–7). The dualistic tendencies of Zoroastrianism, teaching a cosmic struggle between the principles of good and evil, influenced the Jews to view Satan as the archenemy of Yahweh. The postexilic Jews spoke of Satan and his demons as a great negative force tempting humanity to embrace sinfulness, and thus they saw the world as a mammoth battleground between good and evil. Yet because the Jews conceived of Yahweh as the ruler of history, even Satan somehow served to carry out his will.

2. THE HEBREWS ARE PERPETUALLY BOUND TO YAHWEH IN A COVENANT RELATIONSHIP

The second fundamental religious conviction of the Hebrews was that a perpetual covenant relationship exists between Yahweh and the entire community of his chosen people. A covenant is a binding relationship between parties based on solemn promises and obligations and usually sealed by an oath. A great variety of covenants were employed for regulating behavior in ancient times, including those between individuals or between distinct political groups. Many covenants took the form of a superior binding an inferior to obligations. The oath sealing the covenant was always accompanied by symbolic acts such as taking hold of a potent or sacred object. We read that the dying patriarch Jacob asked his son Joseph to swear an oath by placing his hands upon his father's genitals, emblems of fertility: "If now I have found favor in your sight, put your hand under my thigh, and promise to deal loyally and truly with me" (Gen. 47:29, cf. 24:2). Over time the old testicular form of taking an oath was gradually modified to the present custom of swearing on the Scriptures.

The Covenant with Noah

A number of covenants between Yahweh and the Hebrews are mentioned in the Hebrew Bible. Such a covenant is included in the familiar tale of Yahweh's decision to punish the human race for its disobedience by destroying life on earth with a great Flood, adapted from antique Mesopotamian myths involving destructive floods. The biblical account relates that the legendary Noah had found favor with Yahweh. Accordingly, Noah, his family, and a pair of every species of living creature were allowed to survive the deluge on a huge vessel, or ark. We read that Yahweh then established a covenant with Noah and his descendants and with all living creatures, pledging "never again shall there be a flood to destroy the earth" (Gen. 9:11). The sign of this covenant was the rainbow, which the Hebrews imagined as Yahweh's giant bow for shooting arrows of lightning. By placing his weapon in the sky, Yahweh signified his wrath had abated. The biblical narrative also mentions that Yahweh introduced to Noah the privilege of eating meat—provided a creature had been properly sacrificed or slaughtered—a Hebrew explanation for the origin of animal sacrifice and the incorporation of meat in the diet.

The Covenant with Abraham

Yahweh is said to have made a covenant also with Abraham, promising to make the patriarch exceedingly fruitful, "the father of a multitude of nations," and to give him and his descendants the land of Canaan for eternity. The Abrahamic covenant was sealed by a commandment: "Every male among you shall be circumcised. You shall be circumcised in the flesh of your foreskins, and it shall be a sign of the covenant between me and you" (Gen. 17:4–11). Generally, a male who had not been circumcised could not participate in the worship of Yahweh. Circumcision was by no means unique to the Hebrews, however, and was widely performed in antiquity, partly as an initiation rite at puberty consecrating sexual power to a deity. The Egyptians and all other peoples living adjacent to the Hebrews except the despised Philistines practiced the custom. Originally, Hebrew circumcision seems to have been a puberty rite preparatory to marriage. The Hebrews moved circumcision to infancy, requiring boys to undergo the rite eight days after birth to signify their initiation into the covenant community of the Hebrew nation as well as to consecrate their sex organs to Yahweh.

The Covenant at Sinai

Although we noted there is no archaeological evidence of a Hebrew sojourn in Egypt, let alone of a miraculous escape from captivity, the Hebrews believed their most important covenant with Yahweh was made near Mount Sinai after the Exodus, conceived as ratifying all the earlier ones. In this covenant, said to have been mediated by Moses, the Hebrews reputedly promised to worship and obey Yahweh, entering a relationship with their deity analogous to that between a suzerain and his vassals. In return, Yahweh promised to preserve the Hebrews as his chosen people, a special elect community perpetually bound to himself.

3. YAHWEH COMMANDS THE HEBREWS TO OBEY HIS LAW

The Torah

The third fundamental religious conviction of the Hebrews was that Yahweh commands them to obey his law, which sanctified and regulated innumerable aspects of life. The Hebrew religion was strongly earth centered in its supreme preoccupation with following Yahweh's will, expressed in his law. Thus the relationship of Yahweh to the Hebrews was patterned on that of a king to his subjects. The Hebrew Bible, despite its emphasis on Yahweh's legal demands, contains no term strictly equivalent to the English word *law.* The Hebrew word *torah* is often translated "law," though a broader and more exact meaning is "instruction" or "guidance." The first five books of the Hebrew Bible (Genesis, Exodus, Leviticus, Numbers, and Deuteronomy) came to be designated the Torah. The final four books of the Torah contain numerous collections of laws. The Hebrews understood the laws of the Torah as divinely given, and thus they regarded any legal infractions as sins against the will of Yahweh.

The Book of the Covenant and the Ten Commandments

We read that the Hebrews, when entering into the covenant at Sinai, promised to obey Yahweh's law in return for his protection and for being his "holy nation" of chosen people (Exod. 19:6). In short, Yahweh set the Hebrews completely apart from others in exchange for their commitment to honor a collection of laws embracing numerous aspects of life, the so-called Book of the Covenant, material inserted into the Sinai narrative in the book of Exodus centuries after a Moses would have lived (Exod. 20:22–23:33). For the most part, the Book of the Covenant betrays a long history of legal development and reflects an adaptation of Canaanite and other laws to the covenant tradition. The core of Yahweh's legal demands is concisely formulated as the Ten Commandments, also called the Decalogue, which linguistic analysis also shows to have undergone a lengthy evolution (Exodus 20:1–17, Deut. 5:6–21).

Lex Talionis.   Yahweh is often depicted in the Book of the Covenant and elsewhere in the Hebrew Bible as wrathful and vengeful, liable to violent outbursts of temper, one whose will is meant to be obeyed. He demanded the death penalty for numerous transgressions of his law. His vengeance is directed toward those who disobey his commands or oppose his will. Vengeance was a firmly set rule of law among the Hebrews. Their early legal collections reflect the principle of *lex talionis*, or law of equivalent retribution, demanding strict compensation for damage. This meant the taking of "life for life, eye for eye, tooth for tooth, hand for hand, foot for foot, burn for burn, wound for wound, stripe for stripe" (Exod. 21:23–25). As brutal as the principle seems on its face, *lex talionis* actually represented some advance in legal policy by barring both unlimited revenge and an infliction of punishment exceeding the crime.

Laws Protecting Human Beings.   Despite Yahweh's wrath, he was capable of compassion and forgiveness, and he demanded a commitment to truth and justice by his chosen people. Sections of the Book of the Covenant provide for the welfare of orphans and widows. We read also that slaves enjoyed certain rights: "When you buy a Hebrew slave, he shall serve six years and in the seventh he shall go out free, for nothing" (Exod. 21:2). Slavery was universally practiced in the ancient Near East. Two sources of slaves for the Hebrews were prisoners of war and debtors. In terms of the latter, women were reduced to slavery more often than men. Sometimes they were sold specifically into concubinage. We read that "when a man sells his daughter as a slave," the owner could claim her as a concubine for himself or his son, though she could be redeemed and have her contract voided for a price if she did not please the owner (Exod. 21: 7–9).

LAWS IN LEVITICUS AND ELSEWHERE REGARDING SACRIFICIAL WORSHIP

The priests in the kingdoms of Israel and Judah were state officials who collected both animals and produce as sacrifices or taxes. Guardians of the sacred traditions, the priests sacrificed animals and offered commodities to Yahweh on behalf of the Hebrew community. The Hebrews regarded sacrifices and offerings as a means not only of providing sustenance for Yahweh but also winning rewards from him. Many laws in the biblical narrative revolve around sacrificial worship, exemplified by the systematic treatment of various categories of sacrifices in Leviticus 1–7. Leviticus, which may be characterized as a book setting down the principles of worship, also classifies clean and unclean animals for sacrifice as well as for purely human consumption (Lev. 11, cf. Deut 14:3–20). Animal sacrifice involved draining the blood of the victim, burning at least part of the animal (especially the fat) on the altar, and applying its blood to the altar by the priest. Regarded as the seat of life of all living beings, blood was Yahweh's property and reserved for his nourishment, and thus the Hebrews were prohibited from eating meat still containing blood (Ex. 24:6, Deut. 12:23–24, Gen. 9:4–6, Lev. 17:11). One category of animal sacrifice, a burnt offering, was burned whole on the altar, while another form involved consigning only parts of the animal to the altar, the rest of the carcass being reserved for the consumption of the offerers or the priests. The Hebrew Bible also prescribes non-bloody sacrifices utilizing grain, frankincense, and wine.

The Prophets Demand That Sacrifices and Worship Be Grounded in Ethical Living.   The great prophets active from the eighth to the sixth centuries BCE seldom refer directly to the law, but they condemn mere forms of worship as insincere and are emphatic in teaching that sacrifices are pleasing to Yahweh only when offered by individuals living in accordance with his ethical requirements. Thus we read angry words in Amos about miscreants who "trample the head of the poor into the dust of the earth, and turn aside the way of the afflicted" (Amos 2:7). The prophets' censure of the Hebrews for violating the moral underpinning of the law was of incalculable influence in shaping the professed ethical sentiments of medieval and modern times.

THE DEUTERONOMIC LAWS

Deuteronomy, the fifth book of the Torah, purports to be an oration delivered by Moses, though its much-modified core was almost certainly derived from the scroll discovered when the Temple was being repaired about 622 BCE under King Josiah of Judah. We saw that this scroll was referred to in the biblical narrative as a "book of the law" (2 Kings 22:8). Josiah was inspired by the work to effect a sweeping cultic purification, characterized by brutal measures to eliminate all non-Yahwistic practices and all deities except Yahweh. The king ordered the killing of priests touched by other religious traditions and the abolition of every Yahwistic shrine except the Temple at Jerusalem.

The core of Deuteronomy—chapters twelve through twenty-six—serves as the most extensive Hebrew collection of laws. Many of its legal prescriptions are parallel to those in the Book of the Covenant, though much of the material is unique. Reflecting the cultic purification of Josiah, the Deuteronomic legal corpus includes considerable religious instruction calling for the centralization of the cult and its sacrificial system at a place never mentioned by name, but the Temple at Jerusalem was clearly intended. The laws emphasize the obligation of worshiping Yahweh alone, a requirement echoed in the famous confessional statement known as the Shema: "Hear, O Israel: The Lord our God is one Lord; and you shall love the Lord your God with all your heart, and with all your soul, and with all your might" (Deut.

6:4–5). Although the Shema was later incorrectly interpreted as an expression of monotheism, this great formulation declares only that Yahweh must not be worshiped in conjunction with any other deity.

The Law during the Exilic and Postexilic Periods

With the destruction of the Temple by Nebuchadnezzar and the deportation of many members of the Judean nobility to Babylon at the opening of the sixth century BCE, the ancient faith endured because the exiles continued to observe the law. The question naturally arises about where the Judeans—customarily called the Jews from the time—worshiped in Babylonia. Some scholars suggest this period witnessed the birth of the synagogue as a substitute for the Temple, though documentary evidence is lacking. Over the centuries the synagogue evolved into the central institution for teaching the Jewish faith and served as a meetinghouse where prayers were offered to Yahweh and the law was read and expounded. Ceremonies in the synagogue took place in the full view of participants, who were no longer confined to outer courtyards, as they had been at the Jerusalem Temple.

We noted that the Persian ruler Cyrus the Great issued an edict in 537 BCE permitting the Jews to return to Palestine for the rebuilding of the Temple. By this time the law had become an independent entity long loosened from its old moorings in Temple worship. The returning Jews vigorously emphasized the law, which served both to set them apart from the rest of the world and to rebuke what they considered false. Thus they assiduously practiced their dietary laws—the detailed regulations concerning forbidden and permitted foods—and strictly observed both the Sabbath and circumcision as a means of maintaining themselves as a separate and distinct community. In short, the Jews were reluctant to extend Yahweh's law to the rest of humanity, for only they were his chosen people. Only they could truly enjoy the benefits of knowing him.

The Law in Later Jewish History

The characteristic feature of medieval and later Judaism was its continued stress on obedience to the law. Thus to be a Jew was to keep the law in order to sanctify every aspect of life. After the Jerusalem Temple was destroyed by the Romans in 70 CE, allegiance to the law enabled the Jews and their religion to survive in a world they found increasingly alien and forbidding.

4. YAHWEH IS A SPIRITUAL BEING

The fourth and final fundamental conviction of the Jewish religion—though not fully developed until after the completion of the Hebrew Bible—was that Yahweh is a spiritual rather than a material being. For many centuries after the Hebrews adopted Yahweh as their national god, they regarded him as an anthropomorphic deity, one having human attributes. They believed, for example, he walked about on the earth as people do. We read in the book of Genesis that Adam and Eve "heard the sound of the Lord God walking in the garden in the cool of the day. . . ." (Gen. 3:8). Thus the early Hebrews thought of Yahweh as one who walked in human fashion, perhaps preferring the most comfortable period of the day for the activity, and who had sufficient weight to make a sound as he moved over the ground. By the time Nebuchadnezzar carried many of the Jewish leaders into their Babylonian captivity in 597 BCE, however, the priests and prophets were cautiously moving away from anthropomorphism. Yet even in this period the priest-prophet Ezekiel describes the appearance of Yahweh—radiant in his glory—as a "likeness as it were of a human form" (Ezek. 1:26–27). Although the doctrine of the immaterial nature of Yahweh finds no undisputed place in the Hebrew Bible, medieval Jews—under Islamic influence—treated biblical anthropomorphism as metaphorical and proclaimed that their god could neither be seen nor heard, a spiritual being who was remote but cared for them like a father. Yet a vestige of the concept of a material god lingered in the attribution of maleness to the deity, who is described as King, Lord, Father, and Husband in the biblical narrative (Ps. 74:12; Isa. 1:24, 63:16; Hos. 2:16). Scholars point out that the later religion of Christianity represents an extreme form of anthropomorphism, with the deity revealing himself in the form of the person Jesus.

THE DEVELOPMENT OF DOCTRINES OFFERING A FUTURE HOPE

Death and Afterlife

Sheol.   Besides their four fundamental convictions about Yahweh, the Hebrews developed other key doctrines, most notably those concerning hope for the future. Hope for the future is a frequent theme in the Hebrew Bible, articulated for life on earth and later envisioned for a world beyond human experience. For centuries the Hebrews lacked a clear concept of human destiny beyond the grave, for they held to the vague idea of Sheol, a dreary abode below the earth where the dead lingered on without memory of their former lives (Gen. 37:35, Ps. 88:3–12).

Immortality of the Soul.   In the postexilic period, and especially in the Hellenistic period after the death of Alexander the Great in 323 BCE, concepts surrounding death and afterlife underwent fundamental alterations. Jewish texts from the Hellenistic and Roman periods betray several irreconcilable beliefs about the afterlife. One doctrine making inroads among the Jews at the time was a belief in the immortality of the soul, but not the raising of the body. This notion was inherited from the Greek religion and reflects the Platonic idea that body and soul are separate entities, the soul constituting the true essence of a person. Central to the doctrine of the immortality of the soul is the belief that the soul is liberated from the imprisoning body at death to seek a higher life.

The Season Sarcophagus. This partly preserved Jewish marble sarcophagus from Rome shows two Victories holding a medallion decorated with an elaborate seven-branched candelabrum (menorah), the chief symbol of the Jews in antiquity. Flanking the central scene are the Four Seasons represented by winged male figures (only Autumn remains intact). Three cupids underneath the medallion are busy trampling grapes in a vat ornamented with lion mask spouts. Their wine is sacred to the god Dionysus, whose cult promising an afterlife was widespread in the Roman Empire. Although the interpretation is disputed, some investigators suggest the bereaved family borrowed from non-Jewish mythological symbolism to express hope for an afterlife. c. 250 CE. Museo Nazionale Romano, Rome.

Resurrection.   A related but opposing belief gaining ground was that of resurrection, or the revival of the entire psycho-physical person after a period of death. Apparently this concept was borrowed from Zoroastrianism, the Persian religion, which seems to have profoundly influenced the development of Greek thought and, later, the beliefs of Judaism, Christianity, and Islam. A blanket term, resurrection covers several similar concepts, but essentially means the soul will be rejoined with the body at the end of time. The doctrine is often fused with notions of final rewards and punishments. The only unambiguous reference to resurrection occurs in the very late book of Daniel, where we read that at the termination of the age, "many of those who sleep in the dust of the earth shall awake, some to everlasting life, and some to shame and everlasting contempt" (Dan. 12:2). This portrayal does not include the consignment of the resurrected dead to a heaven or a hell, an idea nowhere appearing in the Hebrew Bible. We also read that the resurrection will come with the arrival of the divine warrior Michael (Dan. 12:1), a celestial prince, or archangel, who reflects the elaborate angelology developing in postexilic times, often attributed to Zoroastrian influence. The evolving doctrine of resurrection was far from universal among the Jews of the ancient world, however, and the belief remains a matter of personal choice in present-day Judaism, a religion that has always emphasized the arena of this world rather than any possible afterlife.

Messianic Hope and Apocalyptic Literature

A Messiah as a Monarch and Military Deliverer.   Another aspect of the attitude of hope for the future revolved around the idea of a Messiah, a term derived from the common biblical Hebrew word meaning "anointed one." The rite of anointing was mandatory for accession to the kingship, and the Hebrew Bible applies the designation Messiah, or anointed one, most often to kings, though also on occasion to high priests and others. Additional figures are described as anointed ones. We read that when the kingdom of Judah was under threat from the Assyrians and later the Babylonians, the prophets Isaiah and Jeremiah foretold a Yahweh-sent Messiah, a future king of the house of David who would rule in glory and righteousness. This hope of a king overcoming oppressive powers by force of arms remained widespread during the period of Roman rule.

A Messiah as a Divine Savior.   Other Jews developed a fundamentally different vision of the messianic hope, expecting not a military deliverer but a divine savior who would come through cosmic miracles and cataclysms. Apparently this concept of the Messiah was derived from the figure of Saoshyant, the Savior in the Zoroastrian religion. The Persians believed that Saoshyant—born supernaturally of a virgin—would resurrect all the dead on the Day of Judgement and then vindicate the righteous and condemn the faithless.

The Influence of Apocalyptic Literature.   The idea of the Messiah as a divine savior was highly influenced by apocalyptic literature, that is, ecstatic writing attempting to describe through the hidden meanings of cryptic language the final struggle between Yahweh and the forces of evil. Writers of apocalypse interpreted history as an ascending series of evils that would culminate with a supreme climax of wickedness in the near future. They encouraged the faithful by promising Yahweh's speedy intervention to terminate the present world order, reward the righteous, and damn the ungodly. Arising in the writings of Zoroastrianism, apocalyptic literature became more fully developed in Judaism, where the genre flourished from about 200 BCE until the close of the first century CE. We encounter the enigmatic figure of the Son of Man in a number of these texts. Originally regarded as a symbol of the children of Israel (as depicted in Daniel 7:13–18), in later writings (as the pseudepigraphical work of Enoch) the Son of Man becomes a messianic figure, a preexistent heavenly being in human form, who will come in glory at the end of earthly time in association with the divine kingship of Yahweh.

Visions of messianic hope characterized first-century Judaism and framed the environment in which Jesus of Nazareth lived and thought. The calamitous Jewish uprisings against Rome in the years 70 CE and 135 CE were largely the product of such fervent messianic expectations. We saw these two revolts ended with disastrous defeats bringing the Jews to the brink of destruction. Thereafter they turned away from intense messianic hope to emphasize the practice and study of the Torah.

THE HEBREW BIBLE AS LITERATURE

The Contents

The Torah.   The sacred texts of Hebrew law, teachings, prophecies, and religious experiences came to be regarded as one unit, though they were stored on a large number of different scrolls. They formed the twenty-four books of the Hebrew Bible (the Christian Old Testament was taken from the Hebrew Bible but differently arranged and divided, so that the total number of books is thirty-nine for most Protestant denominations, with additional books accepted as sacred in the Eastern Orthodox and Roman Catholic churches). The Hebrew Bible is divided into three main sections: the Torah, the Prophets, and the Writings. We noted that the Torah consists of the first five biblical books—Genesis, Exodus, Leviticus, Numbers, Deuteronomy—which Christians usually refer to as the Pentateuch (from the Greek *pentateuchos*, five scrolls). Essentially, the Torah is in the form of a narrative running from the stories of creation to the death of Moses. We saw that the basic meaning of the Hebrew word *torah* is instruction or guidance having the force of divine law. The entire Torah offers instruction or guidance about the nature of Yahweh, the covenant relationship with him, and the behavior he demands of his chosen people. The last of these is represented by the major collections of law in the last four books of the Torah. Although the Torah has traditionally been attributed to Moses, biblical scholarship indicates these books actually resulted from a lengthy process of compilation of various texts from different periods.

The Prophets.   The Prophets are subdivided into the Former Prophets and the Latter Prophets. The so-called Former Prophets consist of Joshua, Judges, Samuel, and Kings, with both Samuel and Kings separated into two books in the Christian Scriptures. The Former Prophets are actually historical books showing many signs of composite authorship. They continue the narrative from the death of Moses to the Babylonian exile. We noted that scholars refer to these texts, plus Deuteronomy, as the Deuteronomic history because of their common viewpoint. The Latter Prophets are classified according to length as the "major" prophets (Isaiah, Jeremiah, and Ezekiel) and the Twelve (Hosea to Malachi). The purported utterances of the Twelve appear together as the Book of the Twelve, though they are separated and designated the Minor Prophets in the Christian Bible.

The Writings.   The remaining eleven books belong to the Writings (or Hagiographa), a collection demonstrating a considerable range in content and style. The traditional arrangement in the Hebrew Bible is Psalms, Proverbs, Job, Song of Songs, Ruth, Lamentations, Ecclesiastes, Esther, Daniel, Ezra-Nehemiah, and Chronicles, with both Ezra-Nehemiah and Chronicles separated into two books in the Christian Scriptures and the order of Prophets-Writings reversed. As a whole, the Writings are essentially postexilic books, with parts dating as late as the third and second centuries BCE, though the earliest material originated in the period of the monarchy, if not earlier. Daniel, Ester, Ezra-Nehemiah, and Chronicles are history books covering the period from the Babylonian exile to the return. Proverbs, Job, and Ecclesiastes are classified as wisdom literature, writings in which sages offer their views, a very ancient genre in the Near East. The book of Proverbs contains many wise sayings or teachings about how to attain rich rewards in life, with obedience to the will of Yahweh usually mentioned as a prerequisite. The book of Job questions the rather casual optimism about life found in Proverbs, for we read that although Job obeys Yahweh, he is afflicted with much suffering. Ecclesiastes breathes a bitterly despairing and skeptical outlook on life, even offering the maxim "be not righteous overmuch" (Eccles. 7:16). The treasured book of the Psalms, consisting of hymns, or songs of praise, was compiled from older lyrics for use in the postexilic Temple. The Song of Songs is a collection of explicitly erotic love poems, in which a woman and her lover arouse one another sexually. The book of Ruth is a gripping short novel opposing the practice of discriminating against foreigners. The book of Esther, on the other hand, celebrates national and religious hatred. The author tells a story of an unsuccessful plot to kill the Jews living in the Persian Empire during the reign of one of its kings, but Esther, employing shrewdness and the weapon of sensuality, causes the slaughter to be directed against the accusers of the Jews. The book of Lamentations consists of five poems expressing intense grief over the siege and fall of Jerusalem. The book of Daniel tells a dramatic tale about a legendary Judean youth deported to Babylon in the early sixth century BCE by King Nebuchadnezzar. Marking the beginning of Jewish apocalyptic literature, the book of Daniel revolves around colorful accounts of the hero's wonders and his visions regarding the future of the world.

THE CANON OF THE HEBREW BIBLE

The Assembly at Jabneh (c. 90 CE).   The various literary units, oral and written, of the Hebrew Bible were formed from about 1200 to 100 BCE, with progressive stages of adding, subtracting, rearranging, and merging. By the second century BCE most of the books of the Hebrew Bible, as known today, were informally accepted as a scriptural standard—or canon—though the books of the Torah contained the laws regulating the Jewish community and thus enjoyed preeminent rank. Yet there was still considerable fluidity concerning standardization. Certain religious groups within the broad spectrum of Judaism seem to have had reservations about whether several books in the Writings should be recognized as authoritative, particularly Ezekiel (sometimes conflicting with the requirements of the Torah, exemplified by the differences between Ezekiel 46:6 and Numbers 28:11), Song of Songs (explicitly erotic), Ecclesiastes (negative and skeptical), and Esther (no mention of Yahweh). Moreover, the period from the second century BCE to the late first century CE witnessed a literary explosion producing numerous miscellaneous sacred books intended to serve as additional Writings. Apparently bitter debates took place concerning their authority. Jewish tradition affirms that about 90 CE an assembly of rabbis—teachers of the law—began deliberating at the small Palestinian coast town of Jabneh (Greek Jamnia), which served an important center of Jewish learning after the Roman destruction of the Temple, to fix the boundaries of the Writings.

The Septuagint. Apparently one of the related discussions of the rabbis concerned a translation of the Hebrew Bible into Greek by Jewish scholars working in Alexandria from the third to the first centuries BCE. Presumably intended for the Greek-speaking Jews in Egypt, this translation came to be known as the Septuagint, from the Latin word *septuaginta,* meaning seventy, because of an old legend that some seventy (or seventy-two) Jewish scholars were involved in the endeavor. The Septuagint is commonly abbreviated by the Roman numeral LXX.

The Apocrypha or Deuterocanonicals. The Septuagint included a number of books not belonging to the traditional canon (1 Esdras, Wisdom of Solomon, Sirach, Judith, Tobit, Baruch, the Letter of Jeremiah, additions to Esther, Susannah, Bel and the Dragon, the Song of the Three Children, and the four books of Maccabees). These works, composed between about 200 BCE and 100 CE, enjoyed a wide circulation among Hellenized Jewish communities. A number of them are important for shedding light on cultural or historical developments in the later Hellenistic and early Roman periods, notably 1 and 2 Maccabees, which separately record the story of the Jewish struggle for independence from Seleucid rule in the second century BCE. The additional books in the Septuagint, though regarded as edifying, failed to win final recognition in the Jewish religion as strictly canonical. Yet the language of much of the early Christian church was Greek, and the Septuagint became its Bible and only scripture at first. Most of the extra Septuagintal books—now generally termed the Apocrypha or the Deuterocanonicals—remain in the official biblical texts of both the Roman Catholic Church and, with additional Septuagintal material, the Eastern Orthodox Church. Protestant Christians either exclude the books altogether or print them in a separate section between the Old Testament and the New Testament.

The Pseudepigrapha. Another reported concern of the rabbis at Jabneh was the popularity of a body of highly diverse literature deriving from the same period as the Apocrypha and also intended as Writings. These books were ascribed, more often than not, to ancient biblical notables such as Abraham or Moses to enhance their authority. Although this practice represented nothing new, these particular pseudonymous Jewish works are conventionally termed the Pseudepigrapha. They are valuable sources for understanding the extraordinary ferment in Judaism at the time.

The Rabbinic Conclusion. The rabbis eliminated as canonical the Apocrypha and Pseudepigrapha but retained the three controversial books from the Writings: Ezekiel, Song of Songs, and Esther. Thus the canon of the Hebrew Bible had been essentially settled by the opening of the second century.

JEWISH PARTIES OR SECTS
IN THE FIRST CENTURY CE

The Pharisees

In the period between the outbreak of the Maccabean revolution in the second century BCE and the emergence of Christianity in the first century CE, heated party differences arose over how the devout Jew should interpret the tenets of faith in the daily world. Broadly defined, the Judaism of the first century, far richer in its complexity than later, encompassed various groups venerating the Torah and its holy traditions. The best known today are the Pharisees, though we must guard against a tendency to exaggerate their numbers. Rising in the second century BCE, the Pharisees were strictly orthodox in their loyalty to the Torah through dietary rules, fasting, tithing, prayer, circumcision, and Sabbath observance. They embraced beliefs in the resurrection of the body, life after death, and the advent of the Messiah, apocalyptic ideas presumably borrowed from the religion of Zoroastrianism. They fostered the synagogue as an institution of worship distinct from the Temple. Although castigated in the Christian Gospels, the Pharisees appear to have been held in high esteem by the Jewish masses for their Jewish exclusiveness and narrow piety. We saw that after the destruction of the Temple in 70 CE, the Pharisees established a center of Jewish learning at the coastal town of Jabneh.

Sacred Literature: The Two Talmuds.   The influence of the Pharisees on the development of what became normative Judaism was decisive. Although they honored the written law, the Pharisees were zealous in promoting the authority of the unwritten law, an unwieldy mass of orally transmitted and preserved expositions on the meaning of the Torah. This Oral Law seemed essential to the Pharisees because the Torah left many demands undefined, exemplified by its deficiency in providing an explicit explanation of what activities constitute work in relation to the prohibition of work on the Sabbath. Thus the Oral Law interpreted the Torah and applied its teaching to all aspects of life. During the last half of the second century CE this legal oral tradition of the Pharisees was compiled and arranged in the rambling work known as the Mishnah, which was produced by the rabbis, interpreters of the Jewish law and sharers of ideology with the Pharisees. The Mishnah and the Gemara (later commentaries and elaborations on the Mishnah) were incorporated in the two great Talmuds developed by generations of rabbinic scholars in the centuries after 200 CE. One Talmud originated in Roman Palestine, the Palestinian Talmud, and the other in Babylonia, the Babylonian Talmud. Overshadowing the Palestine Talmud in influence and importance, the Babylonian Talmud remains, next to the Bible, the principal written source of authority for the Jews.

The Rabbis.   The term rabbi arose in the first century CE to denote teachers of the Jewish law. At this time the rabbis came from the ranks of ordinary people and generally worked part time in trades such as carpentry. Defining themselves in the tradition of the Pharisees, the rabbis espoused teachings that became enshrined in

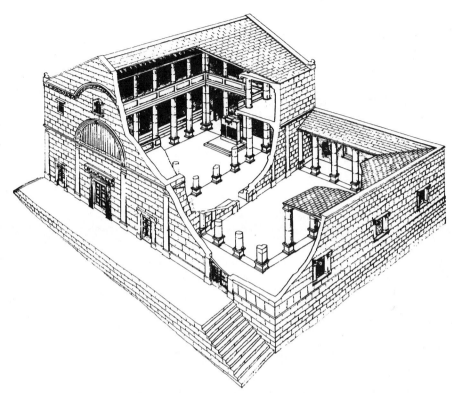

Reconstruction of the beautifully ornamented synagogue at Capernaum, now partly restored. Built of imported white limestone (now dated to the fourth century CE), the synagogue contained a permanent shrine for housing the Torah, a column-supported gallery for women and children, and an attached colonnaded portico and court, the last probably serving as a community school and providing overnight accommodations for travelers.

rabbinic Judaism, the form of the Jewish religion becoming normative by the second century CE. The rabbis could be found interpreting the Torah in the synagogue. We noted that early synagogues served to supplement the restored Temple cult at Jerusalem. The institution was well established by the first century CE, with synagogues flourishing in all the important towns of the Mediterranean world. Worship in the synagogue did not include sacrifice, as in the Temple, but revolved around prayer and the reading and interpreting of the Torah.

THE SADDUCEES

Opposing the Pharisees were the Sadducees, a party speaking for the interests of the ruling establishment, the upper-class priests in control of the Temple, and the affluent commercial and landed interests. The notable Jewish historian Josephus, writing in the late first century CE, tells us that the Sadducees' ties to the ruling class cost them popularity with the masses. Supporters of ancient Jewish religious traditions, the Sadducees opposed innovations such as the doctrine of resurrection of the dead and life after death, claiming these beliefs had no foundation in the Torah. They looked to a strict observance of the Torah to hold the Jewish community together, especially esteeming those provisions concerning the sacrificial cult of the Temple. We continue to hear of them as a party until sometime after the destruction of the Jerusalem Temple in 70 CE, when Judaism lost its priesthood and propitiatory sacrifices to become a religion dominated by rabbis and centered in the synagogue.

THE ZEALOTS

A third Jewish party, the Zealots, had emerged by the onset of the Jewish revolt in 66 CE. They were part of a coalition characterized by extreme opposition to Roman rule. The coalition embraced certain fanatics called the Sicarii, or Assassins, who carried concealed weapons to murder their opponents, and included other groups led by pretended kings and messianic figures. After the fall of Jerusalem in 70 CE, a last desperate group of Zealots fled to the fortress of Masada perched on lofty cliffs near the western shore of the Dead Sea, managing to hold out in the face of a bitter Roman siege until the year 73. Josephus tells us they committed mass suicide to avoid capture.

THE SAMARITANS

A fourth religious group, the Samaritans, are sometimes identified with those left behind in what had been the northern kingdom at the time of the Babylonian exile, though we find no clear evidence of their existence as a distinctive community in Palestine until postexilic times. They built their own temple on Mount Gerizim near the ancient site of Shechem and accepted as canonical only their own version of the Torah, which stresses Gerizim as the center of cultic life. They claimed to be Israelites preserving in an unblemished manner the religion of the northern kingdom. By the time of Jesus of Nazareth the relationship between the Samaritans and other Jewish groups had become extremely bitter. The Samaritans still survive as a small community in their ancestral home. Governed by a high priest, they retain their own traditions, including animal sacrifice, thus adhering to a religion clearly distinct from rabbinic Judaism.

THE ESSENES

A fifth Jewish group, the Essenes, separated themselves from the world to practice an abstemious devotion to the law and to await the end of historical time. Rejecting violence and force, the Essenes passively watched for Yahweh to bring in his kingdom. Thus they withdrew into seclusion, either in desert settings or in villages. Their devout religious communities rigorously observed the Sabbath, steadfastly refused to bear arms, and dutifully engaged in much fasting. Josephus reports they believed the body imprisons the soul, the latter to be rewarded or punished in the afterlife for the deeds performed in this world. Thus they accepted the idea of the immortality of the soul, but not bodily resurrection. Josephus also tells us these extreme ascetics excluded women and shunned marriage, but he mentions that one group of Essenes took wives merely to propagate. Like the Sadducees and the Zealots, the Essenes virtually disappeared with the fall of Jerusalem in the year 70, leaving Jewish leadership to the Pharisees and rabbis.

THE DEAD SEA SCROLLS

Scholarly opinion once widely accepted the view that the Essenes established a communal settlement at a site now called Khirbet Qumran on the northwest shore of the Dead Sea, depositing their manuscripts in nearby caves. This interpretation of the site as an Essene community has come under serious attack. Archaeological finds indicate that the complex at Qumran served as a fortress and was held by armed Jews at the outbreak of the Jewish revolt in 66. Archaeology also suggests that the stronghold was captured by the Romans, perhaps soon after the fall of Jerusalem in the year 70.

Hundreds of scrolls, some almost complete, but others in fragments, have been discovered near the ruins of Qumran and in neighboring areas since 1947. Labeled the Dead Sea Scrolls and dating between the second century BCE and the first century CE, this vast trove of manuscripts includes both traditional biblical texts and previously unknown works. We find copies of books of the Hebrew Bible, biblical commentaries, hymns and prayers, apocryphal and pseudepigraphical works, and unique sectarian compositions. A growing number of scholars interpret the scrolls as a collected library of important Jewish works hidden by Jews fleeing the Roman army from 67 to 73 CE. The collection nowhere mentions the name Essenes and seems to reflect the beliefs and aspirations of many diverse groups. The manuscripts are invaluable for contributing to our understanding of Judaism in all its varieties during the last centuries before the emergence and spread of Christianity. Conspicuous among the several genres represented in the scrolls is a distinctive Jewish apocalyptic literature, typified by its elaborate description of a holy war between the forces of light and darkness, reflecting Zoroastrian dualism. Writers of such material believed they were living in the last days and expected a messiah to establish a kingdom of heaven. Apparently some of this thinking was reflected in early Christianity. Moreover, scholars have identified numerous verbal parallels between the scrolls and the New Testament, particularly the Gospel of John.

THE PROBLEM OF THEODICY

Although the Jews developed fundamental concepts about Yahweh, they wrestled with a weighty theological problem focusing on their deity's rewards and punishments. This issue was closely linked to their belief in a special covenant relationship with Yahweh. In the biblical tradition, the covenant at Sinai included the promise that the Hebrews would reap earthly rewards for obedience to Yahweh's law but suffer earthly punishments for disobedience. Some Hebrews found this idea untenable because numerous people who obeyed the law suffered horrid afflictions, though others who disobeyed the law enjoyed wealth and apparent happiness. The doubters asked difficult questions: Why do children and the righteous often suffer, while the wicked prosper?

A number of thinkers and writers attempted to vindicate the character of their deity in the face of doubts arising from evil in life, an endeavor now known as theodicy. Thus theodicy attempts to explain why a supreme being of goodness would create a world where upright people suffer. One possible resolution would be for Yahweh to meet out rewards and punishments in an afterlife, an idea scarcely appearing in the Hebrew Bible. Yet beliefs about an existence beyond the grave had made inroads among the Jews after the Babylonian exile and seem to have been very popular during the Hellenistic and Roman periods. We noted the Pharisees taught the resurrection of the body and the Essenes believed souls were imperishable.

Other Jews thought the book of Job provided the most satisfactory response to the problem of theodicy. Job is presented to the reader as a righteous man afflicted with a loathsome disease and deprived of his children and possessions. His friends carry on an extensive dialogue with him, attempting to show that he is being punished for sin. Yet Job has not sinned, and he finally appeals directly to Yahweh for an answer. Yahweh speaks, denying that all suffering is the result of wickedness, all prosperity the result of righteousness. He declares his ways and wisdom are beyond human grasp. This instruction to Job that Yahweh's judgments are unfathomable and should never be questioned became the normative Jewish explanation for suffering. In short, the Jews simply dismissed the issue altogether. Later, the Christians too would find the problem of theodicy troublesome, but that is another story.

CHAPTER XII

GREAT POWERS OF WESTERN ASIA: ASSYRIA, CHALDEAN BABYLONIA, LYDIA

We now turn again to Mesopotamia, whose history was traced through the reign of Hammurabi in chapter 5. After the death of this extraordinary Amorite king, probably around the middle of the eighteenth century BCE, the Kassites from the east began entering the region. They extended their control over Babylonia in southern Mesopotamia in the early sixteenth century BCE, ruling for more than four hundred years until the Elamites struck fatally at their power in the twelfth century BCE. For the next half millennium the center of political activity in Mesopotamia shifts from Babylonia to its northern neighbor Assyria. The Assyrians become the first people to carve out an empire embracing almost the entire Near East, governing through an official policy of terror and brutality. Yet the seventh century BCE witnessed the decline and ultimate ruin of the huge Assyrian realm, the victim of internal weaknesses and external forces. The Assyrian capital of Nineveh fell to allied invaders in 612 BCE, despite the support of a reinvigorated Egypt (commonly called Saite Egypt in this period after its capital of Sais in the western Delta).

The victors divided the lands of the Assyrian Empire. The Medes living northeast of Assyria took their share, as did the Chaldeans inhabiting lower Mesopotamia. The Chaldeans were the chief successors to the Assyrian Empire. Their brilliant Neo-Babylonian (or Chaldean) Empire dominated a vast area stretching from Mesopotamia to the borders of Egypt. Yet the Chaldean triumph was all too brief, for the Persians from what is now Iran captured Babylon in 539 BCE, less than a century after the fall of Nineveh, and by rapid conquest extended their control westward to the Mediterranean and into Egypt and eastward to the Indus.

KASSITE BABYLONIA (c. 1595–1160 BCE)

The death of the famed Babylonian monarch Hammurabi, probably about 1750 BCE, was followed by a series of revolts leading to the rapid disintegration of his empire and the division of Babylonia into three parts: the central region remaining under the control of kings of Babylon, the southern section now being held by a new dynasty of raiders known as the Sealanders, and the northeast portion and the middle Euphrates region coming under the rule of invading Kassites, a peoples of obscure origin who probably had occupied the foothills of the Zagros Mountains in Iran before descending into Babylonia. Around a century and one-half later the Hittites

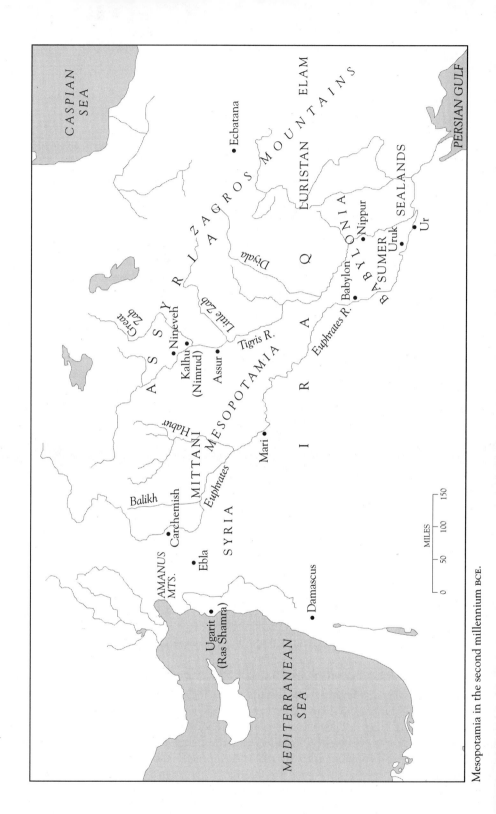

Mesopotamia in the second millennium BCE.

swept down the Euphrates to invade Mesopotamia from their home in Anatolia. They captured the city of Babylon about 1595 BCE, bringing the dynasty of Hammurabi to an inglorious end, but the Hittites soon withdrew, and both Babylon and the Sealand kingdom fell before renewed Kassite attacks. ·

Although the Kassites ruled Babylonia for more than four hundred years, from around 1595 to 1160 BCE, their meager textual remains do not permit us to assign their language to any known family. Apparently the cultural gap between the Kassites and that of the settled Babylonians was quite substantial, but the invaders adopted the culture of their subjects. The Kassites' religion, language, and social institutions had become thoroughly Babylonian within a century. By then the foreign origin of these highlanders was betrayed by little more than the small decorated stelae they had introduced for recording land grants, the molded bricks they employed to form figures in relief for decorating their buildings, and the Kassite names borne by some of their kings.

Apparently the Kassite kings, who were drawn from a small military aristocracy, presided over a mild, unoppressive government and provided their people with substantial periods of peace. Yet in the mid-twelfth century BCE the Elamites struck the Kassite kingdom with a deadly blow, thus terminating the longest dynasty in the history of Babylon. Babylonia then came under the rule of local dynasties. In the first millennium BCE the Kassites returned to the Zagros Mountains, where they generally maintained a degree of autonomy until after the time of Alexander the Great. They disappear from history in the first century CE.

ASSYRIA (c. 2300–612 BCE)

EARLY HISTORY (c. 2300–911 BCE)

The Land of Assur.   The Assyrians inhabited a narrow strip of rolling fertile land in northern Mesopotamia, eventually calling their compact domain the Land of Assur after their heavily fortified city of the same name on the middle Tigris. The city itself was named for the god of war, Assur, the chief deity in the Assyrian pantheon. Even today we apply a Greek form of the deity's name—Assyria—to the ancient Land of Assur. This country was blessed with considerable stone for building projects and moderate rainfall, both in contrast to its southern neighbor of Babylonia. Although what became the Assyrian state centered on the city of Assur, Nineveh served as a second major settlement. Also on the Tigris, Nineveh lay more than a hundred miles north of Assur and provided a splendid view of the foothills of the lofty Taurus range.

Historical and Cultural Links with Babylonia.   Not much is known about the earliest Assyrians, but by about 2300 BCE their homeland in northern Mesopotamia was ruled by the Sargonic kings of Akkad and later by the monarchs of the Third Dynasty of Ur. Clearly, Assyrian history and culture was closely linked with Babylonia.

For example, the Assyrians used cuneiform symbols to write their Semitic language, now called Old Assyrian, one of the main dialects of Akkadian.

Swaying Fortunes (c. 2000–1365 BCE).   With the collapse of the Third Dynasty of Ur about 2000 BCE, Assyria briefly emerged as an independent and relatively influential state. By the early second millennium BCE, as noted in chapter 8, Assyrian merchants had established flourishing colonies at various sites in eastern Anatolia, trading tin and textiles for copper, silver, and gold. Beginning about 1850 BCE, however, Assyria fell under the control of a succession of outside rulers, the inauguration of a period lasting for five centuries. Assyria became first a dependency of Amorite Babylonia and second, from about 1650 to 1360 BCE, a client of Mitanni. Because the trade routes between Babylonia and Armenia followed the course of the Tigris River, the Assyrian homeland was the scene of constant struggles between contending parties throughout this period of subjugation. The hardy Assyrian farmers and shepherds were transformed by these never-ending wars and centuries of outside domination into fierce warriors, developing a militaristic spirit that has forever characterized them.

Assyrian Expansion and Decline (c. 1365–911 BCE).   The first truly powerful Assyrian state emerged after Egypt brought Mitanni to its knees in the middle of the fourteenth century BCE. King Assur-uballit I (c. 1365–1330 BCE) recovered Assyrian independence and inaugurated a policy of expansion. Following the destruction of the Hittite Empire and the decline of Egypt shortly after 1200 BCE in the wake of the incursions by the dreaded Sea Peoples, Assyria filled the political vacuum and soon supplanted Babylonia as the chief military power in Mesopotamia. King Tiglath-pileser I (c. 1115–1077 BCE) even extended Assyrian rule briefly to the shores of the Mediterranean. Following his death, however, Assyria experienced more than a century of decline, with Arameans and other enemies pushing almost to the gates of Assur.

THE ASSYRIAN RESURGENCE (C. 911–745 BCE)

From the Accession of Adad-nirari II to the Death of Assurnasirpal II (c. 911–859 BCE). By the early ninth century BCE the kings were again mounting long raids, and Assyria swiftly became the principal power of the ancient Near East. This new period of Assyrian expansion began during the reign of Adad-nirari II (c. 911–891 BCE), who pushed the Assyrian frontiers east of the Tigris and down to the middle course of the Euphrates. The king also took control of some valuable trade routes east of Assyria and drove the Arameans out of the Tigris valley. His grandson Assurnasirpal II (c. 883–859 BCE) should be credited as the real founder of what historians term the Neo-Assyrian Empire. His armies extended Assyrian rule over many of the small kingdoms that stretched from Assyria westward to the Mediterranean. Assurnasirpal had a well-deserved reputation for resorting to savage torture and butchery during military campaigns, though a positive result of Assyrian expansion was the

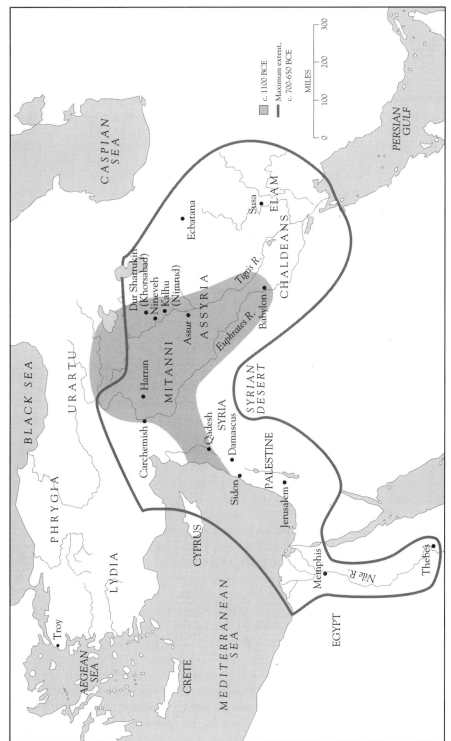

The Assyrian Empire.

further spread of Mesopotamian culture. He may have been the first Assyrian ruler resorting to a policy of mass deportations. The king and his successors dispersed conquered peoples around the Assyrian Empire on a massive scale to ensure imperial security and obtain forced labor, exemplified by his decision to bring defeated Aramean tribes from Syria to Assyria, where they were put to work constructing palaces and monuments. Assurnasirpal was a great builder, and he transformed Kalhu (biblical Calah, modern Nimrud) on the Tigris into the chief administrative city in Assyria. His magnificent palace here was filled with treasures, a number of which are now in the British Museum.

Shalmaneser III and His Weak Successors (c. 858–745 BCE).   Assurnasirpal was succeeded by his son Shalmaneser III (c. 858–824 BCE), who embarked on a campaign of conquest west of the Euphrates and pushed deep into northern Syria and Palestine. Yet revolts in Assyria at the end of his reign led to a period of gradual decline. The state was burdened with inept kings and a weak central government during the first half of the eighth century BCE, when the new kingdom of Urartu in the northeast encroached more and more on Assyrian territory and dominated the Syrian vassals.

THE CENTURY OF GREATEST EXPANSION (C. 745–627 BCE)

Tiglath-pileser III (c. 745–727 BCE).   Assyrian fortunes revived when the usurper Tiglath-pileser III, perhaps of royal blood, came to the throne about 745 BCE, ushering in the century of greatest Assyrian expansion. The first in a series of powerful rulers, Tiglath-pileser reorganized the army and embarked on a program of military conquest.

By this time the Kassite kings had long since been pushed out of Babylonia, and their weak native successors were unable to resist various invaders sweeping over the region. Among the intruders was a vigorous tribal group known as the Chaldeans, who had taken possession of the extreme southern part of Babylonia, now called Chaldea. Because the Chaldeans frequently attacked Assyria from the south, Tiglath-pileser began to intervene in Babylonian affairs. He captured the city of Babylon and conferred its kingship upon himself. Although his extensive campaigns against the great rival power of Urartu were only partly successful, he turned westward and pushed the Urartians out of northern Syria. We noted in chapter 10 that Tiglath-pileser devastated the kingdom of Israel for plotting against him, converting its outlying territories into Assyrian provinces. Then he incorporated Aramean Damascus in the Assyrian Empire. Now he ruled a vast stretch in the eastern Mediterranean, from the Taurus Mountains in the north to the border of Egypt in the south.

Tiglath-pileser established a system of roads and a regular messenger service to improve communications throughout the empire. He consolidated his conquests by appointing governors in some territories and using native kings in others to administer law, collect taxes, and recruit soldiers for the Assyrian army. His military success was made possible in part by the use of heavy infantry and cavalry, the latter supplied with iron weapons, superb horses, and war chariots.

Shalmaneser V (726–722 BCE).   Tiglath-pileser's son Shalmaneser V was faced with a troublesome coalition between Egypt and Israel and the refusal of the latter to pay its assigned tribute. Shalmaneser marched his Assyrian warriors to the very gates of Samaria, the capital of Israel. Although he seems to have died in battle, his successor Sargon II finished the task. Samaria endured a three-year siege but finally fell about 722 BCE. The Assyrians then abolished the kingdom of Israel, annexed its territory, and deported to Assyria many thousands of its leading citizens, thereafter known as the Ten Lost Tribes of Israel.

Sargon II (721–705 BCE): The First of the Sargonids.   Sargon II, probably another usurper, took his name from the great Sargon of Agade ruling some fifteen hundred years earlier. Historians conventionally refer to the last kings of the Assyrian Empire as the Sargonids, of whom four—Sargon II and his descendants Sennacherib, Esarhaddon, and Assurbanipal—astonished the Near Eastern world with their extensive conquests and magnificent monuments. Sargon himself moved the capital from Kalhu to a new site northeast of Nineveh called Dur-Sharrukin, or City of Sargon (modern Khorsabad). Reliefs once adorning the huge royal palace of the new capital are among the treasures of the Louvre.

Most of Sargon's time was spent fighting. The chief campaign of his reign, an invasion of the kingdom of Urartu, took place in 714 BCE. The Assyrians ravished the richest provinces of Urartu and left the kingdom defenseless. Soon the Urartians were faced with swift-moving invaders from the north, the Cimmerians, a warlike people who inflicted deadly blows. The Cimmerians were prevented from pushing into Assyria in 705 BCE only by the prompt military response of Sargon, though he fell in battle. Deflected from Assyrian territories, the wild barbarian horde pushed west into Anatolia, where they overthrew the large kingdom of Phrygia, the realm of the legendary Midas, and then pressed violently against the fabulously wealthy kingdom of Lydia, a new power in the western part of the peninsula. Eventually the Cimmerians came under the yoke of the Lydians and were gradually absorbed into the native population of western Anatolia.

Sennacherib (704–681 BCE).   Sargon's son Sennacherib, experienced as an administrator and soldier, enlarged and consolidated the empire. He rebuilt the ancient city of Nineveh (across the Tigris from modern Mosul) to serve as the worthy new capital of a great empire. Many-gated Nineveh was fortified with double walls having a circumference of more than nine miles. Sennacherib adorned the botanical garden of the capital with plants and trees brought from all parts of the empire, and he constructed a long canal—a marvel of civil engineering—to carry fresh water to the city from mountain streams some thirty miles away. The king's palace, constructed on an immense artificial platform, was decorated with rich woods, marble, and ivory. Sennacherib had developed a keen interest in promoting new techniques in irrigation and bronze casting, but he was forced to spend most of his time quelling uprisings in his far-flung empire.

After King Hezekiah of Judah became entangled with Egypt and the Phoenician and Philistine cities against Assyria, an angry Sennacherib swept through

Palestine with fire and sword in 701 BCE. He captured Phoenician and Philistine towns and surrounded Jerusalem. Lord Byron lamented the siege of Jerusalem with his familiar lines beginning, "The Assyrians came down like the wolf on the fold." The chastened Hezekiah paid an enormous tribute and remained a fearful and loyal vassal throughout the remainder of his reign.

Sennacherib's reign was badly marred by a series of unusually bitter wars against Babylonia and its chief ally, Elam. He gained control over northern Babylonia—the south remained under firm Chaldean rule—by placing one of his younger sons on the throne of Babylon, but the newly elevated king was betrayed to the Elamites and presumably slain. Sennacherib soon made the fateful decision to end effective Babylonian opposition once and for all. In 689 BCE he marched into Babylon, internationally revered for well over a millennium as a center of religion and culture, and massacred its inhabitants. Sennacherib then ordered the destruction of the sacred city, an almost unthinkable deed that included leveling the temple of Marduk and transporting the statue of the god to Assyria. Such sacrilege caused widespread terror and resentment, even among the Assyrians.

Esarhaddon (680–669 BCE). In 681 BCE the brutal Sennacherib was murdered by two of his own sons while praying in a temple, a death widely regarded as divine punishment. Earlier, he had designated his youngest son, the energetic Esarhaddon, as his rightful successor, a decision arousing intense sibling jealousies and ultimately leading to Sennacherib's assassination. Esarhaddon hastened to Nineveh to face his usurping brothers, but they fled after many of their soldiers deserted to him. His initial act was to atone for his father's sacrilege by rebuilding Babylon, symbolically molding one brick with his own hands.

Esarhaddon directed his chief campaign at Egypt, for the Nubian rulers of the kingdom had repeatedly intrigued with several of the vassal rulers owing allegiance to Assyria. Esarhaddon invaded Egypt in 671 BCE, vanquishing its army and proclaiming himself king. This was the maximum expansion of the Assyrian Empire. Upon his departure, however, the Nubian king (Taharqa) returned, fomented a rebellion, and expelled the occupying forces. Hastening back toward Egypt, Esarhaddon fell sick and died on the way.

Assurbanipal (668–627 BCE). Esarhaddon's son Assurbanipal was the last great king of Assyria. Assurbanipal was left to carry out the attack planned against Egypt by his father, and his army managed to take the city of Memphis and the entire Delta. Yet the new Assyrian ruler had to fight constantly to retain his inheritance. He became involved in a war in Babylonia against his brother Shamash-shum-ukin, another son of Esarhaddon. Before his untimely death, Esarhaddon had proclaimed Shamash-shum-ukin as the crown prince of Babylon and Assurbanipal as the legitimate heir to the throne of Assyria. Shamash-shum-ukin, installed as king of Babylon, apparently resented his subordinate status to his brother in Nineveh and eventually became involved in anti-Assyrian plots hatched by the Chaldeans, the Elamites, the Egyptians, and others. With the aid of the Elamites, Shamash-shum-ukin attacked the Assyrian garrisons in Babylonia in 652 BCE. Yet the outbreak of a civil war in Elam soon forced the Elamites to return home. The Assyrians seized the initiative and cleared southern Babylonia of Chaldean forces. Next they marched against the rebel king, besieging Babylon for three years, its defenders resorting to cannibalism and other desperate measures to remain alive. The storied city was finally captured in 648 BCE, but Shamash-shum-ukin threw himself into the flames of his burning palace to avoid capture.

The furious Assurbanipal hunted down the surviving rebels, boasting "I fed their corpses—cut into small pieces—to the dogs, the swine, the wolves, the vultures, the birds of heaven, and the fish of the deep." Then proceeding to crush the Elamites, Assurbanipal marched through the whole of their country and devastated their cities, beginning in 647 BCE. Never had the Assyrian Empire seemed so invincible, but its dazzling façade was beginning to show cracks, some of which were self-imposed. Assurbanipal's horrible vengeance upon Elam, for example, left this important buffer state in shambles and opened his eastern borders to attack by the hostile Medes. The Median kingdom, situated northeast of Assyria, was on the rise and refused to pay tribute. Meanwhile the vigorous new Saite dynasty in Egypt had asserted its independence and expelled the occupying Assyrian garrisons. Yet when Assurbanipal died in 627 BCE, all of his father's Assyrian Empire—with the exception of Egypt—remained essentially intact. The king had even won the addition of Lydia in western Anatolia as a tributary ally. Nineveh was still the largest and most magnificent city in the world, and Assurbanipal's library there contained some 20,000 cuneiform tablets. At this time Assyria must have appeared at the height of its power to the casual observer, but in reality the empire was on the verge of extinction. The end came so quickly and completely that details remain elusive.

THE DESTRUCTION OF ASSYRIA (626–605 BCE)

The Revolt of Nabopolassar (626 BCE).   The major figure after the death of Assurbanipal was the Chaldean leader Nabopolassar, who was acting as the Assyrian governor of southern Babylonia. By seizing the kingship of Babylonia in 626 BCE, Nabopolassar not only inaugurated the final Babylonian dynasty but also laid the foundation for the vast realm historians call the Neo-Babylonian (or Chaldean) Empire. For the next eleven years the Assyrians and the Chaldeans attacked and counterattacked one another. In the meantime Nabopolassar formed an alliance with the powerful Median king—ancient Greek writers know him as Cyaxares—for the purpose of conquering and dividing Assyria.

The Destruction of Nineveh (612 BCE).   The desperate Assyrians were supported only by Egypt, now alarmed that Scythian and other nomadic tribes from the north were pouring over the upper frontiers of the Assyrian Empire to menace all of Syria-Mesopotamia. Yet the Chaldean and Median alliance ultimately spelled Assyrian disaster. The dismantled Elamite state was no longer able to block the Medes, who stormed and destroyed the ancient Assyrian capital of Assur in 614 BCE. Then the Chaldeans and the Medes, aided by Scythians, launched a horrible assault against Nineveh in 612 BCE. They astonished the world by taking the proud city, obliterating its palaces and temples with flames. Although a remnant of the Assyrians fled a hundred miles west to the city of Harran, they would survive a mere three years before falling into the hands of the Babylonians and the Medes.

Battle of Carchemish (605 BCE).   A grim epilogue followed. The remaining Assyrian forces, despite the armed support of King Necho II of Egypt, were decisively defeated by the Babylonians in a battle near Carchemish on the upper Euphrates in 605 BCE. Most inhabitants of the ancient Near East celebrated the death blow to the detested Assyrians, who had made the world tremble for three centuries. A few years earlier, in response to the crumbling of the Assyrian Empire, the biblical prophet Nahum had roared: "All who hear the news of you clap their hands over you. For upon whom has not come your unceasing evil?" (Nah. 3:19). The most hated people of antiquity, the Assyrians were so completely exterminated or brutally enslaved that they eventually disappeared without a trace from the face of the earth.

Territorial Gains of the Conquerors.   In the meantime the victors divided the spoils. The Medes took extensive territories not only in eastern Anatolia but also in the old Assyrian provinces north and east of the Tigris. Their vassals, the Persians, would soon rule ancient Elam and eventually the entire ancient Near East. The Chaldeans gobbled up the western reaches of the Assyrian Empire, thereby ruling a vast domain that stretched from Babylonia to southeast Anatolia and down to the borders of Egypt.

ASSYRIAN CULTURE

ARCHAEOLOGICAL DISCOVERIES

Sir Austen Henry Layard and Hormuzd Rassam.   Beginning in 1845 the dauntless English archaeologist and later diplomat Sir Austen Henry (christened Henry Austen) Layard brought Assyria out of obscurity by excavating two huge mounds of debris beside the Tigris, exposing the remains of both Kalhu and Nineveh. His discoveries stunned the world. Layard and his helpers unearthed vast archives of cuneiform documents, brilliant reliefs, and monumental sculptures such as massive winged bulls and great sphinxes. At the site of Nineveh he uncovered the palace of Sennacherib as well as extraordinary artworks, though his most important find here was the royal archives, including the great library of Assurbanipal. Layard carried to the British Museum many cuneiform texts that later would aid in the decipherment of the Sumerian and Akkadian languages and also would permit the reconstruction of much of the history and literature of Assyria and Babylonia. Layard's assistant, Hormuzd Rassam, was a native of the city of Mosul across the Tigris from the site of Nineveh. After Layard entered political life, the British Museum retained Rassam to continue the archaeological work at Nineveh, where he discovered the remainder of the royal library plus many splendid Assyrian and Babylonian antiquities now in the British Museum.

STATE AND SOCIETY

The King.   Assyria was essentially a military state depending on the ruthless efficiency of the army for exercising dominance. The overwhelming power of imperial Assyria was embodied in the king, regarded as the earthly representative and instrument of the supreme deity Assur. Almost all of the Assyrian kings were forceful figures who spent the campaign season in the field and much of the rest of the year hunting. The king was also a priest and as such was burdened by numerous time-consuming and complicated magico-religious duties. He presided over the chief religious celebrations of Assyria and Babylonia, most notably the New Year Festival, and took part in numerous rituals. The king consulted oracles on all matters of importance. Divine displeasure was thought to be revealed through certain signs, such as a lunar or solar eclipse, both of which were interpreted to portend the death of the monarch. A surrogate then temporarily occupied the throne for a hundred days, after which the substitute was apparently put to death to give the gods the kingly death that had been foretold.

The Queen and the Crown Prince.   The Assyrian queen was treated with deference, for she was not only the principal wife of the king, who linked the gods and the people, but also the mother of the crown prince. She and the royal concubines lived in a harem guarded by eunuchs. A queen might play a powerful role at court, especially if she held the important office of regent during the minority of her kingly son. The crown prince was elaborately trained for his role as future ruler. Although peaceful and orderly succession could be disrupted by the ambitions or jealousies of younger sons and other members of the royal family, the possibility of endless dynastic crises at the death of a king was largely averted by the strong hereditary character of the Assyrian monarchy. Each reigning sovereign chose his successor from among his sons and made certain that the new king-designate was endorsed by the other members of the royal family, the nobles, and the high officials of the realm.

Social Classes under the Royal Family.   To administer the empire, the kings created an extensive central bureaucracy that included generals, high priests, and provincial governors. These top royal officials were drawn from the Assyrian nobility, the highest of the four social classes under the royal family. Although our understanding of Assyrian social gradations remains patchy, the next rank seems to have been a professional class of merchants, bankers, scribes, artisans, physicians, and the like. The professional class helped to bring prosperity to the kingdom, but industry and commerce were scorned as unworthy of a military people. Accordingly, these pursuits were conducted for the Assyrians mainly by foreigners, especially the Arameans and the Hebrews. Next came an ill-defined class of agricultural workers and soldiers ranking much lower than the professional class but well above the slaves. Slaves were generally recruited from indebted families and prisoners of war. They enjoyed certain rights, and some managed to enter a profession or even gain a high administrative post.

Law. We noted that the history of Assyria was linked both culturally and politically with Babylonia. Assyrian legal collections were based on the laws of Hammurabi and other Babylonian models, though Assyrian penalties tended to be more severe. The Assyrians—like the Hebrews—imposed their harshest punishments for behavior lowering the birth rate, such as homosexual activity and abortions. The penalty for certain cases of homosexual anal intercourse was castration. Yet homosexual activity is well attested, whether between men and men or between men and boys. Moreover, homosexual activity with male temple prostitutes was sanctioned by ancient religious tradition, as was sexual behavior involving female temple prostitutes. Abortion, on the other hand, was a criminal offense of extreme consequence. Any woman shown to have undergone the procedure was executed by impalement, her body left unburied. In contrast to Babylonian legal practice, Assyrian law completely subjugated women. A husband could inflict corporal punishment, even mutilation, upon his wife. He was free to put an adulterous spouse to death, and the right of divorce fell entirely within his hands.

THE ARMY

The Assyrian army—the most powerful military machine the ancient Near East had ever witnessed—was the king's primary instrument for enforcing his will upon the empire. At first the army was drawn mainly from the Assyrian peasants in times of warfare, but as the empire expanded, the kings organized an immense standing army. With provisional governors recruiting fighting men from all over the empire, Assyria was capable of putting into the field a force of well over a hundred thousand men. The Assyrians had acquired skills in smelting iron from the Hittites, and by the early ninth century BCE their army had become the first to employ iron weapons on a large scale, one reason for its astonishing victories.

Eventually the Assyrians forces were divided into four branches: light infantry, heavy infantry, chariotry, and cavalry. The light infantrymen were mainly slingers and archers. Clad in a short tunic, they fought without defensive weapons. The heavy infantrymen, the mainstay of the army, were armed with spear, sword, and dagger, and they were protected by armor, high conical helmets, and tall shields. Crack heavy infantry units provided the model for the powerful Greek phalanx of later times. The chariotry was famous for its archers riding on very efficient two-wheeled chariots. Each vehicle carried one or two bowmen, a couple of shield bearers, and a driver. After exhausting their arrows, the charioteers were prepared to wield lances. The cavalry, the newest branch of the army, was gradually superseding the chariotry. Cavalrymen were armed with a small bow or a long spear and rode without saddle or stirrups. In the days before the cavalry had fully evolved, a mounted, shield-bearing attendant rode alongside each cavalryman to hold the reins of both their horses, thereby freeing the archer's hands for firing at a gallop. By the Sargonid period, however, cavalrymen rode solo as true cavalry. The Assyrians imported superb horses—probably from Anatolia, Syria, and Iran—for the use of the chariotry and cavalry.

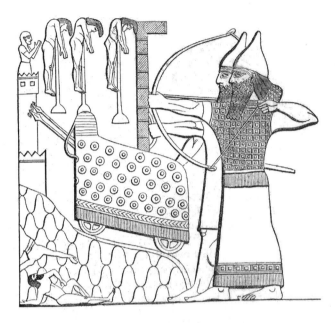

Drawn from a relief found at Nimrud (ancient Kalhu), this scene of Assyrian warriors before a besieged city shows a battering ram drawing up to the walls while archers provide covering fire, with a grisly depiction at the top of naked captives impaled on stakes.

Among the specialized units of the army was a corps of engineers, its members contributing to the besieging of fortified towns by digging tunnels, filling in moats, and the like. The Assyrians were masters of siege warfare. They undermined enemy walls with various siege weapons, exemplified by catapults and battering rams, and on occasion they moved wheeled platforms against such walls to position themselves on the same level with their foes.

The Assyrians reduced their conquered opponents to obedience by inflicting unspeakable atrocities, thereby spreading terror over great distances and minimizing the necessity for actual military action. Inhabitants of captured towns might have their hands, ears, noses, and genitals cut off. Sometimes the victims were skinned alive, blinded, burned to death, or impaled on stakes.

RELIGION

Much of Assyrian art, literature, law, and religion was based on Babylonian models. In terms of religious beliefs and practices, the Assyrians were quite aware of the great debt they owed to the Babylonians (and through them to the earlier Akkadians and Sumerians). Assurbanipal, while campaigning in Elam, discovered a statue of the goddess Ishtar that had been carried from the city of Uruk some 1500 years earlier. The king returned the image to its ancient Sumerian site as an act of piety. Both the Babylonian and the Assyrian priests taught that deities, though present everywhere, were most easily approached in the temples. Priests enjoined worshipers to observe the cycle of the agricultural year through fertility rites, of which the most important was still the New Year Festival.

Assur.   Not surprisingly, the deities of the Assyrians and the Babylonians were much the same, except for the high god. The supreme national deity in Assyria was the war-god Assur, originally the local god of Assur, the holy city and first capital of the country. Eventually Assur was elevated above all other divinities and acquired the imposing title Lord of the Universe. Because Assur had gradually absorbed many features of prominent Mesopotamian deities such as Enlil and Marduk, his theology lacked distinctive focus. Yet his role as a personification of the political interests of Assyria was made absolutely clear. The Assyrians placed his symbol—a winged disk—on standards their fighting forces carried all over the ancient Near East.

Demons.   Although the Assyrians believed deities helped to safeguard the passage through life, their religion inculcated an extreme fear of evil spirits. Innumerable demonic forces required appeasement by charms and priests. They were everywhere. One of them, the terrible female demon Lamashtu, stole infants from their mothers' breasts. Such ideas furthered the Assyrian policy of ruling through fear, for subject peoples were absolutely terrorized by horrible tales about hosts of dreaded supernatural beings.

Divination.   One prominent aspect of the Assyrian religion was divination, the attempt to foretell future events or discover hidden knowledge by occult or supernatural means. Practitioners of divination employed special techniques such as inspecting the configuration and color of sheep livers, interpreting dreams, and observing the stars and planets. The most important method of divination for formulating state policy was astrology. Although the Assyrians made discoveries in astronomy while watching for solar and lunar eclipses, they observed the heavens to make predictions about affairs of state, thereby promoting astrology at the expense of astronomy. Yet they achieved some success in predicting eclipses, and they recognized and named the five visible planets.

MEDICINE

The Assyrians ascribed disease to supernatural origin, but they realized the physical symptoms of illness could be treated, sometimes successfully, by medical procedures and drugs. Thus they confronted disease not only with magic and incantation but also with medicines, believing both methods of treatment might aid in expelling the demons thought to cause the malady. The Assyrians catalogued hundreds of drugs, some containing quite unsavory ingredients. The efficacy of these medicinal substances must have varied considerably.

ART AND ARCHITECTURE

Jewelry and Ivories.   Despite their austere military life and policy of maintaining supremacy through terror, the Assyrians encouraged astounding artistic endeavors. They exhibited a love of bright colors, perfumes, and luxury. The Assyrians, or the artisans they hired from all over the empire, created magnificent pieces of metalware in bronze, gold, and silver. Archaeologists working at the site of the fortress city of Kalhu discovered royal tombs heaped with gold jewelry of exquisite quality. Assyrian ivories, too, are remarkable for their skill of execution. Worked in a variety of ways, ivory was carved into objects such as boxes, spoons, combs, plaques, and fig- urines of people or animals, though most examples consist of small incised panels applied as ornamentation to furniture, doors, screens, and other things.

Royal Palaces.   While exhibiting a certain freshness and originality, Assyrian archi- tecture suggests a logical development from Old Babylonian buildings, with addi- tional inheritances from the Hurrians, Hittites, Egyptians, and others. The heavily walled royal palaces display the ostentatious grandeur so prized by Assyrian kings and were designed as a complex of rooms built around a series of courtyards. Four of the greatest were the massive residences built by Assurnasirpal II at Kalhu, Sargon II at Dur-Sharrukin, and Sennacherib and Assurbanipal at Nineveh. An Assyrian royal palace was usually erected on a huge platform that was level with the tops of the thick walls surrounding the city. Splendid gardens surrounded the palaces, but the kings added a grisly note by hanging the heads of conquered rulers in the trees. Like other Mesopotamian buildings, the palace was built chiefly of sun-dried bricks, though crucial parts of the exterior walls were covered with baked bricks, which were embellished with multicolored glazes, the glazing technique having been trans- mitted to Assyria from Egypt by way of Syria. Stone was easily obtainable in Assyria, in contrast to Babylonia, permitting walls to be faced with ornamental upright stone slabs that were incised with monumental figures.

The Palace of Sargon II at Dur-Sharrukin.   The unfinished royal citadel of Sargon II at Dur-Sharrukin, begun about 720 BCE, was flanked by three modest temples, a lofty painted ziggurat, armories, and splendid dwellings for high officials. The entire palace-city complex covered a square mile. The royal residence itself was far more sumptuous than the religious buildings and contained more than two hundred rooms and courtyards, including the harem, servants' quarters, treasuries, guard rooms, and state apartments. Essential to every Assyrian palace was a brightly painted throne room used by the king for receiving tribute-bearing vassals and ambassadors. Appar- ently the throne room and other chambers at Dur-Sharrukin were topped with brick barrel vaults, which formed semicylindrical ceilings, as in a tunnel.

Portal Figures.   In the Hittite tradition of carving huge portal figures of sphinxes and lions intended to enfeeble evil influences and enemies, the Assyrians flanked entrances to royal palaces with colossal limestone guardian creatures in the form of winged bulls or lions having heads of ornately bearded men. These portentous fig- ures are not true statues in the round but are attached to stone slabs, reflecting the fact that Assyrian sculpture was chiefly in relief. Moreover, the mythical creatures combine a front view at rest with a side view in movement, a contrivance necessi- tating the addition of fifth legs on the sides.

Reliefs.   Although the smaller palaces were decorated with economical mural paintings, sculptors embellished the great royal residences with pictorial friezes in

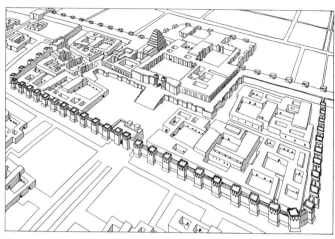

Reconstruction of the fortress city built by Sargon II at Dur-Sharrukin (modern Khorsabad), surrounded by towered walls with seven gates. The fortification walls enclosed an entire square mile of buildings and courtyards, with the huge royal palace (top center) erected on a high platform. The religious complex stood just west of the palace and included a small painted ziggurat and several temples. Begun in 717 BCE, the lavishly adorned palace-fortress was abandoned as the Assyrian capital after Sargon was killed during warfare in 705 BCE.

low relief carved on huge upright slabs of stone lining the lower parts of interior walls. More than life-size, the Assyrian reliefs tell stories with a wealth of detail and portray historical events with seemingly remarkable accuracy. Scenes stress the Assyrian ideal of brutal and masculine power. The dominant figure is the king, his greatness recorded in unmistakable terms by skilled artisans summoned from all over the Near East. The two most common themes are macabre royal conquests and successful royal hunts. Although the kingdom of the gods is occasionally symbolized, exemplified by two hands emerging from the clouds to represent Assur, the kingdom of the monarch receives preeminent attention. Because the king was the earthly representative and instrument of heaven, the sculptors treat all aspects of his existence, even his dining, as divinely significant.

The Assyrian sculptors excelled more so than any others in the ancient Near East in creating a sense of naturalism and spatial illusionism. The famous relief called *The Great Lion Hunt*, executed about 650 BCE at the palace of Assurbanipal at Nineveh, seemingly breathes dynamism into stone through its sense of motion, its straining muscles and swelling veins. Yet this monument also projects an illusion of almost unbearable ferocity and mayhem that is typical of Assyrian reliefs. Now at the British Museum, the work portrays Assurbanipal shooting down lions that have been released from cages and have no chance of escape. Behind his chariot lies a scene of unrelieved carnage showing dying and dead lions riddled with far more arrows than needed to kill them. In a detail depicting a dying lioness, the helpless creature still snarls defiantly, though her hindquarters have been paralyzed by an arrow piercing her spine.

This colossal winged bull with the head of an ornately bearded man once guarded a doorway of Assurnasirpal II's great palace at Kalhu (modern Nimrud), excavated by Layard. Locked in their stone slabs, even the great winged beasts are classified as relief rather than sculpture in the round. Such figures mark the height of Assyrian relief in the attention to detail and the power of the imagery. c. 870 BCE. Alabaster. British Museum, London.

ASSURBANIPAL'S LIBRARY AT NINEVEH

His ruthlessness notwithstanding, Assurbanipal left a valuable legacy to the modern world: his magnificent library at Nineveh. The most important single collection of cuneiform tablets, Assurbanipal's library is now largely in the British Museum and remains an indispensable guide to Mesopotamian literature. The king's enormous collection brought together some 20,000 tablets bearing texts mainly of Babylonian origin. We find omens, rituals, prayers, incantations, wisdom literature, and many other subjects, along with masterpieces such as the Epic of Gilgamesh and the Myth of Creation. Reflecting his passion for erudition, Assurbanipal boasts in a famous inscription that he could "read abstruse tablets whose Sumerian is obscure and whose Akkadian is hard to construe. . . ."

THE NEO-BABYLONIAN EMPIRE (612–539 BCE)

After the collapse of the Assyrian Empire at the end of the seventh century BCE, four powerful states flourished briefly in the Near East: the Neo-Babylonian (or Chaldean) Empire extending from Mesopotamia to the Egyptian border, Media in Iran and eastern Anatolia, Lydia in western Anatolia, and Saite Egypt. The chief successors to the Assyrian Empire were the Chaldeans, a Semitic-speaking tribal people who had settled in southern Babylonia near the Persian Gulf by the second half of the ninth century BCE. They adopted Babylonian traditions and played a prominent role in the Gulf trade. Although the Chaldeans dominated the Near East for less than a century, they brought about the last great period of cultural creativity in ancient Babylonia.

THE EARLY KINGS (626–562 BCE)

Nabopolassar (626–605 BCE). We noted that the Chaldean leader Nabopolassar, who was also the Assyrian governor of southern Babylonia, seized the throne of Babylonia in 626 BCE and inaugurated the final Babylonian dynasty, known to historians as the Chaldean (or Neo-Babylonian) dynasty. Allying himself with the Medes, Nabopolassar participated in the wars that destroyed the tottering Assyrian Empire. We are able to follow these rapidly unfolding events through a series of invaluable Babylonian chronicles. After the fall of Nineveh, the Medes focused on consolidating their conquests in eastern Anatolia, leaving Nabopolassar in virtual control of Assyria. In 610 BCE the Chaldeans and the Medes crushed the remnant of the Assyrian army near the northern city of Harran, and the surviving Assyrians retreated to Carchemish on the upper Euphrates in Syria. The new Egyptian king Necho II, alarmed by the prospect of the Medes and the Chaldeans upsetting the balance of power in Mesopotamia and Syria, decided to provide maximum support for the remaining Assyrians. In the meantime the aging Nabopolassar entrusted Nebuchadnezzar, his eldest son, with the command of the Chaldean army, and in 605 BCE the crown prince decisively defeated the powerful Egyptian army in a bloody battle near Carchemish, forever ending the possibility of an Assyrian revival. The energetic Nebuchadnezzar chased the panic-stricken Egyptians southward and might have followed them into their country but for the news of King Nabopolassar's death.

Nebuchadnezzar II (605–562 BCE). A worthy successor of his father, Nebuchadnezzar II hastened back to Babylonia and secured the throne. The remarkable king pushed his frontiers to the Persian Gulf, the Taurus Mountains, and the borders of Egypt, thereby carving out a large empire embracing Mesopotamia and Syria-Palestine. The Neo-Babylonian Empire, representing the final triumph for ancient Babylonia, briefly functioned as the principal political power in western Asia, maintaining its grasp until the Persians captured Babylon in 539 BCE. Political relations with Media to the east were friendly, and Egypt was constrained within its borders, but opposition from the vassal state of Judah caused considerable unrest. We saw

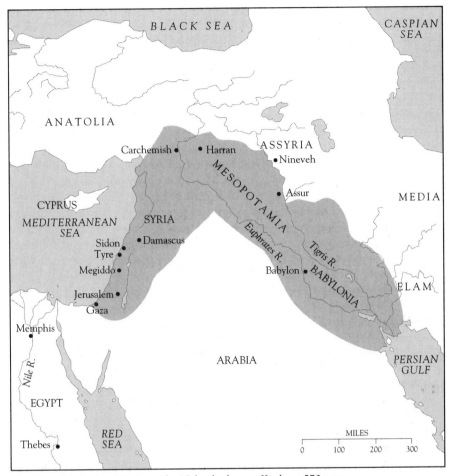

The Neo-Babylonian Empire under Nebuchadnezzar II, about 570 BCE.

in chapter 10 that Nebuchadnezzar's most famous victory was his conquest of Jerusalem and Judah, with the deportation of thousands of leading citizens to Babylonia. The Jews generally prospered in Babylonia, where they developed farmlands and embarked upon commercial ventures.

THE LATER KINGS (562–539 BCE)

Nabonidus (556–539 BCE).   Nebuchadnezzar's three immediate successors, ruling between 562 and 556 BCE, had brief, disappointing reigns. Two of them were murdered during rebellions. The conspirators of the second assassination conferred the kingship on Nabonidus, who was not of the royal house of Nabopolassar. Ascending the throne in 556 BCE, Nabonidus had served as a diplomat of high ability under two Chaldean kings. He was a native of Harran, the final seat of Assyrian power, where his aged mother served as the high priestess of the god Sin. Both the king's complex personality and his later actions contributed, through a confusion of names, to the legends of madness told of Nebuchadnezzar in the biblical book of Daniel.

Nabonidus favored the moon-god Sin of his birthplace over Marduk, the ancient and honored patron of Babylon, and he zealously attempted to elevate his preferred deity as the supreme god of the empire. In obedience to a divine command in a dream, Nabonidus rebuilt the great temple of the god Sin at Harran, destroyed when the city was captured from the Assyrians in 610 BCE, and the king bestowed special attention on other centers of moon worship. His slighting of Chaldean spiritual sensibilities enraged the priests of Marduk in Babylonia and weakened the unity of the state.

The most curious feature of Nabonidus' reign was his abandonment of Babylon for the distant oasis of Teima in northwest Arabia, where he remained about ten years, leaving his son Belshazzar as regent in Babylon. Scholars have offered many intriguing suggestions to explain Nabonidus' exile, ranging from personal to politico-economic reasons. The devotion of the ancient Arabs to the moon-god, worshiped under various names, must have been a major consideration. Perhaps the king was attempting to forge a great Chaldean trading empire in Arabia by establishing colonies along important trade routes, which would have shifted the center of the empire southwestward. The Babylonians considered the Arabian venture an act of sheer madness. Moreover, Nabonidus' prolonged absence from Babylon prevented the New Year Festival from taking place, for only he could play the kingly role in these fertility rites. The repeated cancellations fueled the resentment of the population against him.

While Nabonidus was in Arabia, trouble was brewing in the Near East between the Persians and their overlords, the Medes. The Persians were a scattered tribal group of Indo-European speakers who had settled in southwestern Iran, encroaching on Elam. Perhaps Babylonian intrigue encouraged the Persian ruler Cyrus II, usually called Cyrus the Great, to rebel against the Medes. After successfully challenging and annexing Media in 550 BCE, Cyrus embarked on a series of brilliant military campaigns that brought Lydia—then ruled by King Croesus—and other important territories into his grasp. Meanwhile, according to a lurid story in chapter five of the biblical book of Daniel, the doom of both the crown prince Belshazzar and the Neo-Babylonian Empire was foretold when a disembodied hand wrote a fearful message of warning on a palace wall during an evening feast. There is no extrabiblical confirmation for the account in Daniel, but clearly Cyrus' ambition meant the vast Chaldean realm was now in mortal danger. The aging Nabonidus, probably more than seventy by this time, hurried home from Arabia to find an entrenched pro-Persian faction that had been captivated by the reputation of Cyrus for clemency and religious tolerance. Ominously, the priests of Marduk welcomed overtures from the Persian king, who promised to grant them special privileges in return for their support. Cuneiform evidence insists Babylon fell without a battle when Cyrus appeared before its gates in 539 BCE, with both the Jews and the Chaldeans warmly greeting the Persian ruler as a liberator. Although the fate of Nabonidus remains uncertain, Cyrus preserved the ancient religious institutions of Babylon and accorded the city utmost respect. He then established Persian rule throughout the old Neo-Babylonian Empire, everywhere showing tolerance for local customs and religious practices.

CHALDEAN CULTURE

THE CITY OF BABYLON

Nebuchadnezzar's reign represented the height of Chaldean prosperity and power. Determined to restore Babylon as the preeminent city of the ancient Near East, he ordered its rebuilding in sprawling opulence. The German archaeologist Robert Koldewey began making painstaking excavations at the site in the final years of the nineteenth century and discovered considerable information about the celebrated city, including its roughly square plan. Apparently Nabopolassar initiated and Nebuchadnezzar completed construction of a great bridge having limestone and brick piers that spanned the wide Euphrates, which flowed through the city. Nebuchadnezzar enhanced Babylon with numerous temples, palaces, roads, gates, and walls. He improved the defense system by rebuilding massive inner and outer walls protected by deep moats supplied with water from the connecting Euphrates.

The Ishtar Gate.   The main streets of Babylon ran at right angles and led to the outside world through great bronze gates in the city walls. The most famous of these broad avenues, known today as Procession Street, passed through the magnificent Ishtar Gate and provided the route along which images of the gods were carried during the New Year Festival. The forty-foot high Ishtar Gate was dedicated to Ishtar, the goddess of sexual love and war, and was flanked by towers rising almost a hundred feet in the sky. Koldewey carried the gate to Berlin, where the reconstructed edifice is now displayed in the Staatliche Museum. The most spectacular monument surviving from ancient Babylon, the Ishtar Gate is faced with glazed and molded bricks bearing the stylized figures of yellow dragons (symbolizing Marduk) and bulls (symbolizing the storm-god Adad) marching in raised relief on a background of vivid blue. Like the other great crenellated gate-towers of ancient Babylon, the Ishtar Gate was laid on an underground foundation as deep as its walls were high.

Palace and Ziggurat.   Nebuchadnezzar designed an enormous palace for himself at Babylon. The complex included a profusion of wings and inner courts, its magnificent construction embellished with glazed tile reliefs and many additional forms of decoration. The palace included a Museum that Nebuchadnezzar and his successors filled with inscriptions and statues reflecting the already ancient history of Mesopotamia. Although the project was initiated by Nabopolassar, Nebuchadnezzar completed the refurbishing of the great temple of Marduk, the Esagila, and its associated famous ziggurat, the Etemenanki. The colossal Etemenanki dominated Babylon and may have been the origin of the biblical story of the Tower of Babel that offers an explanation for both the scattering of peoples over the earth and the wide variety of spoken languages.

Beautifully reconstructed in Berlin, the dazzling Ishtar Gate was built at the entrance to the inner city of Babylon by Nebuchadnezzar II about 575 BCE. The ornamental façades of the gate were faced with blue-glazed bricks and adorned with figures of sacred dragons and bulls covered with a rich yellow-brown glaze. Staatliche Museen zu Berlin–Preussisher Kulturbesitz, Vorderasiatisches Museum.

The Hanging Gardens.   Classical writers describe the Hanging Gardens of Babylon as a splendid expanse of natural beauty rising up in tiers and planted with all sorts of trees nourished by a mechanism bringing water up from the river. They ranked these royal gardens, popularly attributed to Nebuchadnezzar, as one of the Seven Wonders of the World. Yet the Hanging Gardens are not mentioned in any known texts from Babylon and have not come to light through excavation. Perhaps the classical writers confused Babylon with Nineveh, where the Assyrians are known to have created sumptuous vistas through their royal gardens watered by intricate engineering works.

LANGUAGES: ARAMAIC AND LATE BABYLONIAN

We saw that the Semitic-speaking Arameans were nomads emerging from the Syrian Desert in the second half of the second millennium BCE to threaten and eventually occupy territories in Syria and along the Euphrates. These intruders carved out petty kingdoms in Syria and formed a strong ethnic element in Assyria and Babylonia. The nomadic background of the Arameans helped them become the chief traders in the vast area stretching from the Persian Gulf to the Mediterranean. Their trading activities spread their language, Aramaic, which superseded Akkadian as the lingua franca of the Near East from the seventh century BCE until the Arab conquest well over a millennium later. One reason for the success of Aramaic was that the Arameans had adopted a variant of the Phoenician alphabet, permitting them to write their practical script with ink on papyrus and leather rather than to record in cuneiform on bulky clay tablets. These developments produced extensive language changes in Assyria and Babylonia, with Aramaic gradually replacing various dialects of Akkadian as the spoken tongue. Although the Chaldeans used Aramaic as the vernacular, they continued to employ Late Babylonian (a successor of Akkadian) for religious texts and the recording of astronomical observations.

RELIGION AND ASTRONOMY

The Chaldean culture was essentially a continuation of the Mesopotamian heritage in city planning, art and architecture, law, literature, trade and commerce, and government. In terms of religion, the Chaldean kings restored old sacred monuments and made the traditional pronouncements praising Marduk as the head of the pantheon. The Chaldeans, like the earlier Mesopotamians, practiced an astral religion. They believed the sun and the moon were gods in their own right, and they identified the other deities with planets or stars. The practice of worshiping each divine being on a separate day led to the inauguration of a seven-day week, which the Romans later adopted and passed on to the modern world.

Divination, the attempt to predict future events by supernatural means, was a prominent feature of Babylonian civilization. The Babylonians believed the deities communicated their will to humankind by various signs in the entrails of animals, in dreams, in the manner smoke rises from a fire, in celestial phenomena, and the like. Chaldean Babylon is remembered for its astrologers, who studied the movements of the heavenly bodies for divine guidance in daily activities. Yet their work

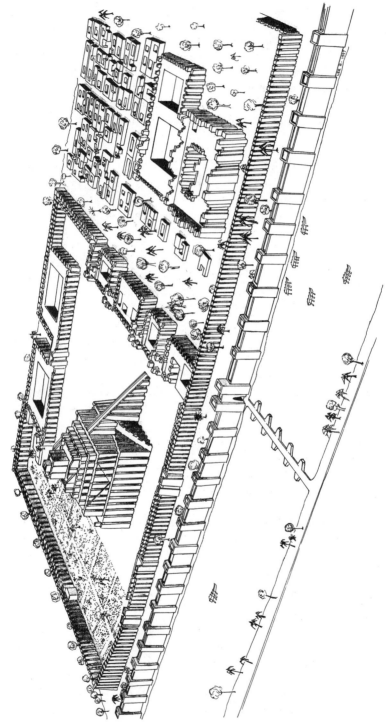

Reconstruction of the center of Babylon during the reign of Nebuchadnezzar II, showing the ziggurat Etemenanki and the great temple Esagila.

represents a turning point in the history of science because important astronomical discoveries resulted from their careful observations of the heavens. The most gifted astronomers and scientists in all of Mesopotamian history, the Chaldeans calculated the approximate length of the solar year, though continuing to use a lunar calendar. They also mapped the heavens and accurately predicted eclipses of the moon and sun.

THE SAITE REVIVAL IN EGYPT (664–525 BCE)

THE PRINCIPAL KINGS

Psamtik I (664–610 BCE).   Egypt had been in eclipse since the twelfth century BCE and ruled in part by kings from Nubia and Libya. After the powerful Assyrian ruler Assurbanipal gained control of much of Egypt from a Nubian king in the seventh century BCE, he administered his new acquisitions along the Nile by appointing Egyptian princes as local governors. Assyrian power was now waning, however, and in 664 BCE a prince named Psamtik (Psammetichos in Greek), the vassal ruler of the western Delta town of Sais, proclaimed himself king of Upper and Lower Egypt. Successfully expelling the Assyrians and consolidating the country, Psamtik I founded the remarkable Twenty-sixth Dynasty, commonly called the Saite period, after the town of Sais. Saite rule lasted well over a century and witnessed an amazing revival of Egyptian splendor.

Necho II (610–595 BCE).   The long-reigning Psamtik was succeeded by his son Necho II in 610 BCE. The balance of power in western Asia was now shifting radically, for the rump of the Assyrian Empire faced utter ruin at the hands of the Chaldeans and their allies. We saw that Necho attempted to bolster the tattered surviving fragment of the Assyrian armies at a savage battle near Carchemish on the upper Euphrates in Syria in 605 BCE, yet his forces were routed by the Chaldeans under the crown prince Nebuchadnezzar. Saite Egypt was compelled to withdraw from both Syria and Palestine, but Necho continued to foment anti-Babylonian sentiment in the region.

In the meantime the ambitious Necho had initiated construction of a canal from the Nile to the Red Sea, though the project may have been abandoned. We know he sent ships along the coasts of the Red Sea to increase trade with Arabia and East Africa. The Greek historian Herodotus tells us of an amazing naval expedition the king dispatched down the Red Sea. The sailors appeared in the Mediterranean three years later, having successfully circumnavigated Africa.

Ahmose II (570–526 BCE).   One notable feature of the Saite period was the strong influence of Greeks and Phoenicians in Egyptian commerce. Many Greeks had crossed the Mediterranean to set up a flourishing trading colony at Naucratis on the mouth of the Nile near Sais. The establishment of Naucratis and other Greek-controlled trading centers in Egypt helped propel the kingdom into a new period of commercial prosperity. After the usurper Ahmose II (better known as Amasis, the

Greek version of his name) seized the throne in 570 BCE, he regulated the lucrative trade with the Aegean by confining Greek traders to the city of Naucratis. Ahmose is credited also with encouraging a revival of traditional forms in art and architecture. Artisans restored ancient temples and revived the strong sculptural style of the Old Kingdom, thereby fostering a nationalistic renaissance. The awakening also produced a popular literature extolling the rise of the Saite kings.

Saite Egypt Succumbs to Persia (525 BCE)

This astounding renewal of Egyptian culture was soon threatened by the rise of the superpower Persia. The Persian king Cambyses, eldest son of Cyrus the Great, crossed the borders of Egypt in 525 BCE and enjoyed a decisive victory. He deported the last of the Saite kings, Psamtik III (526–525 BCE), to the Persian city of Susa, and venerable Egypt became another satrapy (province) of the Persian Empire.

LYDIA (c. 685–540 BCE)

The kingdom of Lydia in the western part of Anatolia embraced fertile valleys and mineral-rich mountain ranges. Its inhabitants, the Lydians, spoke an incompletely understood tongue in the Anatolian subgroup of Indo-European languages. Their early compact state was blocked from the sea by the Ionian Greeks on the west coast—a district called Ionia—yet Lydia lay astride the main trade routes linking the Aegean and inner Anatolia. The Lydians used their many assets to build a powerful commercial empire. They are remembered also for their bountiful harvests and numerous flocks and herds.

The Principal Kings

Gyges (c. 685–652 BCE).   The history of Lydia before the seventh century BCE remains rather obscure. Except for a few imperfectly understood inscriptions, our fragmentary knowledge of this period comes from Assyrian royal annals and the colorful accounts of Greek writers. Herodotus made the Lydian kingdom the subject of many of his most fascinating stories. Lydia became powerful under its Mermnad dynasty, ruling from about 685 to 546 BCE. The dynasty was founded by the semilegendary Gyges—Gugu in the Assyrian records—who murdered the former king, married his wife, and usurped the throne, according to Herodotus' riveting narrative. Gyges raided Greek cities in Ionia and embarked on a program of territorial expansion. When his kingdom was terrorized by the unruly Cimmerians, who were then in the process of overthrowing the kingdom of Phrygia east of Lydia, he succeeded in repulsing the invaders. Yet the horde returned in 652 BCE, pillaging and raping in Lydia, taking the capital of Sardis, and killing Gyges, though the Cimmerians were gradually enfeebled in later years by plagues and by wars with Lydia and Assyria.

Alyattes (c. 610–560 BCE).   Lydia became a major political power in the Near East under Gyges successors, the third of whom, Alyattes, was forced to vie with Media for control of eastern Anatolia. After the Medes and the Chaldeans destroyed the Assyrian Empire, the Median king Cyaxares marched westward to claim his share of Anatolia. Five years of warfare between the Medes and the Lydians proved indecisive, though Alyattes and his forces managed to push eastward to the Halys River (modern Kizil Irmak). On May 28, 585 BCE—a date provided by modern astronomers—the warfare came to a sudden halt when the opposing armies became terrified by an eclipse of the sun. The two sides concluded an alliance treaty designating the Halys River as the border between the Lydian and the Median states. Thus Lydia now reached far beyond its original frontiers to include territory formerly belonging to Phrygia.

Croesus (560–547 BCE).   Alyattes' son Croesus conquered most of the Aegean seaboard and reduced all the Ionian Greek cities except fiercely independent Miletus to the status of subject allies. Apparently the Ionian Greeks were not overly resentful of their Lydian overlords and benefited economically from the enforced political ties. Moreover, Croesus greatly admired Greek culture, and his close contacts with his Ionian vassals led to his Hellenization. He made an alliance with Sparta in the southern part of the Greek mainland and lavished spectacular gifts upon Delphi in central Greece, besides subsidizing construction of the gigantic temple of Artemis at Ephesus on the west coast of Anatolia. Fragments from the temple columns, now at the British Museum, are inscribed "dedicated by King Croesus."

LYDIAN CULTURE

The king's proverbial wealth—reflected in the simile "rich as Croesus"—came from precious metals. Lydia was blessed with vast deposits of gold, silver, and electrum (a natural alloy of gold and silver), accumulations greatly facilitating the development of its commercial empire. The Lydians made an enduring contribution to the world of commerce by inventing metallic coins, which were soon adopted by the Greeks, as a medium of exchange for goods and services. The Lydians certified the weight and value of their coins by stamping them with an official seal usually depicting the head of an animal. Gyges struck coins of electrum and stamped them with a lion's head as an emblem of his kingship. Croesus' earliest coins, also of electrum, were stamped on one side with the facing heads of a lion and a bull. Later he seems to have abandoned electrum in favor of a bimetallic system of pure gold and pure silver coins. Perhaps his silver coins were intended, in part, as a medium of exchange with the Ionian and mainland Greeks, both of whom were now producing silver coins themselves.

The Lydian kings constructed a towering citadel for themselves on a rocky spur above the capital of Sardis. The nearby royal necropolis contains enormous tumuli, or artificial mounds erected over burial chambers. Turning to the smaller arts, the Lydians were praised for their fine textiles and jewelry. They decorated their creations with both Eastern and Western motifs, clearly reflecting their role as intermediaries between Asia and Greece. The Lydians are remembered for their love of music and dancing. They are credited with inventing a famous but lost mode in music and a form of the ancient stringed instrument called the kithara.

A Lydian gold coin, with
lion and bull design,
struck during the reign of
Croesus (560–547 BCE).

Fall of Sardis (546 BCE)

Extending in western Anatolia from the Halys to the Aegean, Lydia reached the
zenith of its power under Croesus. Yet Persia, ominously craving land, was now on
the rise. When the Persian ruler Cyrus the Great successfully challenged and annexed Media in the mid-sixth century BCE, Croesus feared his next objective might
be Lydia. Through an envoy, Croesus sought the advice of Apollo's oracle at Delphi.
Herodotus reports the oracle replied that if Croesus attacked the Persians, "he
would destroy a great empire." Interpreting the enigmatic prophecy favorably, Croesus took the initiative and marched his troops across the Halys into eastern Anatolia to prevent the Persians from pushing into his kingdom. Cyrus made a grueling
march from his capital of Susa and clashed with the Lydians in a gory but inconclusive battle. With winter approaching, Croesus returned to Sardis to prepare for op-
erations the following year. Cyrus followed stealthily and caught the Lydians
completely by surprise. He captured Sardis in 546 BCE and attached the Lydian kingdom to the Persian Empire. Most of Anatolia fell swiftly into Cyrus' hands. Once
again Miletus managed to retain its independence, though the other Greek cities of
Ionia were annexed to Persia. In the meantime Lydia became the chief western
satrapy of the Persian Empire.

CHAPTER XIII

PERSIA

We saw in the last chapter that the Chaldean triumph at the destruction of the Assyrian Empire was brief, for the Persians captured Babylon in 539 BCE, less than a century after the fall of Nineveh. This was a remarkable achievement considering that the conquerers had been an obscure Iranian tribe, vassals of the Medes, just over a generation earlier. The Persians rapidly extended their rule eastward to the Indus and westward to the Mediterranean and into Egypt. The Greeks of Ionia in western Anatolia came under their control, leading to a period of close contact between the Near East and Europe. The great Persian Empire, notable as a model of moderation and restraint, governed the various peoples of the ancient Near East and beyond for around two hundred years, until collapsing at the hands of Alexander the Great in the fourth century BCE.

THE EARLY MEDES AND PERSIANS IN IRAN

The Medes and Persians gradually spread over the western half of the Iranian plateau during the first half of the first millennium BCE. Linked by a common tribal and linguistic background, they were descendents of Indo-European speakers calling themselves Aryans and migrating southward from the Russian steppes—the preferred theory of their place of origin—into the vast area between the Ganges and the Euphrates rivers. The newcomers became a dominant aristocracy in the areas they occupied. Some of the Aryans settled on the Indian subcontinent, while others turned westward onto the Iranian plateau. The latter—among whom were the Medes and Persians—pushed as far as the Zagros range forming the western frontier of the Iranian plateau, further movement being blocked by well-established kingdoms such as Urartu and the states of Mesopotamia. The usual name of their place of settlement—Iran—is derived from the ancient term Aryan.

The Geographical Setting

The Medes settled in the northwestern corner of the Iranian plateau, while the Persians became established in the southwest, which they called Parsa (roughly equivalent to the modern province of Fars). The Ionian Greeks gave the name Persis to the whole of Iran, after Parsa, and eventually this designation was rendered in English as Persia. Westerners, influenced by the Greeks, have long used the term Persia as a name for ancient Iran.

The Iranian plateau served in antiquity as a great land bridge between central and western Asia. This vast region is famous for searingly hot summers and brutally cold winters, one of the harshest settled areas on the face of the earth, though Cyrus the Great is said to have praised its rigorous geography and climate for producing good fighting men. The plateau extends from the eastern edge of Mesopotamia in the west to the Indus River valley in the east, from the Caspian Sea in the north to the Persian Gulf and the Gulf of Oman in the south. An uninviting salt desert stretches across much of the south, while the lofty Elburz range, with some volcanic peaks towering more than 18,000 feet, stands guard over the northern perimeter of the plateau and impedes access to the Caspian Sea. The considerably lower and more hospitable Zagros range in the west runs southwestward along the eastern border of Mesopotamia to the Persian Gulf. Only here in the western part of the plateau—the cultivatable valleys of the chain—did favorable conditions permit extensive settlement, though most of its relatively arid land was more suited for pasturage than agriculture. Iran was not without important assets, however, for the lower mountain slopes yielded timber, and the land was rich in deposits of marble, alabaster, lapis lazuli, turquoise, iron, copper, tin, and lead. Herds of sheep provided wool for textiles, and agriculture was possible along the edge of the desert with proper irrigation.

The Kingdom of Media

We saw that the Medes settled in the northwestern region of the Iranian plateau. Fierce warriors known for breeding splendid horses, the Medes are first mentioned in Assyrian records in the ninth century BCE. Herodotus—the sometimes unreliable source of much of our information about ancient Iran—credits a shadowy figure he calls Deioces with uniting the Medes into a single kingdom. The Medes built a capital called Ecbatana (modern Hamadan), which was favorably placed on the eastern end of the primary trade route from Iran to Mesopotamia through the Zagros Mountains. We know the Medes suffered frequent Assyrian incursions, and tradition maintains that nomadic Scythian tribes from the north attacked western Iran just before the middle of the seventh century BCE, managing to dominate the region for twenty-eight years.

Cyaxares (625–585 BCE).   Herodotus tells us the warrior king Cyaxares pushed the Scythians out and reasserted Median royal authority. Cyaxares greatly improved the organization of the army—probably on the Assyrian model—and adopted Scythian-style mounted archers. Then he extended his rule over neighboring peoples, including the Persians. Cyaxares soon turned his attention toward Assyria, whose kings had frequently plundered Media and exacted tribute. He captured Assur in 614 BCE, afterward concluding a treaty with Nabopolassar of the Neo-Babylonian Empire. The two allied forces stormed the Assyrian capital of Nineveh in 612 BCE. The Medes benefited substantially from the fall of Nineveh and the destruction of the Assyrian Empire. While Cyaxares left Mesopotamia, Syria, and Palestine to the

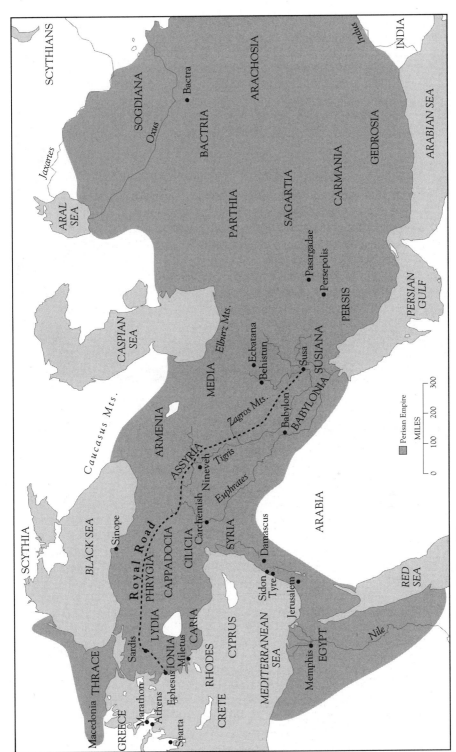

The Persian Empire under Darius I, about 490 BCE.

This exquisite gold decorated comb, from a Scythian royal tomb on the northern coast of the Black Sea, was crafted by Greek artisans in the region and shows Scythians in combat. The heavily armored rider in the center prepares to strike a fatal blow at his enemy, whose fallen horse has been mortally wounded. c. 400 BCE. The Hermitage, St. Petersburg.

Chaldeans, he expanded westward as far as central Anatolia, absorbing the venerable kingdom of Urartu on the way. He clashed with tough Lydia, which was then pushing eastward from western Anatolia. Herodotus reports that a five-year period of armed conflict between the Medes and the Lydians promptly ended during a battle in 585 BCE, when "day was suddenly turned into night" by a solar eclipse the combatants interpreted as an intercession by angry gods. Concluding an alliance, Cyaxares of Media and Alyattes of Lydia fixed the Halys River as the dividing line between their two kingdoms, and the treaty was sealed by the marriage of Cyaxares' son Astyages to the daughter of the Lydian king.

Astyages (585–550 BCE).   The ancient Near East enjoyed a rare period of political stability, held fast for about three decades by the Medes, Chaldeans, Lydians, and Egyptians. The last Median ruler, Astyages, ruled a vast realm reaching from western and southwestern Iran to central Anatolia, but his vassal Cyrus of Persia challenged him with rebellion in 550 BCE. When Astyages marched against Cyrus, his own army revolted and handed him over to his opponent, perhaps an indication he was tyrannical and unpopular with his subjects. Although Cyrus became the master of the Medes, he treated them with honor and appointed them to high office.

THE PERSIAN EMPIRE

At first the Persians were but a scattered Indo-European tribal group in Iran. By the early seventh century BCE they were occupying Elamite back territory in southwestern Iran, the mountainous terrain they called Parsa. Here they absorbed much of the Elamite culture. When the Assyrians marched through Elam, beginning in 647 BCE, and crushed its political centers, the Persians extended their rule over some eastern parts of Elamite territory. In the meantime the Persians swore allegiance to Assyria and later to Media.

CYRUS THE GREAT (559–530 BCE)

The Achaemenid Dynasty.   The ruling family of the Persians claimed descent from a shadowy figure called Haxamanish, more familiarly known under the Greek form of the name, Achaemenes. Thus the Persian dynasty is called Achaemenid. The Achaemenid rulers were relatively insignificant until Cyrus II, justifiably called the Great, ascended the throne in 559 BCE.

The Cyrus Legend.   Although Cyrus gained the kingship by regular channels, in later times Herodotus and others reported miraculous tales of his birth and youth comparable to the legends told of the infancy of Moses and the childhood of Sargon of Agade. Herodotus tells us that Cyrus' maternal grandfather was none other than Astyages, king of Media. After having a frightening dream in which his daughter Mandane expressed contempt for him, Astyages arranged for her to marry his Persian vassal Cambyses rather than some noble Mede who might attempt to dethrone him. The match produced Cyrus. When another dream warned Astyages that Cyrus would replace him, he commanded a military officer named Harpagos to kill his infant grandson. Harpagos was unwilling to execute the dreadful deed and hid the baby with mountain shepherds. When Astyages learned of the insubordination, so the story goes, he ordered the dismemberment and decapitation of Harpagos' own son, serving him for dinner to the disobedient officer, who was unaware of what he was eating until the lid was raised to reveal the final course, his son's head. For years Harpagos waited for his revenge. In the meantime we hear that Cyrus was reunited with his real parents in Persia. When he gained the Persian throne and revolted against Median overlordship, Astyages sent Harpagos against him, but the officer and many of his troops deserted to Cyrus.

Rebellion against Media (550 BCE).   We are uncertain whether Cyrus and his Median overlord Astyages were actually related. As to Cyrus' conquest of Media, he organized the Persian tribes in a successful rebellion against Astyages in 550 BCE and then welded the Medes and Persians into a single state. Cyrus had been ruling from Pasargadae deep inside Persia, but the new circumstances rendered the city inadequate in terms of location and prestige. Thus he selected an additional administrative center, the old Median capital of Ecbatana, which provided an excellent base for the enlargement of a united Iran.

Conquest of Lydia (546 BCE).   Cyrus lulled the Chaldeans into lethargy and then swept westward on a mission of conquest that produced the largest and greatest of all Near Eastern empires. Fabulously wealthy Croesus attempted to protect his western Anatolian kingdom of Lydia by expanding eastward across the Halys River, reportedly after his envoy had consulted the Delphic Oracle in Greece. The Persians and Lydians fought an indecisive battle at the Halys. The lateness of the campaign season then prompted Croesus to retire to his capital of Sardis—a hilltop fortress believed to be impregnable— but Cyrus pursued him secretly and captured the city in 546 BCE.

Conquest of Ionia (546 BCE).   Cyrus then dispatched his generals to annex the city-states of the Ionian Greeks on the Anatolian coast. These wealthy commercial cities had been under a mild Lydian yoke, but Cyrus demanded their complete surrender. Although Miletus submitted without a struggle and was granted special status, the others had to be captured one by one. The military activity in Ionia brought the Persians into discord with the mainland Greeks, who were dismayed by the hostile acts against their Asian kin. This rivalry would eventually lead to a great war between two adversaries.

Fall of Babylon (539 BCE).   Having pushed his western boundary to the sea, the intrepid Cyrus then campaigned in the east and northeast, bringing Bactria and other large territories under Persian control. His next objective was Chaldean Babylonia. Cyrus took advantage of the unpopularity of its monarch, Nabonidus, who had ignored affairs at home and alienated the priests of Marduk as well as many others. In 539 BCE the armies of Cyrus rumbled into Babylonia and soon entered venerable Babylon with little resistance, signaling the beginning of a centuries-long union of southern Mesopotamia with Iran. Semitic-speaking peoples had dominated Mesopotamia and the adjoining lands for more than two millennia, but now their place as rulers was taken by the Indo-European Persians.

Exercising the same religious tolerance for which many of his successors were noted, Cyrus restored the worship of Marduk, an indication he would rule not as a foreign potentate but as a Babylonian. We saw in chapter 10 that he issued a decree permitting the Jewish exiles to return home from Babylonia and rebuild their Temple at Jerusalem. The Jews praised Cyrus in their Bible, referring to him in the book of Isaiah (45:1) as Yahweh's "anointed," a term usually reserved as a title for a king of Israel or Judah. The Hebrew word meaning Yahweh's anointed is rendered in English as messiah, a divinely appointed savior. The description of Cyrus as a messiah in the Hebrew Bible signifies the very high esteem in which the Jews held him.

The conquest of Babylon gave Cyrus the entire Neo-Babylonian Empire, including Syria and Palestine, and carried Persian power all the way to the borders of Egypt. Wherever he expanded, Cyrus courted the good will of his new subjects by showing them the utmost respect.

Death (530 BCE).   Cyrus spent the remainder of his reign consolidating his hold over the Iranian plateau and protecting the northeastern frontier from warlike tribes, finally losing his life east of the Caspian Sea in 530 BCE while fighting an obscure tribe of nomads—the Massagetai—who were led by a warrior queen named

The white limestone tomb of Cyrus the Great, commissioned before his death in 530 BCE, stands near the ruins of the Persian royal residence at Pasargadae. Though colossal, the austere structure reflects Cyrus' personal modesty. Its design resembles the wooded tombs of his ancestors.

Tomyris. Cyrus' body was carried to Pasargadae and placed in an enormous, austere limestone tomb he had designed to resemble the gabled wooden tombs of his early ancestors on the Iranian plateau. At one time, according to the ancient Greek historian Arrian, a succinct message from Cyrus was inscribed upon the monument: "O man, I am Cyrus, the son of Cambyses, who founded the Persian Empire and was King of Asia. Grudge me not therefore this monument."

Originating as the petty prince of a rather insignificant tribe, the wise and capable Cyrus had accomplished the amazing feat of carving out the huge Persian Empire, which nearly reached its maximum extent under his leadership. At the time of his death the empire of the Persians extended from the steppes of Asia in the far northeast to the Aegean and Mediterranean seas in the west and down to the borders of Egypt. For the next two centuries, until the spectacular conquests of Alexander the Great, the Persian kings controlled most of the vast region of southwestern Asia.

CAMBYSES II (530–522 BCE)

Cyrus the Great was succeeded by his son Cambyses II. Herodotus depicts him as a madman and a tyrant, telling us he committed acts of savage violence such as kicking his pregnant wife (who was also his sister) to death, shooting the son of one of his closest advisers with an arrow merely to demonstrate his skill in archery, and ordering the secret murder of his brother Bardiya. Such lurid tales of Cambyses' viciousness are highly questionable and probably reflect Herodotus' use of prejudiced sources.

Conquest of Egypt (525–522 BCE).   Apparently Cyrus had made preparations for a conquest of Saite Egypt to carry Persian rule into Africa. When Cambyses attacked the kingdom in 525 BCE, its Greek mercenaries committed treason, and the Persians enjoyed a resounding victory. Cambyses deported the last of the Saite rulers, Psamtik III, to Susa and had himself installed on the throne, though not as a foreign monarch but as a legitimate king of Egypt.

Cambyses intended to use Egypt as a base for carving out a substantial African empire. He pushed Persian control far into the desert west of the Nile and also mounted a thrust against Nubia, successfully conquering southward beyond the First Cataract, though Herodotus accuses him of inadequately provisioning his army. In 522 BCE Cambyses left Egypt, now firmly in his grasp, to return home. We hear that he had received word of a revolt in Persia, perhaps led by his brother Bardiya or by an imposter named Gaumata claiming to be Bardiya. Uncertainty surrounds these events, though we know Cambyses died on the way, possibly by his own hand in a fit of despair, but more probably from an accidently self-inflicted dagger wound received while hurriedly leaping on his horse.

DARIUS I (522–486 BCE)

The Bisitun Inscription.   An aggressive young army officer named Darius, an Achaemenid prince, rushed to Persia and eventually ascended the throne. Darius I went to considerable effort to advance his version of how he gained the kingship, recorded in his famous Bisitun inscription on a large Median rock face high above the main caravan route from Ecbatana to Babylon. Darius presents himself as the legitimate successor of Cambyses. The inscriptions tells us Cambyses murdered his brother Bardiya and that the people of Persia were unaware of the deed. Later a false Bardiya—the imposter Gaumata—arose and led them in rebellion against Cambyses. Following the death of Cambyses, Darius himself killed the usurper to keep the kingship in the Persian royal family. The textual story is supplemented by a huge relief showing Darius standing in triumph in the presence of bound rebel leaders, his foot resting on the prostrate body of the overthrown ruler. Many scholars find this official account incredulous. Some are persuaded that the true Bardiya ascended the throne legitimately upon the death of his brother, whereupon he was murdered by Darius, who invented the story about Gaumata to cover his tracks. Others suggest Darius actually crushed a dangerous rebellion. The truth simply eludes us.

DARIUS' IMPERIAL ORGANIZATION

Twenty-eight-year-old Darius was confronted with an empire embroiled in rebellion when he took the throne in 522 BCE. Apparently many of his subjects regarded him as a usurper and a liar who had murdered the true Bardiya. He fought with steel determination for at least a year before restoring peace in all quarters of the empire. Once in secure control, Darius devoted much of his thirty-six-year reign to providing the empire with a new form of state organization. He proved through these efforts to be an outstanding lawgiver and administrator.

The Army.   The core of the standing army was composed of the infantry detachments known as the Ten Thousand Immortals, their ranks filled by hand-picked Medes and Persians. Herodotus tells us the strength of the Immortals was never allowed to fall below the designated number, a new recruit immediately replacing a fallen warrior. They were armed with bows, spears, and swords and were further protected by light wicker shields covered with hide. In battle they wore a cloth headdress and a colorful tunic, sometimes over a metal scale shirt. An elite thousand of the force served as the king's bodyguard. The Immortals were accorded special privileges, exemplified by their right to bring concubines and servants on campaigns. The regular standing army also included the chariotry, but the more flexible cavalry had become more important. The superb cavalry units generally fought at a distance and overwhelmed foes with a storm of arrows launched from light bows. On occasion the Persians brought elephants or camels into battle, and in moments of extreme crisis they attached slashing blades to their chariots and rode furiously through enemy ranks. The standing army was reinforced during times of major conflict by a troop levy from subject peoples, though this practice was often inimical to the maintenance of military quality and loyalty.

The Kingship.   The empire was ruled by an absolute hereditary monarch. At Darius' accession the Persian kingship still lacked the numerous emblems of royal authority used advantageously by the older Near Eastern monarchies to enhance the power of the state. He decided to surround his kingly office with ceremony and protocol, adapting various symbols and practices he had observed among the Medes and others. Darius dazzled ordinary mortals through his opulence of dress and surroundings. He was clearly distinguished from others by his gold scepter, long square beard, magnificent earrings and bracelets, high flat-topped tiara (a crenelated crown was reserved for special occasions), flowing robe of purple embroidered with gold, fine crimson trousers, and booted feet. He sat under an ornate purple canopy. An elaborate system of royal etiquette prevailed at his court, including the practice of falling prostrate before the king upon approaching his person. The complex, rigid court protocol engendered an aura of royal mystery and signified that the king's sovereignty was sanctioned by the divine. Thus his word was law in all earthly matters. His great authority was reflected in his imposing official title: the Great King, King of Kings, King in Persia.

Capitals and Court.   Persian kings ruled from four capitals. While their most important administrative center was the former Elamite capital of Susa, they moved in the summer to the cooler heights of the old Median capital of Ecbatana. They also maintained royal residences in their homeland cities of Pasargadae and Persepolis, the latter serving as a great ceremonial site.

This limestone relief from Persepolis shows the enthroned Darius I and his heir apparent Xerxes receiving in audience a high court official, who touches hand to lips in a gesture of respect and stands behind a pair of incense burners. Both king and prince wear crowns as well as the long, square-tipped beards signifying royalty. Because Persian society viewed the king as a descendant of the gods, he was surrounded by an elaborate court ceremonial. c. 490 BCE. Archaeological Museum, Tehran.

The King of Kings was surrounded by an extensive court that functioned as his central government and was composed of relatives, nobles, and high government officials, all attired in long flowing robes and high, fluted felt hats. The royal harem of wives and concubines, which was headed by the principal queen, often exercised considerable influence over affairs of state and sometimes gave birth to political and social intrigue. The court was assisted by a great professional bureaucracy—headed by nobles—which administered the empire.

Satrapies. Darius' innumerable subjects were governed on the basis of a system begun by Cyrus and modeled on the Assyrian imperial practice of dividing an empire into provinces, or satrapies, to use the Persian term. With the exception of the homeland of Persia, virtually the entire realm was organized into some twenty satrapies (the number was increased under later rulers), each required to pay a fixed annual tax or tribute. This provincial system, which allowed different peoples to maintain their own customs and religious practices, was the greatest achievement of the Achaemenids, helping them rule the empire with relative success for more than two centuries.

Satraps. Each of the satrapies retained a measure of autonomy under the administration of a local governor, or satrap, appointed by the king from the nobility or the royal family. The three primary duties of the satraps were to command the provincial armed forces, to enforce the king's laws, and to collect imperial taxes. These men enjoyed immense power and tended to become kinglets, especially during the last years of the empire. Darius checked satrapal power by establishing a traveling bureaucracy—Greek sources refer to these officials as the "king's eyes" and "king's ears"—who made unannounced inspections throughout the empire and reported their findings directly to the king.

Roads and Communications.   The King of Kings also controlled the provincial system by providing a remarkable network of imperial roads, no doubt built for their economic and commercial benefits as well. One of these, the famous Royal Road, was the first long highway in the world. Running from the old Elamite capital of Susa—Darius' most important imperial center—to Sardis in Lydia, the Royal Road was later extended to Ephesus on the Aegean coast, with a total length of almost 1700 miles. Other excellent roads linked important cities such as Memphis, Babylon, Ecbatana, Pasargadae, and the royal residence of Persepolis. These imperial post roads made rapid communications possible throughout the empire, including the referral of important satrapal business to the king for decision. The system operated with relays of mounted messengers carrying official letters. Post stations every fourteen miles allowed a courier to pass the royal mail to a rested messenger with fresh horses. Although donkey and camel caravans took ninety days to travel the Royal Road, royal envoys on horseback carried the king's commands across its entire length in about a week. Herodotus was rightly impressed that "neither snow, nor rain, nor heat, nor gloom of night" stopped the royal messengers. Darius also dug a vital canal between the Nile and the Red Sea, perhaps a completion or reopening of the water connection begun by Egyptian king Necho II around 600 BCE. Now ships enjoyed direct access from the Mediterranean to the Red Sea, from where they could sail on to the Persian Gulf and the Indus. Thus unbroken waterways connected the eastern and western ends of the empire.

Aramaic and Other Languages of the Empire.   We saw in the last chapter that the Semitic tongue Aramaic had replaced Akkadian as the lingua franca of the Near East in the seventh century BCE. Aramaic served as the general means of communication throughout the Persian Empire. Although Aramaic was probably the most widely used administrative language of the imperial government, the languages of the empire were as varied as its peoples and included Elamite in Elam, Late Babylonian (a successor of Akkadian) in Babylonia, Egyptian in Egypt, and Greek in the cities of Ionia on the western Anatolian coast.

Old Persian and Avestan.   The Persians themselves spoke an Indo-European tongue now called Old Persian. Scribes eventually learned to write this language in cuneiform, Akkadian providing the prototype, but apparently Old Persian cuneiform was restricted to royal inscriptions on stone monuments. The famous Bisitun inscription was engraved in Old Persian, Late Babylonian, and Elamite. We know from texts and inscriptions that a closely related Indo-European language— now commonly called Avestan—was employed for Persian sacred writings.

The Legal System.   Acting as the last court of appeal, the king used his judicial authority to exert control over local affairs. Darius ordered a codification of Egyptian law, but we find no convincing evidence he established a system of imperial law throughout the empire. Apparently traditional laws remained in effect for the various peoples under Persian rule, though the king could impose his will by issuing royal edicts having the force of law. His tomb inscription mentions hope that his subjects might live in harmony to ensure "that the stronger does not smite nor destroy the weak."

Economic Development. The early empire enjoyed considerable prosperity. While the financial structure of the government was put on a sound footing by a policy of systematic taxation, the state stimulated the economic health of the empire by promoting agriculture and trade, providing a common system of weights and measures, and issuing a gold coinage. Wealth was chiefly based on land and agriculture. Although most land remained under the control of native peoples, the king rewarded relatives and other favorites with land and large estates in various parts of the empire. The task of actually producing agricultural wealth fell to small-scale farmers, hired agricultural workers, and slaves, the last having been brought back from successful wars. Meanwhile the state invested its funds to improve the vital irrigation system and to encourage various manufacturing enterprises. The imperial government also created an admirable network of roads, already discussed, which fostered the development of trade.

One notable method of storing wealth was to form melted gold and silver into ingots, whose value depended on weight. Thus ingots had to be weighed if used as currency for business transactions. We saw in the last chapter that the Lydians and Greeks had issued metal coins, of which value (quality and weight) was certified by the stamp of the issuing ruler or civic authority. Accordingly, coins were a convenient medium of exchange for goods and services. Darius initiated a Persian imperial coinage modeled on the old Lydian system. The handsome Persian gold coin known as the daric—the name probably derived from Darius—bore an idealized representation of the king as an archer. Only the king enjoyed the right of issuing gold coins, but the satraps were permitted to strike silver or bronze coins. Clearly, Darius inaugurated his standardized coinage and other economic measures to unify the Persian commercial world. Meanwhile banking houses, particularly in Mesopotamia, grew rich by lending money at high interest rates. The later empire was marked by economic decline, however, resulting partly from unsettled political conditions, partly from the removal of huge sums of hard money from the economy through overtaxation. Although a large proportion of taxes were paid in produce, vast hordes of gold and silver tribute in the form of ingots rested indefinitely in the royal treasury. The removal of so much precious metal from circulation resulted in widespread inflation that worsened with time.

ADDITIONAL EXPANSION UNDER DARIUS

The Indus Valley and the Southeastern Corner of Europe. Darius followed an aggressive expansionist policy and added large tracts to the Persian Empire. About 516 BCE he managed to conquer eastward as far as the Indus River and possibly beyond. Yet Europe remained outside his grasp. Perhaps as early as 514 BCE, Darius approached the Hellespont, the narrow strait connecting the Black Sea and the Mediterranean and separating Asia and Europe at the site of present-day Istanbul.

This gold daric, struck around 330 BCE, portrays
the king as an archer with a bent knee.

He crossed on a bridge of boats engineered by the vassal Ionian Greeks to launch a
campaign against the European Scythians north of the Black Sea. Herodotus depicts
the Scythian venture as a complete disaster, but we must give Darius credit for securing strategic territories in the southeastern corner of Europe. The Persians annexed a large part of the coast of Thrace—the region west of the Black Sea—and
then extended their rule along the northern shore of the Aegean as far as the kingdom of Macedonia. Thus they now controlled the approaches to Greece from Asia
and, what is more important, the Black Sea grain trade through the Hellespont,
vital to the economic well-being of the Greek world. With Darius' expansion into
Europe, the powerful Persian Empire had reached its fullest extent. Perhaps the
King of Kings thought the conquest of mainland Greece was but one step away.

Ionian Revolt (499–494 BCE).   A development of particular importance took place
when the Ionian Greeks rose in rebellion against Persian rule in 499 BCE. They had
grown discontent over ever-mounting taxation, forced military service, and existing
forms of local government. The Ionians appealed for assistance to the cities of their
motherland. Sparta refused to be drawn into this volatile confrontation, though
Athens, deeply concerned over Persian control of the Black Sea trade and
Achaemenid ambition in mainland Greece, sent the rebels limited aid, amounting
to only twenty-five ships. Apparently the revolt took the Persians by surprise. They
initially mounted feeble efforts against the Greek offensive, but the Persians finally
crushed the rebellion with severity in 494 BCE.

Invasion of Greece (490 BCE).   To punish the mainland Greeks for their interfer-
ence, Darius ordered a seaborne assault against Greece, thereby beginning a confrontation known as the Persian Wars. The expedition he dispatched in 490 BCE
culminated in the famous battle of Marathon. The Greeks, chiefly Athenians, were
ensconced in the hills and waiting for reinforcements from Sparta. Although considerably less numerous than the Persian forces, the Greeks held the favorable position above the Marathon plain. They descended from their camp to take the
Persians by surprise. The charging Greek line reduced the Persians to hand-to-hand
combat, piercing their light uniforms and shields with long, thrusting spears and
slashing swords. The Persians were forced to return to Asia. Determined to avenge
his honor, Darius began making preparations for an invasion on a grand scale. The
planning came to a sudden halt in 486 BCE with the outbreak of a revolt in Egypt
and the death of the King of Kings.

Xerxes (486–465 bce)

Invasion of Greece (480–479 bce).   Darius' son and successor Xerxes quickly suppressed the rebellion in Egypt, where his extreme ruthlessness signaled a reversal of traditional Persian moderation. In 482 bce he put down a revolt in the city of Babylon with naked force. Xerxes then sought revenge against the mainland Greeks for his father's humiliation at Marathon, announcing, "I shall pass through Europe from end to end and make it all one country." In 480 bce he appeared on the borders of Greece at the head of a huge fighting force that had crossed the Hellespont and marched along the shores of the Aegean. At first the Persians enjoyed success, exemplified by the capture of Athens and the burning of its Acropolis. Yet Xerxes soon witnessed the destruction of a large part of his fleet in the narrow bay of Salamis. The dispirited king returned home to oversee other responsibilities, and in 479 bce the troops he had left behind fell before the Greeks at the battle of Plataea. The Persians never returned to Greece and soon lost all their European territory. Xerxes' reign marks the end of imperial expansion. He retired to the royal city of Persepolis, where he was occupied with building projects and administrative affairs until harem plots brought about his assassination in 465 bce.

The Empire in Decline: The Later Achaemenids (465–330 bce)

Artaxerxes III (359-338 bce).   The Persian Empire survived for almost another century and a half but was rocked during much of this period by economic decline, intrigues, assassinations, and rebellion. Its rulers relied heavily on Greek mercenaries and demonstrated only occasional flashes of intelligence and vigor. The declining empire gained a short respite during the reign of Artaxerxes III, who came to the throne in 359 bce. Artaxerxes put down a number of determined revolts in Phoenicia, Syria, and Egypt, but this able ruler was poisoned before he could consolidate his position.

Darius III (336–330 bce).   The last of the Achaemenids, Darius III, was a distant member of the royal family, now nearly destroyed by assassinations. Darius succeeded in suppressing another Egyptian rebellion, but time was running out for the Persian Empire. Philip II of Macedonia, having already consolidated the mainland Greeks under his rule, planned to eradicate Persian dominion over the Ionian Greek cities, but he was assassinated before setting out for Anatolia.

Alexander the Great Conquers the Persian Empire (334–325 bce).   In the spring of 334 bce, however, Philip's son Alexander the Great crossed the Hellespont with an army of Macedonians and Greeks, the most powerful military machine the ancient world had ever assembled. Darius III—mistakenly assuming the youthful Alexander would fail—had made no serious preparations to resist the invasion and repeatedly panicked during battle. Yet Alexander did not enjoy easy victories, for the Persians made a respectable stand against his superior forces and generally fought with valor.

Alexander was inspired by a burning ambition to carve out a larger empire than that of the Achaemenids. He stormed into Anatolia, killing a large proportion of

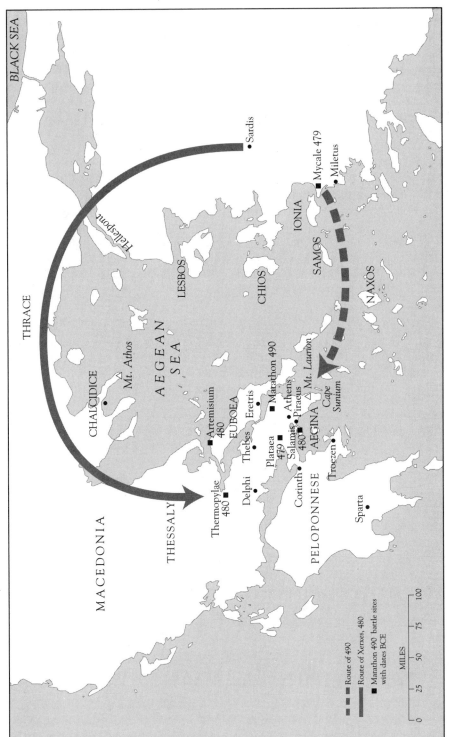

The Persian invasions of Greece, 490 and 480–479 BCE.

the Greek mercenaries in the employ of the Persians, and in 333 BCE he marched south into Syria. Darius finally advanced against the intruder near the town of Issus but experienced overwhelming fear and fled before the outcome of the battle was clear, abandoning his army, his mother, his wife, and his infant son. The Persian troops—instantly losing heart at the sight of their king's cowardice—broke ranks and ran. Alexander then began taking the storied empire piecemeal. After conquering Egypt, he turned eastward and met Darius for a final battle in Mesopotamia. Rather than choosing the natural defensive site of the Tigris River, Darius offered battle near Gaugamela—east of modern Mosul—and was decisively defeated in October of 331 BCE, afterward again turning his chariot in terrified flight. Alexander continued to pick up the pieces of the empire. When Persepolis fell to the invader in April 330 BCE, he burned the magnificent city in retaliation for the destruction of the Athenian Acropolis and also to symbolize the collapse of Achaemenid rule. During the same year Darius III was killed while fleeing from the conqueror on the road to Bactria, apparently by a satrap who feared the broken king would capitulate to the enemy. The assassination gave Alexander title to the Persian Empire, but he had to fight another five years to subdue the eastern satrapies. His realm then stretched from Greece to the borders of north India, but in 323 BCE, while planning an expedition to conquer Arabia, the celebrated conqueror fell ill and died at the age of thirty-three. Important elements of Persian culture survived during the succeeding Hellenistic period, when Iranian affairs were directed by the Greek-speaking Seleucids. The Parthians, ruling from around 170 BCE to 224 CE, adopted Achaemenid traditions, as did their Sasanian successors. We turn in the next chapter to explore the salient features of the widely diffused Persian culture.

CHAPTER XIV

PERSIAN CULTURAL ACHIEVEMENTS

The long survival of the Persian Empire is a tribute to its builders—Cyrus, Cambyses, and Darius—who ruled with tolerance and moderation. Far larger than any previous political unit, the empire brought together in a generally harmonious manner widely differing peoples occupying extensive territories ranging from the deserts of Africa to the snow-topped mountains of Armenia and the frontiers of India. Much of the success of the empire can be attributed to Darius' system of imperial government, discussed in the previous chapter, which continued with little change until the end of the Achaemenid era.

The Achaemenids drew largely on the achievements of subject peoples to forge an amazing degree of cultural unity throughout the empire, one of the chief characteristics of their responsible and generally peaceful rule. This cultural heritage, in part surviving the conquest of Alexander the Great, was most notably expressed in religion, art, and architecture.

ZOROASTRIANISM

The Achaemenid kings, at least from the time of Darius, were receptive to many of the principles of Zoroastrianism, an Iranian religious tradition based on the teachings of the prophet Zarathushtra, the familiar Zoroaster of Greco-Roman tradition. This ancient pre-Islamic faith of Persia is still practiced, chiefly by small groups of Zoroastrians in isolated pockets of Iran and, in much greater numbers, by the Parsees along the west coast of India, who emigrated from Iran a millennium ago under religious pressure from the Muslims. Although Zoroastrianism is now a minor religion embraced by only about 150,000 adherents around the world, the period of Achaemenid rule witnessed its spread as a potent force throughout most of western Asia. Equally significant, Zoroastrianism represents the most enduring legacy of ancient Persia and has profoundly influenced Judaism, Christianity, and Islam, all owing great debts to this remarkable faith.

IRANIAN RELIGION BEFORE ZOROASTER

The Magi and their Rites.   The early development of Zoroastrianism is shrouded in uncertainty. Apparently the pre-Zoroastrian religion of Iran was a composite of the beliefs and practices of the invading Aryans and the indigenous peoples among whom they settled. By early historical times this amalgamated, polytheistic religion seems to have been dominated by an influential caste of hereditary priests known as the Magi. Reflecting their nomadic background, the pre-Zoroastrian priests did not build temples but conducted their services on hilltops or mountains. Their religious life revolved around performing three sacred ceremonies: lighting or maintaining sacred fires, making animal sacrifices, and drinking a sacred intoxicant made from the juice of the haoma plant. This hallucinogenic beverage, an offering to the gods, was prepared by pressing and pounding the stems and stalks of haoma plants to obtain the juice, which was then filtered and drunk by the celebrants. Despite considerable scholarly effort, the identity of the haoma plant of this time remains elusive. All we know with certainty is that the drinking of its mind-altering juice was a central rite not only of the primitive religion of Iran but also of the similar religion of northwest India, though the beverage was called haoma in Iran and soma in India. In both Iran and India the euphoric intoxication induced by the powerful drug of the drink was thought to purvey a glimpse of immortality and a sense of unity with the gods.

Daevas *and* Ahuras.   Like their cousins practicing the Vedic religion in India, the early Iranians divided their deities into two categories, namely the *daevas* (*devas* in Sanskrit) and the *ahuras* (*asuras* in Sanskrit). In Iran the *daevas* were regarded as malevolent and the *ahuras* benevolent, but this system was reversed in Vedic India. Thus Iranian and Indian religion underwent a widening rift, resulting from the gods of one becoming the demons of the other. The greatest of the benevolent deities in Iran was known as Ahura Mazda, or Wise Lord. One of the lesser *ahuras* doing his will was Mithra (Mitra in Sanskrit), regarded as a god of loyalty, justice, war, and victory.

THE REFORMATION OF ZOROASTER

Sources.   A drastic reorientation of the Iranian religion occurred under the forceful message of the reforming prophet Zoroaster, one of the great religious figures of all times. Unfortunately, our sources about his life and teachings are fragmentary and often contradictory. The Zoroastrian sources consist of the Avesta—the Zoroastrian scriptures—and various later religious texts. Scholars generally agree that the oldest part of the Avesta is formed by the Gathas, or hymns, composed in archaic language and reputedly the very words of the great prophet himself, though preserved orally for centuries before being written down. The Gathas stand as the foremost source of information about the life and teachings of Zoroaster. Our chief non-Zoroastrian sources about the prophet are Greek and Roman writers such as Plato, Pliny, and Plutarch, though they freely mix fanciful lore with authentic materials.

Life and Message.   Zoroaster seems to have been active no later than the sixth century BCE and possibly many centuries earlier. He lived somewhere in eastern Iran. The traditional account of his infancy and later life is replete with miracles. We are told that Zoroaster, born of a virgin, began to wander the earth in a quest for truth at the age of twenty, culminating when he was thirty in a revelatory vision of Ahura

Mazda that inspired him to preach the cardinal tenants of the true religion. Although the details of his teachings are uncertain and the subject of dispute, perhaps we can sketch the main thrust of his reform of the ancient Iranian religious system. Zoroaster was committed to the establishment of religion on an ethical basis, an element conspicuously absent from the old Indo-Iranian religious tradition. The prophet expressed wrath at animal sacrifice, or at least the cruelty of cutting the throats of fully conscious bulls, and he censured the intoxicating and perhaps orgiastic behavior accompanying the rite. He retained the ritual use of sacred fire, regarded as a symbol of the divine entity known as Truth. He condemned all the *daevas* as demonic beings but regarded the *ahuras* as the good spirits of the universe. Above all, Zoroaster stressed the supreme power of Ahura Mazda.

The Supremacy of Ahura Mazda.   Ahura Mazda was associated with the principles of infinite wisdom, light, truth, and righteousness. Zoroaster identified him as the one uncreated god of the universe and the source of all goodness. According to the Gathas, the prophet taught that Ahura Mazda fashioned both heaven and earth as well as the moral order. Thus Ahura Mazda alone is worthy of worship. Moreover, the Wise Lord is invisible, changeless, omniscient, omnipresent, and absolutely beyond human understanding.

The Spenta Mainyu and the Amesha Spentas.   Zoroaster explained that Ahura Mazda fashioned the physical world in seven stages: the first was sky, the second water, the third earth, the fourth vegetation, the fifth animals, the sixth humankind, and the seventh fire. Passages in the Gathas lead to the conclusion that Ahura Mazda created the universe through the Spenta Mainyu, or Holy Spirit, regarded as his divine attribute rather than a being apart from him. Additionally, Zoroaster explained that Ahura Mazda created the Amesha Spentas, or Holy Immortals, six celestial beings (conceived also as archangels), who were brought forth to aid in the task of fashioning and governing the world.

Cosmic Dualism.   Deeply rooted in Zoroaster's thought was the importance of choosing good over evil, truth over falsehood. This basic dualism was later expressed in terms of a struggle of two opposing principles for control of the universe, namely, Spenta Mainyu (the Holy Spirit) and Angra Mainyu (the Evil Spirit), subsequently known as Ahriman. As an attribute of Ahura Mazda, Spenta Mainyu is the bringer of Truth, whereas Ahriman encompasses the Lie. Thus the very essence of the Evil Spirit is falsehood. The ethical dualism engendered by Ahriman took on cosmic proportions. While Ahura Mazda leads the forces of goodness, Ahriman directs those of evil, filth, and death. Hosts of divine beings serve as warriors on the righteous side of Ahura Mazda to fight the demons, noxious creatures, and archfiends following the detestable evil of Ahriman. Zoroaster regarded all of the *daevas* of the pre-Zoroastrian religion as Ahriman's offspring and the demons in his army.

Zoroaster urged his followers to join the forces of Ahura Mazda against the demonic powers of darkness by speaking the truth and resisting evil. He taught that all humans are born in a sinless state and are endowed with the free will to serve the

The fire altar, depicted on this Sasanian coin, was prominent in ancient Zoroastrianism, whose priests taught that fire is a manifestation of Ahura Mazda. They kept fires perpetually burning in the open air to link heaven and earth.

good or the evil side. They remain accountable for their choices and have a clear moral responsibility, in the words of the Gathas, to follow the way of righteousness: "Within the span of this life of Earth / Perfection can be reached by fervent souls. / Ardent in zeal, sincere in their toil."

Beyond Death.   Zoroaster's teachings constitute the first systematic treatment of eschatology, that is, a system of doctrines concerning the afterlife or the end of the world. The Gathas frequently refer to the fate of humanity beyond death. Each soul is evaluated in an individual judgment. People accumulating a preponderance of good thoughts, words, and deeds are said to enter an afterlife of unimaginable bliss, but those weighed down by misdeeds plunge into hell. Described in ghastly detail in the *Vision of Arda Viraz,* a work probably written down in the ninth century CE, Zoroastrian hell is truly terrifying. The hero of the book, the righteous sage Viraz, visits the other world to learn the fate of the dead. After viewing the rewards of heaven, he travels through "the jaws of hell" to see the horrors within and finds that an appropriate punishment is meted out for every earthly offense, many of which involve sexual taboos. The sage witnesses the soul of a man who had participated in sexual intercourse with a menstruating woman on earth being tormented by demons, who constantly pour "the menstrual discharge of women" into his mouth. The righteous Viraz sees the souls of the wicked enduring many other dreadful punishments, including "the heat of swiftly blazing fire" and incessant beatings. Scholars suggest his vision of the other world is the ultimate source of Dante's *Divine Comedy.*

LATER DEVELOPMENTS

The Three Saviors and Resurrection.   The horrors of divine punishment are mercifully temporary because Zoroastrianism provides for the eventual redemption of the souls in hell. Zoroaster's later followers spelled out doctrines pertaining to the deliverance from hell in great detail. They explained that three saviors—born to unblemished virgins from Zoroaster's preserved semen—will appear at intervals of a thousand years to perfect the world and reclaim humanity from evil. Presiding over the final millennium of finite time, the last savior (Saoshyant) will bring to completion the mission of preparing humanity for the termination of the world and the establishment of the eternal kingdom of Ahura Mazda. A general resurrection of the dead in heaven and hell will occur at the end of his mission on earth. At the raising of the dead, souls will be reunited with their bodies. The wicked will then be purified to join the righteous, all speaking with one tongue in praise of Ahura Mazda.

Meanwhile, in a final battle, Ahura Mazda and his heavenly hosts will conquer Ahriman and his demons before destroying them and every trace of their evil in a mighty conflagration. The wonderfully restored world will then enter an eternal age of paradisiacal joy devoid not only of the torment and sin of the past but also of the curse of human aging and decay. In the history of religion, Zoroastrianism remains one of the very few faiths providing for the universal salvation of humanity. We should note also that its dualism is temporary, for Ahura Mazda is assured of ultimate triumph. In short, Zoroastrianism tends toward monotheism through its teaching that the evil principle will no longer exist in the eternal age of Ahura Mazda.

Syncretism.   Zoroastrianism slowly spread throughout most of western Asia following the death of its great prophet but was subject to much compromise and syncretism, or union, with other beliefs. The Zoroastrianism of the Achaemenid period underwent many changes in the face of a strong contest between those ascribing to the pure form of Zoroaster's teachings and those supporting the deeply rooted Iranian religious traditions. We find evidence of the reintroduction of the haoma rite and the acknowledgement of subordinate deities to Ahura Mazda.

Zoroastrianism during the Macedonian, Seleucid, Parthian, and Sasanian Periods (330 BCE–651 CE). After the Persian Empire was lost to Alexander the Great in the fourth century BCE, Zoroastrianism experienced a heavy blow as a wave of Greek influence swept through the old Achaemenid lands. Alexander's death in 323 BCE was followed by intense fighting among his generals for his empire. Seleucus gained possession of Persia and other territories, the inauguration of the Seleucid era. The Seleucids continued the policy of undermining Zoroastrianism with Greek elements, but by the mid-third century BCE their power in Persia had come under attack from all sides. The nomadic Parthians, who had settled in northeast Iran, began to expand into Seleucid domains and carved out an empire stretching from the frontiers of India to the borders of Mesopotamia. They continued to rule these vast territories until the middle of the third century CE. Regarding themselves as heirs of the Achaemenids, the Parthian rulers adopted the old title King of Kings and sanctioned Zoroastrianism, though syncretism continued apace.

A nationalistic Persian dynasty—the Sasanian—revolted in southern Iran at the beginning of the third century CE. The Sasanians swiftly wrested control of the empire from the Parthians and ruled until 651. Presiding over a new period of cultural brilliance, the Sasanian kings vigorously promoted a syncretic Zoroastrianism, now the official religion of the state. Judaism, Christianity, Hinduism, and Buddhism were also represented in the empire, and the population supported additional faiths such as Mithraism and Manichaeism. Mithraism was based on a strong allegiance to the *ahura* Mithra, a powerful figure in the pre-Zoroastrian pantheon. Linked to the sun, Mithra was thought to uphold the natural rhythms of nature and the harmonious relationships among humankind. Much earlier, the popular god had made his way westward into the Roman Empire, where he encountered implacable hostility from the early Christians. Although Mithra (Mithras in Greco-Roman tradition) left a conspicuous mark on Christian doctrine, he was violently suppressed by the Christians after they associated themselves with the power of Rome in the early fourth century. The dualistic sect known as Manichaeism, an additional rival of early Christianity from Persia, blended various doctrines of Zoroastrianism, Buddhism, Christianity, and other faiths. Manichaeism attracted Augustine of Hippo before he made his famous conversion to Christianity in the late fourth century. Like Mithraism, Manichaeism was ultimately stamped out in the Roman Empire by the growing power of Christianity.

The Muslim Conquest and the Decline of Zoroastrianism.   Sasanian Iran was weakened by extended wars against the Roman Empire and later against its surviving eastern half, often called the Eastern Roman Empire or the Byzantine Empire. Muslim Arab warriors conquered the debilitated Sasanian state in the seventh century CE. The bulk of the population was converted to Islam by intense persuasion or coercion, though somehow a small group of Zoroastrians persisted in their faith. As religious persecution intensified in the eighth and ninth centuries, a number of the remaining Zoroastrians fled from Iran and found asylum in India, where they are known as the Parsees—after their native Persia—and their religion is called Parseeism. A few thousand Zoroastrians, identified by the Muslims as Gabars (infidels), have managed to survive in isolated pockets of present-day Iran, clinging tenaciously to their beleaguered faith in the face of strict Islamic rule.

Sacred Literature and Religious Ceremonies

The Avesta.   Zoroastrians treat the Avesta, their scriptures, as if directly inspired by Ahura Mazda. The sacred work was composed over a long span, probably extending from the time of Zoroaster to the reigns of the Sasanians. The Avesta was handed down orally in the dialects known as Gathic and Avestan until the Sasanian period and then committed to writing. Because Gathic and Avestan had become exceedingly difficult to understand by that time, the Avesta was provided with a translation and later a commentary in Pahlavi (Middle Persian), the official language of the Sasanian Empire.

The Avesta is fragmentary in its present form, chiefly because considerable Zoroastrian sacred literature was destroyed in the aftermath of the Arab conquest. We noted that scholars generally regard the Gathas, the hymns associated with Zoroaster, as the oldest part of the sacred work. The extant Avesta is used chiefly for intricate ceremonies and contains five subdivisions, including the Yasna, the main liturgy. The Yasna embraces the Gathas and a collection of prayers and liturgical formulas focusing on the preparation and offering of haoma, an observance meant to lead worshipers to the contemplation and adoration of Ahura Mazda.

Zoroastrian Worship in Antiquity.   Although the details of Zoroastrian rites and observances in ancient Iran are disputed, we saw that Zoroaster retained the use of fire. Reliefs above the tombs of Darius and his successors depict kings worshiping before a sacred fire in the presence of a winged figure signifying Ahura Mazda. Fire altars in open-air sanctuaries are the only structures built by the Persians having an incontestable religious purpose. Zoroastrian priests kept fires perpetually burning on the altars to dispel darkness and express the glorious nature of Ahura Mazda. Conceived as a symbol of truth, fire was thought to emanate from the abode of Ahura Mazda and to provide a strong link between heaven and earth.

The reintroduced haoma ceremony served as the central rite of ancient Zoroastrianism. The juice of the haoma plant was prized for imparting extraordinary hallucinatory experiences and great spiritual gifts. In antiquity the sacramental haoma was probably partaken by the entire community, not just the priests, its powerful drug said to have produced an exhilarating sense of contentment and joy without causing any harmful effects whatsoever. The Zoroastrians regarded haoma as far more than a sacramental extract from a mystical plant, however, for Haoma was also a heavenly being whose actual presence was conveyed to the partakers through the potent juice. The divine Haoma was believed to act as both sacrificial victim and priest in the ancient haoma rite, dying in the extraction of the juice but then overcoming death and offering a foretaste of eternal life to those nourished by his sacred drink. Scholars note that the ancient haoma sacrifice represents a remarkable forerunner of the Christian Eucharist.

Unfortunately, scholars are unable to disentangle the worship of the ancient Zoroastrians from that of the current devotees of the faith. Present-day Zoroastrian priests conduct many of the rites in temples, where they venerate and perpetually burn the sacred fire, its flame conceived as the visible sign of Ahura Mazda's guiding presence. Worship includes praying to Ahura Mazda and reciting the Avesta. Performed by priests in special attire, the central rite of Zoroastrianism remains the offering of haoma juice—now devoid of hallucinogenic properties—along with bread, water, and other elements to Ahura Mazda to aid humans in their quest for righteousness and salvation.

ZOROASTRIAN INFLUENCES ON JUDAISM, CHRISTIANITY, AND ISLAM

Zoroastrian teachings found their way into other religions. We saw in chapter 11 that postexilic Judaism borrowed various concepts from Zoroastrianism, including a demonic Satan, clearly a version of Ahriman. Later, about 250 BCE, apocalyptic literature began to appear in Jewish circles. This style of writing claims to reveal things normally hidden and to unveil the future. Showing an almost certain debt to Zoroastrian thought, Jewish apocalyptic literature includes doctrines such as an evil Satan, an angelic hierarchy, heaven and hell, judgment after death and at the end of the world, resurrection of the body, a cosmic dualism of good and evil forces led respectively by the archangel Michael and by Satan, and a future Savior and messianic kingdom in which righteousness will prevail. The early Christians incorporated these beliefs circulating within ancient Judaism as essential doctrines in their own religion. Moreover, although directly derived from Jewish writings (the pseudepigraphical book of Enoch and the apocryphal book of Tobit), the seven spirits of God mentioned in the book of Revelation in the New Testament (Rev. 1:4) probably have their ultimate origin in the Holy Immortals and the Holy Spirit of Zoroastrianism. Zoroastrian doctrines also pervaded Islam, for the prophet Mahomet gravitated toward Jewish and Christian thought rooted in Zoroastrianism. He seems to have been profoundly influenced by the eschatology originating in Zoroastrianism,

Persian metalwork shows a particular appreciation for the animal
form, which was skillfully adapted for decorative effects. The
handle of this splendid gold rhyton, or drinking horn, takes the
form a winged lion, depicted as a vibrant, watchful animal.
5th century BCE. Archaeological Museum, Tehran.

with rewards for the righteous and torments for the wicked. Thus Islam included beliefs in the resurrection of the body, judgment day, heaven and hell, Satan, demons,
and a hierarchy of angels.

ART AND ARCHITECTURE

SMALLER ARTS

We saw that the notable Achaemenid culture was essentially a blend of diverse elements. Persian imperial art was shaped by techniques, styles, and motifs borrowed
from lands such as Assyria-Babylonia in the northwest, Greece in the west, Egypt in
the south, and India in the east. Yet the Achaemenids unified their eclectic art with
a distinctive Persian stamp and purpose. Persian admiration for graceful form is reflected in the smaller arts, exemplified by aesthetically pleasing stone and pottery
vessels. Achaemenid artisans also excelled in metalwork, seal cuttings, and jewelry.

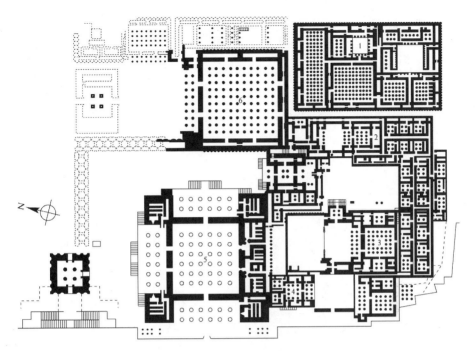

1. Treasury
2. Harem
3. Palace of Xerxes
4. Palace of Darius I
5. Audience hall of Darius I
6. Throne hall of Xerxes
----- Partially excavated

Plan of Persepolis.

Metalworkers commonly decorated their creations with hybrid animal figures and animal motifs, the continuation of an ancient Iranian tradition.

Susa

The Persians are famous for their architecture. Prior to Cyrus' rapid conquest of a huge empire, the Persians had little need of monumental structures. Cyrus and his successors, believing their cities should reflect imperial power and wealth, created magnificent metropolitan settings on a scale the world had never seen. Darius I marshaled artisans from around the empire to construct a huge new palace at the old Elamite capital of Susa, his chief administrative center. The influence here of the Assyro-Babylonian style is clearly evident, for the royal palace was erected around large interior courtyards, while the walls were decorated with griffins, lions, and bulls, all formed of brightly colored molded and glazed brickwork.

Persepolis

Darius transferred some ceremonial functions from Susa to the more specifically Persian site of Persepolis, spectacularly situated near the edge of the lofty mountains

Reconstruction of the audience hall, or Apadana, where the king received dignitaries. With its lofty columns and monumental stairways, the great building dominated Persepolis.

Reconstruction of the western portico of the Apadana, showing the king elevated on a portable throne to review the procession of the annual New Year Festival. Each of the three porticoes of the Apadana was graced by twelve lofty limestone columns supporting the beams of the cedar roof timbers. About sixty-four feet high, the fluted columns stood on cylindrical stone bases and were crowned by massive double-bull capitals.

above the Persian Gulf. The Achaemenids achieved their greatest architectural triumph by erecting a magnificent palace complex at Persepolis. Darius built many of the palace buildings and the harem. Construction continued under Xerxes and was essentially completed by Artaxerxes I. Workers began the project by leveling a mountain slope to make a vast terrace, which received the palace complex. The terrace was reinforced by a massive retaining wall of rectangular limestone blocks on three sides, the remaining side backing into a sizeable slope. A magnificent double reversing stairway led to the huge Gate of All Lands at the top of the terrace, a gateway flanked by colossal Mesopotamian-inspired winged bulls. The main buildings, which were fashioned of gray limestone from adjacent mountains, were erected on a platform approached by additional flights of stairs. Excavations indicate that Darius built an immense audience hall that archaeologists term the Apadana, said to have accommodated 10,000 people, while Xerxes initiated and probably completed construction on the still larger audience hall known as the Hall of a Hundred Columns.

The characteristic architectural feature at Persepolis was the soaring columned hall, not borrowed from elsewhere but rooted in ancient Iranian prototypes. The columns in the audience halls of Darius and Xerxes were more widely spaced than those in Egyptian buildings, resulting in the light and airy effect typical of Achaemenid palaces. The vividly painted stone columns supporting the Hall of a Hundred Columns reached a height of forty feet. Each member of this forestlike profusion was slender and carefully fluted in the Greek manner. Although the floral designs of the bases and capitals of the columns suggest Egyptian influence, the capitals were topped by the forequarters of a pair of bulls or lions, a Persian innovation. These paired creatures supported the painted heavy beams of the imported cedar roof timbers.

Darius' great audience hall was approached by two ceremonial double staircases, which are entirely faced with reliefs depicting an honor guard of armed Immortals as well as long lines of foreign dignitaries from client states, representatives from the satrapies, Persian and Median courtiers, and other officials, all probably originally sparkling with applied color. The subjects have passed through the Gate of All Lands and are depicted climbing the stairs to the audience hall. Bearing gifts or tribute, they have come to pay homage to the enthroned Darius and to his standing son Xerxes during the sacred New Year Festival. All activity centers around the image of the King of Kings, the usual focus of Achaemenid art, and probably represents actual ceremonies taking place at Persepolis during the important celebration. Although perhaps inspired by Assyrian reliefs, the Persian figures are more rounded, naturalistic, and organically unified. Apparently Darius employed talented Ionian Greek artisans to carve the reliefs, for the crisp layers of overlapping garments and the beautifully pleated folds of drapery reflect the Archaic style of Greek sculpture.

We noted that Alexander the Great burned Persepolis in 331 BCE, an unfortunate act symbolizing the collapse of two centuries of humane Achaemenid rule. The standing ruins of the great palace complex—chiefly stairways, columns, doorways, and window jambs—still reflect the legendary grandeur of the city. Alexander transferred the scepter of imperial power from Asia to Europe. The many eventful centuries embracing the remainder of ancient history center on developments in the European world.

BIBLIOGRAPHY

The following selection lists informative works in English, many with detailed references to more specialized studies and to original sources in translation. Readers are encouraged to familiarize themselves also with the various scholarly journals presenting current research on the ancient Near East.

GENERAL STUDIES

Burney, Charles. *From Village to Empire: An Introduction to Near Eastern Archaeology.* Oxford: Phaidon, 1977.

The Cambridge Ancient History. Vols. 1–2, 3d ed. Vols 3–4, 2d ed. Cambridge: Cambridge University Press, 1970–91.

Gibson, McGuire, and Robert D. Biggs, eds. *The Organization of Power: Aspects of Bureaucracy in the Ancient Near East.* 2d ed. Chicago: Oriental Institute of the University of Chicago, 1991.

Hallo, William W., and William K. Simpson. *The Ancient Near East: A History.* 2d ed. Fort Worth, Harcourt Brace, 1998.

Knapp, A. Bernard. *The History and Culture of Ancient Western Asia and Egypt.* Chicago: Dorsey, 1988.

Kuhrt, Amélie. *The Ancient Near East.* 2 vols., London: Routledge, 1995.

Leick, Gwendolyn. *A Dictionary of Ancient Near Eastern Mythologies.* London: Routledge, 1991.

Lloyd, Seton. *The Art of the Ancient Near East.* London: Thames and Hudson, 1961.

Moorey, P. R. S. *The Ancient Near East.* Oxford: Ashmolean Museum, 1987.

Nissen, Hans J. *Archaic Bookkeeping: Early Writing and Techniques of Economic Administration in the Ancient Near East.* Trans. Paul Larsen. Chicago: University of Chicago Press, 1993.

Nissen, Hans J. *The Early History of the Ancient Near East, 9000–2000 B.C.* Trans. Elizabeth Lutzeier with Kenneth J. Northcott. Chicago: University of Chicago Press, 1988.

The Oxford Encyclopedia of Archaeology in the Near East. Ed. Eric M. Meyers. 5 vols. New York: Oxford University Press, 1996.

Pope, Maurice. *The Story of Decipherment: From Egyptian Hieroglyphic to Linear B.* London: Thames and Hudson, 1975.

Pritchard, James B., ed. *Ancient Near Eastern Texts Relating to the Old Testament.* 3d ed. Princeton: Princeton University Press, 1969.

Sasson, Jack M., ed. *Civilizations of the Ancient Near East.* 4 vols. New York: Scribner's, 1995.

HUMAN ORIGINS AND PREHISTORY (CHAPTERS 1–2)

Angela, Piero, and Alberto Angela. *The Extraordinary Story of Human Origins.* Trans. Gabriele Tonne. Buffalo: Prometheus, 1993.

Bailey, G. N., and P. Callow, eds. *Stone Age Prehistory: Studies in Memory of Charles McBurney*. Cambridge: Cambridge University Press, 1986.

Binford, Lewis R. *In Pursuit of the Past: Decoding the Archaeological Record*. London: Thames and Hudson, 1983.

Burenhult, Göran, ed. *People of the Stone Age: Hunter-Gatherers and Early Farmers*. San Francisco: HarperSanFrancisco, 1993.

Clark, Grahame. *Economic Prehistory: Papers on Archaeology*. Cambridge: Cambridge University Press, 1989.

Cohen, Mark Nathan. *Health and the Rise of Civilization*. New Haven: Yale University Press, 1989.

Cohen, Mark Nathan. *The Food Crisis in Prehistory: Overpopulation and the Origin of Agriculture*. New Haven: Yale University Press, 1977.

Cunliffe, Barry, ed. *The Oxford Illustrated Prehistory of Europe*. Oxford: Oxford University Press, 1994.

Dickson, D. Bruce. *The Dawn of Belief: Religion in the Upper Paleolithic of Southwestern Europe*. Tucson: University of Arizona Press, 1990.

Ehrenberg, Margaret. *Women in Prehistory*. Norman: University of Oklahoma Press, 1989.

Fagan, Brian M. *People of the Earth: An Introduction to World Prehistory*. 7th ed. New York: Harper Collins, 1992.

Fagan, Brian M. *World Prehistory: A Brief Introduction*. 2d ed. New York: Harper Collins, 1993.

Gamble, Clive. *The Palaeolithic Settlement of Europe*. Cambridge: Cambridge University Press, 1986.

Gowlett, John A. J. *Ascent to Civilization: The Archaeology of Early Humans*. 2d ed. New York: McGraw-Hill, 1993.

Greene, Kevin. *Archaeology, an Introduction: The History, Principles, and Methods of Modern Archaeology*. Philadelphia: University of Pennsylvania Press, 1995.

Haviland, William A. *Human Evolution and Prehistory*. 3d ed. Fort Worth: Harcourt Brace, 1994.

Henry, Donald O. *From Foraging to Agriculture: The Levant at the End of the Ice Age*. Philadelphia: University of Pennsylvania Press, 1989.

Hodges, Henry. *Technology in the Ancient World*. New York: Knopf, 1970.

Johanson, Donald, Lenora Johanson, and Blake Edgar. *Ancestors: In Search of Human Origins*. New York: Villard, 1994.

Johanson, Donald, and Blake Edgar. *From Lucy to Language*. New York: Simon and Schuster, 1996.

Larsen, Clark Spencer, Robert M. Matter, and Daniel L. Gebo. *Human Origins: The Fossil Record*. 2d ed. Prospect Heights, Ill.: Waveland, 1991.

Leakey, Richard. *The Origin of Humankind*. New York: BasicBooks, 1994.

Leroi-Gourhan, André. *The Dawn of European Art: An Introduction to Palaeolithic Cave Painting*. Trans. Sara Champion. Cambridge: Cambridge University Press, 1982.

Lewin, Roger. *Human Evolution: An Illustrated Introduction*. 3d ed. Boston: Blacknell Scientific Publications, 1993.

Lieberman, Philip. *Uniquely Human: The Evolution of Speech, Thought, and Selfless Behavior.* Cambridge, Mass.: Harvard University Press, 1991.

Mellaart, James. *Çatal Hüyük: A Neolithic Town in Anatolia.* New York: McGraw-Hill, 1967.

Mellaart, James. *The Neolithic of the Near East.* London: Thames and Hudson, 1975.

Mellars, Paul, ed. *The Emergence of Modern Humans: An Archaeological Perspective.* Ithaca, N.Y.: Cornell University Press, 1990.

Nitecki, Matthew H., and Doris V. Nitecki. *Origins of Anatomically Modern Humans.* New York: Plenum, 1994.

Pericot-Garcia, Luis, John Galloway, and Andreas Lommel. *Prehistoric and Primitive Art.* London: Thames and Hudson, 1969.

Price, T. Douglas, and Gary M. Feinman. *Images of the Past.* Mountain View, Calif.: Mayfield, 1993.

Rasmussen, D. Tab, ed. *The Origin and Evolution of Humans and Humanness.* Boston: Jones and Bartlett, 1993.

Renfrew, Colin, and Paul Bahn. *Archaeology: Theories, Methods, and Practices.* New York: Thames and Hudson, 1991.

Sandars, N. K. *Prehistoric Art in Europe.* 2d ed. Harmondsworth, England: Penguin, 1985.

Shreeve, James. *The Neanderthal Enigma: Solving the Mystery of Modern Human Origins.* New York: William Morrow, 1995.

Sieveking, Ann. *The Cave Artists.* London: Thames and Hudson, 1979.

Stringer, Christopher, and Clive Gamble. *In Search of the Neanderthals: Solving the Puzzle of Human Origins.* London: Thames and Hudson, 1993.

Trinkaus, Erik, and Pat Shipman. *The Neanderthals: Changing the Image of Mankind.* New York, Knopf, 1993.

Wymer, John. *The Palaeolithic Age.* New York: St. Martin, 1981.

Yakar, Jak. *Prehistoric Anatolia: The Neolithic Transformation and the Early Chalcolithic Period.* Tel Aviv: Tel Aviv University, 1991.

The Early Mesopotamians (Chapters 3–5)

Algaze, Guillermo. *The Uruk World System: The Dynamics of Expansion of Early Mesopotamian Civilization.* Chicago: University of Chicago Press, 1993.

Bermant, Chaim, and Michael Weitzman. *Ebla: A Revelation in Archaeology.* New York: Times Books, 1979.

Boecker, Hans Jochen. *Law and the Administration of Justice in the Old Testament and Ancient East.* Trans. Jeremy Moiser. Minneapolis: Augsburg, 1980.

Bottéro, Jean. *Mesopotamia: Writing, Reasoning, and the Gods.* Trans. Zainab Bahrani and Marc van de Mieroop. Chicago: University of Chicago Press, 1992.

Carter, Elizabeth, and Matthew W. Stolper. *Elam: Surveys of Political History and Archaeology.* Berkeley: University of California Press, 1984.

Collon, Dominique. *Ancient Near Eastern Art.* Berkeley: University of California Press, 1995.

Collon, Dominique. *First Impressions: Cylinder Seals in the Ancient Near East.* 2d ed. London: British Museum Publications, 1993.

Cooper, Jerrold S. *Sumerian and Akkadian Royal Inscriptions.* Vol. 1. New Haven: American Oriental Society, 1986–.

Crawford, Harriet. *Sumer and the Sumerians.* Cambridge: Cambridge University Press, 1991.

Dalley, Stephanie. *Mari and Karana: Two Old Babylonian Cities.* London: Longman, 1984.

Dalley, Stephanie, trans. *Myths from Mesopotamia: Creation, the Flood, Gilgamesh, and Others.* Oxford: Oxford University Press, 1991.

Frankfort, Henri. *The Art and Architecture of the Ancient Orient.* Harmondsworth, England: Penguin, 1970. Reprint, New Haven: Yale University Press, 1996.

Frankfort, Henri. *The Birth of Civilization in the Near East.* London: William and Norgate, 1951.

Henrickson, Elizabeth F., and Ingolf Thuesen, eds. *Upon This Foundation—the 'Ubaid Reconsidered: Proceedings from the 'Ubaid Symposium, Elsinore [Denmark], May 30th–June 1st 1988.* Copenhagen: Museum Tusculanum Press, 1989.

Hinz, Walther. *The Lost World of Elam: Re-creation of a Vanished Civilization.* Trans. Jennifer Barnes. New York: New York University Press, 1973.

Jacobsen, Thorkild. *The Treasures of Darkness: A History of Mesopotamian Religion.* New Haven: Yale University Press, 1976.

Kramer, Samuel Noah. *History Begins at Sumer.* 3d ed. Philadelphia: University of Pennsylvania Press, 1981.

Kramer, Samuel Noah. *Sumerian Mythology: A Study of Spiritual and Literary Achievement in the Third Millennium B.C.* Rev. ed. New York: Harper, 1961.

Kramer, Samuel Noah. *The Sumerians: Their History, Culture, and Character.* Chicago: University of Chicago Press, 1963.

Liverani, Mario, ed. *Akkad: The First World Empire.* Padua: Sargon, 1993.

Lloyd, Seton. *The Archaeology of Mesopotamia.* Rev. ed. New York: Thames and Hudson, 1984.

Lloyd, Seton. *Foundations in the Dust: The Story of Mesopotamian Exploration.* Rev. ed. London: Thames and Hudson, 1980.

Matthiae, Paolo. *Ebla: An Empire Rediscovered.* Trans. Christopher Holme. London: Hodder and Stoughton, 1980.

Van de Mieroop, Marc. *Society and Enterprise in Old Babylonian Ur.* Berlin: D. Reimer, 1992.

Moorey, P. R. S. *Ancient Mesopotamian Materials and Industries: The Archaeological Evidence.* Oxford: Clarendon Press, 1994.

Moortgat, Anton. *The Art of Ancient Mesopotamia: The Classical Art of the Near East.* Trans. Judith Filson. London: Phaidon, 1969.

Oates, Joan. *Babylon.* Rev. ed. London: Thames and Hudson, 1986.

Oppenheim, A. Lee. *Ancient Mesopotamia: Portrait of a Dead Civilization.* Rev. ed. Chicago: University of Chicago Press, 1977.

Pettinato, Giovanni. *Ebla: A New Look at History.* Trans. C. Faith Richardson. Baltimore: Johns Hopkins University Press, 1991.

Postgate, J. N. *Early Mesopotamia: Society and Economy at the Dawn of History.* London: Routledge, 1992.

Potts, Timothy. *Mesopotamia and the East: An Archaeological and Historical Study of Foreign Relations ca. 3400–2000 BC.* Oxford: Oxford University Committee for Archaeology, 1994.

Reade, Julian. *Mesopotamia.* Cambridge, Mass.: Harvard University Press, 1991.

Roaf, Michael. *Cultural Atlas of Mesopotamia and the Ancient Near East.* New York: Facts on File, 1990.

Roux, Georges. *Ancient Iraq.* 3d ed. London: Penguin, 1992.

Saggs, H. W. F. *Babylonians.* Norman: University of Oklahoma Press, 1995.

Saggs, H. W. F. *Civilization before Greece and Rome.* New Haven: Yale University Press, 1989.

Saggs, H. W. F. *The Encounter with the Divine in Mesopotamia and Israel.* London: Athlone, 1978.

Saggs, H. W. F. *The Greatness That Was Babylon: A Survey of the Ancient Civilizations of the Tigris-Euphrates Valley.* Rev. ed. London: Sidwick and Jackson, 1988.

Stein, Gil, and Mitchell S. Rothman, eds. *Chiefdoms and Early States in the Near East: The Organizational Dynamics and Complexity.* Madison, Wis.: Prehistoric Press, 1994.

Tigay, Jeffrey H. *Evolution of the Gilgamesh Epic.* Philadelphia: University of Pennsylvania Press, 1982.

Woolley, Leonard, Sir. *Ur 'of the Chaldees': A Revised and Updated Edition of Sir Leonard Woolley's Excavations at Ur.* Rev. by P. R. S. Moorey. Ithaca, N.Y., Cornell University Press, 1982.

The Egyptians (Chapters 6–7)

Aldred, Cyril. *Egyptian Art: In the Days of the Pharaohs, 3100–320 BC.* London: Thames and Hudson, 1980.

Aldred, Cyril. *The Egyptians.* Rev. ed. London: Thames and Hudson, 1984.

Aldred, Cyril. *Akhenaten: King of Egypt.* London: Thames and Hudson, 1988.

Bagnall, Roger S. *Egypt in Late Antiquity.* Princeton: Princeton University Press, 1993.

Bourriau, Janine. *Pharaohs and Mortals: Egyptian Art in the Middle Kingdom.* Cambridge: Cambridge University Press, 1988.

Breasted, James Henry. *Ancient Records of Egypt.* 5 vols. Chicago: University of Chicago Press, 1906–1907.

Breasted, James Henry. *Development of Religion and Thought in Ancient Egypt.* London: Hodder and Stoughton, 1912.

Budge, E. A. Wallis, Sir. *The Book of the Dead: An English Translation of the Chapters, Hymns, etc., of the Theban Recension.* 2d ed. London: Kegan Paul, Trench, Trübner, 1909.

Butzer, Karl W. *Early Hydraulic Civilization in Egypt: A Study in Cultural Ecology.* Chicago: University of Chicago Press, 1976.

David, A. Rosalie. *The Ancient Egyptians: Religious Beliefs and Practices.* London: Routledge and Kegan Paul, 1982.

David, A. Rosalie. *The Egyptian Kingdoms.* New York: Peter Bedrick, 1988.

Edwards, I. E. S. *The Pyramids of Egypt.* Rev. ed. Harmondsworth, England: Viking, 1986.

Edwards, I. E. S. *Tutankhamun, His Tomb and Its Treasures.* New York: Metropolitan Museum of Art, 1976.

Forman, Werner, and Stephen Quirke. *Hieroglyphs and the Afterlife in Ancient Egypt.* London: British Museum Press, 1996.

Gardiner, Alan, Sir. *Egypt of the Pharaohs: An Introduction.* Oxford: Clarendon Press, 1961.

Glanville, S. R. K., ed. *Legacy of Egypt.* 2d ed. Oxford: Clarendon Press, 1971.

Griffiths, J. Gwyn. *The Conflict of Horus and Seth from Egyptian and Classical Sources.* Liverpool: Liverpool University Press, 1961.

Harris, J. R., ed. *The Legacy of Egypt.* 2d ed. Oxford: Clarendon Press, 1971.

Hawkes, Jacquetta. *The First Great Civilizations: Life in Mesopotamia, the Indus Valley, and Egypt.* New York: Knopf, 1973.

Ions, Veronica. *Egyptian Mythology.* Rev. ed. New York: Peter Bedrick, 1983.

James, T. G. H. *Ancient Egypt: The Land and Its Legacy.* London: British Museum Publications, 1988.

James, T. G. H. *An Introduction to Ancient Egypt.* London: British Museum Publications, 1979.

James, T. G. H. *Pharaoh's People: Scenes from Life in Imperial Egypt.* London: Bodley Head, 1984.

James, T. G. H. *A Short History of Ancient Egypt: From Predynastic to Roman Times.* London: Cassell, 1995.

Katan, Norma Jean, with Barbara Mintz. *Hieroglyphs: The Writing of Ancient Egypt.* Rev. ed. London: British Museum Publications, 1985.

Kemp, Barry J. *Ancient Egypt: Anatomy of a Civilization.* London: Routledge, 1989.

Kozloff, Arielle P., and Betsy M. Bryan with Lawrence M. Berman. *Egypt's Dazzling Sun: Amenhotep III and His World.* Cleveland: Cleveland Museum of Art, 1992.

Lichtheim, Miriam. *Ancient Egyptian Literature: A Book of Readings.* 3 vols. Berkeley: University of California Press, 1973–1980.

Lucas, Alfred. *Ancient Egyptian Materials and Industries.* 4th ed. Rev. J. R. Harris. London: E. Arnold, 1962.

Malek, Jaromir, ed. *Egypt: Ancient Culture, Modern Land.* Norman: University of Oklahoma Press, 1993.

Mertz, Barbara. *Red Land, Black Land: Daily Life in Ancient Egypt.* Rev. ed. New York: Peter Bedrick, 1990.

Morenz, Siegfried. *Egyptian Religion.* Trans. Ann E. Keep. London: Methuen, 1973.

Quirke, Stephen, and Jeffrey Spencer, eds. *The British Museum Book of Ancient Egypt.* London: Thames and Hudson, 1992.

Redford, Donald B. *Akhenaten: The Heretic King*. Princeton: Princeton University Press, 1984.

Redford, Donald B. *Egypt, Canaan, and Israel in Ancient Times*. Princeton: Princeton University Press, 1992.

Reeves, Nicholas. *The Complete Tutankhamun: The King, the Tomb, the Royal Treasure*. London: Thames and Hudson, 1990.

Ruffle, John. *Heritage of the Pharaohs: An Introduction to Egyptian Archaeology*. Oxford: Phaidon, 1977.

Shafer, Byron E., ed. *Religion in Ancient Egypt: Gods, Myths, and Personal Practice*. Contributors, John Baines, Leonard H. Lesko, and David P. Silverman. London: Routledge, 1991.

Simpson, William Kelly, ed. *The Literature of Ancient Egypt*. New Haven: Yale University Press, 1972.

Smith, W. Stevenson. *The Art and Architecture of Ancient Egypt*. Rev. ed. with additions by William Kelly Simpson. Harmondsworth, England: Penguin, 1981.

Stierlin, Henri. *The Pharaohs, Master-builders*. Paris: Terrail, 1995.

Strouhal, Eugen. *Life of the Ancient Egyptians*. Trans. Deryck Viney. Norman: University of Oklahoma Press, 1992.

Stead, Miriam. *Egyptian Life*. Cambridge, Mass.: Harvard University Press, 1986.

Trigger, Bruce G., et al. *Ancient Egypt: A Social History*. Cambridge: Cambridge University Press, 1983.

Trigger, Bruce G. *Early Civilizations: Ancient Egypt in Context*. Cairo: American University in Cairo Press, 1993.

The Hittites and Their Neighbors (Chapter 8)

Akurgal, Ekrem. *The Art of the Hittites*. Trans. Constance NcNab. London: Thames and Hudson, 1962.

Beal, Richard H. *The Organization of the Hittite Military*. Heidelberg: C. Winter, 1992.

Beckman, Gary. *Hittite Diplomatic Texts*. Ed. Harry A. Hoffner, Jr. Atlanta: Scholars Press, 1996.

Bittel, Kurt. *Hattusha: The Capital of the Hittites*. New York: Oxford University Press, 1970.

Gurney, O. R. *The Hittites*. 2d ed. London: Penguin, 1990.

Hoffner, Harry A., Jr., trans. *Hittite Myths*. Ed. Gary M. Beckman. Atlanta: Scholars Press, 1990.

Lloyd, Seton. *Early Anatolia: The Archaeology of Asia Minor before the Greeks*. Harmondsworth, England: Penguin, 1956.

Lloyd, Seton. *Early Highland Peoples of Anatolia*. London: Thames and Hudson, 1967.

Mallory, J. P. *In Search of the Indo-Europeans: Language, Archaeology, and Myth*. London: Thames and Hudson, 1989.

Macqueen, J. G. *The Hittites and Their Contemporaries in Asia Minor*. Rev. ed. London: Thames and Hudson, 1986.

Mellaart, James. *The Archaeology of Ancient Turkey*. London: Bodley Head, 1978.

Piotrovsky, Boris P. *The Ancient Civilization of Urartu*. Trans. James Hogarth. London: Cowles, 1969.

Sandars, N. K. *The Sea Peoples: Warriors of the Ancient Mediterranean, 1250–1150 BC*. Rev. ed. London: Thames and Hudson, 1985.

Wilhelm, Gernot. *The Hurrians*. Trans. Jennifer Barnes. Warminster, England: Aris and Phillips, 1989.

THE PHOENICIANS AND OTHER EARLY SEMITIC SPEAKERS (CHAPTER 9)

Aubet, María Eugenia. *The Phoenicians and the West: Politics, Colonies, and Trade*. Trans. Mary Turton. Cambridge: Cambridge University Press, 1993.

Baramki, Dimitri. *Phoenicia and the Phoenicians*. Beirut: Khayats, 1961.

Curtis, Adrian. *Ugarit (Ras Shamra)*. Cambridge: Lutterworth, 1985.

Harden, Donald B. *The Phoenicians*. 2d ed. London: Thames and Hudson, 1971.

Herm, Gerhard. *The Phoenicians: The Purple Empire of the Ancient World*. Trans. Caroline Hillier. New York: Morrow, 1975.

Matthiae, Paolo. *Ebla: An Empire Rediscovered*. Trans. Christopher Holme. London: Hodder and Stoughton, 1980.

Moscati, Sabatino, dir. *The Phoenicians*. Milan: Bompiani, 1988.

Moscati, Sabatino. *The World of the Phoenicians*. Trans. Alastair Hamilton. London: Weidenfeld and Nicolson, 1968.

THE HEBREWS (CHAPTERS 10–11)

Ackroyd, Peter R. *Studies in the Religious Tradition of the Old Testament*. London: SCM Press, 1987.

Aharoni, Yohanan. *The Archaeology of the Land of Israel: From the Prehistoric Beginnings to the End of the First Temple Period*. Ed. Miriam Aharoni. Trans. Anson F. Rainey. Philadelphia: Westminster, 1982.

Anderson, Bernhard W. *Understanding the Old Testament*. 4th ed. Englewood Cliffs, N.J.: Prentice-Hall, 1986.

Baron, Salo Wittmayer. *A Social and Religious History of the Jews*. 2d ed. 18 vols. New York: Columbia University Press, 1952–1983.

Ben-Tor, Amnon, ed. *The Archaeology of Ancient Israel*. Trans. R. Greenberg. New Haven: Yale University Press, 1992.

Bright, John. *A History of Israel*. 3d ed. Philadelphia: Westminster, 1981.

Clements, R. E., ed. *The World of Ancient Israel: Sociological, Anthropological and Political Perspectives*. Cambridge: Cambridge University Press, 1989.

Cohen, Shaye J. D. *From the Maccabees to the Mishnah*. Philadelphia: Westminster, 1987.

Dothan, Trude. *The Philistines and Their Material Culture*. New Haven: Yale University Press, 1982.

Dotham, Trude, and Moshe Dotham. *People of the Sea: The Search for the Philistines*. New York: Macmillan, 1992.

Drews, Robert. *The End of the Bronze Age: Changes in Warfare and the Catastrophe ca. 1200 B.C.* Princeton: Princeton University Press, 1993.

Finkelstein, Israel. *The Archaeology of the Israelite Settlement.* Jerusalem: Israel Exploration Society, 1988.

Finkelstein, Israel, and Nadav Na'aman, eds. *From Nomadism to Monarchy: Archaeological and Historical Aspects of Early Israel.* Jerusalem: Israel Exploration Society, 1994.

Flanders, Henry Jackson, Jr., Robert Wilson Crapps, and David Anthony Smith. *People of the Covenant: An Introduction to the Hebrew Bible.* 4th ed. Oxford: Oxford University Press, 1996.

Golb, Norman. *Who Wrote the Dead Sea Scrolls?: The Search for the Secret of Qumran.* New York: Scribner's, 1995.

Gottwald, Norman K. *The Hebrew Bible—A Socio-Literary Introduction.* Philadelphia, Fortress, 1985.

Gottwald, Norman K. *The Hebrew Bible in Its Social World and in Ours.* Atlanta: Scholars Press, 1993.

Grant, Michael. *The History of Ancient Israel.* London: Weidenfeld and Nicholson, 1984.

Herrmann, Siegfried. *A History of Israel in Old Testament Times.* Rev. ed. Philadelphia: Fortress, 1981.

Kempinski, Aharon, and Ronny Reich, eds. *The Architecture of Ancient Israel: From the Prehistoric to the Persian Periods.* Jerusalem: Israel Exploration Society, 1992.

Matthews, Victor H., and Don. C. Benjamin. *Social World of Ancient Israel, 1250–587 BCE.* Peabody, Mass.: Hendrickson, 1993.

Mazar, Amihai. *Archaeology of the Land of the Bible, 10,000–586 B.C.E.* New York: Doubleday, 1990.

Miller, J. Maxwell, and John H. Hayes. *A History of Ancient Israel and Judah.* Philadelphia: Westminster, 1986.

Neusner, Jacob. *The Classics of Judaism: A Textbook and Reader.* Louisville: Westminster/John Knox, 1995.

Olyan, Saul M. *Asherah and the Cult of Yahweh in Israel.* Atlanta: Scholars Press, 1988.

Olyan, Saul M. *A Thousand Thousands Served Him: Exegesis and the Naming of Angels in Ancient Judaism.* Tübingen: J.C.B. Mohr, 1993.

Pagels, Elaine. *The Origin of Satan.* New York: Random House, 1995.

Pettinato, Giovanni. *Ebla: A New Look at History.* Trans. C. Faith Richardson. Baltimore: Johns Hopkins University Press, 1991.

Redford, Donald B. *Egypt, Canaan, and Israel in Ancient Times.* Princeton: Princeton University Press, 1992.

Sandmel, Samuel. *The Hebrew Scriptures: An Introduction to their Literature and Religious Ideas.* Oxford: Oxford University Press, 1978.

Shanks, Hershel, ed. *Ancient Israel: A Short History from Abraham to the Roman Destruction of the Temple.* Washington: Biblical Archaeology Society, 1988.

Soggin, J. Alberto. *A History of Ancient Israel.* Philadelphia: Westminster, 1985.

Tubb, Jonathan N., and Rupert L. Chapman. *Archaeology and the Bible*. London: British Museum Press, 1990.

THE ASSYRIANS, CHALDEANS, AND LYDIANS (CHAPTER 12)

Barnett, R. D. *Assyrian Sculpture in the British Museum*. Toronto: McClelland and Stewart, 1975.

Beaulieu, Paul-Alain. *The Reign of Nabonidus, King of Babylon, 556–539 B.C.* New Haven: Yale University Press, 1989.

Brinkman, J. A. *Prelude to Empire: Babylonian Society and Politics, 747–626 B.C.* Philadelphia: Babylonian Fund, 1984.

British Museum. *Assyrian Sculpture*. Cambridge, Mass.: Harvard University Press, 1983.

Contenau, Georges. *Everyday Life in Babylon and Assyria*. London: Edward Arnold, 1954.

Frame, Grant. *Babylonia 689–627 B.C.: A Political History*. Istanbul: Nederlands Historisch-Archaeologisch Instituut te Istanbul, 1992.

Grayson, A. Kirk. *Assyrian and Babylonian Chronicles*. Locust Valley, N.Y.: J. J. Augustin, 1975.

Grayson, A. Kirk. *Assyrian Royal Inscriptions*. Wiesbaden: O. Harrassowitz, 1972–.

Grayson, A. Kirk, et al. *The Royal Inscriptions of Mesopotamia*. Toronto: University of Toronto Press, 1987–.

Frankfurt, Henri. *The Art and Architecture of the Ancient Orient*. 4th ed. New Haven: Yale University Press, 1970.

Hooke, S. H. *Babylonian and Assyrian Religion*. Norman: University of Oklahoma Press, 1963.

Lloyd, Seton. *The Archaeology of Mesopotamia: From the Old Stone Age to the Persian Conquest*. Rev. ed. London: Thames and Hudson, 1984.

Lloyd, Seton. *Foundations in the Dust: The Story of Mesopotamian Exploration*. Rev. ed. London: Thames and Hudson, 1980.

Luckenbill, Daniel David. *Ancient Records of Assyria and Babylonia*. Chicago: University of Chicago Press, 1926–1927.

Neugebauer, O. *The Exact Sciences in Antiquity*. 2d ed. New York: Dover, 1969.

Oates, Joan. *Babylon*. London: Thames and Hudson, 1979.

Olmstead, A. T. *History of Assyria*. New York: Scribner's, 1923.

Oppenheim, A. Leo, trans. *Letters from Mesopotamia: Official, Business, and Private Letters on Clay Tablets from Two Millennia*. Chicago: University of Chicago Press, 1967.

Parpola, Simo, ed. *State Archives of Assyria*. Helsinki: Helsinki University Press, 1987–

Parrot, Andre. *The Arts of Assyria*. Trans. Stuart Gilbert and James Emmons. New York: Golden Press, 1961.

Rolle, Renate. *The World of the Scythians*. Trans. F. G. Walls. Berkeley: University of California Press, 1989.

Roux, Georges. *Ancient Iraq*. 3d ed. London: Penguin, 1992.

Sack, Ronald H. *Images of Nebuchadnezzar: The Emergence of a Legend*. Selinsgrove, Pa.: Susquehanna University Press; London: Associated University Presses, 1991.

Saggs, H. W. F. *Babylonians*. Norman: University of Oklahoma Press, 1995.

Saggs, H. W. F. *Everyday Life in Babylonia and Assyria*. Rev. ed. New York: Dorset Press, 1987.

Saggs, H. W. F. *The Greatness That Was Babylon: A Survey of the Ancient Civilizations of the Tigris-Euphrates Valley*. Rev. ed. London: Sidgwick and Jackson, 1988.

Saggs, H. W. F. *The Might That Was Assyria*. London: Sidgwick and Jackson, 1984.

The Medes and Persians (Chapters 13–14)

Bengtson, Hermann, ed. *The Greeks and the Persians: From the Sixth to the Fourth Centuries*. Trans. John Conway. New York: Delacorte, 1968.

Boyce, Mary. *A History of Zoroastrianism*. 3 vols. Leiden: E. Brill, 1975–1991.

Boyce, Mary, ed. and trans. *Textual Sources for the Study of Zoroastrianism*. Manchester: Manchester University Press, 1984.

Boyce, Mary. *Zoroastrianism: Its Antiquity and Constant Vigour*. Costa Mesa, Calif.: Mazda, 1992.

The Cambridge History of Iran. Vols. 1–3. Cambridge: Cambridge University Press, 1968–1983.

Cohn, Norman. *Cosmos, Chaos and the World to Come: The Ancient Roots of Apocalyptic Faith*. New Haven: Yale University Press, 1993.

Colledge, Malcolm A. R. *The Parthians*. London: Thames and Hudson, 1967.

Cook, J. M. *The Persian Empire*. London: Dent, 1983.

Culican, William. *The Medes and Persians*. New York: Praeger, 1965.

Curtis, John. *Ancient Persia*. Cambridge, Mass.: Harvard University Press, 1990.

Duchesne-Guillemin, Jacques, trans. *The Hymns of Zarathustra: Being a Translation of the Gāthās Together with Introduction and Commentary*. Trans. from the French by Mrs. M. Henning. London: John Murray, 1952.

Duchesne-Guillemin, Jacques. *Religion of Ancient Iran*. Bombay: Tata, 1973.

Farksa, Ann. *Achaemenid Sculpture*. Istanbul: Nederlands Historisch-Archaeologish Instituut in het Nabije Oosten, 1974.

Frye, Richard N. *The Heritage of Persia*. Cleveland: World, 1963.

Frye, Richard N. *The History of Ancient Iran*. Munich: C. H. Beck, 1984.

Ghirshman, R. *Iran from the Earliest Times to the Islamic Conquest*. Harmondsworth, England: Penguin, 1954.

Godard, André. *The Art of Iran*. Trans. Michael Heron. Ed. Michael Rogers. New York, Praeger, 1965.

Malandra, William W., trans. and ed. *An Introduction to Ancient Iranian Religion: Readings from the Avesta and Achaemenid Inscriptions*. Minneapolis: University of Minnesota Press, 1983.

Moorey, P. R. S. *Ancient Iran*. Oxford: Ashmolean Museum, 1975.

Nigosian, S. A. *The Zoroastrian Faith: Tradition and Modern Research*. Montreal: McGill-Queen's University Press, 1993.

Olmstead, A. T. *History of the Persian Empire: Achaemenid Period*. Chicago: University of Chicago Press, 1948.

Porada, Edith. *The Art of Ancient Iran: Pre-Islamic Cultures*. New York: Crown, 1965.

Roaf, Michael. *Sculptures and Sculptors at Persepolis*. London: British Institute for Persian Studies, 1983.

Schmidt, Erich F. *Persepolis*. 3 vols. Chicago: University of Chicago Press, 1953–1970.

PICTURE CREDITS

Chapter 1 8, 10 Rainbird, Robert Harding Picture Library 12 The Diagram Group 13 Gilles Tosello 19 Color Photo Hans Hinz 22 Naturhistoriches Museum, Vienna, Austria **Chapter 2** 29, 30 James Mellaart 34 Scientific American, Inc., illustration on page 80 by Particia J. Wynne from "Megalithic Monuments," by Glyn Daniel, July 1980 **Chapter 3** 54 Giraudon, Art Resource, NY **Chapter 4** 62 The Oriental Institute, University of Chicago 66 Scala, Art Resource, NY 67 University Museum, University of Pennsylvania, Philadelphia 72 Hirmer Foto Archive **Chapter 5** 77 Hirmer Foto Archive 79 Reunion des Musees Nationaux 81 British Museum **Chapter 6** 113 Hirmer Foto Archive 116 Foto Marburg, Art Resource, NY 121 National Geographic Society, artist William Bond **Chapter 7** 135 Tony Stone, ©David Austin 138 Trigger et al., *Ancient Egypt: A Social History*, fig. 3-2, Cambridge University Press 141 Metropolitan Museum of Art; New York 142 British Museum 148 The Grand Rapids Art Museum; David Roberts, lithograph, gift of the Wedge Foundation 149 Giovanni Belzoni **Chapter 8** 169 Hirmer Foto Archive 170 Josephine Powell, Photographer, Rome, Italy 171 National Geographic Society **Chapter 9** 186 The Israel Museum, Jerusalem 188 Lee Reynolds 192 Oriental Division, The New York Public Library, Astor, Lenox and Tilden Foundations **Chapter 10** 204 Lee Reynolds 213 Scripture Union, used by permission 215 Alinari, Art Resourse, NY 216 Hirmer Foto Archive **Chapter 11** 221 Abington Press 229 Alinari, Art Resourse, NY 235 Scripture Union, used by permission **Chapter 12** 254 The Royal Institute of British Architects and the University of London 255 British Museum, London 260 Bildarchiv Preussischet 262 Lee Reynolds 266 Courtesy of The Archaeological Exploration of Sardis **Chapter 13** 270 National Geographic Society 273, 276 The Oriental Institute, University of Chicago 279 The American Numismatic Society **Chapter 14** 286 The Ancient Art and Architecture Collection Ltd. 290 Josephine Powell, Photographer, Rome, Italy 292, 293 Dr. Heiko Krefter

INDEX

Arrangement of material within entries is predominantly chronological.
References in italics denote illustrations.

Hebrew/Jewish, 196–197, 224–227
Hittite, 166
Old Babylonian, 83–86
Persian, 276–278
Third Dynasty of Ur, 80–81
Layard, Sir Austen Henry, 248
lead, 268
Leah, 195
Leakey, Louis, 5
Leakey, Mary, 5
Leakey, Richard, 5
Lebanon, 176, 179, 182
Lebanon Mountains, 176, 189
legal texts. *See* law
Legend of Keret, 182
Leviticus, Book of, 217, 224–226
    and sacrifice, 225–226
lex talionis, 85–86, 225
library, of Assurbanipal at Nineveh, 247–248,
    255
Libya/Libyans, 127, 152, 263
Libyan Desert, 91
life cults, 15
linen, Egyptian, 125
lingua franca, 191, 261, 277
lions, 169, 171, 253, 265–266, 291, 294
literature
    Assyrian, 248, 251
    Babylonian, 248
    Egyptian, 117–118, 123, 129, 130, 183
    Hittite, 168
    Mesopotamian, 53
    Persian, 284
    Ugaritic, 180–182
    See also Dead Sea Scrolls, Hebrew Bible,
        Hebrews, law
Lot, 195
Lower Egypt, 98, 102–103, 268
lugal, 51
Lugalzagesi, 55, 75–76
lunar month, 21. *See also* calendar
Luwian/Luwian speakers, 160–161, 173
Luxor, Temple of, 139–140, *140*, 141
Lydia/Lydians, 173, 239, 245, 247, 256, 258,
    264–266, 270, 272, 277
    attached to Persian Empire, 265–266
    culture, 265
    principal kings, 264–266
    trade, 264

Ma`at (deity), 106, 110, 129, 144
ma`at (eternal principles), 109–110
Maccabean Revolt, 212
Maccabees, Books of the, 233

Macedonia/Macedonians, 211, 279–280
Magi, 283–284
magic. *See* religion and magic
Mahomet, 289
mail/messenger service, Persian, 277
"major" prophets, 221–222
Malachi, 222
Malachi, Book of, 231
Malta, 187
Manasseh, 209–210
Mandane, 271
Manetho, 98–99, 108, 129, 132
Manichaeism, 287–288
Marathon, battle of, 279–280
Marathon, plain of, 279
marble, 268
Marduk (deity), 84, 87, 246, 252, 258–259, 261,
    272
Mari, 76, 82, 157
marriage
    Assyrian, 250
    Egyptian, 124–125
    Hebrew, 218
    Old Babylonian, 86
    Sacred, of Sumer, 59
    Sumerian, 73–74
Marseilles, 187
Mary, mother of Jesus, 23, 108
Masada, 215, 236
Massagetai, 272–273
mastaba, 111, *111*, 112, 116, 120, *120*
masturbation, 58, 105
matriarchy, 39
mathematics, Sumerian, 69
Media/Medes, 156, 173–177, 247–248, 256, 258,
    264–267, 274–275, 294
    Cyrus of Persia gains control of Median
        territory, 270
    map, 269
    Median-Lydian alliance, 270
    principal kings, 268, 270
medicine/drugs
    Assyrian, 252
    Egyptian, 130–131
    Sumerian, 69
Medinet Habu, mortuary temple of Ramses III
    at, 151
Mediterranean climate, 197
Megiddo, 136, 210
Memphis, 103, 110, 112, 114, 127–128, 149,
    246, 277
Menes. *See* Narmer
menhirs, 34
Menkaure, 117